D1228808

A River and Its City

A River and Its City

*The Nature of Landscape
in New Orleans*

Ari Kelman

UNIVERSITY OF CALIFORNIA PRESS
Berkeley · Los Angeles · London

This book has been made possible through a grant
from the Louisiana Endowment for the Humanities,
a state affiliate of the National Endowment for the
Humanities.

The opinions expressed in this book do not necessarily
represent the views of the Louisiana Endowment for
the Humanities or the National Endowment for the
Humanities.

University of California Press
Berkeley and Los Angeles, California

University of California Press, Ltd.
London, England

Library of Congress Cataloging-in-Publication Data

Kelman, Ari, 1968–.
    A river and its city : the nature of landscape in
New Orleans / Ari Kelman.
        p.   cm.
    Includes bibliographical references and index.
    ISBN 0-520-23432-4 (alk. paper)
    1. Urban ecology—Louisiana—New Orleans.
2. Human ecology—Louisiana—New Orleans.
3. Mississippi River—History.   I. Title.
HT243.U62 L685   2003

304.0'09763'35—dc21   2002016558

Manufactured in the United States of America

12   11   10   09   08   07   06   05   04   03

10   9   8   7   6   5   4   3   2   1

The paper used in this publication meets the minimum
requirements of ANSI/NISO Z39.48–1992 (R 1997)
(Permanence of Paper). ●

Contents

Illustrations

Acknowledgments

To acknowledge all of the debts, large and small, financial, intellectual, and social, that I have accrued while working on this project would take hundreds of pages; to pay them all back, several lifetimes. Suffice it to say that I would not have completed this book without the help that I received from the people and institutions listed below. As a confused graduate student in the History Department at Brown University, I benefited greatly from working with and learning from Volker Berghan, the late Bernard Bruce, Mari Jo Buhle, Howard Chudacoff, Cate Cooper, Doug Cope, Jerry Davila, Nathaniel Frank, Gabrielle Friedman, Tom Gleason, Cherrie Guerzon, Tim Harris, Joan Lusk, Josh Marshall, James McClain, the late Bill McLoughlin, Karen Mota, Ed Rafferty, Tom Skidmore, Muriel Soenens, Jim Sparrow, and Gordon Wood. Lucy Barber, whom I met at Brown, has since read long sections of this book, lent a sympathetic ear more times than I can recall, and shared her influential ideas about cities and public space. Zach Morgan, my closest friend from graduate school, has always reminded me that sometimes it is a good idea to put one's work aside. Through the years, our bike rides, road trips, and long conversations have kept me smiling and thinking.

In my two years living in Norman, Oklahoma, while working at the University of Oklahoma, I was lucky to find generous colleagues and wonderful friends: Ben Alpers, Molly Boren, Gavin Bridge, Graham Burnett, Adam Cohen, Julie Cohen, Deborah Dalton, Julia Ehrhardt, Julie Gozan, Rob Griswold, Kathy Gross, Sandy Holguin, Al Hurtado, Tina

Kambour, Tom Keck, Cathy Kelly, Bradley Kirsch, Scott Kirsch, Debra Klebesadel, Lynne Levy, Carolyn Morgan, Bob Nairn, Josh Piker, Bob Rundstrom, Francesca Sawaya, Karin Schutjer, Bob Shalhope, Circe Sturm, Zev Trachtenberg, Sarah Tracy, Bret Wallach, and Melanie Wright. Paul Gilje, David Levy, Gregg Mitman, and Don Pisani all led by example, as they taught me how to be a professional historian. The brilliant and warm-hearted Randy Lewis always found ways to make me laugh aloud, even as he improved this book immeasurably with his keen eye and sharp wit. David Boren welcomed me into a huge family at O.U. Along with Steve Gillon, who became my mentor, trusted confidant, advisor, and friend, President Boren created a scholar's paradise at the O.U. Honors College.

My good fortune has continued since I arrived in Denver, Colorado, where I now teach at the University of Denver. Robert Anderson, Liz Andrews, Thomas Andrews, Eric Arnold, Luc Beaudoin, Penelope Canan, Fred Cheever, Marjorie Levine-Clark, Michael Levine-Clark, Paul Colomy, Paul Dewen, Yasmaine Ford-Faggan, Leah Garrett, Mike Gibbs, Peter Golas, Joyce Goodfriend, Carol Helstosky, Lauren Hirsch, Pam Hughes, Nita Johnson, Len Kapelovitz, Jen Karas, Linda Kosten, Patricia Nelson-Limerick, Catherine O'Neil, Nancy Reichman, Meg Steitz, Susan Sterett, Nancy Litwack-Strong, Peter Strong, Steven Strong, Ingrid Tague, and Josh Thurman all have eased my transition to living a mile above sea level—unfortunately, that description makes these folks sound a bit like Sherpas, rather than the outstanding coworkers and companions they are. Don Hughes has taken me under his wing, an ideal spot for an environmental historian to learn and grow. From the moment I met them, Abbey Kapelovitz and Gregg Kvistad have always been good-humored and helpful, providing support, sound advice, and plenty of laughter along the way. Both Mark Fiege and Jared Orsi read rough drafts of this book and gave outstanding advice, reflected in the final product. Susan Schulten also made this a much better monograph by suggesting numerous subtle changes and sharing stories from her own adventures in publishing. She has been an outstanding colleague and co-conspirator.

Without dedicated archivists, the unsung heroes of the historical profession, this book would not exist. I wish to thank collectively the staffs at the Filson Club, the Historic New Orleans Collection, the Kentucky State Historical Society, the Library of Congress, the Louisiana Division of the New Orleans Public Library, the Louisiana State Museum Historical Research Center, the National Archives, the New York Public Library, the Southeast Architectural Archive at Tulane University, the Special Collections Division at Tulane University, the Special Collections Division at the University of Kentucky's King Library, and the Supreme Court Archives at the University of New Orleans's Earl K. Long Library. Marie Windell at UNO, Joan Caldwell and Bill Meneray at Tulane, John Magill and Sally Stassi at the Historic New Orleans Collection, Wayne Everard at the New Orleans Public Library, and Shannon Glasheen at the Louisiana State Museum all showed particular interest in this project and took extra time from their very busy schedules to offer assistance above and beyond the call of duty.

Numerous other scholars, friends, and family members, scattered across this and other countries, have helped me at various times by offering encouragement, insights, and critiques. Thanks to Robin Bachin, Peter Baldwin, John Barry, Felicity Beede, Herman Bennett, William Borah, Jeanne Boydston, John Brooke, Kathy Brosnan, Bob Bruegemann, Tom Buchanan, Peter Caron, Craig Colten, Teresa Cooper, Danielle Cover, Albert Cowdrey, Bill Cronon, Adina Davidson, Josh Davidson, Mark Davidson, Rachel Davidson, Mike Davis, Bill Deverell, Betsy Farley, Mike Feldman, Sam Feldman, Jon Festinger, Lucia Festinger, John Findlay, Caitlin FitzSimons, Rich Gale, Glen Gendzel, Paula Geyh, Laelia Gilborn, Jesse Goff, Julie Goff, Nina Hellman, Sarah-Anne Henning, Arnold Hirsch, Greg Hise, Andrew Hurley, David Igler, Lynn Iler, Jill Jacobson, Mary-Anne Janacek, Julie Kleinman, Matt Klingle, Ruth Knack, Ed Lyon, Neil Maher, Ben Maygarden, John McNeill, Betsy Mendelsohn, Jennifer Mitchel, Claudia Morgan, Jennifer Morgan, John Morgan, Eric Mumford, Bill Newby, Caroline Nobel, Philip Nobel, Kisten Nolan, Max Page, Larry Powell, Sara Pritchard, Ivy Restituto, Martin Reuss, Andrew Rosen, Maya Rosen, Hal Rothman, Mary Ryan, Paul Sabin, David Sampliner, Judy Schafer, John Schumann, Richard Sewell, Todd Shallat, Diane Shaw, Bryant Simon, Amy Stelljes, Audrey Stout, Ellen Stroud, Joe Sullivan, Greg Summers, Paul Sutter, Jay Taylor, Johnathan Veitch, Steve Wacksman, David Wain, Sarah Walker, Louis Warren, Craig Wedren, Craig Werner, Steve Whitfield, Craig Wilder, Donald Worster, Janet York, Stephanie Yuhl, Liz Zale, Corrinne Zimmerman, and Gabi Zolla. The Hermans, Shael, Helen, and Dara, welcomed me into their home in New Orleans, and Shael taught me about Louisiana's culinary culture and legal system. Karl Jacoby and Conevery Bolton Valencius read early drafts of this book, and their incisive yet always kind comments prompted me to hone my argument. Joe Rosen and Judy Smith, my in-laws, have always been there for me. And my loving parents, Sam and

Anna Kelman, deserve as much credit for this book as I do (but none of the blame). They raised me to cherish a good argument, to love ideas, and to think hard about the past.

I wish to thank several institutions for providing financial assistance. An American Historical Association Littleton-Griswold grant allowed me to do much of the research for the first chapter of this book. Generous funding from the Graduate School and the Department of History at Brown University covered many of my expenses during the two years that I lived in New Orleans. A Williams Research Grant from the Historic New Orleans Collection underwrote a preliminary trip to New Orleans to explore the city's archives. A fellowship from the John Nicholas Brown Center for the Study of American Civilization freed me to devote an entire summer to uninterrupted writing. A sizable subvention grant from the Louisiana Endowment for the Humanities has helped to keep this book relatively affordable. The National Endowment for the Humanities sponsored my attendance at an edifying summer institute in Chicago, "The Built Environment of the American Metropolis" (1999), which helped me organize my thoughts as I began the process of revising. I would like to thank all of the other participants in that institute whom I have not mentioned elsewhere in these acknowledgments. The University of Denver's Division of Arts, Humanities, and Social Sciences, along with the Louisiana Endowment for the Humanities, provided money that enabled me to travel to New Orleans and find the illustrations scattered herein. The University of Oklahoma Honors College bought the computer on which this book was written and allowed me to teach half-time for a year so that I could focus on my research. And the Graduate School at the University of Oklahoma paid for the preparation of this book's index.

I must single out the contributions of a dedicated, talented, and caring group of scholars who served as my graduate advisors at Brown and have continued to offer counsel in the years since. They have worked endless hours with excellent humor for the good of this project. No matter how many times I thank Andrew Isenberg, Naomi Lamoreaux, James Patterson, and John Thomas, I can never adequately express the respect and gratitude that I feel for them. Drew arrived at Brown at a fortuitous moment for me, as I was casting about for a dissertation topic. He taught me about environmental history, offered crucial comments on this project, and never failed to do a favor when asked. Naomi urged me to train my eye on economic relationships and gave advice that helped me transform a dissertation into a book. From the moment I arrived at Brown,

Jim inspired me with his work ethic, scholarship, and commitment to pedagogy. He is a model for young professors. Jack attempted to show me the proper way to read, to teach, and to write. Through no fault of his own, he succeeded only in part; nonetheless, I thank him for his efforts. He has been a good friend and benevolent taskmaster.

Two anonymous readers and Sarah Elkind, all toiling for the University of California Press, presented me with a dazzling array of excellent suggestions for how to improve this book. I thank them all for their input. As with all of the other people and institutions that I have acknowledged here, they deserve much credit for this book's publication; the mistakes that remain are my fault alone. Years ago, when I was still struggling with my research, Monica McCormick, my stalwart editor at U.C. Press, gave me the confidence that I had stumbled onto a topic worthy of a book. In the years since, she has shepherded me through the publication process, given guidance when asked, and remained upbeat about my project and prospects even when I had my doubts. As this book neared completion, Roberta Englemann, Andrew Frisardi, Laura Harger, and Randy Heyman stepped in to offer valuable and much-appreciated assistance.

Finally, I dedicate this book to my love, Lesley. I spend much of my time studying the past, but it is the thought of our future together that sustains me.

Nature's Highway to Market

In a remote corner of northwestern Minnesota, springs bubble from beneath the earth's surface, reaching daylight almost 1,500 feet above sea level and 2,500 miles from the end of a winding journey through the heart of North America to the Gulf of Mexico. This is the source of the Mississippi River. At the start of its travels, the Mississippi is a tiny brook, but hundreds of other streams will join with it along its course to the gulf, accounting for the famed river's greatness. Thirty miles into its journey, the Mississippi slips through the surrounding countryside at just one hundred cubic feet per second. Then, another 350 miles farther along, the first of its major tributaries, the Crow Wing, tumbles into the trunk stream, and as quickly as that the Mississippi swells to formidable size. The swift way that the Mississippi gulps up the Crow Wing provides a key to understanding the great river: what we think of as one stream is actually a system of more than one hundred thousand smaller watercourses joined under a single name. That name, then—the Mississippi—no matter how it dances on the tongue, like gurgling water, is more a matter of convenience, a shorthand for human uses, than a truly descriptive label.[1]

The Mississippi system's magnitude shames hyperbole into understatement. The river system drains an enormous area (figure 1), reaching within approximately 300 miles of the shores of the Atlantic Ocean and within roughly 500 miles of the Pacific coastline. From the steep eastern slope of the Rocky Mountains to the west side of the rolling Allegheny range, ten entire states, significant parts of twenty-two others, and large sections of two Canadian provinces lie within the sweep of the Mississippi River's drainage basin. This area encompasses approximately 1,200,000 square miles, or, more dramatically, in excess of 40 percent of the continental United States.[2]

The vastness of this territory yields a riparian system of surpassing unpredictability and complexity, with behavior shaped by events in places as far removed from one another as Idaho and New York. For instance, a sudden landslide in Colorado's mountains sends debris hurtling into valleys below. Flash floods then sweep that material into rivers that eventually twist their way into the Mississippi. A hard autumn rain in the flatlands of Indiana runs off into streams that ultimately also find their way into the river system, again increasing the trunk stream's flow. Heavy snow in western Pennsylvania melts in a spring thaw, and that water too eventually joins the Mississippi. Add to this the effect of human settlements throughout the river's drainage system: each time a town builds a mall, a parking lot, or a new subdivision, or a farmer clears a tract of land, local rivers swell and their waters finally empty into the Mississippi.

At St. Louis the Missouri River, the longest of the system's tributaries, joins the Mississippi. Or is it the other way around? Today most people consider the Mississippi the trunk stream, but the Missouri is by far the system's longest river, having already traveled more than 2,000 miles from its headwaters when it meets the Mississippi.[3] Had French explorers stumbled on the Missouri first, we likely would now know it as the world's greatest river. Instead, the European conquest of the continent traveled from east to west, so we call the confluence of these two rivers the Mississippi, relegating the Missouri to regional fame while the Mississippi is internationally known.

Approximately 150 miles farther south of St. Louis, the Ohio River joins the Mississippi at an Illinois town that Anglo-European settlers optimistically named Cairo. For miles below Cairo, the two renowned rivers appear intent on maintaining distinct identities after having made long journeys from their sources—the Ohio has traveled almost 1,000 miles, while the Mississippi has come even farther than that.[4] For a time, the Ohio seems to challenge the Mississippi for supremacy in the trunk stream's bed, as the two mingle only reluctantly, with the Ohio's blue water and the darker Mississippi flowing separately for miles before finally uniting as a single muddy current.

Far downstream of Cairo, between Natchez and Baton Rouge, the Mississippi's last major tributary, the Red River, enters the trunk. Below

Map of the United States, showing the Area Drained into the Mississippi River

Figure 1. The Mississippi River drains an area extending from Montana to New York and from Alberta to the Gulf of Mexico. Courtesy of the Special Collections Division, Tulane University.

the Red, streams emanate from the Mississippi instead of emptying into it; they are distributaries rather than tributaries. This is where the Mississippi has built its delta, but we must not be confused by the sweeping phrase "Mississippi Delta," commonly used to name an ill-defined region, steeped in mythology. Places such as Memphis and Jackson are part of the river's flood plain, and as such were once located in its delta, but today those cities are part of the delta only in cultural terms. "Delta" blues notwithstanding, when geologists speak of the Mississippi Delta they refer to an area south of the Red River.[5]

The process of delta formation is an example of what geologists call "dynamic sedimentation."[6] To understand what this means, imagine you have a garden hose with the water pressure turned high. Make a small cut in the hose near the spigot and steadily slip sand into the rushing water. The sand will be pushed along by the confined water's current. Now put the hose's nozzle into a shallow pool. Where the hose meets open water the current dissipates, and the sand is deposited. If you wait long enough, a small beach appears near the hose's nozzle: you have created your own delta. The Mississippi builds its delta similarly, but the river is better equipped for the task. In the words of one of the Mississippi's early historians, it carries the "the marl of the Rocky mountains, the clay of the Black mountains, the earth of the Alleghenies, the red loam, washed from the hills at the sources of the Arkansas and Red Rivers," until it arrives at the Gulf of Mexico.[7] Where it empties into the gulf, the Mississippi's current weakens, and over millennia it has built its delta by depositing sediment drawn from throughout its system, an area including much of the interior of the continent.

The Mississippi's delta is otherworldly, so interminably flat that one scholar says "nine-tenths of [it] is sky."[8] It is a place of seemingly endless, interconnected marshes, swamps, and bayous, with little solid land anywhere in sight. Cattails, irises, mangroves, and a wide variety of grasses thrive in the delta's soggy environment. Muskrats, otters, minks, raccoons, and of course alligators all inhabit this watery world, while crawfish, or "mudbugs," as locals call them, burrow in a constantly replenished supply of muck. Much of the delta remains a wetland wilderness—a great place for a fish, or perhaps even a fishing trip, but a forbidding location to build a city. Yet that is exactly what people have done there.

In the midst of the delta, approximately a hundred miles from the Mississippi's mouth at the gulf, the meandering river turns sharply to the south, then abruptly snakes east and as quickly heads north, finally returning to a southeasterly course. In 1718, Jean-Baptiste Le Moyne, sieur de Bienville, placed French Louisiana's capital in the resulting crescent, on rare high ground deposited by the river. The location, which a local Native American guide had pointed out to Bienville approximately two decades earlier, seemed ideal because it lay near a portage between the Mississippi and a lake, later named Pontchartrain, which leads eventually to the gulf. Because it was virtually surrounded by water (see figure 2), the city Bienville founded was called L'Isle de la Nouvelle Orléans (the Island of New Orleans); today it is known as New Orleans or the Crescent City.[9]

When Bienville gazed at the Mississippi's muddy waters, he did not contemplate the power of fluvial tectonics, the vagaries of accretion and erosion, or the difference between the river's deltaic and flood plains. He saw only a magnificent system of watery roads, a tapestry of commercial empire woven from the strands of the river system's watercourses. Bienville read the geography of the Mississippi Valley as surely as we might read a map, and he saw the unmistakable imprint of divine providence. Viewing God and what he called "Nature" as parts of a whole, Bienville perceived the river as a gift, a treasure map carved into the continent. For several reasons, his perceptions made sense. Before our era

Figure 2. The city of New Orleans is almost completely surrounded by water: the Mississippi River is in the foreground and Lake Pontchartrain in the background of this photograph (ca. 1940s). Courtesy of the Special Collections Division, Tulane University.

of paved roads, rails, or air travel—all technologies circumventing the vagaries of geography—rivers served as highways of commerce. And the Mississippi system provided the most magnificent collection of highways in the world, including more than fifteen thousand miles of navigable streams, a system shaped like a large funnel with its spout pointed at New Orleans.[10] In Bienville's mind, this strategic location guaranteed that from the capillaries of backcountry brooks, to the veins of larger tributary rivers like the Ohio and the Missouri, and finally to the artery of the trunk stream itself, commerce, the lifeblood of the continent, would inevitably flow downstream on the Mississippi system to market at New Orleans.

Bienville chose New Orleans's location based on this felicitous reading of the river system, which he saw as the city's greatest asset, but his enthusiasm for the river's commercial benefits blinded him to many of the challenges of building a city in the delta. One might say he focused on New Orleans's "situation" while ignoring the hazards of its "site." Geographer Peirce Lewis writes that *situation* "is what we commonly mean when we speak of a place with respect to neighboring places";[11] in the present context, then, it refers to the advantages that Bienville believed New Orleans would enjoy compared to other cities. Not only would it stand near the mouth of an enormous system of navigable waterways that promised to carry trade its way, but the Gulf of Mexico would lie downstream, a gateway to the ports of the Americas, the Caribbean, and Europe. In short, New Orleans's situation would offer a commercial metropolis unparalleled access to the continent's interior as well as to markets throughout the Atlantic World of trade.

If New Orleans's situation seemed perfectly crafted by a kindly God working through Nature, its local environment, or "site," which Lewis defines as the "actual real estate which the city occupies," proved quite frustrating to settlers.[12] When Bienville and other boosters cast the river as New Orleans's benefactor, they ignored a host of environmental obstacles that later were to plague the city: the river's current (commerce could flow downriver to New Orleans, but traders returning home, upstream, faced a difficult passage); horrifying epidemics, exacerbated by a steamy climate, that swept through the city regularly during the eighteenth and nineteenth centuries; the silt-choked passes at the river's mouth, which often blockaded the Mississippi; municipal drainage, ranging from terrible to nonexistent, because much of the local terrain lies below sea level while sitting atop a high water table; and the threat of catastrophic flooding—the result of the local topography, the river that had created it, and the delta's damp climate. Each of these features embodied the dynamism of the city's environs, dynamism that belied Bienville's reading of geography and Nature as uniformly, or at least predictably, benevolent.

Early accounts of New Orleans catalog the settlement's environmental woes while remaining optimistic about the city's long-range prospects.[13] One visitor, Pierre-François-Xavier de Charlevoix, a Jesuit priest who toured New Orleans in 1722, noted that the "justest notion you can form of it is, to imagine to yourself two hundred persons...on the banks of a great river, thinking upon nothing but putting themselves under cover from the injuries of the weather." Even though Charlevoix worried for the colonists, he nonetheless envisioned a bright future for the city, writing that "Rome and Paris had not such considerable beginnings...and their founders met not with those advantages on the Seine and the Tiber, which we have found on the Mississippi, in comparison of which, these two rivers are no more than brooks." As a result, he predicted that "this wild and desert place, at present almost entirely covered over with canes and trees, shall one day...become the capital of a large and rich colony." Charlevoix, Bienville, and countless others who later commented on the city's relationship with its surroundings believed that the promise of New Orleans's situation outweighed the shortcomings of its site. Henry Murray, a traveler who visited the city in the mid-nineteenth century, summed up this viewpoint: "New Orleans is surprising evidence of what men will endure, when cheered by the hopes of an ever-flowing tide of all mighty dollars and cents."[14]

In Charlevoix's and Murray's observations one catches a glimpse of what the river has meant to New Orleans: despite a host of environmental woes, people have settled there because they believed that the Mississippi would make them rich, or at least keep food on their tables.[15] Promised financial gain, though, is only a portion of the river's significance for the city, and just one piece of the story of the relationship between New Orleans and the Mississippi that this book tells. As I researched and wrote, it became clear to me that the interactions between a vast, urban center and the continent's largest, most dynamic watercourse often appear inscrutable. The river has offered no written records—none of the traditional tools historians use to understand the past—while the city's residents have left far too many documents for a lone scholar to grapple with in a lifetime. Therefore, I sought an unusual methodology to understand the ties between river and city: I turned to where New Orleans and the Mississippi collide, where the urban meets what often has been called the natural—the riverfront.

Reading New Orleans's riverfront as both a natural artifact and a cultural form proved rewarding, because throughout the city's history, by custom and law, the river's banks have been public. As a result, competing interests have struggled for control of the waterfront, for the right to shape that space, sometimes to open it for public access and use, at other times to wall it off for commercial purposes exclusively. I discovered in these contests much about what the river has symbolized to people. And because the waterfront has been public, a broad cross section of New Orleanians (the inelegant term for residents of the city) have had a voice in shaping that space physically and culturally, as well as in determining its best uses. In short, the waterfront provided me with a useful tool for understanding the river's significance for the city.

Still, this discovery fulfilled only half of my goals for this project, in which I hoped to understand and convey not only people's conceptions of the river, but also how the river shaped New Orleans. In other words, I wanted to demonstrate that the relationship between river and city has been reciprocal. The waterfront proved an excellent source in this case as well, because the river has played a critical role in the contests to control and define its banks. Whether materially, through floods, erosion, and deposition, or more abstractly, in its impact on the way people think about New Orleans, the river has been an active participant in the city's development. For instance, urbanists write of "cognitive mapping," the unspoken, unwritten ways that people understand cities in which they live.[16] For most New Orleanians the river has been the most important mental *and* physical landmark in the city, shaping not only ideas about the city, but also molding it spatially.

After studying the waterfront, I arrived at this book's main insights, which can be summed up by paraphrasing Mark Twain: reports of the deaths of public space and so-called nature in U.S. cities are exaggerated. This is not to say that our urban areas are all marked by glorious public spaces. This is hardly true, particularly if one compares typical U.S. cities to their European counterparts. Nor do I claim that U.S. metropolitan areas are green havens, ecological paradises where the flora and fauna are healthy, the air clean, and the water pure. Instead, I attempt to demonstrate that public space and nature remain a vital part of urban America, alive if not always well, and that contemporary discourse that is often filled with dirges for both is overstated. Before elaborating on these points, let me clarify some of the language critical to understanding my arguments.

Literary critic Raymond Williams's book *Keywords,* quoted so often by environmental historians that it risks becoming a cliché, says that "nature is perhaps the most complex word in the [English] language" because of its countless definitions, which have depended not only on the time and place the word has been used, but also on who has done the using. Taking up where Williams left off, many scholars now argue that nature, once thought to be static and immutable, is actually a pliable social construction.[17] Cornfields on a big Nebraska farm, Yosemite National Park, the Mississippi River: for some people, each of these represents nature. For others, however, the fields are an artifact of technology, marred by pesticides, herbicides, and monoculture; the park is an engineered landscape, first altered by Native Americans and later by Anglo-Europeans drawing on pastoral images; and the river is an artificial drainage ditch, starved by dams, straitjacketed by concrete banks, and choked by toxic sludge. The point is well taken: nature is a complicated and historically contingent concept, as much the creation of social processes as a fixed, material reality.

But this point of view also raises an important question: if nature is a social construction, how can I meaningfully claim that it has shaped New Orleans? The answer is that social constructions have causative weight. Just because their meanings change in different times and places, depending on users and uses, does not mean social constructions have no impact on history. For an example, one need only think about race, now widely viewed as a constructed concept but still recognized as a powerful historical agent. Another answer, of equal importance, is that while I accept that nature is socially constructed, I am not so steeped in postmodern scholarship as to see it *only* in this light. *Nature,* I argue, is also a blanket term covering a variety of material things, such as winds, tides, and pathogens, just to name a few. Indeed, people, measurable biological entities, are also part of nature—but more on that later.

How, then, do I deal with this precarious word? How can nature have meaning or analytical heft if it changes guises so often? When possible, I specify exactly what I mean when writing of nature, though in some places I found it difficult, even counterproductive, to avoid the word entirely. In service of brevity, I sometimes use the word *nature* as shorthand where I am confident my meaning is clear. More importantly, when historical actors I discuss used the word, I do so as well when writing about them. At those times, where I can, I draw out what people meant when referring to nature; I see this as another way of interpreting people's relationship with their environment and clarifying their understanding of what they deemed natural.

Two other terms demand attention. Williams explores neither the word *public* nor *space* in *Keywords*—although they are, particularly in tandem, nearly as complicated as *nature. The public* is, perhaps more than any other phrase in modern parlance, bandied about by pundits. Like *nature* in today's eco-friendly cultural climate, *the public* conveys powerful moral authority and a sense of unassailable righteousness; it is a benchmark term, against which politicians and policies are measured. The public has schools, which, according to experts, are in trouble. Increasingly, its health is scrutinized: the public should smoke less, eat more vegetables, and walk briskly at least thrice weekly. The public is everywhere—indeed, we are part of the public—but it is also nowhere, because rarely is the public defined. The public, then, again like nature, is a social construction; its meanings are fluid and historically contingent. Yet, as with nature, I argue that the public is also material, and though there is not one, single, normative public, particular publics can be quantified and defined. As a result, I have tried, whenever possible, not to refer to the public without stating who or what I mean. Likewise, when actors in the text discussed the public, I explain to whom I think they referred.

Space, regrettably, may be as complex. Here I follow postmodern geographers who seek a "reassertion of space in critical social theory." These scholars, who often draw on the pioneering work of Michel Foucault, have rightly argued that spaces are products of power relationships.[18] Unlike these geographers, however, who often view space only as a product of discourse, as representation or an abstraction, this book usually remains rooted in physical space, on the ground in New Orleans. This is not to suggest that discourse plays no part in producing space. It does, but not alone. I contend that space is a product of political, economic, and cultural contests, *as well as* material forces. If that sounds too theoretical, do not worry. Although the public in this book is often shaped by people's understanding of that word, it is still composed of identifiable individuals. And even though perceptions also shape the spaces that the public occupies, those spaces almost always remain *terra firma*.

Definitions aside, most misapprehensions about the demise of urban nature are rooted in the centuries-old view that cities are solely an expression of human culture, antithetical to the natural world. And though the nature/culture dichotomy has been thoroughly debunked in some quarters of the academy recently, the vast majority of urbanists, when they write about the nonhuman world at all, still echo Lewis Mumford's claim that "as the pavement spreads, nature is pushed away."[19] Vestiges of this argument linger even in the finest urban-environmental histories, including those devoted to blurring the boundary between cities and their natural surroundings, such as William Cronon's masterpiece, *Nature's Metropolis*. Cronon's analysis is almost exclusively focused on economic relationships; he pays little attention to social, cultural, or urban spatial history. As a result, the question of how, or even if, nature is woven into the city's fabric goes unasked. Furthermore, in Cronon's telling, as Chicago grew, the metropolis's relationship with its hinterland devolved from interdependence to urban dominance. By the volume's end—after having read about how corporate capital has sponsored the industrialization of time, the deforestation of the city's surroundings, and the commodification of the agricultural products that once linked Windy City consumers with rural producers—one wonders whether what the author, drawing on Marx and Hegel, calls "first nature" matters at all anymore in the workings of the city.[20]

The same question should be applied even to the work of those scholars most interested in spatial issues, because, with few exceptions, they have overlooked the significance and power of urban nature. Important studies on the "social production of urban space" have either ignored the ways in which the nonhuman world has taken part in producing those spaces—people alone are seen as responsible for the urban form— or depicted nature as passive, as acted upon rather than acting in city life.[21]

An antidote for these misconceptions can be found in the concept of landscape as defined by geographer D. W. Meinig, who writes that "the idea of landscape runs counter to recognition of any simple binary relationship between man and nature. Rather, it begins with a naive acceptance of the intricate intermingling of physical, biological, and cultural features which any glance around us displays." Meinig's words have served as something like a mission statement for the field of landscape studies. The best work in the discipline depicts "all landscapes as symbolic," and "as part of the shared set of ideas and memories and feelings which bind a people together," while recognizing these places as both human and nonhuman constructions.[22] By viewing New Orleans's waterfront in this way, I conclude that the Mississippi, because of what hydrologists call its natural regimen—the unaltered workings of the river— *and* its cultural significance, still plays a role in shaping space and people's perceptions of nature in the city. Like landscape architect Anne Spirn, I believe that "humans are not the sole authors of landscape," a view that rebuts Mumford's argument that where cities advance, nature inevitably retreats.[23] Instead of opposing cities and their nonhuman surroundings, I suggest that New Orleans's waterfront represents a mingling of built and natural environments, and that the production of space in New Orleans has been both a natural and social process. Indeed, the attempt to draw a line between the two is almost always futile.

As people weep for the end of urban nature, they also mourn the demise of public space in cities. In using the riverbanks as a lens to bring New Orleans's relationship with the Mississippi into focus, I conclude that the waterfront has always been, at least by some definitions, a public space, and that it still remains one. As a result, I disagree with scholars who long for a lost golden age when the public played out democratic impulses in urban coffeehouses. I also differ in part with people who, like journalist Michael Sorkin and geographer, environmental historian, and polemicist Mike Davis, deride the modern metropolis as a Disney-style theme park monitored by ubiquitous surveillance cameras.

Such incisive critiques are thought-provoking and deserve credit for spot-lighting the issue of beleaguered urban public spaces. As they demon-strate, there is little doubt that public spaces are besieged in our cities, and those few that remain vibrant are often more closely monitored and tightly controlled today than in the past. Still, these studies do not fully account for the tangled histories of urban spaces, and how the public that used those spaces has changed over time.[24]

In contrast, I argue that to understand the history of urban public spaces one must first grapple with how protean definitions of the public have been across time, and the impact that constant shifts in the mean-ing of that phrase—the public—have had on the production of land-scapes in cities. In short, public spaces are always being reinvented as perceptions of the public shift from era to era. Applying this point has serious repercussions, because the texts framing the contemporary de-bate about public space, like that focusing on urban nature, typically are narratives of steady decline or unraveling: in the past the public con-trolled spaces that were free, open, and plentiful, but now the hegemony of corporate elites over such spaces is absolute. This argument remains useful insofar as it recognizes that the production and control of urban public space have often been determined by power relations. Regardless of its utility, though, this position ultimately fails to account for the fact that the very definition of the public has also been a product of power dynamics, a point that might force scholars, as it has me in this project, to abandon a declension model of history, not to embrace instead a coun-tervailing positivist interpretation, but an alternative characterized by nuance, in which negotiation becomes the mainspring of change over time, and non-elites share power with elites.

In my study of the production of landscapes at New Orleans's wa-terfront across nearly two hundred years, the findings are complicated. The riverfront illustrates that there are many different kinds of public spaces (just as there are many different publics)—recreational, political, cultural, and commercial, to name only a few—and one location, some-times over time and sometimes in an instant, can fall into all of these cat-egories. The point here is not to create a taxonomy of public spaces, but rather to underscore how complex these places are. For instance, it is too simple and historically inaccurate to think of public space as uni-formly unregulated or open to all, what geographer Don Mitchell has labeled "unconstrained space within which political movements can or-ganize and expand into wider arenas." This view represents one ideal-ized form of public space, and at certain times in New Orleans's history, the waterfront has met this lofty standard. More often, however, various municipal institutions, ranging from the French and Spanish colonial authorities to the city council have closely monitored the riverfront, attempting to limit access to what Mitchell, writing about Peace Park in Berkeley, California, labels an "appropriate public."[25] This does not mean that the waterfront has not been public; rather, it has been the site of conflicts over the meaning and application of that word, meanings that have shifted frequently, painfully, and with great effect throughout New Orleans's history. Again, like nature, public space in the city has been historically contingent, culturally constructed, *and* material.[26]

To understand the ways in which the Mississippi's banks have served as a public space, I explore the social history of that landscape, asking who has used the waterfront and for what, as well as who has controlled that space and how they have defined the public for whom it is intended. At the same time, because the waterfront is designated as public in Louisiana's law, I look to legal history to understand that landscape. By reviewing court cases, I examine how the law has variously foreshadowed, mirrored, and echoed changes in the public character of the waterfront. Here, too, definitions changed in different times: sometimes the courts employed an expansive reading of the public's rights to the waterfront; at others they ruled that a small, centralized group of city or state officials had the right to regulate and control that space in the public's interest. Finally, I study the waterfront's cultural history, because, regardless of who has controlled the riverfront in a particular period, or the judicial rulings on the public's rights along the Mississippi's banks, New Orleanians have always perceived the waterfront as theirs, and accordingly have remade that space in small and large ways.[27]

Arguing that the waterfront has been a public space—no matter how complicated such nomenclature may be—is a crucial point because of the central role that such places play in city life. As countless scholars, ranging from Peter Baldwin to William Whyte, from Mary Ryan to Richard Sennett, have argued, public spaces are among the most important determinants of the health of cities: they can be meeting sites, social centers, and gathering places; locations in which to negotiate difference, whether cultural, political, or otherwise, and to recognize common goals, dreams, or ideals; spots that allow cramped urban dwellers, often short on private space, to spread out; and defining landscapes or landmarks, providing a sense of identity for many cities.[28] In my eyes, and as I describe it, New Orleans's waterfront is all of these things. But as a public space at the city's edge, where New Orleans meets the Mississippi, the waterfront is also something else, well worth examining, not only for urban but also environmental historians: it is the location where New Orleanians have often experienced the river's impact on their city and where they have struggled collectively with what the river means to them. The waterfront is the place where New Orleanians have formed opinions about, resolved conflicts over, and decided on the best uses of the river. In other words, my study of New Orleans's waterfront suggests that public spaces in cities may also be important because they serve as spots where people interact with urban nature.

The episodes discussed in this book, often characterized by quests for control of space and the Mississippi, together form a history of the waterfront and, by extension, the city's relationship with the river. Looking back to Charlevoix's era, the river originally represented a promise that a steady flow of trade would find its way to the waterfront. Based on this view of the Mississippi, Bienville founded New Orleans, and many settlers came to the city because they deemed his reading of the landscape prescient. Yet, for all of the region's geographic allure, New Orleans's local environment hindered most efforts at achieving the city's perceived destiny as the seat of an inland commercial empire. So, while New Orleanians often viewed what they called nature as kindly, it could also be unpredictable, fickle, even cruel. This tension—between site and situation—has characterized the city's environmental history, because New Orleanians did not stand pat with the hand the river dealt them. Instead, like people in countless other places throughout U.S. history, they altered their city's site in trying to meet the promise of its situation.

From its settlement, New Orleans has been a commercial metropolis, and commerce abhors chaos. Consequently, to maximize its efficiency and attractiveness as an entrepot, the city's residents have tried to impose their will on their environment. They have attempted to regularize the river and its banks, in the words of journalist John McPhee, to "control nature," while at the same time rationalizing space in the city.[29] Over time, New Orleanians have remade their urban-riparian ecosystem to suit human ends. In doing so, they have believed that they were finishing nature's work, somehow making whole what they deemed incomplete. Most often, the instruments of change they have employed have been property law as well as science and technology. For example, New Orleanians have produced space at the waterfront using the law as an organizing principle or bulwark. They have also built enormous, artificial levees designed to wall off the city from the river's floodwaters, reinforced the river's banks to halt its shape-shifting, and constructed huge riverside warehouses to protect goods stored at the city's port, all as a way of engineering dynamism out of their city's site.

I write in this book about the ways that these efforts have played out at the waterfront. Predictably, there have been unanticipated consequences. Sometimes property law has caused or exacerbated environmental problems, and occasionally, new technologies, designed to render life easier and more predictable, have made surprising demands on the city's residents. This book also explores how the process of rationalizing the riverfront has altered that space's public character. Unregulated spaces typically are less orderly than locations subject to centralized authority. As a result, while many New Orleanians have fought throughout the city's history to keep the waterfront open and public, others, particularly commercial elites, have wanted to consolidate power over that space with an eye toward regimenting it. When they have seized authority at the waterfront, the city's elites have often limited access to that space, arguing that commercial uses best served the public and that commerce required order to thrive. In the words of one of the founders of the field of landscape studies, J. B. Jackson, New Orleans's commercial elites have tried to remake the waterfront as a "space devoted to process rather than to people."[30]

Through their efforts at controlling the river and waterfront, New Orleanians have tried to discipline their environment, to make the unpredictable predictable in service of capitalist development.[31] The result was that throughout much of the city's history, New Orleans grew distant, both culturally and spatially, from the river that sustained it. Whereas the Mississippi formed part of the daily lives of most New Orleanians from the colonial period until the era of Reconstruction, for a century after that the river and its waterfront were off-limits or inaccessible to most of the city's residents. The artificial levees and warehouses lining the waterfront formed a physical barrier between New Orleans and the Mississippi, while the conflation of the riverfront's public character with commercial endeavors further alienated many people from that space. In short, by the mid-twentieth century, sepia-toned images of the river flowing by the city were little more than vestiges of public memory lingering from the antebellum era.

At first glance, this may seem like another retelling of the tragic tale running through many environmental and urban histories—the degradation of the natural environment and the enclosure of public space at the hands of economic elites. And yet, New Orleans's reciprocal relationship with the Mississippi adds complexity to these well-worn stories. By examining episodes in which non-elite residents of the city have succeeded in maintaining the waterfront's status as a mixed-use, public space, I highlight the role that common people have played in shaping that landscape. At the same time, I focus on the Mississippi's ongoing participation in creating landscapes in New Orleans, arguing that the river has been an actor in the production of urban space.

Chapter 1 of this book opens in the years immediately following the Louisiana Purchase, when a New York attorney, recently arrived in New Orleans, successfully sued the city for title to a parcel of the Mississippi's riverfront. The resulting controversy dragged on for almost two decades. This chapter reveals the importance that the Mississippi and its banks held for New Orleanians in the aftermath of the city's colonial period, exploring the disparate ways that different segments of the city's population viewed public space and the river. The second chapter also pivots on a conflict over the Mississippi's banks, this time during the era of steamboats on the river in the 1830s, when the municipal government attempted to remake the mixed-use, public waterfront as a steamboat port. This chapter examines the impact that a river-based technology had on people's perceptions of the Mississippi, as well on as time and space more broadly. Chapter 2 concludes with a discussion of why, in 1836, New Orleans divided into three independently governed submunicipalities, after competing interests, unable to agree on how best to administer the waterfront, ultimately split the city into thirds.

The divided city eventually reunited in 1852. But only a year later New Orleans faced another crisis, when a massive yellow-fever epidemic gripped the city, killing nearly ten thousand people in approximately four months. Chapter 3 chronicles this epidemic. It suggests that the outbreak might have been minimized had New Orleans's commercial community not maintained a stranglehold on the city's public sphere by forcing the press to remain silent about the scourge. Commercial elites then unwittingly further encouraged the epidemic's spread when they refused to close the city's port by instituting a quarantine at the waterfront, demonstrating their hard-won control over that public space. The third chapter concludes with an exploration of the ways in which the epidemic, seemingly a "natural disaster," forced New Orleanians to rethink their city's relationship with the Mississippi and what they labeled nature.

Chapter 4 is set in the years after the Civil War, when the city struggled to revive its flagging economy. In the 1870s, New Orleanians lured trunk railroads to the city by offering generous land grants along the waterfront, beginning a process in which portions of that space were privatized over time. The discussion in this chapter then moves into the dawn of the Progressive Era, when the city created a quasi-public organization to administer the waterfront, the Board of Commissioners of the Port of New Orleans, or Dock Board. The Dock Board overhauled the riverfront, employing scientific management of space to rationalize the city's port by constructing huge warehouses to keep goods stored there safe from the delta's climate. Ironically, though the Dock Board championed its choices by pointing to the public character of the riverbanks, it nonetheless ensured that fewer New Orleanians than ever before would have access to the waterfront, raising a question into high relief: who or what, exactly, was the public New Orleans?

The 1927 flood is the subject of chapter 5. No event in the city's history has been more significant in shifting people's perceptions of the Mississippi, as New Orleanians witnessed the river at its most dynamic and unpredictable, while also facing their own culpability in creating what many people at the time recognized as a human-constructed catastrophe. This book concludes with an epilogue, focusing on New Orleans in the late 1950s and early 1960s, when a coalition of student activists, urban professionals, and environmentalists banded together to defeat a proposed riverfront expressway slated for construction between the Mississippi and the city's French Quarter. The so-called freeway fighters founded their resistance on the contention that the river and city were fundamentally linked along the waterfront. This episode completes the book's arc, because after their victory, the coalition members convinced city officials to reopen the disputed portion of the waterfront as a multi-use, public space.

Finally, in writing this book I discovered that not only have nature and public space always been a part of the urban fabric in New Orleans—indeed, they still are—but also that, along the city's waterfront, these two slippery concepts and material entities are inextricably intertwined. Much of this book, then, is devoted to demonstrating how changing definitions of the public informed people's perceptions of the Mississippi; how New Orleanians' understandings of what they called nature shaped the production of landscapes in the city; how the public, as it was constantly being redefined, fought for control of urban space and the river; and how the Mississippi itself impinged on all of the above, on the ways in which nature and the public were defined in New Orleans, and on the ways in which space was produced in the city. This is a story of a river and its city.

CHAPTER 1

A Batture Laid Out for the
Particular Use of the Public

WHO OWNS BIG MUDDY'S MUD?

On May 23, 1807, an audience at the superior courthouse of the Territory of Orleans waited to hear the outcome of the case *John Gravier v. Mayor, Aldermen, and Inhabitants of the City of New Orleans*. Among the onlookers, three men were especially interested. One of them, Edward Livingston, attorney for the plaintiff and a renowned New York City politician, had arrived in Louisiana just three years earlier. The other two, Louis Moreau-Lislet and Pierre Derbigny, both prominent members of New Orleans's Creole (in this book meaning Louisiana-born) elite, provided counsel for the city. After a short wait, the court's decision was likely evident in Livingston's barely concealed glee and the fury that Moreau-Lislet and Derbigny struggled to contain. The three presiding judges ruled unanimously: Jean Gravier's title to the batture—defined as the part of the Mississippi's banks remaining covered in times of high water and uncovered during low—fronting the Faubourg (false city or suburb) St. Mary was secure.[1]

Perhaps the justices believed that such an unwavering verdict would silence controversy surrounding what was becoming known as the batture case. If so, they underestimated people's investment in the dispute, largely because they misunderstood the significance of the Mississippi and its waterfront for New Orleanians. Rather than settling the issue, by ruling for Gravier the court inflamed an array of interests resolved to fight for the batture. The concerned parties included New Orleanians who valued the batture as a public space; riparian proprietors who feared for their land values; New Orleans's Conseil de ville (city council), which hoped to consolidate its control over the riverfront; and President Thomas Jefferson, who believed that the batture was a key part of his plans for what was then known as the West. Because of the high stakes and the characters involved in the case, what might have been a local legal and land-use dispute spilled outside the confines of the territorial courtroom into the streets of New Orleans, and eventually found its way to Washington, D.C.

The origins of the batture case can be traced to several conflicts simmering in New Orleans in the years immediately before and after the Louisiana Purchase. For instance, the cultural and diplomatic disputes that flared between the French, Spanish, and Americans vying for control of the Mississippi fueled the discord.[2] The contested nature of property rights in New Orleans also contributed to the dispute, because adherents to the civil-law tradition predominating in Louisiana and the common-law-influenced legal system in place throughout the rest of the United States fought over the city's waterfront. Additionally, clashing perceptions of the Mississippi, and what people called nature, played a role in the controversy. The fight also centered on competing notions of the proper use of urban space in New Orleans, as the combatants involved in the case were concerned with controlling the riverfront at a time when shifting definitions of public rights transformed that landscape into a battleground. Finally, the batture case serves as a reminder that the Mississippi has played a key role in shaping space in New Orleans, because the river, through its geomorphological processes, was an active participant in the conflict. Indeed, the Mississippi had touched off the hostilities when it deposited the disputed terrain—the batture itself.

Although people founded New Orleans, the city could not have existed without the river. Through dynamic sedimentation, the Mississippi built not only its delta, but also its natural levee (from the French *lever*, to raise), and on the river's levee New Orleanians built their city (figure 3). Levee formation occurs when alluvial rivers, which periodically leave their beds, stretch out on their flood plains. In the years prior to the construction of the artificial levees that line the Mississippi today, when the river overtopped its banks, its muddy water, after spreading out, lost current. Without a current keeping sediment suspended, heavy material dropped out first, leaving lighter sediment in suspension, to be deposited farther from the river's bed. As a result of

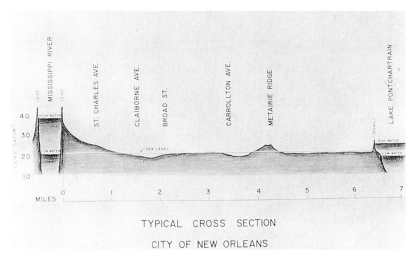

TYPICAL CROSS SECTION
CITY OF NEW ORLEANS

Figure 3. This cross section of the city demonstrates how the terrain slopes away from the Mississippi. Through the turn of the twentieth century, the city extended only to the vicinity of Claiborne Avenue. Note how high above the city the river flows, confined only within its levee, particularly at times of high water. Adapted from the *Report on the Drainage of the City of New Orleans* (1895), courtesy of G. Joseph Sullivan, General Superintendent, Sewerage and Water Board of New Orleans.

this deposition pattern, over millennia, alluvial ridges formed, flanking the Mississippi, sloping gently away from the stream like long sedimentary ramps: the river's natural levees.[3]

This topography helps explain part of the waterfront's significance throughout New Orleans's history. Rare high ground has always held great value in the city, because prior to the advent of sophisticated drainage technologies, the river's levee provided the only suitable foundation for building in the delta's soggy environment. Early planners took advantage of this geological gift, placing the city on the river's eastern levee. At that time, New Orleans was composed of what we now call the French Quarter, a grid six blocks deep from the river and twelve blocks wide along the waterfront. The highest point of the natural levee was approximately twenty feet above sea level, and from that apex the local terrain sloped back to a cypress wetland at the city's rear (figure 4). Beyond what New Orleanians called the "backswamp," which lay as much as ten feet below sea level, stood Lake Pontchartrain.[4] Because New Orleans is nestled in the crook of one of the river's crescent-shaped meanders, to the west, east, and south the city is bounded by the river's levee. The shore of Lake Pontchartrain stands to the north. Like anywhere else

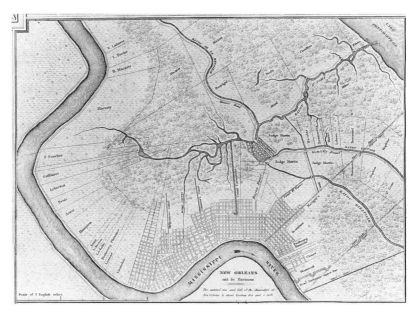

Figure 4. Until the end of the nineteenth century, when powerful drainage pumps reclaimed the swamps at the city's rear, New Orleans backed to massive wetlands (map dated 1829). Courtesy of The Historic New Orleans Collection.

in the Mississippi's delta, New Orleans is surrounded by a wet world composed of terrain that is not quite land.

The batture case, one of the most intense and enduring of the conflicts over the waterfront in the city's history, focused on a portion of muddy sediment deposited on the river side of the levee just upstream from the French Quarter (figure 5). The Mississippi inundated that parcel of muck for much of the year, leaving it dry only during periods of low water. Like the river's natural levee and delta, the batture also was a product of dynamic sedimentation. To understand how the batture came to be, imagine New Orleans situated within a quarter-moon crescent. The French Quarter lies cupped in the lower portion of the crescent, with the Mississippi represented by the C shape itself. As the Mississippi flowed by the city in an era before concrete bank revetment, it scoured out sediment from the shore opposite the French Quarter, the so-called West Bank, because that terrain faced the brunt of the current as the river turned along the lower part of the crescent. Meanwhile, on the East Bank, particularly just upstream from the French Quarter, the river deposited material in relatively calm water, slowly forming what became known as the batture. With the power of its current, and the sediment

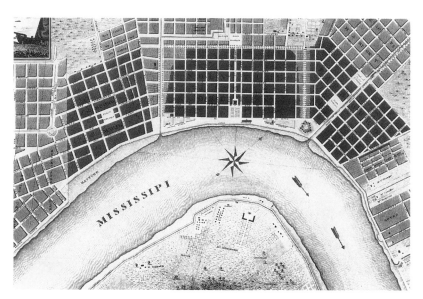

Figure 5. The disputed batture terrain lay just upstream from the French Quarter, fronting the Faubourg St. Mary (map dated 1817). Courtesy of The Historic New Orleans Collection.

staining its waters, the Mississippi eroded vast chunks of earth from one part of its banks while depositing new land at another spot—the river gaveth and the river tooketh away.

To casual observers, the batture might have seemed like an anonymous stretch of mud, but its history heralded the controversy swirling around it after the Purchase. The St. Mary batture abutted a parcel of land the Jesuit order had owned for much of the French colonial period in Louisiana. When the Jesuits were expelled from the colony in 1763, the French administration subdivided and sold off their lands, with the terrain fronting the batture falling into the hands of Bertrand Gravier in 1785. After further dividing his holdings into smaller plots, Gravier sold them in the 1790s. He named the *faubourg* he founded after his late wife, Mary. When Gravier died in 1797, his brother Jean acquired the remaining unsold portion of the Faubourg St. Mary.[5] The tale might have ended there, with the foundation of one of the city's first suburbs, but the story grew more complex in the wake of the Louisiana Purchase.

In 1803, Gravier gazed at the accreting batture in front of the Faubourg St. Mary and saw profit potential in the silt. No seer, Gravier was a savvy speculator who recognized the value of land in postcolonial New Orleans. But his plan for the batture was complicated because he owned none of the riparian lots in the *faubourg*. Nonetheless, he reclaimed a portion of the batture in front of the settlement by erecting an artificial levee to keep approximately four hundred square feet of sediment dry year-round. Gravier later justified his behavior by noting that he had never sold off the batture itself, though buyers had snapped up the riparian lots years earlier.[6] This plan to reclaim the deposited land seems to have progressed until Gravier attempted to prohibit people from using the St. Mary batture. His actions, which likely had seemed harmless or eccentric until then—why bother a respected member of the community while he wanders in the riverside muck?—suddenly aroused protests from New Orleanians, who, in dry seasons, were accustomed to using the batture for storage, landfill, and a promenade.

At this early stage of the dispute, two distinct views of the riverfront emerged: on the one hand, Gravier's vision of neatly divided plots of real estate, reclaimed land commodified and rationalized by private-property rights; on the other, an open waterfront, available for common use, as had been customary throughout the city's history. There was a choice, in other words, between capitalizing on the waterfront's new-found economic potential and maintaining the community's venerable rights to use that space in a variety of commercial and noncommercial ways. In response to a series of protests from aggrieved New Orleanians, the Conseil de ville backed the latter position, proclaiming the area open to the "public," though it failed to account for who or what was included in such a broad conceptual category.[7] Following that resolution, Gravier, seemingly chastened, abandoned his improvements—for a while.

The council's declaration arose out of a combination of factors: Louisiana's civil-law heritage, local custom, and the legislators' desire to consolidate control of the waterfront. When the United States purchased Louisiana, French and Spanish laws were in place in New Orleans.[8] Those two nations drew much of their legal scholarship, particularly on the subject of riparian law, from ancient Roman sources. Although the batture's rightful ownership ultimately evolved into a hotly contested topic, in 1804 the council simply followed local laws, which stated that the banks of navigable rivers were publicly held. That portion of the civil law hinged on what is called a servitude, defined as the "limitations on ownership established by law for the benefit of the general public."[9] In the batture's case, the applicable servitude stated that while a landowner could hold title to the property abutting a navigable river, the public retained access to the riverbanks. This servitude had shaped custom in New Orleans, and the waterfront had remained open from the city's founding, though the appropriate public had always been defined by the French and Spanish authorities. All public lands, after all, had belonged to the crown throughout the city's colonial period. With the American purchase of Louisiana, however, the people became sovereign, and the council had to compete with other parties in the city for the role of guardian of the public's best interests.

Early in the batture controversy, few residents of New Orleans knew of the legal scholarship designating the banks of Louisiana's navigable rivers as public. What New Orleanians did know was the meaning that the riverbanks held for them. The waterfront was the border where the human and nonhuman worlds mingled, the center of New Orleans's urban-riparian environment. Every day, people interacted with one another and with the Mississippi at the riverbanks. In many ways the waterfront defined the city. Market, municipal entryway, port, and promenade, in post-Purchase New Orleans, it provided the city's most important public space, a landscape from which people marveled at the city's commerce, multicultural character, and relationship with the Mississippi.

Although located on the city's margin, the waterfront stood at the core of life in New Orleans. It was the key to orienting oneself in the city not only because of the myriad uses New Orleanians made of the riverbanks, but also because of the city's layout. At the time of the Purchase, New Orleans was home to fewer than ten thousand people, and pedestrians could stroll the city's length and breadth in a morning, going about their business in a town marked by architectural uniformity with a European flair, and straight but muddy streets. Huge fires had swept through New Orleans in 1788 and 1794, and few structures of more than four stories tall stood in the rebuilt city. With no architectural monuments save for St. Louis Cathedral, in what is now known as Jackson Square (figure 6), and the Ursuline Convent, the massive Mississippi hugging New Orleans in its crescent embrace dwarfed all human constructions, making the riverfront the city's most noteworthy feature.[10]

The waterfront dominated New Orleans physically not just because of the prominent place it occupied in people's mental maps of the city, but also because of the region's topography. All of New Orleans lay on the river's natural levee, but the high ground immediately adjacent to the Mississippi took on special significance. The highest point of the river's natural levee in New Orleans stood between ten and twenty feet above sea level. Twenty feet may sound paltry, but when compared with neighboring terrain, much of it below sea level, New Orleans's levee had always been a great mountain in the delta's flatlands. Then, shortly after the city's founding, the threat of flooding had forced New Orleanians to augment the natural levee, rais-

Figure 6. St. Louis Cathedral dominates the scene at Jackson Square, as people promenade on the levee in the foreground (1855). Courtesy of The Historic New Orleans Collection.

ing it higher as a barrier between the city and the river's floodwaters. Through the years, New Orleanians had built the artificial levee taller, elevating the riverbank still higher above the surrounding land. The combined effect of the region's geology and this technological innovation staggered the senses: the farther one traveled from the river in New Orleans, the lower the ground.[11] The Mississippi and its levee loomed above the city, drawing all eyes to the riverfront, as to the pulpit of a cathedral.

The local environment increased the riverfront's significance for other reasons as well. Because the delta is dominated by wetlands, there were no viable land routes into the city in its early years. As a result, the riverfront typically provided the point of ingress and egress for travelers, traders, and residents of New Orleans. The high ground along the waterfront served as the city's front door; it usually was the first site greeting people as they arrived in New Orleans and the last thing they saw when leaving. Consequently, the waterfront often emblazoned itself in people's memories, the most enduring image that travelers carried with them of New Orleans. In narratives they penned after visiting the city, tourists time and again remarked on the awe-inspiring spectacle of the roiling Mississippi and its waterfront perched above New Orleans.

But the waterfront's importance was not merely an accident of topography, augmented by human ingenuity. For cultural reasons, too, New Orleanians valued the levee. The city's founders, recognizing the importance of the Mississippi, memorialized the waterfront, in some respects turning it into sacred space, by laying out the town's main plaza, the Place d'armes (now Jackson Square), fronting the river, with St. Louis Cathedral at the plaza's rear. The outcome was a profound sense of the union between river and city, as well as the sacralization of the Mississippi.

From the sacred to the profane, elevated above the city physically, the riverfront also provided a waterside promenade where New Orleanians and their visitors enjoyed cooling breezes wafting off the river. One observer in early-nineteenth-century New Orleans noted that when the climate became stifling, "the Levee after sunset is crowded with company, who having been confined all day to their houses, seldom miss this favourable opportunity of breathing a little fresh air."[12] Paved with gravel made from oyster shells and planted with orange trees, the levee provided a mall that afforded people an opportunity to stroll, taking in the sights and smells of the life in New Orleans while admiring the city's relationship with the river.[13]

And over time, the waterfront's economic significance also grew for the city, as the site next to the Place d'armes housed New Orleans's most important bazaar (today's French Market), as well as the city's port. Because of the Mississippi's great depth in front of New Orleans—approximately two hundred feet at the French Quarter's upstream boundary—the city enjoyed a deep-water port. Flatboats, keelboats, and all manner of sailing vessels lined up at the riverfront, creating a captivating commercial spectacle that observers often likened to a "forest of masts."[14] Traders haggled in countless languages at the city's port, making it a multicultural hub and one of the capitals of the Atlantic World. The riverfront was the heartbeat of the city's commercial enterprise, and it was there that New Orleanians measured their economic pulse. With no financial markets to interpret, and no leading economic indicators to consult, interested parties needed only to look to the riverfront for their business news. A mass of ships and bustle at the waterfront meant good tidings, while lulls signaled flagging commerce.

In seasons of low water, the Mississippi's batture served as one of the waterfront's most important spots, whose significance in New Orleans tended to stem from the way people used it rather than from its exchange value. Because of the city's topography, flooding and drainage were year-round problems in the days before an effective system of levees, in conjunction with electric drainage pumps and canals, reclaimed much of the swampy ground in New Orleans. Therefore, New Orleanians used the batture as a source of much-needed landfill to raise their property higher above the surrounding swamps, marshes, and bayous (figure 7). The

Figure 7. New Orleanians used the riverbanks, including the batture, for a variety of purposes: a storage site, a source of soil for fill, a pedestrian mall, and a port (image dated 1841). Courtesy of The Historic New Orleans Collection.

batture also served as an open storage spot where people kept goods, ranging from firewood to nonperishable foodstuffs. And lastly, the batture merits our attention because it served as the point of interface between the city and river. The batture was a kind of contested terrain that was entirely part neither of New Orleans nor of the Mississippi; as geologists have said of the whole of the delta, it was "between earth and sea, belonging to neither and alternately claimed by both."[15] As a result, it served as a symbolic landscape, characteristic of New Orleans's unique relationship with the Mississippi. The batture embodied the vague boundary between city and the river.

A NEW YORKER'S KEEN EYE FOR REAL ESTATE

The batture controversy likely would have ended with Gravier's censure by the city council had Edward Livingston not settled in New Orleans in 1804. Although Livingston came from New York, his family had established close ties to Louisiana prior to his arrival in New Orleans. His older brother, Robert, along with James Monroe, had served as the chief negotiator in Paris during the Louisiana Purchase. And Edward himself had been a rising star among the nation's Democratic-Republicans prior to running afoul of President Jefferson during the Aaron Burr conflict in 1801. Then, before coming to New Orleans, Livingston had sullied his reputation further in Jefferson's eyes by accruing a humiliating debt while serving in public office in New York, when one of his subordinates had absconded with nearly fifty thousand dollars from the city's treasury. In the acquisition of Louisiana, Livingston saw a chance for a clean slate, and he practically sprinted for New Orleans, leaving his disgrace behind in Manhattan.[16]

Livingston brought with him to the Crescent City an American perspective on property rights, a New Yorker's eye for the value of riparian land, a debtor's nose for easy money, and one of the keenest legal minds in the nation. Upon arriving in New Orleans, Livingston looked for an angle that would yield fast profits. When he trained his gaze on the St. Mary batture, Livingston believed that he had "found a business that will ultimately prove extremely profitable."[17] It remains unclear how Livingston and Gravier connected, but most deponents in the batture case believed that the New Yorker had solicited the case, furthering the impression that the lawyer was a rapacious speculator. Regardless, Gravier hired Livingston after the New Yorker agreed to take the case without promise of a fee. He accepted instead a guarantee that, if victorious, he would receive a portion of the spoils: a parcel of the Mississippi's waterfront. Content with those terms, Livingston brought suit against the city in October 1805.

After a long series of delays, the court ruled on the case in May 1807. In his opening argument, Livingston had claimed that because the disputed alluvium had begun accreting prior to the final sale of the riparian lots in the *faubourg,* and because the batture was not included in those sales, Gravier retained title to the land. The defendants' attorneys, Moreau-Lislet and Derbigny, had responded by marshaling an array of official papers suggesting that Gravier had never secured title to the batture. The two Creole lawyers had also stated that a riparian servitude guaranteed the public the right to use the alluvium, nullifying Gravier's claims. For support of their contention, they had called a host of witnesses, "all of whom proved that as long as they remembered...the inhabitants of the town had used the Batture for supplying themselves with building sand, and earth for filling up the streets and lots." Those witnesses had also testified that whenever anybody had built a structure on the batture in the past, the city had torn it down.[18]

In retrospect, that last bit of testimony raises questions about what kind of public space the waterfront had been in New Orleans prior to

the Purchase, illustrating that it is simplistic to call a space public without defining one's terms. If the space was public, why had the city torn
down structures on the waterfront? Who was included in the public that
was entitled to access the waterfront? What were those people allowed
to do there? And who, ultimately, controlled the waterfront landscape?

The structures in question had been built by people left homeless after
the fire of 1794. Although the city government had allowed squatters to
live on the waterfront following the blaze, eventually colonial authorities insisted that the temporary dwellings had to come down. When the
homeless people living next to the river resisted, officials removed the
shanties, demonstrating that although non-elite New Orleanians could
use the waterfront, the colonial administration ultimately controlled that
space.[19] In other words, the waterfront landscape had been public but
well regulated, its uses and users confined within parameters approved
by a centralized government apparatus. Thus it seems that the Creole attorneys' insistence that the batture was a public space obscured as much
as it revealed, suggesting that the public in New Orleans was far more
unified than the events following the fire of 1794 indicate.

Because of the complicated makeup of the public in New Orleans,
whereas Livingston's case remained relatively simple, the Creole attorneys argued a much more complex point. The New Yorker benefited
from representing a single party, while Moreau-Lislet's and Derbigny's
clients included the government and people of New Orleans. In short,
the Creoles fought for groups with often conflicting viewpoints on the
public character of the riverfront. Consequently, Livingston founded his
arguments on a relatively straightforward reading of private-property
rights: Gravier held title to the land in question, and therefore it belonged
to him; he could use it or dispose of it in any way he chose. On the other
hand, Moreau-Lislet and Derbigny attempted to prove that the batture
was public, a far more tangled notion of property. With a common
enemy to fight in 1807, the Creole attorneys and their clients avoided
the question of what exactly they meant when calling the waterfront public. But that issue was to emerge later in the dispute and would resurface
repeatedly throughout the city's history.

In explaining their decision in favor of the plaintiff, the justices of the
territorial court focused on four points. First, Gravier's property reached
the Mississippi's waters; second, batture accretions belonged to the
riparian-property title holder; third, the batture had begun accumulat-
ing while Gravier owned the property, and therefore the alluvium composed part of his holdings; fourth, because Gravier had never sold the

batture, he retained title to the accretion. As a result of these findings, in their unanimous ruling of May 23, 1807, the judges found Gravier's title to the land valid.[20] With the court's decision in hand, Livingston believed that he had found the means to dispatch his debt and rehabilitate his good name. He did not know that the batture controversy was only beginning.

Within days of his victory, Livingston sank an additional investment of seventy-seven thousand dollars into the batture and began contemplating improvements on his property. He hoped to turn his piece of the waterfront into a private port, likely to accommodate the steamboats his brother Robert was building back east with an eye toward navigating the Mississippi system. Livingston planned first to erect a new artificial reclamation levee to keep the batture dry year-round. Once the new levee was there, he would construct a navigation canal and a large building on the site. With his plans complete, Livingston hired African-American laborers, but much to his chagrin, each day when the workers arrived at the waterfront, a mob gathered, driving them away from the disputed terrain.[21]

As the summer wore on, this strange tableau continued: shortly after Livingston's laborers arrived next to the Mississippi, an appointed guard began beating a drum. At that signal, a crowd gathered to chase off the workers. The mob apparently recognized that if Livingston completed his private port, he would gain control of that portion of the riverfront, threatening its public character. It is unclear whether the rioters used the batture for storage, a promenade, a source of fill, or for some other purpose. Regardless, they made it clear that they were unwilling to allow Livingston to privatize any part of the waterfront. By demonstrating next to the Mississippi, the mob's members also asserted their place as part of the public in the city. And since, for the moment, the mob's interests matched those of the city's government and most elites, the authorities did not attempt to bring the rioters to heel, even though they were ignoring the rule of law. Livingston finally snapped in late August, contacting the territorial governor, William Claiborne, to demand that he uphold the court's ruling.[22]

As New Orleanians protected their access to the batture by warning away Livingston's workers, the Conseil de ville also sought to improve its uncertain status at the waterfront. At nearly the same time that Livingston wrote to Claiborne, the council appealed to the governor, asking him to intervene in the dispute. The council implored Claiborne to try a new strategy to end the conflict, suggesting that he inform President Jefferson of the controversy and ask the federal government to claim title to the riverside sediment, as colonial administrators had before the Purchase. Claiborne wrote to Jefferson, noting his fear that if the federal government did not step in, there might be "much bloodshed," and as he awaited a reply, the crisis escalated.[23]

On September 15, 1807, Livingston brought matters to a head by sparking what he thought would be a sympathetic spectacle at the waterfront. The previous day he had hired constables to protect his workers, but to no avail; the mob had triumphed again. On the morning of September 15, Livingston sent word to Claiborne that his laborers would commence work at noon, and he worried that the mob might "change the insolence of riot into the crime of murder." At twelve o'clock sharp, Livingston arrived at the batture with his workmen. Conscious of the era's racial politics, Livingston had hired whites only that day, hopeful that racial allegiances might trump spatial politics. It is possible that Livingston also recognized that white workers, carrying the full prerogatives of citizenship, could claim status as part of the public whose rights were protected at New Orleans's waterfront. Nonetheless, events transpired just as they had all summer.[24] As Livingston's workers gathered, a guard pounded a drum, summoning protesters, and a crowd of nearly four hundred people congregated to protect their rights. Claiborne then arrived on the scene and addressed the mob, scolding them to allow the courts to decide the matter and "retire in peace to [their] respective homes." He reassured the crowd that the matter was not settled, explaining that he had sent word to Jefferson. He then agreed to dispatch an envoy to Washington to communicate the rioters' grievances to the president. Having exacted the governor's word, the crowd dispersed.[25]

Following the events of September 15, Claiborne and the city council prepared papers asking the federal government to claim authority over the batture. After receiving news of Livingston's courtroom victory and plans for the batture, as well as of the riverfront riots, Jefferson quickly redressed what he saw as an egregious wrong and a threat to stability in newly acquired Louisiana. Invoking the controversial Squatters Act of 1807, Jefferson directed the secretary of state, James Madison, to have Livingston evicted from the contested terrain. Although Jefferson never admitted as much, his decision was hasty and quite likely illegal. Regardless, on January 25, 1808, the U.S. marshal in New Orleans, Le Breton D'Orgenois, arrived at the batture, ejected Livingston's workers, and seized the property in the name of the federal government. Although Livingston promptly secured an injunction against D'Orgenois, the marshal ignored the court order and removed the workers again in the following days.[26]

THE SAGE FROM MONTICELLO

Ironically, though Claiborne had hoped to contain the controversy by turning to the federal government for aid, his actions instead transformed the case from a local to a national issue. And in turning to Jefferson, Claiborne involved an ego and sharp mind at least equal to Livingston's, as well as an individual whose concern for the fate of the Mississippi could match that of most New Orleanians. Biographers of both Jefferson and Livingston have examined the batture case briefly, concluding that the president injected himself into the fray because of his personal antipathy for Livingston. They point to Jefferson's rage over the New Yorker's ties to Aaron Burr and the black eye Livingston had given to Jefferson's beloved political party with his involvement in the Manhattan embezzling scandal. Another student of the batture case indicates that Jefferson had twin goals in entering the controversy: first, keeping the fragile peace in Louisiana, and second, antagonizing Livingston, an unpopular figure in New Orleans, to earn political capital with the city's powerful Creole elites.[27] What scholars have failed to address is the president's interest in the spatial and environmental aspects of the case. Jefferson had a vested interest in an open and accessible Mississippi, a river he had never seen, but one that nonetheless had shaped his career, since it was the West's fight for a free Mississippi that initially had spurred Jefferson to dispatch ministers to buy New Orleans, leading to the Louisiana Purchase, among the defining moments of his presidency.

Jefferson's close ties to the Mississippi were forged in the years after the American Revolution. At that time, the federal government began assisting its land-hungry citizens, eager to settle the Mississippi Valley, by sponsoring the conquest of the region's Native Americans. The government also began negotiating treaties with foreign nations, designed to secure the western settlers' rights to navigate the region's highway of commerce, the Mississippi system. In the controversies surrounding those negotiations, Jefferson learned what the river and its banks meant to the West.

The importance of the Mississippi for westerners was simple: the river promised economic survival. As early as 1780, a struggling Kentucky settler, John May, linked western land values with open navigation of the river, writing to a business associate that prosperity in the region depended on whether Spain would allow trade on the lower Mississippi.[28] In 1785, another settler, David Wood Meriwether, summed up the river's significance in a letter to a friend who considered moving near what later was to be the city of Louisville. Meriwether wrote that weeks earlier a group of traders, finding the river open, had reputedly reached New Orleans. Of the event's importance he wrote in homespun prose: "If this be true we Shall have a fine cuntry in a short time...and with out a trade I think we shall ever remain poor."[29] For the West, an open Mississippi meant flowing commerce and high land values; a closed river spelled ruin.

When John Jay, the minister charged with negotiating a commercial treaty with Spain after the Revolutionary War, suggested that the United States give up the river's navigation in exchange for other diplomatic objectives, westerners erupted in outrage. In 1786, Jay stated that without ceding control of the Mississippi to Spain for a term of twenty-five years there could be no treaty. Representatives of western settlers responded that a treaty marred by such terms would be "cruel, oppressive, and unjust."[30] Jay never signed a treaty with Spain, his efforts scuttled by the aggrieved westerners.

The meaning of an open Mississippi to the West crystallized for Jefferson during Jay's negotiations. Throughout the troubled talks, western settlers espoused an argument based on what might be labeled a kind of ecological diplomacy—long before the term "ecology" became fashionable—suggesting that because the Mississippi was the only outlet for their trade, the "God of nature...intended it for a Common from the creation." They asked people to "trace the Mississippi from the ocean—survey the innumerable rivers which water your western territory, and pay their tribute to its greatness—then we ask, can the God of wisdom and nature have created that vast country in vain?"[31] These entreaties were based on an interpretation of nature common to the late eighteenth century: divine providence had created the nonhuman world to serve the interests of people. Although Jefferson was posted in Paris at the height of Jay's negotiations with Spain, his correspondence indicates that he was aware of the turmoil in the West.[32] And the settlers' interpretation of nature's and the river system's meaning was to mold the future president's convictions about the Mississippi, ultimately shaping his ideas regarding the free use of the river throughout his career.

In 1790, when Jefferson became secretary of state, he composed a list of reasons why the United States possessed a right to free use of the Mississippi, placing at the top the will of "Nature." Use of the river, though, was not enough for Jefferson; he understood that without access to its banks, free navigation of the stream meant little. In a letter to William Carmichael, a United States minister in Spain, Jefferson explained: "The right to use a thing comprehends a right to the means necessary to its use, and without which it would be useless."[33] He founded his claims on the writings of natural-rights philosophers Hugo Grotius, Samuel Pufendorf, and Emmerich de Vattel, gleaning his argument from their work on Roman riparian law. Jefferson concluded that "rivers belong to the public. [Most likely, when talking about the "public" he was referring to citizens of the fledgling republic.] The use of the banks belongs also to the public…as the use of the river itself does."[34] In studying the Mississippi question, Jefferson decided on two key points: first, Nature intended the river to be open for the West; and second, without access to its banks, the Mississippi was useless to western settlers. Years later, Jefferson's involvement in the negotiations with Spain, his inquiry into Roman sources, and the conclusions he drew all were to influence his actions in the batture controversy.

Two themes—the will of Nature, and the public character of the river and its banks—continued driving Jefferson's Mississippi policy, but westerners, still fuming because the river remained in Spanish hands, eventually threatened to secede.[35] In 1795, when Thomas Pinckney negotiated the treaty with Spain that later bore his name, he averted that disaster by securing not only free use of the river, but also a so-called American deposit in New Orleans. For six years after that, westerners navigated the Mississippi freely, landing with their goods at the deposit in the city. And with American trade in New Orleans booming, westerners increasingly depended on the Mississippi. In 1802, James Madison summed up the river's significance for settlers, noting that "the Mississippi to them is everything. It is the Hudson, the Delaware, the Potomac, and all the navigable rivers of the Atlantic States, formed into one stream." Because of the deposit's importance, westerners were outraged when Spain closed New Orleans to American trade on October 16, 1802. Correspondents at papers such as the *Kentucky Gazette* derided the decision as "astonishing and truly lamentable."[36] In the days following, westerners again threatened secession if the federal government could not guarantee them use of the Mississippi and its banks.

President Jefferson observed the rising tide of western protest and responded by redoubling efforts, then already under way, to acquire New Orleans.[37] With the news that Spain had agreed to retrocede Louisiana to France, Jefferson shifted diplomatic energies from Madrid to his minister in Paris, Robert Livingston. In January 1803, Jefferson, under pressure from the inflamed West, reinforced Livingston by sending James Monroe to Paris. On April 29, 1803, the duo signed the Louisiana Purchase, securing use of the Mississippi and its banks for the people of the United States.[38] For over twenty years, Jefferson had spent countless hours studying the Mississippi Valley's landscape from afar and the vagaries of riparian law, while musing on the will of Nature. He had come to view the Mississippi and its banks as spaces held publicly in trust for the citizens of the nation; and with the Louisiana Purchase, he believed that he finally could rest assured that they belonged to the United States. For these reasons, when Jefferson received news that Edward Livingston wished to enclose a portion of the batture for private gain, threatening the calm in Louisiana, he greeted the threat decisively. Years earlier, Jefferson had written to Livingston's brother Robert, while he negotiated the Purchase, "there is on the globe one single spot, the possessor of which is our natural and habitual enemy."[39] In that letter Jefferson had referred to New Orleans, and in his eyes the younger Livingston made himself the nation's foe with his effort to privatize the batture.

COMPETING INTERESTS

Even before Jefferson had Livingston evicted from the batture, a brutal pamphlet war had begun in New Orleans in the wake of the territorial court's decision. On one side stood Livingston and his few local allies, armed with the court's decision in the case. Representatives of New Orleans's government, members of the city's Creole elite, riparian proprietors, other residents of the city, and eventually Jefferson stood on the other. In a series of broadsides the antagonists outlined their positions, revealing the issues at stake in the controversy: who should control the waterfront and what should be done with it; the proper place of the Mississippi in New Orleans's dynamic urban-riparian environment; and the future of Louisiana's legal system. In short, the pamphlets describe conflicting views on property rights, public space, and people's perceptions of the river and the land that it had created.

The first pamphlet, published by Derbigny in the summer of 1807, outlined the case from the defense attorneys' perspective. Derbigny's tract exacerbated the unrest already surrounding the court's decision, and, coupled with extensive newspaper coverage of the case, likely spurred the mob hindering Livingston's workers. After restating the batture's his-

tory, Derbigny arrived at the meat of his argument: the laws of France
applied in the dispute, laws which held that accretions on the banks of
navigable rivers belonged to the ruling sovereign. In the batture's case,
the U.S. government was sovereign, and thus the land belonged to federal authorities. Therefore, Derbigny argued, the court had mistakenly
upheld Gravier's title to the land. The land was public (for Derbigny, this
probably meant, most importantly, that it did not belong to Livingston),
he suggested, but owned by the federal government whose authority held
sway.[40] Jefferson, in particular, found Derbigny's brief compelling, and
used it later as justification for his having evicted Livingston from the
batture.

Derbigny's pamphlet touched on another issue as well: the credibility
of the common-law-trained superior-court justices who had decided the
case. Although the judges had consulted and cited civil-law sources in
their decision, their backgrounds struck Derbigny as an unfair imposi-
tion of common-law-influenced jurisprudence in a civil-law jurisdiction.
He decried this injustice, claiming that Louisiana's legal heritage had
been bastardized by judges working "in a country whose language, manners, usages, and even sometimes whose law, are little familiar to
them."[41] Derbigny no doubt intended his critique to garner support from
Louisiana's legal community, already struggling to maintain the civil
law's primacy in the wake of the Purchase.[42] At the same time, Derbigny's
arguments invested the batture with an ethnic identity. The American
judges who had ruled in the case not only had misread Louisiana's law,
he suggested, but had also failed to comprehend the significance of the
region's environment. In fact, they had misjudged the waterfront's
significance because they were Americans, strangers in a strange land
whose laws and landscapes were equally mysterious.

Derbigny's discussion of the waterfront's importance for New Orleans—describing the riverfront accretion as a boon to the city, a gift on
which it rested—is the most revealing part of the pamphlet. Using this
line of argument to confer legitimacy on his position, Derbigny tapped
into one of the most powerful creation myths in New Orleans, a story
that went back to the era of the city's founding: "nature," working
through its agent, the river, favored the city and would nurture it. Derbigny explained that the "batture seems to have been fortunately placed
there to favor the building of the city." He acknowledged that without
the river's assistance "New-Orleans would perhaps never have existed."
Revealing the city's continuing dependence on the river and batture, he
noted: "In a country like lower Louisiana, where neither mountains nor

hills are to be seen; where not a single stone exists that is not brought thither...it is easy to conceive how valuable must be a mass of sand and mud incessantly renewed by the bounty of the river." He announced that the alluvium was necessary "for the building of a large and commercial town, and to repair the losses of the soil which is perpetually falling away, owing to its natural slope, and its situation below the level of the river." Here, Derbigny explored the dynamic qualities of the river and the city's environment.[43] Although New Orleans faced environmental hardships, the kindly Mississippi had given the city the natural levee, and continued to provide the much-needed soil of the batture for building. In sum, the Mississippi—and by extension, nature—insured that New Orleans could exist and prosper.

At the same time, Derbigny related another, darker side to the river, a contrasting view that further demonstrated the dynamism New Orleanians saw in their surroundings: one moment the Mississippi could be an ally, the next, without warning, an adversary. Derbigny warned that without the Mississippi's sedimentary assistance, New Orleans would cease to exist. He recounted the danger of digging in the city, which risked "creating infectious and pestilential quagmires." Betraying serious concerns about large-scale development near the Mississippi, he suggested that the river might obliterate the waterfront if Livingston completed his proposed improvements; and he cautioned that if the New Yorker tampered with the stream's current, the Mississippi could not be trusted to maintain its course, that it would likely leave the city's port dry.[44] Derbigny raised these specters to warn his audience that if the Mississippi were mistreated, it might lash out at the city. He used this discussion of New Orleans's unpredictable surroundings to imply that the riverfront must remain open and public, available to all of the city's residents struggling with the delta's constantly shifting environment.

Derbigny's concerns should not be misread as evidence of a nascent environmental consciousness. Instead, what he and New Orleanians had that Livingston did not have was experience with the river and the delta that it had created. While Livingston imagined a private port, carved out of clearly delineated private property at the batture, New Orleanians remembered the lessons of their environmental history. Lore abounded in the city, recounting floods as recent as those in 1785, 1791, and 1799, when water had stood in the French Quarter. Locals also were wary of the river's geomorphology. They knew that even though the Mississippi might deposit yards of batture accretions in one spot, it could also erode land elsewhere, seemingly on a whim. Finally, New Orleanians, subscribing to the era's medical misconceptions, believed that digging in the city gave rise to murderous epidemics by releasing foul, pestilential vapors into the air. Each of these convictions suggested a cautious approach to improving the waterfront.

Livingston took Derbigny's cue, as he too began publishing pamphlets, evidence entered into New Orleans's court of public opinion. In December 1807, he responded to Derbigny with a point-by-point rebuttal of the Creole's arguments. The most important issue covered in Livingston's pamphlet was his contention that the batture belonged to its adjacent riparian proprietors, and because the court had upheld Gravier's title, the batture was his.[45] With his arguments in print, Livingston awaited the federal government's response to Claiborne's distress call, certain that it would back the court's ruling.

Accordingly, Livingston was bitterly disappointed when news arrived from Washington that Jefferson frowned on the court's decision. Then the president's choice to evict Livingston changed the conflict's tenor. After Marshal D'Orgenois seized Livingston's section of the batture, the New Yorker portrayed himself as an oppressed party in the conflict. In May 1808, Livingston traveled to Washington to confront the president, but Jefferson brushed him off. Irate, Livingston wrote a falsely conciliatory note, full of veiled threats, to Secretary of State James Madison, who coolly replied that Jefferson had passed the case on to Congress.[46] In a final letter to Madison, Livingston explained that he had shown restraint by not challenging Jefferson's authority in New Orleans. The New Yorker claimed that he had not wanted to expose New Orleanians to a "degrading spectacle of a court unable to execute its decrees, or the afflicting one of a violent struggle, perhaps a bloody conflict, between the ministerial officers of the judicial and Executive power." Livingston concluded in dramatic style, warning that he would not continue to nurture infant American democracy in Creole Louisiana.[47]

Forced off his land, having failed in his mission to appeal to Jefferson, Livingston went public with his plight, firing off a new series of pamphlets designed to unmask the president as a villain. In the first of these broadsides, Livingston focused on the sanctity of private-property rights in the United States. He argued that Jefferson had trampled the sacred principles of the Revolution, and so protested, "I am an American citizen! I live in a country professedly under the government of the United States, and which is entitled as well by justice as by law, and the sacred stipulation of treaty to the protection of private property!" He went on to issue a warning, angling to hook property holders nationwide: "If the

power then, exercised against me be legal, there is no security for any
one, and we all hold our property by the precarious tenure of another's
will—A mere allegation suggested by malice, repeated by folly, and whis-
pered in secret to the presidential ear, may in a moment deprive us of our
only means of existence."[48] Livingston's goal was clear: he hoped to tap
into the young nation's anxieties about governmental tyranny. Such
tirades, though, did little to improve his position in New Orleans.

In focusing on property rights as the key to the controversy, Livingston
revealed views that for many New Orleanians seemed incompatible with
their city's dynamic environment. Before arriving in New Orleans, Livingston had lived in Manhattan, where he likely had acquired his perspective on the best methods for developing a municipality's waterfront.
One scholar of New York's legal history, Hendrik Hartog, has noted that
Manhattan's financially strapped Common Council used land grants as
a way of developing the city's port, leaving private citizens who promised to improve the land in control of a portion of the waterfront during Livingston's residence in Gotham. Hartog argues that turning the
waterfront over to private ownership was a method of planned development for the city that served the public's interests.[49] With the New
York waterfront as his primer, Livingston may have considered vacant,
riparian land as wasted land, inefficiently and irrationally organized.

In his pamphlet of 1808, Livingston illustrated that while he shared
Derbigny's opinion that the batture was a gift from nature, this point led
the two attorneys to different conclusions. Livingston acknowledged that
the batture grew constantly, increasing in value because of its uses in
New Orleans. But the New Yorker believed that the alluvium should be
owned and controlled by individuals who would develop the waterfront.
Livingston was making a characteristically American promise: he would
transform useless land, closely akin to wilderness, unpredictable at best
and perhaps even dangerous, into a productive economic resource. Livingston would capitalize on the river's benevolence, taking raw materi-
als—the batture's soil—and finishing them. In sum, he would make good
on nature's promise to New Orleans. And so, while Derbigny argued
that the batture should remain public, Livingston hoped to privatize the
waterfront. Saddled with debt, Livingston viewed the batture as a speculator's dream—a parcel of land not only rising in value, but also increasing in size without additional investment. The batture needed only
the steady hand of private ownership to maximize its benefits. Privatization of property, Livingston implied, served the public good. Anything

less than privatization risked squandering the river's gift to the city, a theme that was to recur again and again whenever disputes cropped up over land use at the waterfront.

In several publications that followed Livingston's pamphlet into print, it became clear that questions of private versus public control of the waterfront and people's perceptions of nature represented the broadest chasms separating the New Yorker and the majority of his opponents in New Orleans and Washington. The shock that Livingston evinced over his eviction from the waterfront was genuine. He could not believe that New Orleanians and Jefferson had deprived him of property with title validated by a court of law. Livingston's outrage was founded on a reverence for private-property rights so common among residents of the young republic that it resembled an inherited trait, woven tightly into the fabric of the nation's collective consciousness.[50] Such a view of property was predicated on the supposition that land, seemingly a static commodity, could and should be bought and sold. This position, however, clashed with local custom and law in New Orleans. In the delta, the environment refuted visions of all land, particularly riparian land, as inert and predictable, especially along the Mississippi's banks, where the process of dynamic sedimentation took place in the short span of human time. In the batture's accretion many New Orleanians glimpsed the power and unpredictability of the river. As a result, as Derbigny stated in his pamphlet, they coped with this dynamism communally, in part by keeping the waterfront public.

Louisiana's legal scholars amplified this argument in the *Digest of the Civil Laws Now in Force in the Territory of Orleans,* published at the height of the controversy, in the spring of 1808.[51] The *Digest* codified Louisiana's commitment to its civil-law heritage, guaranteeing that, regardless of the conflict's outcome, in the future the Mississippi's riverfront was to remain a public space in the eyes of the law. In book 2, article 6, the *Digest* dealt with navigable rivers, relating that their use was "allowed to all members of the nation." Article 8 explained that "the use of the shores of navigable rivers or creeks, is public." Echoing the superior court's decision in the original batture case, the article went on to state that "nevertheless, the property of the river shores belongs to those who possess the adjoining lands."[52] With these two articles, the *Digest* protected the property rights of riparian landholders, while at the same time establishing the servitude that guaranteed the public's right to use the Mississippi's banks and batture in the future. What the *Digest* did not do was clarify what or who that public was—a question that was to haunt New Orleans throughout its history.

Following the publication of the *Digest,* New Orleans's Creole elite mustered several new tracts into the pamphlet war that sounded the theme of the river's and delta's unpredictability, as well as the batture's public character. The first tract included official documents from the colonial period, along with testimony from approximately fifty members of the city's leading families, all refuting Livingston's spurious claim that riparian proprietors had privatized portions of the riverfront in the past. The Creoles reiterated that any time private buildings had been constructed on the batture prior to the Purchase, "their owners were obliged to throw them down by order of the government." The pamphlet hammered away at one issue: following local custom and law, the city's government had never allowed riparian proprietors to use the waterfront for personal gain. That is, because the Mississippi's banks had never been held privately, it followed that they had always been open "for public uses."[53]

Three other publications closely followed the Creoles' memorial, each produced by Julian Poydras, the territory's congressional representative. Poydras had much to lose if Livingston controlled the batture. Twenty years earlier, Bertrand Gravier had sold him a parcel of riparian land in the original St. Mary subdivision. Livingston's proposed batture development stood across from that property, threatening Poydras's view of the river and his access to the waterfront. As a result of his personal stake in the conflict, coupled with a gift for hyperbole and a keen sense of the riverfront's importance to the city, Poydras's publications provide tasty rhetorical morsels in comparison to the humdrum fare cooked up by the other pamphleteers. In just one representative instance, Poydras claimed that the New Yorker was guilty of "an offence against the laws of nature...perverting her most bountiful gifts, and converting them into so many scourges, curses, and maledictions."[54] For Poydras, it seemed that Livingston had no respect for the Mississippi, the delta's environment, or the people of New Orleans.

The congressman's publications restated and refined the ongoing discussion of why the Mississippi's waterfront had been always public and why it should remain so in the future. Poydras dealt in depth with environmental concerns, echoing Derbigny's warnings that if the river was misused it would inevitably strike back at the city. He worried especially that Livingston's "mischievous work of destruction" would alter the river's course and current. Harping on the dangers of releasing foul odors into the humid air, Poydras also claimed that Livingston's canals would "become putrid and stinking...and occasion a general pestilence in the country." Accordingly, he stated that privatizing a section of the waterfront would "inevitably have rendered New Orleans the horror of strangers, and the tomb of its inhabitants."[55] In sum, Poydras joined his contemporaries, evoking the river's power in arguing that misdirected efforts at altering the waterfront would prompt retribution from "nature" and the Mississippi.

Poydras offered a second compelling reason for maintaining the public status of the Mississippi's banks: he predicted that as commercial activity increased in the city, the waterfront, which served as New Orleans's port, would gain significance. As a result, he hacked his way through the thicket of complicated legal issues surrounding the controversy, stating that "the question is not about alluvion, public roads, batture, nor even about the bed of the river and its banks. The real question relates to the resumption of the best and, indeed, only seat for the port of New Orleans."[56] Poydras reminded his readers that the waterfront already filled to capacity with trade vessels during busy seasons of the year, and he argued that giving up control of the city's port to private individuals would be suicidal for a commercial metropolis. He recognized that the landscape opposite the Faubourg St. Mary promised to be among the city's most valued spaces, and, he surmised, to privatize any portion of such a valuable financial resource would be a colossal blunder for the community.[57] In short, the Mississippi's banks had to remain public for economic as well as environmental reasons.

Poydras also stated a third, previously ignored argument supporting a publicly held waterfront: the importance of urban aesthetics. In dealing with this theme in his pamphlets, Poydras suggested that the city's close ties to the river were crucial in creating what modern students of the controversy might call "a sense of place" in New Orleans.[58] By the time that Livingston became aware of the batture, observers had long commented on the beauty of the city's waterfront, on the views of New Orleans available from the Mississippi and of the river from the city. Poydras argued that Livingston's actions would inevitably lead to similar claims, ultimately despoiling the waterfront. He summed up this fear by declaring that Livingston would have altered the "delightful aspect of the harbor and city," and suggested that Livingston's proposed plan for the waterfront "would have intercepted the view which the city now enjoys of the river and opposite country," and "the loathsome appearance of irregular and filthy store houses and stinking canals would have made it look like the doleful abode of death and desolation; and, in truth, it soon would have become so." Finally, he complained that if Livingston and other landowners gained control of the riverfront, "the citizens of New Orleans would have been deprived of the only place where they can go to take an evening walk, so necessary in that hot country, and enjoy the freshness of river air, and the agreeable view of the water."[59] Poydras, a riparian proprietor himself, worried that if Livingston succeeded in his land grab, New Orleans would sacrifice its riverfront to quick and unplanned commercial growth, built on private ownership of land that was environmentally, socially, culturally, and even legally ill-suited to such a convention.

PROPERTY HELD IN COMMON . . . FROM TIME IMMEMORIAL

At the St. Mary batture, the Mississippi participated in the production of landscapes and controversy in the city. As each flood season passed during the conflict, the river carried tons of sediment past the city, dumping a portion on the growing batture (figure 8). Contemporary maps suggest that the muddy shoal had almost doubled in size in less than a hundred years. The monetary value of the land also had grown, especially after steamboats arrived on the Mississippi in 1811, promising boom times for New Orleans. By 1813, New Orleanians estimated the value of the contested portion of the batture at more than five hundred thousand dollars. At that time, Livingston eluded a stalemate by returning to the site of past victories, the courts, where he made a final push to secure control of the batture. He first filed suit in the district court in New Orleans against Marshal D'Orgenois, who had evicted him from the batture in early 1808, seeking to recover the property. Livingston then sued Jefferson in federal circuit court, seeking damages for the president's having ordered his eviction from the batture.[60]

The first case to receive a hearing, Livingston's suit against Jefferson, ended in frustration for the New Yorker when the then-current president, James Madison, tapped a judge loyal to Jefferson to sit on the circuit-court bench, all but guaranteeing victory for the former chief executive. In a move typical of the questionable ethics he had employed throughout the batture conflict, Jefferson had influenced Madison's judicial appointment, threatening to drag the president's good name through the Mississippi mud by exposing the role that Madison had played early in the controversy. Le Breton D'Orgenois, on the other hand, had none of Jefferson's influence and therefore relied solely on the

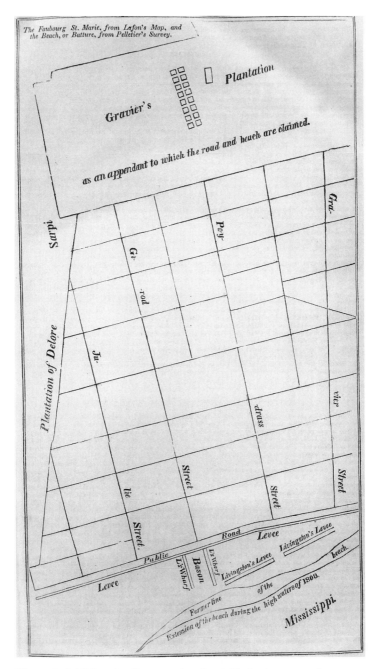

The Faubourg St. Marie, from Lafon's Map, and the Beach, or Batture, from Pelletier's Survey.

Plantation

Gravier's

as an appendant to which the road and beach are claimed.

Sarpi

Gra-

Poy-

Gr-

.rod

Ju-

vier

drass

Plantation of Delore

lie

Street

Street

Street

Street

Road   Levee

Livingston's Levee

Public

Bason

Le Wharf

Livingston's Levee

Livingston's Levee

beach

Levee

Le Wharf

Former line   of the   high waters of 1800.

Extension of the beach during the high waters of 1800.

Mississippi

Figure 8. Additional soil accumulated quickly in the years after Edward Livingston laid claim to the batture. Note the extension of the batture and the depiction of Livingston's improvements at the bottom of the map (1810). Courtesy of the Special Collections Division, Tulane University.

merits of his case at trial. On August 4, 1813, the district-court justices handed down their verdict in the case of *Livingston v. D'Orgenois,* ruling for Livingston. The court once again had granted Livingston possession of the batture.[61]

When Livingston won his case against D'Orgenois in 1813, it seemed that he would finally reap the harvest of eight years of hard work. D'Orgenois, seeking only peace and quiet in his dotage, refused the city's pleas to appeal the court's decision. Then, with Livingston about to begin improvements on his valuable stretch of property, the city secured an injunction preventing him from keeping the "public" from using the batture. Again Livingston returned to court, where he successfully argued for the injunction's dissolution. But even after Livingston's third legal victory, the city continued to harass him. For instance, in the fall of 1814, Livingston, hoping to gain control of his waterfront property at long last, filed suit against Jean Lallemand, a city laborer who had taken soil from the batture for use in a public-works project. The Conseil de ville boiled over, publishing a notice in the papers asserting the public's right to take material from the batture, and guaranteeing legal defense to any citizen arrested for doing so.[62] At the following week's council meeting, city officials, still overheated, agreed to post guards along the riverfront to arrest anyone who "annoyed citizens in the exercise of a privilege which has always existed in favor of the public."[63]

Once again, the language employed by the council in its proclamation raises significant questions, highlighting how complicated public spaces and the public itself could be. Was the council suggesting that it would protect only "citizens'" rights at the waterfront? In other words, were only citizens considered members of the public? If the answer to that question was yes, as it likely was, could Livingston then have excluded slaves or recent immigrants to the city from using the batture? Had he done so, would he have avoided the council's wrath because chattel slaves and newcomers did not enjoy the rights of citizenship? And, if this was in fact the case, how "public" was the waterfront? Although these issues are interesting in retrospect—they underscore the historically contingent nature of the public—nobody at the time gave them much thought.

As the council maneuvered Livingston into a corner, the wily New Yorker worked to regain the offensive. Falling back on his familiarity with the law, Livingston tried to exploit a statute stating that with the approval of twelve local landowners riparian proprietors could shift the location of the levee on their land. In response, in the fall of 1815 the Conseil de ville overturned the levee statute, passing a new law that made the council the final arbiter of any proposed levee moves.[64] In doing so, the council accomplished two goals. First, it asserted its power along the waterfront, beginning a period in which it attempted to consolidate control of the riverfront, as that landscape became increasingly important in New Orleans during the era of steamboats. And second, the council unequivocally demonstrated to Livingston that he would never control the batture on his own terms.

Despite his numerous victories in courtroom skirmishes, by early 1816 Livingston apparently realized that the city would win the batture war. Over the next several years, hoping to end the conflict, he offered the municipality a series of compromises seemingly modeled on the agreements between New York's Common Council and the riparian proprietors who had developed portions of Manhattan's waterfront. But each time Livingston made an offer, the city held out for a better deal. Having turned the tables on the New Yorker, the members of the Conseil de ville hung back and waited. For four more years the conflict dragged on, with Livingston offering increasingly attractive terms and the council demanding greater concessions. Livingston first agreed to allow New Orleanians their traditional right to remove sediment from the batture; he then offered to donate a portion of the batture to the city; later, he promised to construct a new levee. Finally, he guaranteed all of the above, a new public market on a portion of the batture, as well as a wide, public road running adjacent to the property. In September 1820, after wringing additional concessions from Livingston, the Conseil de ville accepted his compromise, certain its control of the waterfront was secure into the future.[65]

Over the first fifteen years of the American period in the city, the batture assumed a significance out of proportion to its size, largely because New Orleanians, confronted with the importance of the riverside sediment, grappled with issues linked to the future of their city: who would control the waterfront, what was that landscape's best use, and what did the river mean to the municipality? Economic interests motivated many of the people who resisted the batture's privatization. Similar processes took place in other cities throughout the nation, a part of the contested emergence of capitalism in U.S. metropolitan areas. Students of urban space have noted that as commercial capitalism took root in cities, people no longer valued spaces for their uses but instead for the amount of capital proprietors could ask in exchange for them.[66] The batture controversy serves as an example of this transition. New Orleanians traditionally had valued the land for its public uses: promenade, storage site and source of landfill. Livingston, on the other hand, coveted the land not only for the use he could make of it, but also for its exchange value. The city's government and residents, outraged by those plans, vetoed Livingston's efforts repeatedly for more than a decade.

Still, to cast the combatants in the controversy as two clear sides in a land-use dispute would be to view the episode through an overly modern lens. Today, environmentalists often analyze conflicts about land in terms of a simplistic dichotomy—development versus preservation—that would only obscure the complex power dynamics present in the battle for control of New Orleans's waterfront. While many common people hoped to keep the batture undeveloped, Livingston's other Creole adversaries, political and commercial elites, were usually prodevelopment. For New Orleans's people of commerce, the waterfront held the key to the future. In place of the empty batture, they, like Livingston, imagined a waterfront crammed with vessels carrying the goods of the West. Yet they sought to preserve the batture's public character, no matter how narrowly they might have defined such a complex concept. Drawing on local custom, the civil law, and a view of the river as a dynamic actor, New Orleans's elites fought side by side with non-elites to keep the batture public, "held in common," as Poydras put it, the way it had been "from time immemorial."[67] Only later did differing views of that contested concept—the public—create additional fault lines in the city's social and spatial fabric.

The batture controversy was not only a land-use dispute, but also a fight about people's relationship with the Mississippi and their ability to control the river. Many New Orleanians believed that Livingston did not respect or understand the river, and they worried that if he gained control of the waterfront, environmental as well as economic disaster would ensue. Livingston, on the other hand, revered private-property rights, and believed that privatization of the waterfront represented the best course for developing the city's port and maximizing the river's benefits. New Orleanians fretted that his vision for the batture ignored the river's power and ability to shape the waterfront. Although the city's residents also wanted to tame the mercurial Mississippi, unlike Livingston, at the time they believed that private control of riparian land was not the best means of achieving that goal. Their experiences with the unpredictability of their environment forced them to recognize that while deeds and titles—words on a page—remained inert, the constantly shifting river did not respect legal guarantees or borders drawn on a map. The Mississippi flowed where it chose, without regard for property lines, some-times rendering such powerful legal artifice little more than a meaning-less fiction. In the riparian servitude, Livingston saw an unacceptable ambiguity between private ownership and public use, while residents of New Orleans found a flexibility in it that allowed them to cope with their dynamic urban-riparian environment.

The river's agency in producing urban space may be the most significant lesson and legacy of the batture controversy. In the delta's en-vironment one finds compelling evidence of the Mississippi's ongoing role in city building. Traditionally, urbanists have explored only the so-cial forces that yield the urban form, but the batture case supports the contention that urban landscapes are not produced by people alone.[68] Forces such as erosion, deposition, fluvial tectonics, and climate also shape cities; in New Orleans the Mississippi plays an important, and often understudied, role in creating the municipal form. In building the natural levee upon which the city sits, and then in eroding or depositing riverfront land in the form of the batture, the Mississippi has constantly asserted its role as an active participant in New Orleans's history.

Following the batture conflict, the city's relationship with the Missis-sippi was to change forever. Although many people still fought to keep the batture public for a host of reasons, the future revealed that for New Orleans's commercial community, the conflict had been a battle for con-trol of the best location for the city's port. And as the city reached its compromise with Livingston, the shifting landscape along the riverfront signaled that change was underway in New Orleans. In 1820, visitors still arrived in the city via the river and marveled at the magnificent wa-terfront. They also likely noted the expansion of the city both up and down the riverbanks. Perhaps most important, the craft on which they arrived may not have bowed to the river's current, since by then steam-boats commonly plied the Mississippi system. That new technology's ar-rival heralded an enormous leap in people's ability to control the river, and with that transition came a rapid shift in the use of New Orleans's waterfront, the public character of that landscape, and related changes in the city's relationship with the Mississippi.

CHAPTER 2

Human Genius, Organed with Machinery

STEAMBOATS ON THE MISSISSIPPI

In the spring of 1811, as Edward Livingston staked his claim to the riverbanks in New Orleans, his older brother, Robert, tried to seize control of the Mississippi itself. The elder Livingston, along with his partners, Robert Fulton and Nicholas Roosevelt (Theodore's great-granduncle), offered the Orleans Territorial Legislature a deal: they would bring their steamboat prototype to the Mississippi in exchange for a monopoly of use on the territory's waterways. The trio, known as the Fulton group, had made similar proposals to legislators throughout the Mississippi Valley, but each governing body had rebuffed them after facing popular outrage at the prospect of a monopoly on the river system. For valley residents, the Fulton group's request smacked of eastern arrogance, of countless episodes in which westerners felt certain that their coastal neighbors had sacrificed the settlers' interests for selfish regional goals.[1] The valley's people had been especially shocked to learn that Robert Livingston, the man they hailed for opening the Mississippi by acquiring Louisiana, had turned his back on the past by attempting to close the river anew. Only in the Territory of Orleans did the Fulton group receive a warmer reception, when the legislature granted them a serious hearing.

No place had more to gain from the arrival of steamboats on the Mississippi than New Orleans, because the city's supposed destiny as the valley's market hinged on traders' ability to navigate the river. By 1811, observers had long viewed New Orleans's commanding situation near the river's mouth as evidence that what they called Nature had chosen the city for greatness. That myth, passed from one generation of boosters to the next, turned on the idea that it would be only a matter of time before the Mississippi's current swept trade downstream, bestowing prosperity on the city. The current: it was inexorable, perpetually in motion, and it guaranteed great riches by bringing trade. It embodied nature's promise to New Orleans, because it traveled in only one direction from throughout the Mississippi Valley: toward the Crescent City. Consequently, New Orleanians typically celebrated their city's relationship with the river.

Sometimes, however, they faced the downside of relying on the Mississippi, as when its current clouded visions of empire by raising questions about access to the valley's upper reaches. Skeptics wondered how New Orleans could control its vast hinterland when the relentless current made upstream navigation so difficult and therefore obstructed commercial traffic. And with good reason, because struggling with the river was an annual rite for traders who floated produce downstream to market on flatboats, often little more than rough collections of planks nailed together, what one critic called a "wooden prison."[2] After arriving in New Orleans, many traders broke their flatboats up and sold the wood along with their other wares, before facing a grueling journey home, either overland or via keelboats on the river. In contrast to flatboats, which, like seed pods or willow leaves, traveled only downstream, keelboats often could be found impersonating salmon, fighting the current. Traveling upstream prior to the arrival of steamboats on the river, then, was no mean feat. Only sails and ideal conditions spared traders hard labor. Otherwise, in shallow water they set long poles in the river's bottom and then pushed their craft along, like Venetian gondoliers (figure 9). In eddies, oars could be used, but most often "cordelling" sufficed as the means of defying the river's current. The cordelle was a long, heavy rope, fastened to a riverboat's bow. The crew's best swimmer paddled ashore with the cordelle clamped in his teeth, like a well-trained retriever. His mates followed in his wake, and once on land they began a months-long game of tug-of-war with the river's powerful current, pulling the vessel upstream.[3]

Arduous, unpredictable, and dangerous—conditions changed constantly, as traders confronted storms, ice floes, or a current made more uncooperative by floodwaters. The commute was also time-consuming, described by one onlooker as "an affair of three or four, and sometimes

Figure 9. Keelboat crew members used one of several grueling methods to fight the Mississippi's current in their journey upstream (1953 reproduction). Courtesy of The Historic New Orleans Collection.

nine months."[4] Thus, for traders, the Mississippi system became home and workshop. Boatmen lived on the rivers, drank from them, bathed in their waters, and zealously studied their habits and nuances. So much time spent on the rivers by traders presented problems for New Orleans's commercial community. Because of the voyage's difficulty, valley traders typically made just one trip to market at New Orleans per year; consequently, the river's unyielding current captivated even New Orleanians who had never faced its might. The city's commercial community, especially, pondered the Mississippi's power, confident that business would boom if people could somehow overcome its flow.[5]

The Fulton group guaranteed that it would do exactly that. The partners offered the territorial government hope that what had been New Orleans's theoretical hinterland, removed from the city by thousands of miles and the river's current, would be within easy reach after steamboats tamed the Mississippi. And the partners did not come to the Territory of Orleans armed only with rhetoric and grand promises. Four years earlier, in 1807, Fulton's and Livingston's steamboat, the *Clermont,* had traveled upstream on the Hudson River, proving the viability of steam-powered river navigation.[6] Following that voyage, the two Roberts had looked west and joined forces with Roosevelt. The three had then built a steamboat designed to withstand the rigors of the Mississippi: the *New Orleans*. With the *New Orleans*'s future beckoning, and the *Clermont*'s past triumph serving as a kind of corporate prospectus, the Fulton group arrived in Louisiana, asking for exclusive rights to navigate the Mississippi and its branches.

Although the fight to maintain the batture as a common was at its peak, the possibility of imposing order on the unpredictable river was too attractive for politicians in the Territory of Orleans to ignore. So, even as Governor Claiborne struggled to keep Edward Livingston from controlling New Orleans's waterfront, he asked the territorial legislature to accept the Fulton group's offer, demonstrating the contingent nature of public space in New Orleans. Although the state's civil code guaranteed that the Mississippi was a public waterway, Claiborne nonetheless explained that he was "confident that the introduction of Steam boats on the Mississippi and its waters, would greatly conduce to the convenience and welfare of the inhabitants of this Territory."[7] At first glance, Claiborne's actions seem hypocritical—how could he fight to keep the batture open while supporting a monopoly on the Mississippi's waters?—but he saw no conflict in his positions. The people of the Territory of Orleans would benefit from the arrival of steamboats on the river;

thus Claiborne, conflating commercial and public interests, believed that the monopoly was congruent with his interpretation of the Mississippi's public character. Confident in his stance, Claiborne continued lobbying until the legislature eventually granted the Fulton group the "sole privilege of using Steam Boats" in the Territory of Orleans late in the spring of 1811.[8]

On the surface, the legislature's choice seems like an instance in which politicians privatized public space in service of economic elites alone. But this reaction in part misreads the past, because the legislators, like Claiborne, believed that they served the people of the Territory of Orleans by granting the Fulton group its monopoly. As a result, their decision illuminates notions, common in the first decades of the nineteenth century, about the best way to maximize the benefits of public natural resources. Monopolies offend our modern sensibilities. We believe that they create unfair advantages for a privileged few, infringe on the public's rights, and tamper with the workings of an ostensibly free market. In the early republic, however, state and territorial legislatures often granted monopolies as a way of spurring economic growth. Government at all levels, cash-poor but craving development, turned to the private sector to construct public works.[9] In exchange for their outlay of capital, corporations received monopolies. In this light, the Orleans Territorial Legislature did not betray its constituents; it embraced the best method it knew of making progress toward prosperity for an ill-defined public.

At the same time, the monopoly grant offers insight into the legislature's views of the Mississippi and what we call technology, then known as "artifice" or "art." Although today we often place technology and pristine environments in opposition, the assemblymen did not fret about setting a machine loose in the gardens of Louisiana. Instead, they hoped that artifice would improve, rather than despoil, the territory's riparian environment. The legislators saw the river as a valuable but unpredictable resource, a watery wilderness that demanded discipline. Although they viewed the river as a gift from nature, it was also an obstacle; its waters led to prosperity, but its current blocked the path to empire. The legislators thus hoped that the Fulton group would civilize the Mississippi by applying the "hand of man," increasing the river's productivity.[10] Beyond obvious and telling gender connotations, such language also demonstrates an abiding faith in the power of artifice. The *New Orleans* could improve the river, render it docile, smooth its rough edges, leaving it a predictable venue hospitable to commerce. In short, the Fulton group could complete

the work that nature had begun. Therefore, the legislature granted the
partners their monopoly, hopeful that the Fulton group would eliminate
one of the hurdles that the river had placed on New Orleans's path to
greatness. Their decision represented a peculiar strain of technological
utopianism: artifice, the legislators seemed to believe, would *necessarily*
serve the public's interests, a theme that has for many people become an
ingrained myth throughout the nation's history.

A half year after the legislature's decision, the *New Orleans* left Pittsburgh, bound for the Crescent City, eventually arriving on January 10,
1812. Although they did not know it then, for New Orleanians that voyage proved to be among the most significant events of the nineteenth century, because it marked the beginning of the era of steam in the city. After
steamboats conquered the Mississippi's current, New Orleans became
the valley's quintessential river city, the most important market in the region. By 1861, so many immigrants had poured into New Orleans, hoping to capitalize on the city's boom times, that its population had exploded more than tenfold from the era of the Louisiana Purchase.[11] For
many observers, it seemed that the hand of man had tamed the river, that
the rise of New Orleans symbolized the possibility of carving civilization
out of wilderness. On the eve of the Civil War, because of the steamboats
and the trade they carried to the city, New Orleans stood on the brink
of its mythic destiny as the seat of an inland commercial empire, poised
to dominate the interior of the continent. Technology appeared finally
to have delivered the Mississippi's promise.

Predictably, the era of steam witnessed profound changes in the city's
relationship with the Mississippi, and developments at the waterfront
reflected some of those shifts. As steamboats seemed to impose order on
the Mississippi, New Orleanians became more confident in their control
of nature. They still extolled the river's virtues, and they also reveled in
their own power to tame the mighty stream. In the same period, the city
built wharves along the waterfront, demonstrating not only a high regard for artifice, but also the spatial demands that technology made on
New Orleans.[12] Construction of those wharves raised a series of related
questions about the riverfront, already becoming familiar in the city.
What was the best use for that space? How could it be improved without alienating the public's rights? Who enjoyed membership in New Orleans's public? That is, who should be allowed to claim space at the waterfront? And who should oversee that space? Even as New Orleanians
experienced decades of unprecedented prosperity born of apparent control of their surroundings, the answers to those questions threatened to

shred the fabric of the city. And throughout the era of steam, though people boasted that they had overcome the river's current, the Mississippi played a part in answering each of those queries. But before New Orleanians could deal with any of those issues, they first had to see whether or not the river itself was a public space.

FIGHTING FOR A RIPARIAN COMMON

Despite the Orleans Territorial Legislature's hopes, the Fulton group did not immediately usher in a commercial and transportation revolution on the Mississippi system, and initially steamboats had only a negligible impact on the region's economy. Although a new era did begin when the *New Orleans* arrived at the Crescent City's waterfront in 1812, the partners' monopoly dissuaded all but the most intrepid entrepreneurs from bringing additional steamboats to the Mississippi. In other words, the legislature's decision to privatize the river in the name of the public had unintended consequences: the monopoly cleared what New Orleanians saw as an environmental obstacle—the river's current—but created a political problem in the valley by consolidating control of the Mississippi's waters in the Territory of Orleans in the hands of the Fulton group alone. As a result, even after 1812, most valley traders still traveled to and from New Orleans without steam power. Five years were to pass after the *New Orleans*'s first journey before someone applied an expansive definition of public space to the waters of the Mississippi system, breaking the Fulton group's monopoly and reopening the river to a wider application of steam technology.

On March 22, 1817, Henry Shreve sat in New Orleans's jail for challenging the Fulton group's monopoly. The story leading to his incarceration has all the makings of an early western novel: a family cutting its eastern roots to find fortune in the rich soil of the Mississippi Valley; death-defying encounters, including a spectacular steamboat explosion; virtuous heroes and wicked villains galore; and, flowing throughout the story, binding its scenes together, the rivers of the Mississippi system. In 1788, Shreve's family settled in western Pennsylvania, on the banks of Washington Run, a tributary of the Youghiogheny River. The Yough—the name rhymes with *sock*—runs into the Monongahela, which meets the Allegheny and Ohio rivers in Pittsburgh. Shreve grew up near Washington Run, always fascinated by life on the rivers. By 1807, he had purchased a keelboat of his own and begun trading on the Mississippi system.[13]

After enjoying five successful years in business, Shreve chose to attack the Fulton group's year-old monopoly. His reasons are lost in the past—indeed, the riverboatman himself left few documentary records, so much of his story has to be pieced together from conjecture and from the primary sources produced by his contemporaries—but profit motive likely played a part in the decision. So too did his views on the public character of the Mississippi. As a child, Shreve had almost certainly heard tales of the valley's fight for a free Mississippi. His family and neighbors had relied on free navigation of the river system and the deposit at New Orleans for economic survival and thus had celebrated the acquisition of Louisiana, confident that the city and the Mississippi would remain open in the future. And Shreve, like so many other settlers in the upper valley, had probably blanched when he had heard that eastern monopolists had gained control of the river in the Territory of Orleans, a development that conflicted with the way many valley residents viewed the Mississippi. During the Fulton group's quest for control of the river, settlers in the valley, as in the years leading to the Louisiana Purchase, had again insisted that the river must remain open as a regional common. It was that vision of a riparian public space, available to anybody who chose to use its waters, that seems to have shaped Shreve's understanding of the Mississippi.

In 1813, Shreve, along with countless other riverboatmen in the valley, became captivated by the power of artifice. The Fulton group's *New Orleans* had recently proven that steamboats could defy the Mississippi's current, and Shreve began designing and operating an updated version of the invention for use on the river system. Although the Fulton group retained its increasingly valuable monopoly, on December 1, 1814, Shreve nonetheless traveled from Pittsburgh to New Orleans aboard the steamboat *Enterprise*. The following spring, when Shreve, laden with cargo, readied to leave the Crescent City, Edward Livingston, acting on the Fulton group's behalf, blocked his way. At the time, Livingston confronted one of the impasses hindering his land grab at the batture. Likely concerned that his family's quest for control of the river, as well its banks, might escalate public sentiment already set against him, Livingston thus skirted another battle at the waterfront; instead of confronting Shreve directly, he offered several local attorneys retainers to work for the monopolists. In effect, he tried to undercut the riverboatman's quest for counsel. Livingston was too late. By that time Shreve had already found a lawyer, Abner Duncan, who, after refusing Livingston's entreaties, secured safe passage for the *Enterprise* out of New Orleans.[14]

In the spring of 1815, with the Mississippi spreading outside of its levees during its annual flood stage, Shreve navigated the river as though it were a series of vast lakes. He traveled upstream away from the brunt of the current, in calm water at the flooded river's margins. The journey to Louisville took the *Enterprise* twenty-five days, and when Shreve arrived he enjoyed a hero's welcome. The first man to captain a steamboat from New Orleans—the Fulton group's vessels had navigated only the lower river to that point—Shreve quickly left for Pittsburgh, arriving there eleven days later. It had taken him just over a month for a journey that previously had often taken six months, and for some observers the event seemed revolutionary. Writers at *Niles' Register* asked, "What prospect of commerce is held out to the immense region of the West, by the use of these boats!"[15] Although some skeptics carped that Shreve's journey had not been a true test of the technology—looking back, hecklers noted that "there was no current. In view of these favorable circumstances, the experiment was not satisfactory"—for most observers the conclusion was obvious: artifice had tamed nature.[16]

Although Shreve had flouted the Fulton group's control of the Mississippi, their monopoly remained intact. Still, in June 1816, Shreve returned to New Orleans aboard another steamboat that he had helped design, the *Washington*. After surviving a boiler explosion on the trip downstream, which killed several passengers aboard the vessel, Shreve arrived in New Orleans, hoping to shatter the monopolists' hold on the river once and for all. Upon hearing of the *Washington*'s arrival, Livingston reputedly proposed that Shreve tell Duncan to give a weak defense in any impending court case, preserving the Fulton group's monopoly. In return, Livingston offered Shreve half an interest in his brother's company. Shreve refused, turning again to Duncan to negotiate his departure from New Orleans, and in mid-October the *Washington* left the city.[17]

Apparently more eager than ever to force a definitive confrontation with the Fulton group in order to open up access to the river, Shreve returned to New Orleans on March 12, 1817, presenting Edward Livingston with a dilemma. Having been outmaneuvered by Duncan twice previously, Livingston was reluctant to press the Fulton group's claim unless he stood ready to take his case before a judge. In late March, the *Washington*'s imminent departure forced Livingston's hand. If Shreve kept coming and going as he pleased, the Fulton group's monopoly would be overturned de facto. Facing that prospect, Livingston sued Shreve. In response, aware that the state legislature had recently begun investigating the Fulton group's privileges, Duncan chose to play upon New Orleanians' perceptions of the Livingston family as greedy swindlers intent on privatizing the city's and the state's most valuable resources. Duncan counseled Shreve to await arrest aboard the *Washington,* certain that a public spectacle at the waterfront would generate sympathy for the riverboatman's efforts to reopen the Mississippi. When the marshal arrested Shreve, a large crowd, perhaps composed in part of people who had protested Livingston's plans for the batture, jeered and threatened to storm the jail.[18]

Shreve spent only one night behind bars. And although the legalities of the *Washington's* departure remained unresolved, he fled New Orleans on March 24, leaving Duncan to handle his affairs in court. Less than a month later, Shreve arrived in Louisville, demonstrating again the possibilities that steamboats held out for improving navigation on the Mississippi system. Shreve achieved legendary status in the valley with that trip upriver. As westerners constructed a regional identity, based in part on the valley's rivers and the steamboats plying them, they cast Shreve as the hero in the story of steam's arrival on the Mississippi. The Fulton group's role did not suit the people of the valley, who were offended by the monopolists' eastern origins and desire to close the river. Over time, early historians and regional commentators created a myth, which then entered the realm of public memory: Shreve alone had conquered the Mississippi system. Of the *Washington's* journey in 1817, one historian wrote that "this was the trip that convinced the despairing public that steamboat navigation would succeed on the Western waters." Another exaggerated that "from this voyage all historians date the commencement of steam navigation in the Mississippi valley."[19] For these authors, it was the rough-hewn Shreve, with his encyclopedic knowledge of the Mississippi and its tributaries, who had made good on nature's promises to the valley.

Of course, the story of steam's arrival on the river system was more complicated than that, especially because the Fulton group retained its monopoly until April 21, 1817, the day when Duncan squared off with the easterners' lawyer in court. After the attorneys presented their cases, Judge Dominick Hall ruled that he had no jurisdiction in the case, dismissing the suit and effectively ending the Fulton group's monopoly. With so few documents revealing Shreve's thoughts, it is hard to determine his views on the river, or on public space for that matter. One can only surmise that, having been raised on the banks of the Mississippi system, surrounded by traders who depended on open access to market in New Orleans, Shreve had imbibed his region's stance on the subject of a riparian common. Or perhaps he was just in it for the money. But his actions later in life, when he fought to keep the Mississippi system safe and open, indicate that Shreve's passion for the rivers ran deeper than a mere desire for financial gain.[20] Regardless, though Shreve should not be hailed for single-handedly inaugurating the era of steam on the Mississippi, as he still often is by biographers eager to lionize the riverboatman, he deserves credit for reopening the river by insisting on a broader definition of riparian public space than that of the Fulton group, the Orleans Territorial Legislature, or Governor Claiborne.

THE ANNIHILATION OF SPACE AND TIME

When Judge Hall handed down his decision, a transportation and technological revolution, which had been proceeding at a halting clip, accelerated. And nowhere was this revolution's impact more obvious than at New Orleans's waterfront—often called the levee—where an ever-increasing quantity of steamboats demonstrated apparent mastery of the Mississippi. The levee presented an awesome spectacle, with a confluence of technologies, goods, and people that was amazing in an age when successful challenges to the boundaries of space and time were just becoming commonplace. In the years between 1817 and 1861, the waterfront became a symbolic landscape, generating awe among observers who exclaimed that "no triumph of art over the obstacles of nature has ever been so complete." Trade vessels of all kinds, not just steamboats but flatboats and sailing ships—with an easier way of traveling upstream available, most keelboats disappeared during the era of steam—lined up in such numbers that onlookers likened the scene at the levee to "a forest of masts."[21] This metaphor, which appeared again and again in nineteenth-century descriptions of New Orleans, mixes images gleaned from the nonhuman world and the realm of human artifice, encapsulating the union of nature and technology that fueled the era of steam on the Mississippi.

Not surprisingly, steamboats were the waterfront's signal feature. In the years between the *New Orleans*'s first voyage and Shreve's journey aboard the *Washington* in 1817, the city's wharf registrar recorded only 7 different steamboats arriving at the waterfront. Then, in a little more than a year following Hall's ruling, 14 new steamboats appeared on the register, accounting for almost 200 arrivals. Those numbers marked just the first trickle of what eventually was to become a flood of steamboats descending on the levee. In 1827, there were more than 100 steamboats afloat on the Mississippi system, and only 5 years later, steamboats made in excess of 1,000 arrivals at New Orleans. On the eve of the Civil War, over 250 steamboats plied the Mississippi system, making more than 3,500 stops at New Orleans's levee.[22]

So many steamboats arriving in the city had a profound impact on observers' perceptions of artifice and the river. In the early republic, few Americans had contact with industrial landscapes or technologies. Therefore, steamboats at the levee (figure 10) awed onlookers with the manifest power of human ingenuity. And the machines became more impressive over time, as designers began placing one deck atop another, like layers of a wedding cake. One, then two, and finally three decks, all stood above a steamboat's hull, towering high over the river. This design created a perceptual contrast for visitors at the levee, who were struck by the vessels' height when set against the open expanse of the Mississippi. Designers also added impressive aesthetic flourishes: lavish gingerbread ornaments; colorful paint; elaborate figureheads from the republican pantheon; and metal sculpture capping the vessels' smoke-stacks. If the sight of the boats did not overwhelm onlookers, their sounds often did. Huge roof bells and ear-splitting steam whistles pro-vided voices for the boats; knowledgeable listeners could identify a ves-sel by its aural signature. Due to their elevation above the river, their growing numbers, and the topography of the city's waterfront, steam-boats seemed ubiquitous in New Orleans. One traveler remarked that "whenever you happen to turn down a street which leads to the river you get the impression that the hundreds of steamboats moored obliquely along the levees with their prows facing the city are advanc-ing in your direction, and without reflecting, you are prompted to move aside and let them pass."[23]

During the era of steam, the waterfront became a commercial carni-val, as riverboats transported an astonishing variety and quantity of goods to market at New Orleans. This merchandise attested to the fer-tility of the valley's soil, the industry of its settlers, and the power of tech-nology. One visitor explained that the "innumerable quantity of barrels, hogsheads, cotton bags, pork hams, apples, bagging & rope &c &c." marked the waterfront as the "market place of the wealth of the West."[24] In 1816, total annual receipts at New Orleans's port already exceeded eight million dollars. In the years following, that figure climbed steadily: to over thirteen million dollars the next year, after Shreve ended the Ful-ton group's hold on the river; to more than twenty million dollars in

Figure 10. Pedestrians stroll the riverfront, amid laborers and piles of goods, as steamboats dominate the scene (1890). Courtesy of The Historic New Orleans Collection.

1825; and to double that number by 1837. By 1840, over five hundred thousand tons of freight arrived at New Orleans's port, valued at nearly fifty million dollars. Ten years later, receipts climbed over one hundred million dollars, and never fell below that mark until the Civil War began.[25]

Even in retrospect, the numbers are mind-boggling, but for people walking the levee, the goods' physical presence must have seemed even more improbable. Following the batture conflict, the waterfront remained open, free of structures limiting access to the riverbanks. In a typical year in the 1830s, a pedestrian could stroll the waterfront amid thousands of reams of paper, boxes of candles and soap, and hogsheads of tobacco; marvel at tens of thousands of barrels of apples, bushels of oats, and animal hides; pay homage to hundreds of thousands of bales of "king" cotton; and contemplate millions of pounds of pork or gallons of whiskey.[26] Today, we are used to supermarkets filled with goods from around the globe. Refrigeration, vacuum packing, airplanes, trucks, and other technologies allow us to buy bagged Florida oranges in the produce aisle, plastic-wrapped Texas beef at the deli counter, and bottled Italian balsamic vinegar in the foreign-foods section. The world's goods are at our fingertips; we buy without thinking about a product's place of origin or how it came to be in our hands. For most antebellum observers, however, New Orleans's levee was a market unprecedented in their experience, a symbol of the power of artifice to bring goods from diverse locales together in one place.

Another feature of the waterfront—the people congregating there—illustrated that steamboats broke down not only geographic borders, but also normally stark spatial divisions separating individuals of different races, classes, genders, and ethnicities. Wealthy cabin passengers disembarked next to destitute deck hands, often recent immigrants, who unloaded cargo, while free people of color and enslaved African-Americans hauled wood to fuel a steamboat's insatiable boilers. A multinational crowd of traders haggled at the levee, shouting out prices in a polyglot chorus, as ladies and gentlemen walked the riverbanks, enjoying the sights and breeze coming off the Mississippi. While visiting New Orleans in 1838, a tourist remarked that the "population passing in the streets, especially on 'the Levee,' and others adjoining the river, is the most amusing motley assemblage that can be exhibited in any town on earth." He noted that "the prevailing language seems to be that of Babel—Spanish, Portuguese, French, English, mixed with a few wretched remains of Choctaw, and other Indian tribes; and all these are spoken in the loudest, broadest, and strangest dialects."[27]

Still, neither the levee nor greater New Orleans was a melting pot in the idealized sense of that metaphor. Many individuals were uncomfortable with the social mixing at the waterfront, just as some people today are put off when confronted by the diverse groups frequenting urban, public spaces. Commenting on the chaotic nature of the levee, one genteel traveler recommended that refined visitors should enjoy the view from a steamboat's topmost deck. He warned that the scene reeked of democracy: "All grades of society, all classes here mingle & commingle in all the peculiarity of their individual character."[28] Still, even if such encounters made some visitors uneasy, at the levee people came into contact with individuals of different backgrounds, upon whom they likely never would have laid eyes under other circumstances. And this feature marked the levee, although it was regulated, as a public space in the expansive way that those words are often used today. The levee was a place where a diverse population gathered and negotiated differences across cultural, racial, or gender lines.

Whiskey from Kentucky distilleries, apples from New York orchards, corn from central-Illinois farms, furs from the Canadian backcountry, cotton from upper Louisiana, cheese from Wisconsin's dairyland, starched visitors from London, Creole traders hawking their wares, African-American firemen cleaning soot from their faces, "Kaintucks" napping beside their battered flatboats, and refined couples ambling arm in arm—all mingled at the waterfront. The potential for movement, for travel to distant lands—a raw, kinetic energy—seemed to hang in the humid air near the river. Observers knew that such a collage of people and goods from places far removed from one another could have been assembled in the western United States only with the help of technology. Such a gathering would have been unlikely, even impossible, before the advent of steamboats on the river system because the lower and upper reaches of the valley had remained separated by a half-year journey. The scenes at the levee, then, represented a triumph of human ingenuity over geography, as steamboats shifted the meanings of time and space.

By what means did steamboats transform New Orleans's riverfront? There were three: their steadily increasing speed, the relative predictability they imposed on the Mississippi, and the inexpensive transit they offered traders. Speed captures the imagination, while cargo capacity and shipping prices seem comparatively prosaic, but diminished shipping costs and soaring capacities aboard steamboats contributed to the rise of New Orleans's port. Each year, as more steamboats carried more cargo—capacity jumped by over 60 percent in the first three decades of the era of steam—cutthroat competition forced shipping prices down. Prior to the arrival of steamboats on the Mississippi, upriver shipping rates from New Orleans typically hovered near five dollars per hundred pounds. By the late 1820s, prices often fell below fifty cents for the same quantity on that route.[29] Consequently, during the era of steam, valley traders shipped more goods to New Orleans than ever before. Heaped in piles along the waterfront, those products accounted for the city's antebellum ascent in status to a regional entrepot.

Despite the importance of shipping costs and cargo capacities, few people, save for traders, paid much mind to them at the time. Instead, speed—representing artifice's apparent triumph over nature—attracted popular raves. After steamboats had conquered the current, velocity became a consuming passion on the river system (see figure 11). In the parlance of the river, the boat credited with the fastest time on a main route—from New Orleans to Louisville or from St. Louis to Pittsburgh—held "the horns." When the *Washington* steamed upstream from New Orleans to Louisville in just under a month in 1817, the feat seemed incredible. Later that year, though, the *Shelby* took the horns when it trav-

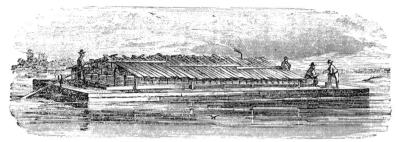

FLATBOAT FROM ST. LOUIS TO NEW ORLEANS, TIME FOUR MONTHS.

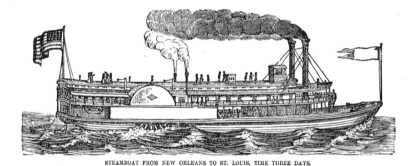

STEAMBOAT FROM NEW ORLEANS TO ST. LOUIS, TIME THREE DAYS.

Figure 11. Steamboats upended people's senses of distance and time (image ca. mid-nineteenth century). Courtesy of The Historic New Orleans Collection.

eled the same route in a little more than twenty days. Then, in 1828, the *Tecumseh* arrived in Louisville only eight days out of New Orleans. By 1850, a passenger could leave New Orleans on Sunday for a Friday engagement in Louisville, confident that she would arrive on time.[30] A river voyage of fifteen hundred miles in a week—the distance and time seem paltry and pokey in our era of supersonic travel, but for New Orleanians at that time, steamboats represented "a complete revolution in the internal navigation of the region."[31]

Steam travel collapsed time and space, as a kind of technological alchemy turned six months' hard labor into one month's comparatively relaxing travel. Less than twenty years later, further innovation transformed the month-long voyage into a journey of less than a week. It seemed as though steamboats had compressed the valley's environs like an accordion, bringing the upper Ohio River and the lower Mississippi together as easily as one might fold a map, leaving Baton Rouge astride Pittsburgh. One commentator wrote of the steamboats' impact: "distance is no longer thought of in this region—it is almost annihilated by steam."[32]

As steamboats shifted the meanings of space and time, they altered New Orleanian's relationships with the Mississippi. That the river's current could be overcome, that people could travel in relative ease and comfort between the city and the valley's furthest reaches, suggested that humans had seized control of the Mississippi. Henry Tudor, visiting New Orleans in 1833, explained that steamboats could clear the "natural obstacle" of the river's current with only the "the exhalation arising from a few tea-kettles full of boiling water."[33] Tudor made an important point about the control of what New Orleanians at the time called nature: prior to the arrival of steamboats on the Mississippi system, people had no idea how much time a journey from the city to an upriver destination might take, or even if such a journey could be completed. During the era of steam, however, people grew confident that they could travel and trade where and when they chose.

Contemporary discussions of the meanings of the Mississippi system reveal people's attitudes about the technological innovations. Conventional wisdom dictated that God and Nature had created the rivers to serve people's needs. One commentator wrote of the river system that "the Creator of the universe has no where on the face of the earth, spread more lavishly the means of human prosperity, or stamped more legibly the lineaments of beautiful and convenient adaptation to the wants and necessities of mankind."[34] These sentiments hearkened back to New Orleans's early boosters, who saw evidence of a divine plan for the city in the valley's geography. But the Mississippi's current had blocked the city's path to riches; it was people who had overcome the current with steamboats, fulfilling nature's promise. Another observer suggested as much, writing that "nature ha[d] been prodigal" in laying out the river system, but "it was left to human skill and energy, to turn her gifts to the best advantage."[35] In sum, artifice had brought order to the Mississippi; people had improved the natural world.

These revelations seemingly tie into a traditional understanding of the role that technology plays in shaping human relationships with the environment: artifice isolates people from the unpredictability of their surroundings, ultimately diminishing their awe for the power of the nonhuman world in favor of reverence for mechanical innovation.[36] For instance, when nineteenth-century western historian Timothy Flint wrote about steam travel, he focused on the impact that juxtaposing the valley's environs—a wilderness—and a technological marvel had on travelers: "A contrast is thus strongly forced upon the mind, of the highest improvement and the latest pre-eminent invention of art with the most lonely aspect of a grand but desolate nature." Flint compared "the most striking and complete assemblage of splendor and comfort, the cheerfulness of a floating hotel...with a wild and uninhabited forest."[37] And yet, not all travelers experienced steamboat journeys as instances of technology dominating the environment. The vessels brought more people than ever before onto the Mississippi system, including upper-class Europeans making "grand tours" of the United States. These tourists served as publicists for the Mississippi, waxing poetic about the river's majesty in a seemingly endless stream of narratives published during the era of steam. In hundreds of memoirs, the steamboats *and* the river played starring roles, sharing the stage. The steamboats were impressive, certainly, but they did not entirely overshadow their surroundings.

But the romantic prose favored by tourists often betrayed an elite sensibility, focusing on aesthetics while ignoring the hard work, skill, and energy that it took to overcome the current. Therefore, travel narratives are imperfect tools for understanding how steamboats shifted observers' views of what they called nature. As upper-crust steamboat tourists dined on sumptuous feasts, or gambled for high stakes in opulent staterooms, such travel must have appeared luxurious. Authors typically disregarded deforestation, for instance, on the Mississippi's banks, a result of the estimated thirty-two cords of wood on average a steamboat's boilers consumed each day.[38] Indeed, in first class it could seem like the boats moved as if by magic, while such illusions were impossible in the superheated atmosphere below the decks, where so-called firemen fed a craft's boiler. These hired hands knew that steamboats were energy-transfer machines: the human energy required to navigate a strong current or to stoke a boiler, and the organic energy stored in the trees that provided power for the vessels. In his study of the Columbia River, historian Richard White suggests that in the past, "human beings knew the river through the work the river demanded of them."[39] The same was true of laborers on the Mississippi. And because no group knew the river better than steamboat pilots, their experiences and recollections spotlight ways in which human perceptions of the Mississippi shifted as steamboats seemingly controlled the river.

During the era of steam, most people in the know agreed that the pilots' jobs—navigating the Mississippi system—were by far the most pressure-packed, if not the most physically demanding, on the river. Under the best of circumstances this task proved daunting, as the unpredictable rivers were choked with fallen trees and other detritus, prone to seemingly aimless and endless meanders, and often so silted in places that even the lightest vessels ran aground. Pilots also confronted the river system's dynamism. Even years of experience, and guides such as Zadok Cramer's *Navigator,* could become useless if a bank caved, a channel shifted, or a thick fog rolled in. Well-known routes sometimes changed as quickly as a hard rain fell. To keep the boats, passengers, and cargo under their supervision safe, pilots studied every riffle, rapid, eddy, twist, and turn found on the Mississippi system.[40]

The pilots' most eloquent spokesman was Samuel Clemens, better known as Mark Twain, the pen name he borrowed from his days working aboard a steamboat. In the 1880s, Twain recalled his apprenticeship as a young cub pilot, writing about his efforts to understand the Mississippi's moods. Diving deep into metaphor, he explained that "the face of the water, in time, became a wonderful book—a book that was a dead language to the uneducated passenger, but which told its mind to me without reserve, delivering its most cherished secrets as clearly as if it uttered them with a voice."[41] Twain suggested that people who worked on the Mississippi understood the river in ways that lay people could not. River professionals communicated with the river, acquiring knowledge only endless hours of labor on its waters could provide.

Twain's reminiscences also suggest that workers recognized that the river's power and unpredictability persisted into the era of steam. Focusing on the Mississippi's dynamism, Twain wrote that "it was not a book to be read once and thrown aside, for it had a new story to tell every day. Throughout the long twelve hundred miles there was never a page that was void of interest, never one that you could leave unread without loss."[42] The moment a pilot stopped reading the river carefully, he risked losing his boat to hazards such as snags—fallen trees—that could pierce a vessel's hull in an instant. Snags were by-products of a dynamic, riparian environment. Because of the instability of the Mississippi's banks, large sections of earth, including "acres of forests," sometimes eroded into the river.[43] Many of these trees sank to the bottom, but portions of others lurked near the surface, threatening river traffic. So Twain and his contemporaries studied the Mississippi, hoping to avoid snags or other hazards that proved that the river was still unpredictable, even to those who knew it best.

In time Twain sadly realized that the intimacy he enjoyed with the river as a result of careful study came with a price. The author admitted that as he became increasingly familiar with the Mississippi he forgot its majesty. "Now when I had mastered the language of this water and had come to know every trifling feature that bordered the great river as familiarly as I knew the letters of the alphabet," Twain wrote, "I had made a valuable acquisition." He also lamented that "I had lost something, too. I had lost something which could never be restored to me while I lived. All the grace, the beauty, the poetry had gone out of the majestic river!"[44] What had been a love affair between Twain and the Mississippi over time became a stale marriage, perhaps still a relationship between intimates, but one devoid of passion.

FROM MUDDY BANKS TO ORDERED WHARVES

As technology imposed order on the Mississippi, making it more predictable and a better place to do business, and as the city's residents pondered the levee, or traveled upstream to Louisville in less than a week, they celebrated the ways that artifice had rendered the mercurial river relatively docile. The Mississippi, for the first time in the city's history, seemed to be under control, and steamboats had been the agents of change. But while the annihilation of space and time may have brought empire within reach for New Orleanians, the surging economy and the presence of a new technology along the levee confused and enlivened ongoing battles over urban space, ultimately leaving the city divided over how best to develop and administer its waterfront in an age of artifice. Steamboats, it turned out, were not simply passive servants of human interests; they, like other transportation technologies, had needs that played out in the production of space in the city. In time, the arrival of steamboats at the waterfront yielded a series of unforeseen consequences in New Orleans that threatened to rip apart the city's delicate spatial fabric.

Prior to the arrival of steamboats on the Mississippi, the river's east bank at New Orleans had remained largely undeveloped, a space called public by the city's citizens. As the furor over Edward Livingston's plans for the batture demonstrated, New Orleanians resisted construction there, fearing that development would jeopardize their right to use the waterfront as a source of landfill, a storage spot, or a promenade. Local custom and law protected those rights, and the waterfront, though commercial, stood open. Pedestrians could stroll the length of the riverbanks, sidestepping piles of goods, the watercraft littering the shore, and the crowds of traders, laborers, and tourists surrounding them. Onlookers enjoyed uninterrupted views of New Orleans and the Mississippi, appreciating the close relationship between the two.

During the era of steam, this relationship began changing. After the voyage of the *New Orleans,* and especially following Judge Hall's ruling of 1817, the waterfront became one of the nation's premier ports, and the stakes involved in administering it increased. As steamboats altered human perceptions of space and time, they also prompted New Orleans to reconfigure its riverfront. This proved to be a contested process, the study of which sheds light on changes in the city's residents' priorities regarding public spaces and their interactions with the Mississippi. Old questions—echoes from the batture controversy—about who should control the riverfront, how that landscape should best be used, and who constituted the public that had a right to access and use the waterfront received additional attention. And new questions, like those surrounding the appropriate amount of space and proper docking location for riverboats and other trade vessels, prompted battles with far-reaching consequences. These fights demonstrated once again the complicated nature of public space in New Orleans and the river's ongoing role in shaping landscapes in the city.

Early in the era of steam, the Conseil de ville claimed stewardship over the waterfront. Although only the Fulton group's steamboats and a rare independent vessel visited New Orleans before 1817, the waterfront nonetheless demanded attention as the council contemplated methods of encouraging and regulating the city's river-borne commerce. With no structures protecting goods at the levee, and few controls over who had access to the waterfront or how it could be used, the port appeared disorganized to commercial elites who believed that centralized control would maximize efficiency, insuring increased profits in the future. Eager to placate the commercial community and to oversee the waterfront, the council passed a port ordinance on December 11, 1816. Included in that law were provisions specifying the areas where vessels should dock, as well as regulations marking the extent of the port. Soon after, the council passed additional ordinances intended to further organize the waterfront.[45]

At first glance, these pieces of legislation hardly seem worthy of attention; yet they began a period of change in the way that New Orleanians produced space along the riverbanks. Steamboats apparently had brought order to the Mississippi by overcoming its current. The port ordinances, in turn, represented the council's efforts at sorting activity along the riverbanks, regulating the waterfront so that commerce could thrive there. The laws claimed terrain exclusively for commercial purposes, insuring that trade vessels would have room to land even as the number of arrivals at the levee increased yearly. In short, the ordinances were an early step in what was to be a lengthy and controversial process in New Orleans: dividing waterfront space into use-based categories—work and play, nature and artifice. For that reason, although these ordinances were not especially expansive, nor did they invest the council with much power, they were significant.

For almost two more decades, the Conseil de ville enacted port laws without generating substantial dissent. Then, in 1835, the river reminded New Orleanians that it too produced space in the city, touching off a two-year controversy at the waterfront. In March of that year, several steamboat captains and New Orleanians petitioned the state legislature to look into conditions at the port in the city's upriver, or American, section. The legislature investigated the claims, finding that the batture forming in that area of the city had grown so large that it rendered the port there useless.[46] In short, the river had ignored laws intended to fix borders along the waterfront, another example of how dynamic sedimentation could undermine property law. As a result, laborers unloading trade vessels at the time had to cross one hundred yards of mud before reaching the levee and the city beyond. Although the committee members recommended amending the laws governing the waterfront, they hesitated before offering their opinion because the issue involved "the jarring and opposing interests of the city of New Orleans."[47]

Those interests broke down along ethnic lines. On one side stood Americans living in the upper part of the city, including the Faubourg St. Mary and development farther upriver. Creole elites—typically residents of the French Quarter and the city's downriver *faubourgs*—opposed the Americans. The Americans hoped to secure municipal appropriations to build new wharves along the waterfront in their district of the city, while Creoles tried to avoid spending funds on a part of the port that they believed was doomed by the river's geomorphological processes. Lurking below the dispute's surface were more troubling issues. Creoles feared that Americans were becoming dominant in the city's commercial and political affairs and that the newcomers might monopolize traffic on the river in the future. In the batture accumulations Creoles saw another gift given them by the Mississippi: silt to dam the Americans' flow of trade. The Americans, on the other hand, worried that Creoles were clinging to their shrinking majority on the Conseil de ville to serve ethnic interests. American council members believed that Creoles, aware that their political decline had begun, saw the wharf issue as a last chance to stem the tide of growing American influence in the city.

A spatial and environmental dimension accompanied these ethnic and political conflicts. Still influenced by the batture controversy, New Or-

leans's Creole commercial elites maintained that building structures at
the waterfront threatened the public's right to access the river and its
banks. Although Creoles on the Conseil de ville had shown that they
were willing to develop the waterfront—Creole council members had
sponsored port ordinances early in the era of steam—they balked before
sanctioning improvements on the scale suggested by their American
counterparts. In contrast, members of New Orleans's emerging American commercial community insisted that the needs of trade superseded
other rights accorded the public at the waterfront. The Americans on the
council evinced a far more instrumental view of the riverbanks, arguing
that the waterfront landscape could serve the public best by bowing to
commerce. Accordingly, they hoped to engineer space at the waterfront
for the circulation of goods, rather than for people's uses. Ultimately, the
state supreme court ruled on the dispute after mulling over the public's
interests and whose responsibility it was to guard those interests. By that
time, though, the controversy had torn the city apart.

In retrospect, the Conseil de ville's meeting of April 4, 1835, became
something of a referendum on nature, technology, and the production
of space in the city, as tempers flared when Councilman Dixon, an American, proposed altering docking positions at the Port of New Orleans.
Dixon insisted that steamboats should be allowed to land opposite the
city's American section, at a site the batture had not yet rendered useless. Supporting Dixon, Councilman McCready, also an American, mentioned the Erie Canal and East Coast railroad construction, warning that
"nature had indeed gifted the state with a magnificent river; but if shack-
les are imposed on the western trade, merchants...will find...other outlets for their produce." McCready's threat resonated for some council
members. The arrival of steamboats on the Mississippi was part of a
transportation revolution taking place nationwide, and some councilmen recognized that artifice, so potentially helpful to New Orleans, could
also threaten its interests. As new transportation technologies emerged,
even the valley's geography could not keep trade flowing exclusively
down the Mississippi. The city must improve its waterfront or risk losing business to other markets, the Americans on the council suggested.
Still, national affairs proved no match for local grudges: when the
amendment came to a vote, it failed along sectional and ethnic lines, leaving the issues unresolved.[48]

As the controversy persisted, a secession movement arose amid the
city's American commercial community. English-speaking activists, convinced that their section of New Orleans would never receive fair treat-

ment from the Creole-dominated council, suggested that the city split along geographic and ethnic lines and argued that the resulting two sections could form autonomous municipalities. The Americans would then administer their portion of the waterfront as they chose, leaving the Creoles to their own devices. If the Creoles insisted on preserving the public's sweeping and therefore anachronistic privileges along the waterfront, then their section could not compete effectively for a share of the valley's trade. That would be their decision, the Americans reasoned. The secessionists suggested that there was no choice other than division for a city fighting pitched battles over the waterfront, its most important natural resource, in an era when New Orleans had to develop its spaces to accommodate emerging transportation technologies or lose business to other markets.[49]

When the Conseil de ville met again on August 13, 1835, sectional ill will pervaded. The mayor addressed the assembly that day, urging comity by acknowledging that waterfront improvements *were* necessary. Then he also demanded patience from the Americans, reminding them that the Mississippi was not so biddable as they implied. Parroting arguments from the batture conflict, the mayor warned that if the river were mistreated, it might wipe out the city's port. Development, he scolded, that did not account for the river's role in shaping the waterfront risked the city's commercial future. In other words, though artifice had served the city well, the mayor did not believe that technology could be trusted to tame the river in every instance. Finally, he cautioned that both by custom and law the levee was a public space. Again referring back to the batture case, he noted that the compromise with Edward Livingston stipulated that the waterfront could be used only for "natural purposes." The mayor warned that building wharves would violate this agreement by imperiling the public's—though he did not explain to whom or what he referred—long-standing right to access an unobstructed riverfront. The American councilmen responded by repeating their commitment to development, suggesting that such a course would not threaten the public designation of the space, but instead better serve New Orleanians' needs in an era of artifice.[50]

On October 16, 1835, the crisis escalated when American property holders and merchants held a protest in the city's Arcade building. At this meeting, Samuel Jarvis Peters, a real-estate developer and former council member, presented a memorial explaining the secessionists' position. Peters reiterated that the batture threatened the upper district of the city, explaining that the Americans hoped to deal with the obstruction by building a huge new wharf along the extent of the riverfront opposite the Faubourg St. Mary. In contrast to the mayor's warnings, Peters indicated that it was the river, not artifice, that should be feared. He begged the question of what impact the wharf would have on people's ability to use the waterfront. Instead he climbed to the moral high ground, suggesting that he and his supporters among New Orleans's American population wanted to avoid splitting the city. The memorial, he claimed, was a last-ditch effort to convince the Creoles to accede to the Americans' demands—an early kind of bayou brinksmanship. After Peters's presentation, the assembly posted the document publicly, a line drawn down the center of the city's alluvial soil.[51]

The Arcade meeting signaled changes in the conflict. Convinced that their section of the city needed waterfront improvements to accommodate the steadily increasing steamboat trade, Americans made clear their contempt for the public's customary rights at the riverbanks. The secessionists' solution to the problem of the river's silting—construction at the waterfront—also suggested how impressed they were with artifice and how progress, an ineffable goal, had captivated them. The allure of the possible, of controlling time, space, and the river, in service of trade, seemed within reach during the era of steam, and the Americans insisted that the city needed to consolidate its already excellent commercial position while it had the chance. Certain that a massive wharf could withstand the river's wrath, the Americans dismissed the Creoles' suggestion that sedimentation could not be stopped and that the Mississippi would not tolerate people tampering with its natural regimen.

Following the Arcade meeting, a writer at the *Bee,* the city's bilingual newspaper, surveyed the conflict. The reporter acknowledged that the riverfront had always been a "public" space. In an age of artifice, though, he claimed that the public's interests had dovetailed with those of the city's commercial community. Therefore, he reasoned, the riverfront should be developed to promote trade and thus the public good.[52] The subtext was clear: each year a growing share of the city's commerce arrived aboard steamboats, and if those vessels required wharves, then wharves they must have. The author believed that old notions regarding the public's interest along the waterfront were outmoded, because New Orleans needed to cement its place as the valley's market or risk losing business to commercial rivals, cities served by transportation technologies like canals or railroads. Nature had been kind to New Orleans; the Mississippi remained the valley's highway of trade; but the city would squander its natural advantages if it did not reshape its waterfront to cater to commercial interests and steam technology.

Responding to the secessionists, the Conseil de ville convened a committee, and on October 27 the council discussed its findings. Anger mounted as Councilman Gaiennie, a Creole, revealed that the committee did not suggest that a wharf should be constructed for the city's upper section. Justifying the decision by pointing to local custom, law, and the river's power, he noted that the public's (still undefined) rights would be alienated by construction, and that the river would destroy the wharf anyway. After Gaiennie concluded, Councilman Caldwell, an American, "appeal[ed] on behalf of the petitioners and their project." In a righteous fury, he warned that the memorialists were a group "who cannot be contented with half measures; who do not brook being tampered with, while they possess the remedy in their own hands and have any recourse and resource; and who must have justice done them." The American insisted that the wharf initiative had to pass, or the city would split; the Creoles were unmoved. When the measure came up for a vote, it failed again along sectional lines.[53]

Following the meeting, the council sent a bill to the state legislature, seeking dissolution of the city into three submunicipalities; on March 1, 1836, the bill passed the house by a six-to-one margin. The next day, the senate passed the bill, five to one. Just over a week later, the *Bee* printed its text, explaining the divided city's system of government. The three submunicipalities (see figure 12) were to be the city's geographic center, or French Quarter, forming the First Municipality; the upriver, American section, the Second; and the downriver *faubourgs,* the Third. Each had a council, all subordinate to a general council and mayor, both of whom had mandates limited to points of common interest between the three districts and no powers of appropriation.[54] The goal of bringing order to the waterfront, a process contingent on dividing that space into use-based categories, had yielded dire consequences: the city had become a confederation of ethnic enclaves, united only by a weak central government and a name that held different meanings, depending on the language in which it was uttered.

Whereas early in the era of steam, the Conseil de ville had sponsored the port's reorganization, by 1836 that policy had divided New Orleans over questions of the river's place in the city and the waterfront's future. These were old issues, but for the first time American commercial elites had shouted down the arguments that Creoles had used since Edward

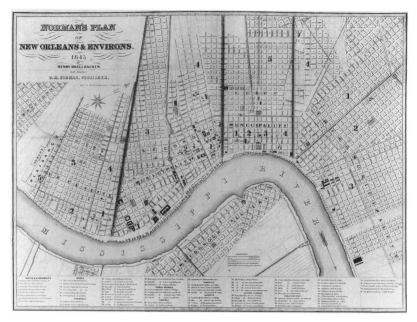

Figure 12. After years of controversy over how best to administer the waterfront, New Orleans was divided into three submunicipalities. Note the dark vertical lines demarking the boundaries in the city in this map (1845). Courtesy of The Historic New Orleans Collection.

Livingston unveiled his batture plans. With steamboats plying the river and workers digging canals and laying rails around the country, the Americans had insisted that the public's traditional prerogatives along the waterfront were antiquated. They accepted that a vaguely defined public had a right to use the waterfront, but restructured who should be included in that category and what rights they had exactly. They had also dismissed the idea that the Mississippi would lash out if people built permanent structures on its banks, a notion that rang false in an age when artifice seemingly controlled nature. Arguments about the public's rights at the waterfront, or the river's overwhelming power, sounded hollow next to the roar of a riverboat's stoked boiler or the shrill of its whistle. The waterfront could be a public space, the Americans allowed, but it would also be devoted more explicitly than ever to commercial purposes. And with the city divided, American commercial elites began imposing their vision of how to produce and use the waterfront landscape—though not without additional controversy.

Ironically, in an era of great technological advances, of ostensibly tamed nature and disciplined urban space, battles over the waterfront became only more heated and convoluted in the wake of the city's division. As the three municipalities organized their now-divided ports, non-elite New Orleanians fought to preserve their rights at the waterfront, still viewing construction there as a threat to that space's public designation. The three municipalities also continued bickering with one another about the riverbanks, scuffles that led to a series of waterfront-related cases ending up before the state supreme court. In its decisions, the judiciary redefined both the municipalities' and the public's rights along the riverbanks, recasting the city's border with the Mississippi as a far more commercial and instrumental landscape than it ever had been in the past.[55] The justices' opinions often mirrored the arguments that American secessionists had put forth in the days leading to the city's division: the public's rights at the waterfront had shifted in the era of steam; people had to accept that artifice demanded new spatial organization and the construction of permanent structures along the Mississippi's banks.

The first of the major waterfront cases decided by Louisiana's supreme court arose out of the controversy that had split the city. The conflict began when Americans in the Second Municipality wasted little time before building the long-delayed wharf fronting the Faubourg St. Mary. As a result of the construction, city residents found their path to the Mississippi blocked. Aware that people could not access the riverbanks in the American section of the city, the council of the First Municipality filed suit against the Second Municipality, invoking the public's right to use the waterfront. The Creoles' suit amounted to a last-ditch effort to halt the Americans' plans for their section of the city's port—spatial sour grapes playing out in the courts.[56]

After the Second Municipality appealed to the state supreme court, the justices ruled in the case of *Municipality No. 1 v. Municipality No. 2*. In its decision, the court allowed that the contested portion of the riverfront was "dedicated to public uses," but it went on to note that "the administration of this space, and the batture on it, is confided exclusively to the second municipality." Thus, while the justices acknowledged that the waterfront remained public, the city government could determine public rights next to the river. The judges continued, reiterating that the public had a "right to take earth and sand from" the batture, but with an important caveat: this right did not supersede "other great objects of the [riverfront's] dedication."[57] With this section of its decision, the court held that building structures at the riverfront, long disputed, constituted a legitimate use of the corporate powers of the councils in an urban and technologically sophisticated era. In other words, if one of the councils determined that wharves better served the public's interests than digging soil from or promenading on the batture, it could build, even if the construction limited people's access to the Mississippi or its accretions.

In this and other cases, the court expanded the role of the municipalities along the riverfront.[58] In terms of the justices' consistently invoking the public's rights, their rhetoric did not change from the era of the batture dispute. What had shifted was the way in which the justices defined New Orleanians' rights and interests, and, by extension, the public itself. Each case's outcome diminished the legal power that the portion of the public made up of non-elite New Orleanians wielded, compared to their elected officials and the city's commercial community, by reiterating that the councils' plans had precedence over non-elite citizens' hopes for the riverfront. In decision after decision, the justices ruled that modern, urban conditions and economic imperatives brought about by technological change had antiquated those ancient rights. Stewardship over the waterfront had to be centralized in the era of steam so that officials could oversee the landscape next to the Mississippi. People who hoped to wander the riverbanks, or dig dirt from the batture, could still do so, but only if a construction site, a steamboat, or a new wharf built by one of the three municipal councils had not already occupied that space.

In the future, the decision to build wharves along the riverbanks was to have profound consequences not only for the waterfront's status as a public space, but also for the city's relationship with the Mississippi. By tilting toward a policy of commercial planning at the waterfront, New Orleans's municipal councils and Louisiana's supreme court established a precedent that became akin to holy writ in the city: riverfront development would serve trade above all else. As time passed, such a position was to render the city far less flexible in dealing with the river and the delta's unpredictable environment. Having bowed to the needs of transportation technologies by investing in costly, static infrastructure, the city later was to find itself less adaptable when facing ecological problems, such as flooding. In short, spatial and economic decisions made during the 1830s were to have environmental repercussions for the city right up to the present day. But at the time, such issues lay in the hazy distance.

THE FLEETING CONTROL OF NATURE,
ARTIFICE, AND PUBLIC SPACE

On a balmy spring evening in 1847, J.D.B. DeBow, one of the Mississippi Valley's best-known and shrewdest economic commentators,
walked New Orleans's waterfront. Gazing at the sun setting over the
river, he cataloged some of the many changes wrought in the city since
the 1812 voyage of the *New Orleans,* noting scores of steamboats
docked at the levee, potent artifice "which acknowledge[d] none of the
powers of air, and await[ed] no tide."[59] Had DeBow climbed to the third
deck of one of those vessels, he could have seen relatively new urban development stretching for miles upriver, shadowing the Mississippi to New
Orleans's border with the neighboring town of Lafayette. Looking downstream, he might have noted that the lower portion of the city had also
grown during the era of steam. Immediately below him, DeBow found
other impressive changes. The waterfront sported a new feature, a symbol of progress to an apostle of commerce like DeBow: so many wharves
had been built out into the Mississippi as it made its crescent-shaped meander that from above the riverbanks resembled a centipede turning a
corner.[60]

DeBow described a remarkably tranquil scene at the waterfront. With
a southerly breeze carrying the briny scent of the gulf to the city, the
"busy hum of life" at the levee was "hushing to repose." Meanwhile,
the Mississippi, personified as a nurturing mother, hugged New Orleans
to its "broad bosom." Amazed by all that he saw next to the river,
DeBow mused that the levee demonstrated the power of "art, science,
and luxury; of discovery and invention; of the interchange between nations, imparting knowledge, harmonizing manners, creating refinement;
of the exchanges of the products of distant climes, supplying nature, and
feeding wants."[61] In DeBow's telling, trade could draw order out of
chaos and beauty from desolation.

For DeBow, the levee evoked "the whole story" of the era of steam,
the triumph of commerce and artifice marching forward in lockstep.
Those two agents of change had spread "civilization," which DeBow
counterpoised with what had recently been untamed "nature": the Mississippi and its banks before steamboats had brought the river and waterfront to heel.[62] DeBow was not alone in reveling in the city's triumphs.
One contemporary study of New Orleans's economic growth suggested
that "between 1830 and 1840 no city in the United States kept pace with

it." Much evidence supported such a conclusion. During the era of steam, the city had blossomed from a colonial backwater into one of the five largest metropolises in the nation, and the third most prolific exporter of goods in the world.[63] As DeBow suggested, spatial and technological transformations, as well as economic indicators, were the catalysts of these developments. Just three decades earlier, the riverbanks had been mostly empty, a broad sweep of mud fronting the city. In those days, the Mississippi had been a wild river, dangling the promise of empire before the city, but out of control. In the span of thirty years, New Orleanians had seemingly ordered their city's built and what they called natural environments, leaving DeBow with the impression that the era of steam could be related as a tale of steady progress, symbolized by changes at New Orleans's waterfront.

DeBow knew that the city's economic growth had been predicated on a series of power struggles: the struggle to overcome the river's current with the power of steam, the struggle to define the type of public space that the Mississippi would be in an age of artifice, and the struggle for control of the riverbanks in New Orleans. In DeBow's estimation, by 1847 those struggles had been resolved. The Mississippi remained open to all comers, and steamboats seemingly had domesticated the river. People had also regulated the waterfront, imposing order where chaos had reigned. As a result, DeBow and other boosters, flush with the city's success, dusted off predictions grown creaky with age, and updated them by propping them against the hulls of steamboats docked at the waterfront: nature, in conjunction with or completed by artifice, had brought New Orleans to the brink of its destiny as the seat of a vast commercial empire.

But DeBow's account of nature, artifice, and public space, all disciplined, ignored an uncomfortable reality in the city: order had been hard to come by and proved harder still to maintain. Although DeBow believed that he saw the whole story of the era of steam on display at the waterfront, his commercial leanings blinded him to many facets of that tale, a complicated interplay of social and environmental factors outside his line of sight. For instance, because of his enthusiasm for what he called progress, DeBow ignored ongoing challenges facing the city as it competed with other markets for commercial preeminence in the valley. He also disregarded strife surrounding the reorganization of the city's port, even as spatial battles raged around him in the 1840s, and he overlooked the catastrophic ways in which steamboats sometimes seemed to rebel against the people who counted on them to tame the river. In short, DeBow told only part of a complicated story. Another competing narrative lurked in the muddy currents of the Mississippi, waited just below decks aboard the steamboats plying the river, and hid among crowds gathered at New Orleans's levee. Although DeBow did not realize it, New Orleanians' control of the valley's trade, the city's waterfront, the steamboats docked there, and the Mississippi often proved illusory.

Even as DeBow celebrated the city's commercial heyday, other markets were diverting business from the Mississippi system. Canal fever gathered momentum throughout the era of steam, and in the years between 1825 and 1848, traders began floating goods on the Erie, Pennsylvania Main Line, Michigan, and two Ohio canals. Later, railroads further loosened the Mississippi system's stranglehold on the valley's trade. By 1852, four trunk lines had completed links to the valley; and in 1853, workers finished laying track across Illinois and Wisconsin to the banks of the Mississippi. With each passing year, more goods from the valley found their way to markets via trade routes other than the river.[64] In short, as the dream of empire in New Orleans came into sharper focus, the long-term reality was actually slipping away.

Still, even as "artificial rivers" and "iron horses" captured a growing portion of the valley's trade, New Orleanians bragged about the power of steamboats and their city's "natural advantages."[65] Into the 1850s, many of the city's commercial elites remained convinced that trade would always flow to market via the north-south river route, rather than west-east on railroads and canals. Such confidence soon proved unwarranted. While steamboats had conquered the Mississippi's current, they had never broken free of its serpentine coils. Thus, for all of New Orleanians' boasts about the annihilation of space and time, the vessels remained bound to the waters of the river system, while canal and railroad engineers reshaped trade routes to suit their whims. In other words, developers armed with cheap labor and blasting powder could overcome even the vagaries of geography. The journey to market via railroads and canals, from west to east, was shorter, quicker, and ultimately cheaper than from north to south on the river to New Orleans, and then to the East Coast, via deep-water shipping.

Eventually, as New Orleans's relative share of the valley's trade diminished, some observers recognized that what they had always lauded as nature's gifts had caused complacency in the city. A few even went so far as to suggest that "providence has supplied us with such immense natural advantages that we have been hitherto content to lay upon our oars, supinely trusting to the superiority of our position." These revelations belatedly caused savvy critics to call for railroad construction, a strategy that they hoped would help the city walk upon the "path of enterprise which will undoubtedly give to New Orleans the destiny intended for her by the bounteous and plastic hand of nature."[66] Again, they wanted to supplement, or complete, the city's natural advantages with artifice, as steamboats had to such great effect in the past.[67] But by that time it was too late; there was little New Orleans could do, as valley traders increasingly floated goods to eastern markets on canals or shipped them overland via railroads.

If DeBow misread New Orleans's economic future, he also failed to grasp that the levee remained a contested, multiuse landscape. In 1847, despite decades of efforts by commercial elites struggling to reshape the waterfront into an orderly space devoted to trade, some segments of the city's population still viewed the riverbanks as public, in the broadest sense of that word. For instance, many African-American slaves, private property whom most New Orleanians would have deemed far beyond even an expansively defined public in the city, capitalized on development at the levee, using it as a staging location from which they escaped bondage aboard vessels headed to the North. Such actions highlight a historical irony: as the Mississippi's banks became increasingly commercial, disciplined, and closely regulated throughout the era of steam, that landscape endured as an open, public space, produced by the people who used it as well as by those who made the laws governing its use. That African-American slaves claimed space for themselves along the levee and aboard steamboats demonstrated how public those spaces were and how contingent such a category could be.

Beginning with the *New Orleans* in 1812, steamboats shifted the meaning of the Mississippi and New Orleans's waterfront for African-Americans. The threat of being sold down the river loomed over slaves in the antebellum period because the Mississippi linked free territory in the North with the South, where slavery was legal. For African-Americans, then, the river's current represented the threat of separation from family, friends, and freedom, and New Orleans's levee signified the horrors of bondage. As steamboats annihilated space and time, however, the vessels once again shifted some African-Americans' perceptions of the waterfront and the Mississippi. During the era of steam, the levee became a site where people of different races mingled and where runaway slaves, therefore, could lose themselves. Not even laws imposing spatial segregation at the waterfront could keep slaves from finding work, stowing away, or occasionally booking passage to freedom aboard steamboats bound for the North.

Anticipating such perceived threats, in 1816 Louisiana passed an act compelling captains of steamboats to sharpen their gaze when looking for runaways. Undaunted, many slaves used the river as a pathway to freedom, leaving Louisiana's legal records peppered with cases in which enslaved African-Americans bolted aboard steamboats headed for the upper valley.[68] In response, slave owners, aware that the vessels "offered such facility to the escape of slaves," lobbied the state to enact more stringent restrictions to limit the number of runaways.[69] In the years between 1835 and 1842, Louisiana passed four laws placing greater responsibility on steamboat captains to keep their vessels free of runaways.[70] But with traffic on the river increasing, New Orleans's levee became busier and the Mississippi still provided an avenue north for many slaves.

One case discussed a runaway attempt that took place on March 20, 1850. After hiding in the crowd at New Orleans's waterfront, a light-skinned slave named Robert booked passage for himself aboard the steamboat *Western World*. Not content to brave the elements on deck, he paid cabin fare, and as an eyewitness recounted, "no suspicions were entertained by any one that said person was a slave." During Robert's journey, despite the anxiety he likely felt, "his deportment was quiet and retiring, and his appearance that of a modest and unassuming gentleman." Eventually, the vessel's chief steward caught on to the ruse and approached the captain, outraged that Robert had violated the era's fragile racial and gender castes by seating "himself at the first table, high up, near the ladies." On March 25, the captain interrogated Robert and threw him off in Memphis. Other passengers grumbled because Robert had been ejected, certain that the "captain would get himself into a scrape" for putting such a fine gentleman ashore. Despite such protests, Robert went to jail, where he waited until a slave catcher brought him back to New Orleans.[71]

Although Robert did not make it to his destination, his case and others like it demonstrate that as steamboats brought distant locales within New Orleans's reach, and the levee filled with multicultural crowds, freedom in the upper valley became accessible to some of New Orleans's enslaved African-Americans. Many runaways suffered grim fates, like Robert's, but others escaped. Their cases suggest that the underground railroad, always shrouded in controversy, may have been misnamed; the path to freedom sometimes began at New Orleans's levee, and then continued on the Mississippi, aboard steamboats bound for the North. Consequently, for some slaves during the era of steam, the waterfront became a more open and public space than ever before and the Mississippi became a river of freedom.

Just as DeBow overstated the city's tight grip on the valley's trade and exaggerated the waterfront's orderly commercial character, he also magnified the certainty of people's mastery of the Mississippi and the steamboats that reputedly had bested the river system's current. In the years before and after DeBow published his meditation, steamboat disasters at New Orleans's levee could have served as metaphors for the city's shaky hold on its built and so-called natural environment. Several riverboats blew up without warning near the waterfront in those years, causing millions of dollars in property damage, killing hundreds of passengers, and ultimately shaking New Orleanians' faith in the efficacy of artifice—if only briefly. While those explosions were a product of a variety of factors, including human error and crude engineering, they also point out that the Mississippi remained a dynamic presence in New Orleans, hardly tamed by technology or always nurturing, as DeBow suggested.

Boiler explosions were a violent outgrowth of the quest to overcome the river's current, because the feature that allowed Mississippi steamboats to travel upstream also contributed to their propensity to explode without warning. The earliest working steamboats in the nation, including the *Clermont* and the *New Orleans,* relied on relatively safe, low-pressure engines for power. Then, over time, the strength and unpredictability of the Mississippi's current encouraged riverboat designers to use high-pressure engines aboard vessels destined for the river. These engines typically had far greater horsepower than their low-pressure forebears, and they could be stoked to extraordinary performance, if necessary, by casting pine knots or other incendiaries into their fireboxes. This feature allowed pilots to fight unexpected currents, power a beached vessel off a hidden sandbar, or outrun competitors in the much-publicized races that often were used to generate business in an increasingly cutthroat marketplace. Eventually, low-pressure engines all but disappeared on the river system. By 1838, only 1 out of 258 steamboats on the Mississippi system employed a low-pressure engine.[72] The high-pressure alternative simply offered too many features to riverboatmen eager to overcome the Mississippi's current.

Although they had many advantages, high-pressure engines sometimes exacted a bloody price. As the number of boats in use on the Mississippi system increased, pilots had to boost speed or lose business, and the number of tragedies on the river grew as firemen stoked overtaxed boilers to gain advantages over rivals. From 1841 to 1848, more than 60 boats blew up on the Mississippi system, killing nearly 550 people.[73] Still, steam technology had become such an integral part of New Orleans's economy that most people accepted explosions as a necessary risk attendant to the city's quest for empire. As the century neared its midpoint, however, a series of three accidents in just a little more than a month took place in the levee's vicinity, close enough to New Orleans so that the city's residents came into direct contact with the carnage. The scenes they witnessed raised questions about risk and danger in a machine age, leaving many people wondering if they actually did control the river or the vessels on it.

The first of the tragedies took place a few minutes after 5:00 P.M. on November 15, 1849. Passengers boarding the steamboat *Louisiana* covered their ears as the vessel's whistle drowned out the last peals coming from the cathedral bell at Jackson Square. Suddenly, as the crew loosed the boat from its wharf, "all the boilers exploded with a concussion." The force of the blast was so great that "large pieces of the boilers were blown hundreds of yards from the wharf." One shard of shrapnel cut through a mule resting at the waterfront, still retaining enough force to kill a horse and driver that were struck next. People throughout the city heard the explosion and rushed to the river. One witness recalled that "a number of bodies, in every conceivable state of mutilation, had been dragged from the wreck, and were surrounded by the immense crowd which had assembled." The shattered *Louisiana* sank to the bottom of the river in less than ten minutes, taking with it "ladies and gentlemen who were vainly struggling to free themselves." In the aftermath, several small boats skimmed their way through the wreckage, plucking survivors from the muddy water. The entire city mourned the dead, conservatively estimated at 150.[74]

In the following weeks, melancholy gripped New Orleans, as people refused to accept the "customary verdict of 'nobody to blame.'" Then, less than a month later, before the city had recovered from the *Louisiana*'s loss, two other disasters rocked the waterfront. The first involved the *Anglo-Norman*, which exploded just upriver from New Orleans, on December 14, 1850. The local press noted that after the *Anglo-Norman* disaster, "a prudent man often bethinks him of the necessity of making his will before he trusts himself to the deck of a steamboat." Just days after that, on December 17, 1850, the *Knoxville* blew up shortly after leaving the wharf in front of the Second Municipality, only a few feet from the site of the *Louisiana*'s destruction. Although relatively minor, the final accident in the trio of horrors left some people badly shaken, questioning their mastery of artifice and the Mississippi. One reporter even wondered if steamboats had begun to do New Orleans more harm than good: "The frequent repetition of such accidents—to call them by so light a name—gives to New Orleans, a character of recklessness, which to say the least is not an enviable reputation."[75]

So blindly confident was DeBow in 1847, he likely still would have crowed about the city's bright future even if he had understood how precarious New Orleans's hold on the valley's trade was, that the crowding at the levee offered African-American slaves ample opportunities to escape, or that people's control of the river and the steamboats on it was far from secure. For too long, New Orleanians had believed that theirs was nature's chosen city; the era of steam had only deepened their convictions. In 1847, transportation technologies siphoning trade from the Mississippi seemed like little more than minor threats to most elites who had grown fat on river-borne commerce. Slaves who managed to turn technology and urban development to their advantage merited attention, but their actions did not constitute a true crisis for the city's slaveholders. And for most New Orleanians, the persistent and unchecked power of the Mississippi and the steamboat explosions resulting in part from battling the river's current usually felt like little more than choppy water along the winding route to empire.

That DeBow ignored these issues is far more revealing than if he had covered each in depth, allowing room for contingency. His faith in commerce, artifice, and the river's benevolence demonstrated that myths sprouting in the fertile soil flanking the Mississippi since the city's settlement had taken deep root during the era of steam: the river, tamed by artifice, would make New Orleanians the rich citizens of an empire. And the waterfront, disciplined for commerce, represented a triumph of the era of steam. DeBow had little time for challenges to his views; thus, what he saw around him inevitably supported what he already suspected was the truth. The consequences of such hubris became evident again in the coming years, as a series of yellow-fever epidemics, culminating with the great scourge of 1853, demonstrated that New Orleans's relationship with the river, and the city's commercial community's control over the waterfront, could sometimes lead to environmental disasters on a grand scale.

CHAPTER 3

The Necropolis
of the South

THE ARRIVAL OF A KILLER

In the spring of 1853, New Orleans seemed like a carefree city. April had
been cool and sunny, and the first part of May followed suit, with few
of the oppressively hot, humid days that can make the delta's climate intolerable.[1] Arriving with seasonal high water on the Mississippi came
flatboats and steamboats loaded with goods from the valley's upper
reaches. The press noted that the city's commercial community, though
spoiled by years of economic growth, was nonetheless pleased, because
"business, universally, has ... been unusually profitable and productive."
A wide range of commodities stood in huge piles at the levee, testifying
to good times fueled by the river. To account for the boom, locals pointed
to the Mississippi and "Nature," arguing that the city stood poised to
become "the greatest commercial emporium on the face of the earth."[2]
Indeed, with the river funneling goods and people to its front door, New
Orleans had grown into one of the five largest metropolises in the nation by midcentury, boasting a population of approximately 120,000
year-round residents in 1853. A year earlier, New Orleans's three municipalities, divided for more than fifteen years over how best to develop
and administer the waterfront, had put their differences aside, recom-
bining as a unified whole.[3] As a result of all of these factors—social, economic, spatial, and environmental—the city appeared to be at the height
of a golden age.

Yet, with hindsight serving as a guide, even in the early spring there were subtle indications at the waterfront that not all was well in New Orleans. On May 23, a recent immigrant to the city fell to his knees near the Mississippi while unloading the *Augusta,* the sailing vessel on which he had arrived in Louisiana. The prostrated man could not work, he said, because of severe body aches, nausea, and a high fever. Irritated by the delay offloading expensive cargo under his supervision, the *Augusta*'s captain grudgingly summoned a physician named Morris Schuppert. At the time, Schuppert almost certainly thought little of the incident. He did not even bother to record his patient's name, noting only that the sick man recovered. After all, the city's waterfront was a space known for producing disease. Following heavy rains over the previous days, the streets adjacent to the levee had "filled with water" and become "saturated with filth and decaying vegetables and animal matter."[4] Perhaps Dr. Schuppert eased any anxieties that he might have felt with the thought that the people living near the river were mostly immigrants, unfamiliar with the delta's climate, and therefore prone to illness.

If Schuppert's first visit to the *Augusta* had not alarmed him, the doctor apparently did grow concerned when he received another summons from the vessel's captain two days later. When Schuppert arrived at the levee that day, he found a second immigrant suffering from symptoms identical to those of the first man. Ultimately, the second man was not as lucky as the first; five days later he died. Two days after that, the *Augusta*'s captain called Schuppert a third time, alerting the physician that something more than filth was amiss at the waterfront. Schuppert then cared for two more immigrant laborers; one recovered, while the other, a man named G. Woetle, entered New Orleans's Charity Hospital, where he died two days later. When doctors, upset by the pattern of illness at the waterfront and the sailor's symptoms, performed an autopsy on Woetle, they found what they described as "two ounces of the black vomit" in his stomach.[5] After months marked by a relatively light caseload, the physicians at Charity Hospital were alarmed to see such a rapid influx of patients whose symptoms fit a familiar pattern. It seemed that yellow fever was loose in the city.

Woetle and his shipmates were among the first of approximately ten thousand people who died of yellow fever over the summer of 1853 in New Orleans. Those killed were all victims of what John Duffy, a historian of public health, has called "probably the worst single epidemic ever to strike a major American city."[6] The scope of the carnage, the horror of a community nearly decimated by disease, may suggest that this episode was unique, set apart from the workings of everyday life in the city. But such a view removes the epidemic from the context of New Orleans's environmental history. Focusing too much attention on the horrific death toll risks portraying the pestilence as beyond human control, as a plague visited on the city by vengeful nature or an angry deity. In fact, the epidemic of 1853, though astonishing in its scale, was almost predictable—at least in retrospect. It was a product of everyday decisions made by people who sought to impose social, economic, and spatial order on their environment. It was an outgrowth of that environment as well, because, although many New Orleanians believed that they had engineered much of the troubling unpredictability out of their city's site during the era of steam, the epidemic of 1853 demonstrated the ongoing power of the non-human world in mid-nineteenth-century New Orleans.

By 1853, yellow fever had killed approximately seventeen thousand people since its first recorded appearance in Louisiana in 1796. After 1810, a major epidemic—one in which a hundred or more people died—had struck the city at least every third year.[7] Still, the 1853 epidemic was unusual not only for its scale, but also for the impact that it had on people's beliefs and priorities. During the epidemic, as yellow fever wiped out almost 10 percent of the city's population, the disease recast New Orleanians' understanding of epidemiology, etiology, and the human body; forced a reorganization of space in the city, as a geography of infectious illness bred horror and panic throughout public and private spaces; altered social and economic relationships; and challenged assumptions New Orleanians had about their city's relationship with the Mississippi River and what they called nature. As a result, the epidemic of 1853 demonstrates how pestilence shaped the urban experience in antebellum New Orleans. At the same time, the events of 1853 underscore the social and spatial dimension of disease outbreaks in the city, because the epidemic was not simply a natural disaster, or an act of God, but an event shaped by human behaviors and attitudes, particularly the way that New Orleanians defined the public in their city and produced the spaces around them.

In May 1853, as doctors searched the contents of Woetle's stomach for omens, New Orleanians remained unaware of what was about to befall them. Although they did not know it, the pieces were in place for yellow fever to run amok in the city: the epidemiological prerequisites necessary to begin an outbreak, the climatic and biological conditions necessary to foster pestilence, the social and spatial setting necessary to spread disease, and the human population necessary to host the scourge.[8] In each case, ideas about space, including bodily spaces, played a role. In New Orleans, members of the city's commercial community believed that spaces functioned best as venues for trade; they should be orderly, marked by clearly delineated borders based on uses to encourage the exchange of goods. This view applied to circumscribed spaces close at hand, such as the levee, but also to distant, relatively unbounded spaces such as the Mississippi system, and even to spaces as far removed as the shipping routes of the Atlantic World and the foreign ports making up the city's network of trade. The epidemic of 1853 demonstrates that such a view of space had consequences, because yellow fever did not respect spatial discipline. It moved through space without regard for the laws of commerce—in fact, those laws often abetted the disease's spread.

For a yellow-fever epidemic to begin, the disease's pathogen must be introduced into a setting where it can flourish. In 1853, the pathogen likely arrived in the city as a stowaway aboard the *Camboden Castle,* a trade vessel that had sailed to Louisiana directly from Kingston, Jamaica, where a yellow-fever epidemic had raged that spring.[9] The *Castle* is the likely point of origin for the disease because it completed its journey to New Orleans up the Mississippi with the *Augusta,* the vessel that carried G. Woetle and his comrades to the city. The *Castle*'s and *Augusta*'s crews later indicated that "there was free communication between the two ships."[10] It is likely that at that time the sailors aboard the *Augusta* first came into contact with the yellow-fever pathogen.

Blessed with historical perspective and a relatively sophisticated understanding of communicable disease, one might ask why the *Castle* left a place stricken by one of the antebellum era's most destructive scourges. The answer is simple: in 1853, yellow fever was as mysterious as it was deadly. And commerce's importance to port cities, coupled with misconceptions about the disease, insured that trade vessels often unintentionally carried pathogens from infected sites to unsuspecting destinations. Yellow fever mystified people throughout the nineteenth century, in part because of its simple costumes—it arrived cloaked in the plain raiment of milder ailments. In relatively benign cases, victims suffered from fever, head and body aches, and nausea: all symptoms common enough to be discounted. More severe cases were marked by chills, photosensitivity, fainting spells, jaundice—thus the disease's name—and gastrointestinal hemorrhages which led to yellow fever's signature symptom, emesis stained dark by blood: the black vomit. Unless victims

spewed the black vomit, yellow fever was typically subtle enough to con-
fuse most antebellum doctors.

In addition to the fear that yellow fever inspired because of its inscrutability, the disease grew still more terrifying because physicians
knew little about either its etiology (origins) or mode of transmission. In
the years before the advent of germ theory, most doctors searching for
the roots of epidemics agreed that vapors rising from marshes or rotting
organic matter, so-called miasmas, or, as it was spelled in Louisiana, miasms, poisoned the air. Miasmatic theory led to other medical misconceptions, such as the theory of "local origin," whereby physicians accounted for epidemics by pointing to local conditions that allegedly had
spawned pestilence through spontaneous generation. Most proponents
of local origin and miasmatic theory extrapolated further. Because they
believed that disease emerged only out of local conditions, these physicians typically stated that yellow fever could not spread beyond the place
that had birthed it. Therefore, the argument went, yellow fever was not
contagious.[11]

New Orleans, surrounded by swamps, dotted with markets where
produce decomposed in the sun, and plagued by bad drainage and heavy
rain, had to guard against the production of miasms or fall prey to epidemics. Guided by such thinking, cautious residents and tourists in New
Orleans had a strained relationship with the city's environs, sensing ill
health in the air they breathed. For instance, when Henry Tudor visited
the city during the winter of 1831, after disembarking at the levee he announced that he had arrived at "the head-quarters of Death." Tudor exclaimed that had it been high summer, he "should scarcely expect to be
alive."[12] For all of the anxiety that the city's environment elicited, in cases
such as the yellow fever epidemic of 1853 the theories of miasms and
local origin provided people with a false sense of security. Convinced
that yellow fever was not contagious, the *Castle*'s captain, for instance,
had ordered his crew to clean the vessel, sprinkling it with lime to rid it
of miasms, before setting sail from Kingston with a clear conscience,
bound for New Orleans and a meeting with the *Augusta*.[13]

Still, questions about the pathogen's arrival linger, particularly because some of New Orleans's physicians accepted that yellow fever was
"transportable," that it could travel from infected places to healthy ones
where environmental conditions then spurred outbreaks.[14] Why, then,
did the city not bar its doors to the *Castle* and other ships sailing from
infected ports? Local commercial elites, people like J.D.B. DeBow,
would have answered that question by pointing to New Orleans's rela-

tionship with the Mississippi, arguing that trade was the city's lifeblood. By 1853, the arrival of vessels like the *Augusta* from far-flung ports was so common as to merit little attention in the city; their presence at the waterfront seemed natural, their rigging part of the forest of masts at the levee. Closing the city to trade by imposing a quarantine at the port thus was a last resort in battles with diseases that New Orleanians barely understood.

This unfortunate coincidence of microbiology and human behavior accounts for yellow fever's arrival in the city. And this mingling of human and nonhuman factors continued after the *Castle* made port, as the pathogen's presence fulfilled only the first of the conditions necessary to start an epidemic. The *Augusta*'s human cargo, including 230 European immigrants, met a second condition by providing a reservoir of suscep- tible hosts for the pathogen to attack. Because people who survive a bout with the disease enjoy immunity for life—yellow fever is a virus like chicken pox in this regard—a steady influx of nonimmune hosts is nec- essary to begin or maintain an epidemic. In New Orleans, frequent new arrivals typically provided an ample reservoir of hosts, and 1853 was no exception. For decades, during the era of steam, the city had drawn tens of thousands of immigrants annually. Then, in the years leading to 1853, the revolutions of 1848 in Europe, coupled with famine in Ireland, had given Europeans already pulled by economic opportunity a push to leave home as well. From 1848 through 1852 more than 160,000 immigrants had arrived at New Orleans's waterfront, and many had stayed in the city. Only New York had welcomed more newcomers in those years.[15]

If the Europeans aboard the *Augusta* unknowingly fostered the epi- demic, another group of immigrants, likely hidden in plain sight aboard the *Castle,* fulfilled a third condition necessary to start an outbreak. These immigrants were female *Aedes aegypti* mosquitoes, the vector that spreads yellow fever. Despite physicians' claims to the contrary in 1853, yellow fever is highly contagious, though it can be transmitted only by female *Aedes aegypti* mosquitoes. When a female mosquito takes a blood meal—as often as twelve times in a month—from an infected host, she gathers nourishment for her eggs as well as a dose of the virus. Once a carrier, she transmits the disease each time she feeds throughout her life, like a flying dirty needle, randomly infecting unsuspecting victims for as long as two months.[16] Where the mosquitoes live year-round, yellow fever can become endemic, meaning it can exist at low levels in the pop- ulation at all times, but in New Orleans, winter freezes usually wiped out the adult insects until spring's higher temperatures arrived, renewing their life cycle, as well as the city's residents' swatting and cursing—and, often, their battles with yellow fever.

Although by most definitions mosquitoes are a part of the natural world, New Orleans provided an especially welcoming home for the insects because of features of its built environment as well as the delta's climate.[17] That the mosquitoes thrived in the Crescent City because of this mingling of features traditionally labeled natural and urban belies any simple opposition of the two. Originally from Africa, *Aedes aegypti* mosquitoes came to the Americas as a by-product of the slave trade, often labeled a kind of "biological revenge" by scholars eager to find morality in the workings of the nonhuman world.[18] Only the luckiest mosquitoes arrived in a city as hospitable to their kind as New Orleans, where warm temperatures, heavy rains, and high humidity suited *Aedes aegypti*. Then, over time, the mosquitoes adapted to city life, in part because concentrated crowds of people provided self-serve buffets.[19] *Aedes aegypti* mosquitoes also prefer laying their eggs in artificial containers, and through the first half of the nineteenth century, most New Orleanians gathered drinking water in cisterns, huge, three-hundred- to five-hundred-gallon cypress tubs "in close proximity" to their homes.[20] In short, as the city had expanded during the era of steam, it had provided additional habitat for mosquitoes, unwittingly making its residents more vulnerable to yellow-fever outbreaks.

Because of these conditions, linked both to the city's so-called natural and built environment, 1853 proved to be a banner year for mosquitoes. In early June, with the yellow-fever pathogen already loose at the waterfront, clouds of mosquitoes darkened the dusk skies above New Orleans. L. H. Webb, a student who found "the mosquitoes troublesome," confessed to his diary that he spent a week fruitlessly trying to drive them from his home with cigar smoke. After fouling his nest, he gave up and "went to bed considerably nauseated."[21] Webb's troubles were commonplace, and by the end of the month, the press acknowledged the problem, admitting: "We have never known the mosquitoes to be half as severe as they are at present." Ironically, though, the papers celebrated the infestation, insisting that pestilence would not visit the city during the coming summer, "for the simple reason that Providence does not afflict us with two curses at one and the same time; and, to add yellow fever to the present terrible visitation of mosquitoes, would be too much for human endurance."[22]

AN OFFICIAL SILENCE

As summer's heat enveloped the delta in 1853, a dangerous set of environmental and social factors collided in New Orleans. With the yellow-fever pathogen present, a huge reservoir of hosts in place, and swarms of vectors buzzing through the air, the stage was set for an epidemic. Surely, then, it was fortunate that E.D. Fenner, a doctor at Charity Hospital, recognized the peril. In the wake of Woetle's autopsy, Fenner recalled that the discovery of black vomit "excited my apprehensions, and caused me to inquire whether anything like yellow fever had been seen by others."[23] But his inquiries must have been discreet, because Fenner failed to spread the alarm. Talk of the disease remained so quiet, in fact, that as late as the third week of June, with hundreds of people already dead, the *Daily Picayune* announced that an epidemic had been "denied by all the most eminent physicians in the city."[24] Why, in the face of such a grave threat, did journalists and physicians apparently behave so irresponsibly?

In part, the forced calm was the work of commercial elites who kept a tight rein on the press and medical community as a way of maintaining both order in the city and their control over the waterfront. Censorship emerging from greed mingled with fear of damaging New Orleans's reputation nationwide and, in turn, the city's dominance of the valley's trade. Based on past experience, New Orleanians knew that press coverage of epidemics would lead to panic that threatened trade by sullying the city's good name. As environmental historian Conevery Bolton Valencius argues, locations can become associated with illness, a damaging reputation that lingers long after an epidemic's end.[25] And by 1853, in some quarters, New Orleans had become known as a "wet graveyard," a perception that many businesspeople believed had limited the city's economic growth.[26] There was some truth to such claims. News of pestilence could halt trade instantly, as hordes of people fled the city. Neighboring areas often then slapped quarantines on New Orleans, further hampering commerce by effectively wresting control of the Mississippi from the city's commercial community. Deprived of workers, consumers, trade, and the benefits of the river, the city's economy foundered during epidemics. For many commercial elites this prospect could seem worse than the possibility of an outbreak. As a result, and because of the conflation of commercial and public interests that predominated during the era of steam, elites and city officials were loathe to give up control of the waterfront, certain that their wisdom and actions served New Orleans's interests.

Following the yellow-fever epidemic of 1847, when approximately three thousand people had died, members of New Orleans's commercial community had begun spreading the word that pestilence had released its grip on the city for good.[27] Elites had worked with physicians to rehabilitate the city's reputation, doctoring statistics and manipulating data. Even while admitting that New Orleans was "sometimes overtaken with epidemics," these boosters had insisted that the city did "not suffer in a fair and liberal comparison, in respect to public health, with many others reputed to be more healthy."[28] Dr. Fenner ruefully explained that "when shown...that the annual mortality of this city, in proportion to population, more than doubles that of any city in Europe or America, they either disregard the solemn truth or flatly deny it." Projecting the image that New Orleans was healthy quickly became a matter of civic duty, as though to raise the alarm that yellow fever had returned to the city would be to strike a blow against commerce, growth, and progress. Fenner mourned that those who dared bring "to light such unwelcome facts" were labeled "enemies to the city."[29] In short, a narrowly defined public's health could be sacrificed to another, ostensibly greater public good: maintaining critical trade relationships during the era of steam.

Forced to worry about their professional credibility and social standing, most of New Orleans's doctors remained quiet about yellow fever when the tell-tale signs of an epidemic began appearing in 1853. As an explanation for the silence, Dr. Morton Dowler pointed an accusing finger at elites in the city, noting that in New Orleans "commerce is King and it is no more permitted to any physician to report cases of fever with impunity in the absence of an epidemic, than to foretell and encompass the King's death." Dowler later raged that an official silence about yellow fever had stopped doctors from protecting the innocent. He stated "that the influences exist, in this city, which prevent the actual state of public health, during the summer months, so far as yellow fever is concerned, from being known to the people."[30]

Joining doctors in silence were journalists—who, in fairness, had observed that fewer than six hundred people had succumbed to yellow fever in the three summers leading to 1853, and so may have believed that the disease really had left the city.[31] Or perhaps they too knew that they had to answer to the city's people of commerce. Years later, Dr. John McKowen advanced the latter theory when he bitterly recalled a meeting between his father and the owner of the *True Delta* newspaper, John McGinnis, after the epidemic of 1853. McKowen remembered that McGinnis "assured my father that the first and last step to success in any undertaking in New Orleans was persistent falsehoods about yellow fever." The physician then railed that the "commercial interests of New Orleans let every newspaper in the city understand distinctly...that any reference to yellow fever in any way whatever would cause the immediate loss of every advertisement."[32] In sum, elites, engaged in a struggle to maintain control of New Orleans's waterfront, and thereby its booming trade, sought control of the press as well.

Regardless of the newspapers' motivations, as hundreds of people sickened in 1853 reporters assured their readers that yellow fever had been permanently banished from New Orleans. Bemoaning the beginning of an exodus from the city, the *Daily Crescent* chided the departing masses for abandoning their homes "now that yellow fever has become an obsolete idea in New Orleans." The most reckless journalists ignored or shouted down physicians who tried spreading news of pestilence in the city—such reports were "hushed up."[33] Dr. Fenner later recalled that he had begged editors to publish warnings about the disease's presence, but, acting under an "erroneous impression of their duty to the public," they had "studiously endeavored to conceal or suppress the true state of affairs." Fenner observed that "the result of this course [was]...to deter some of our more respectable physicians from saying a word about the first cases of yellow fever." And even worse, "to induce many persons who wish to leave the city as soon as yellow fever appears, to remain until they are exposed to imminent danger."[34]

Propaganda alone, however, could not account for the official silence hovering over New Orleans through June and into early July 1853. Several interrelated ideas about the relationship between disease, the environment, and the human body contributed to the city's stoicism as it faced the onset of an epidemic. In 1853, most New Orleanians, like other people around the country, believed that good health was a product of an individual body's relationship with its environment. A healthy body was internally and externally balanced; it existed in harmony with its surroundings, while a diseased body did not. If either a body or its surroundings shifted—for instance, if one's habits became intemperate or one's environment became filthy and began producing miasms—one might become sick with a disease such as yellow fever. Therefore, maintaining bodily and environmental order and balance promised good health, and most New Orleanians thus considered clean air and clean living the best protection against disease.[35]

These ideas about health emerged from and then strengthened currents of class conflict and xenophobia present in New Orleans, offering further justification for keeping news of yellow fever quiet in 1853. Based on erroneous notions about the origin and spread of epidemics, New Orleanians blamed victims of outbreaks for their plight, arguing that the dead and dying had brought misfortune on themselves through bad habits and disrespect for the delta's environment. The press explained that immigrants and the working classes were known to "congregate in damp and unwholesome places, and what with exposure, neglect and want, become the first victims of an epidemic."[36] Therefore, in an era marked by nativism nationwide, epidemics offered environmental justifications for anti-immigrant and class prejudice. In short, the people most New Orleanians believed were likely to contract yellow fever often were not deemed worthy of concern, particularly if prophylactic measures meant commercial sacrifice. Consequently, even as the death toll increased early in the summer of 1853, the epidemic's victims were not a part of the public whose health mattered most in the city.[37] Indeed, because most elite New Orleanians viewed the people who typically contracted yellow fever as outside of the public in the city, it became still easier to justify keeping news of the epidemic quiet and the waterfront open. Once again in the city's history, the contingent nature of the public had emerged clearly and with profound consequences.

Despite the efforts of the commercial community, complicit doctors, and misguided journalists, by mid-July rumors about the disease circulated in the city. But another set of misconceptions about pestilence and urban space caused many people to count themselves safe, maintaining calm in New Orleans long after it was warranted. Because people believed that yellow fever could not spread beyond specific locations, and because the city's upper classes enjoyed spatial mobility—they could avoid diseased spaces—elites remained sure of their safety even as the virus spread. On July 21, the *Daily Delta* finally granted that yellow fever had "attained to the character of a slight epidemic," but it promised that there was nothing to fear because the outbreak was confined near the waterfront, a location notorious for an array of disease hot spots, including slaughterhouses, markets, and open basins—sites that generated filth, charnel, putrid smells, and thus miasms. The area adjacent to the levee also hosted thousands of immigrants living in squalor in "crowded boarding houses."[38] The *Delta*'s assurances seemed reasonable if yellow fever actually was limited to spaces producing miasms, and if diseased bodies posed no threat because the pestilence was not contagious. Therefore, many elites who might have fled despite the press's and medical community's rhetoric stayed in the city, confident that yellow fever would not touch them because it was bound to circumscribed, unhealthy spaces and the bodies of people who frequented those areas.

In the same period, myths about the interaction of the body and the environment placated many longtime residents of New Orleans of all classes. In the article in which the *Delta* soothed its readers by insisting that the epidemic threatened only specific sections of the city, the paper offered additional comfort by pointing out "that the attacks of the malady are confined exclusively to strangers."[39] This assertion emerged out of a half-baked myth, drawn from a recipe including equal parts flawed empiricism and cultural conceit, which suggested that Creoles and the "acclimated"— people who had undergone a process of "seasoning" in which they had become accustomed to the local environment—were immune to yellow fever because of prolonged exposure to Louisiana's climate.[40] In other words, many New Orleanians believed that longstanding ties to the delta fostered immunity to yellow fever by bringing seasoned bodies into concert with the city's otherwise hazardous surroundings.

Although concepts of Creole immunity and acclimation turned largely on myths, some truth lurked behind each. Rarely do more than half of the people who contract yellow fever die, and survivors are immune for the rest of their lives.[41] Thus, the acclimated had not only become accustomed to the local environment, but most likely had also survived a bout with the virus, though few knew it because of the disease's inscrutability. Unless victims manifested telltale symptoms like the black vomit—and then a patient's chances of survival plummeted—misdiagnoses were common. Longtime residents of the city thus founded claims about acclimation in fact, though they didn't understand the origin of their health. The probable explanation for Creole immunity is similar. Yellow fever is an equal-opportunity killer; apparent Creole immunity was not the result of cultural heritage, but more likely a function of surviving early bouts with the disease. Because young children rarely are killed by yellow fever—again, like the chicken pox—and are immune after recovering, it is likely that many Creoles had contracted the disease when young, and then grew up thinking that they never had had it. Blessed with a survivor's immunity, they never sickened as adults. What they called immunity, founded in cultural superiority and ties to the delta's environment, was more likely part of a relatively painless childhood acclimation process.

Finally, lingering consequences of the era of steam's divisive spatial politics also accounted for the silence. When the city had split into separate municipalities in 1836, as was discussed in chapter 2, it did so to smooth the way for waterfront development. And though New Orleans had consolidated in 1852, many of the problems of the divided metropolis remained: most notably the difficulty of mobilizing the municipal government to respond to a crisis. This shortcoming was especially evident in the absence of a board of health in midsummer 1853. Contemporary reports indicate that the board's members had resigned in a huff early in June, after the city council had ignored their entreaties about the arrival of pestilence. Then, as yellow fever killed hundreds of people, the municipal government had engaged in bitter debates, hindering the creation of a more powerful board until late in July. This foot-dragging had deadly consequences. Traditionally, one of the board of health's important roles had been town crier, announcing that an epidemic threatened the city. In 1853, with no board seated, the city's physicians and newspapers used that body's absence as still another excuse for their silence.[42]

All of which explains why, in late July 1853, yellow fever seemed to pose little threat to many New Orleanians. The disease menaced unseasoned newcomers; it struck impoverished people living near the waterfront, surrounded by miasms; and most often, it attacked recent immigrants, who were generally poor, unacclimated, and unaccustomed to the delta's climate. Years later, the satirist and social critic George Washington Cable spoofed Creoles for these attitudes about yellow fever. Cable explained that the Creole "had, and largely retains still, an absurd belief in his entire immunity from attack. When he has it, it is something else. As for strangers—he threw up his palms and eyebrows—nobody asked them to come to New Orleans."[43] Into late July, then, many New Orleanians remained confident about their health. Yellow fever preferred disordered bodies amid disordered surroundings. So long as the epidemic claimed victims near the waterfront, among the city's immigrants and working classes, Creoles, the acclimated, and elites relaxed, certain of their safety, because they were insulated from disease by breeding, spatial segregation, and ties to the environment.

THE PANIC SPREADS

At July's end, hard facts shattered the official silence in the city, leaving a grim mood draped over New Orleans like a shroud. In the month's last week, heavy rain fell from black skies daily, turning the city's thoroughfares into a morass. Worse still, the rain combined with heat and humidity, causing trash in the streets to rot. The filthy conditions prompted complaints about "villainous smells" wafting through the air, not-so-subtle allusions to dangerous miasms.[44] At the same time, yellow fever stained the wards saffron at Charity Hospital, as bodies overflowed into temporary beds placed throughout its halls. From July 16 to 23, more than 425 people died there.[45] Confronted with the death toll, the *Daily Delta* belatedly admitted that "yellow fever prevails in this city to an equal extent, if not surpassing, almost any previous year."[46] Taking measure of the crisis, the city council finally appointed a new board of health, leading one bitter merchant to scoff: "Their creation can do no good—it is too late, lime and resolutions can't save us."[47] With the body count rising daily, the realization swept over New Orleans that a severe epidemic had laid siege to the city while people had sat on their hands.

Many New Orleanians found proof of the epidemic's impact in haunting scenes at the waterfront. In July's last weeks, both Vicksburg and Natchez fulfilled the worst fears of New Orleans's commercial community by imposing quarantines on the city. Abandoned by two of its most important upriver trading partners, business in New Orleans foundered as predicted. Cataloging the economic damage, an alarmed reporter contrasted the levee after the quarantines with its "vast expanse of exposed and almost naked planking," to that same space only a month earlier, when it "was fairly groaning under the immense weight of the freight which lay piled everywhere over its length and breadth, and its whole extended border was lined with ships and steamers."[48] Already, for weeks leading to that point, New Orleanians had skirted the area near the river whenever they could, fearful that the levee was the epicenter of pestilence in the city. Consequently, the waterfront stood empty of both people and goods. The city's most valued public space had been stigmatized as hazardous, best avoided if possible. The commercial community and city officials had lost control of the landscape.

In time, people of all races, classes, and ethnicities became terrified, as the virus seemed to behave strangely, upending time-tested myths in the city, including its supposedly predictable geography, the idea that it thrived only in filthy areas of the city, near the waterfront, amid newcomers and the working classes. In 1853, however, yellow fever seemed to be leapfrogging around town. One concerned resident of the city noted that after "gaining strength by what it fed upon, it began to travel to other and more distant points, to extend its arms, so to speak, in every direction." Not only did the disease appear intent on occupying the entire city, but it also seemed to have lost its taste only for poor, unacclimated victims, causing an observer to warn that it had "acquired strength to attack those who consider themselves impregnable."[49] So oddly did the virus act, one mer-

chant wrote to a friend that "the nature of the disease is universally admitted to be different from former types." As panic spread, rumors circulated that the city faced not yellow fever, but the Black Death itself.[50]

Despite such anxieties, the disease behaved normally, at least epi-
demiologically speaking; the reason that it terrified New Orleanians was
that it ignored ostensibly fixed and absolute spatial boundaries in the
city. In other words, though people did not realize it, the virus traveled
on the wings of its vectors, transgressing borders dividing one section of
New Orleans from the next. It spread throughout the city and populace
without regard for labels people fixed to urban landscapes: filthy or pure,
commercial or residential, even public or private. Such categories proved
meaningless to organisms that moved through space, not socially or economically, but ecologically. A mosquito might bite an immigrant living
in a flophouse near the riverfront, fly a short distance across town, enter
the open window of an ornate home of a Creole commercial scion—a
window left open, ironically, to circulate a healthy breeze within—and
pass along the virus while taking its next blood meal. When yellow fever
traveled throughout the city in this way, it effectively rendered private
spaces public, and did the same to the bodies of people who contracted
the disease. As a result, New Orleanians who had always believed themselves to be immune based on their prosperity, breeding, ties to the delta,
or because they lived in the city's cleanest districts, were shocked when
they sickened. Perhaps more even than the fast-rising death count, this
invasion of private spaces, distant from the river, including elite bodily
spaces, prompted city-wide alarm.

As the epidemic's severity became obvious at July's end, thousands of
New Orleanians returned to the abandoned waterfront, where those who
could afford to flee willingly paid exorbitant fees for passage on the first
available vessel out of the city. One frightened reporter noted that "since
the alarm the number of travelers is increased vastly," while another did
"not think New Orleans has ever been as completely deserted by her
merchants and professional men as she is now." George Washington
Cable later recalled that "porters were tossing trunks into wagons, car-
riages were rattling over the stones and whirling out across the broad
white levee to the steamboats' sides.... The fleeing crowd was numbered
by thousands."[51] Even members of the city council panicked. On July
26 they voted to adjourn until autumn—thinking that would be long
after the epidemic's end. Then, two days later, they voted again with their
feet, when an emergency session of the council lacked the bodies needed
for a quorum.[52]

Many migrants traveled to pastoral locales, seemingly beyond the virus's reach. Resorts scattered on the Mississippi Gulf Coast, including the town of Ocean Springs, were favored destinations for people hoping to outdistance yellow fever. Ocean Springs is located approximately thirty miles east of the point where the Pearl River empties into the gulf, forming Mississippi's boundary with Louisiana. In 1852, the town's fortune's had changed when two men discovered therapeutic minerals in a stream flowing near the village sawmill. With the quick hands of profiteers, they built marble bathing basins on the site. A year later, early in 1853, a New Orleans physician constructed the Ocean Springs Hotel near the baths, on an elevated piece of land, with the gulf on one side and a picturesque salt marsh on the other. The hotel's graceful veranda fronted the marsh, offering visitors views of the ducks, herons, and other waterfowl living in the yard, while breezes blew in off the gulf, keeping guests cool and ostensibly safe from disease.[53]

In 1853, much of Ocean Springs's appeal could be traced to how starkly the beach town's surroundings contrasted with New Orleans's environment. Long before yellow fever arrived in the city, the resort's proprietor had crafted a romantic tableau nestled on the shore. Neither untamed wilderness nor filthy metropolis, the hotel's setting was an idealized "natural" landscape designed to lure people to the coast. Early in the summer, clever advertisements for the hotel ran in New Orleans's papers, playing on the city/country dichotomy already ingrained in readers' imaginations.[54] For instance, one promotion set the city's "fumes of filthy sewers, and the hot breath of radiating walls and streets" against the coast's "cooling brine." As the epidemic became a silent partner for the hotel's management, another ad taunted New Orleanians with "the contrast between the city and the watering places! Here we are all alive to health and recreation and invigorating sports, while with you it is all sickness, death, and desolation!"[55] In this view, the city was dangerous, the countryside safe, a healing environment where people frolicked surrounded by comforting visions of nature.

Ocean Springs traded not only on its setting, but also on its status as a private space. Even as yellow fever attacked the entire city, abandoning its traditional haunts near the river, many New Orleanians still hoped that they could stay healthy by confining themselves to landscapes that were clean, private, and therefore free of the filth and disorderly bodies that generated disease. This faith illustrates that despite lessons which they might have learned during the early stages of the epidemic, many New Orleanians still viewed space socially, geographically, and economically, rather than ecologically, as we might today. Without knowledge of the disease's vector, or an understanding that the virus was contagious, many people thought that it was possible to segregate spaces that they perceived as separate. That is, confused New Orleanians thought that if they insulated themselves from the apparent causes of the epidemic, they could avoid its ravages. For this reason Ocean Springs seemed like an ideally isolated location. Not only did the resort boast healthy coastal environs, including fresh air and crisp breezes, but it was also far enough from the city to stay clean. At the same time, the cost of accessing the resort—steamboat passage and the hotel's rates—kept it private. Therefore, as yellow fever made many of the city's elite and private spaces public and common, the environment and exclusivity of Ocean Springs seemed to promise to keep the disease away. Private space again seemed like safe space.

At the end of July, the contrast between the coast and city highlighted another example in which the inequitable distribution of hardship across class lines played out spatially during the epidemic of 1853. For the most part, those who left New Orleans for the coast—and there was certainly no shortage of them—were wealthy people who purchased geographic mobility and health with cash. One conservative estimate suggested that at least ten thousand New Orleanians fled to coastal resorts during the summer of 1853.[56] Members of the working classes and recent immigrants, however, typically could not afford to leave. They remained in New Orleans, taunted by the accounts of the coast's splendor that were printed in the city's papers or likely shared as stories among the illiterate. For instance, as New Orleanians mourned their dead on July 23, the Grand Summer Regatta took place off Ocean Springs. The next day's papers contained detailed accounts of the sailing race, unwittingly mocking the city's suffering. With pen and ink, one correspondent conjured up pastoral landscapes worthy of Thomas Cole, writing that "little children are ranging the wooded slopes; some dropping pebbles in the stream, others straying along the beach." Another reporter focused on the race itself, "confessing" that he had "never seen a more beautiful sight."[57] Meanwhile, the scene in New Orleans, where close to a hundred people were dying daily, served as a grim foil for the celebrations taking place at the coast.[58]

A FEAST OF HORRORS!

In August 1853 yellow fever inscribed itself deeply onto the city's population, public landscapes, and social order. Stricken people bore the disease's signature on their haunted faces: a yellowish tint that caused even friends to back away in horror. Many others, afraid to venture from home, died alone, leaving undiscovered corpses waiting until foul odors alerted neighbors to a victim's presence. In a failed effort to mask the smell of death and rid New Orleans of miasms, the board of health polluted the air further when it began burning tar at the city's major intersections. As thick, greasy smoke wafted through the air, people avoided the outdoors, leaving the "streets deserted."[59] With the city at a standstill, terrified New Orleanians scanned the papers for death notices, cared for the sick, and prayed that the epidemic might spare them for another day. A. J. Wood, an architect working in the city at the time, wrote that "the faculties are stunned and awed, the senses are oppressed with the deepest gloom. Never have I known such cause for sadness." Another observer, summing up the state of affairs, noted that by the middle of the month "the whole city was a hospital."[60]

This assessment—that the whole city had become a hospital—sheds light on conditions in New Orleans in August 1853: death, normally private and sacred, had become public and all too common. In early August, with countless vectors carrying the pathogen, and thousands of people hosting the virus, the epidemic had statistical probability on its side, as the likelihood of a mosquito spreading the disease from one person to the next reached its apex. The results were terrifying. On August 1, the *Daily Delta* reported that nearly seven hundred people had died from yellow fever the previous week. The next week that number jumped over a thousand.[61] Though staggering, such statistics dehumanize the devastation. To put faces on the tragedy, one might imagine every person in a large apartment complex, or all of the residents of a suburban subdivision, dying in one day from a single cause, and then contemplate repeating such horrors over weeks. New Orleanians read the signs of such carnage all around them. As the daily death toll exceeded two hundred, "every awning post" on the streets was "placarded with funeral invitations," leaving the few remaining pedestrians "melancholy" as they "noticed the names of the dead."[62] Somber processions, looking like parades gone horribly wrong, carried bodies through the gates of the city's cemeteries.

By the middle of August, the only crowded public spaces in New Orleans, besides hospitals, were cemeteries, the so-called cities of the dead. Because much of New Orleans lies at or below sea level, and the city sits atop a high water table, under normal circumstances underground burials were often impracticable and relatively rare until the turn of the twentieth century, yet another example of how the nonhuman world shaped the city's landscapes throughout the nineteenth century. As a result, most of New Orleans's oldest burial grounds are made up of a series of beautiful and elaborate crypts and tombs, where wealthier residents are laid to rest, and row upon row of multitiered vaults, similar to the lockers of a modern morgue, though out-of-doors, which serve as the final resting place for the less affluent (figure 13). Today, these cemeteries are among the most popular of the city's extensive tourist attractions. They have an eerie, gothic, somewhat macabre mood that captivates visitors. During the summer of 1853, however, the cities of the dead served as horrifying symbolic landscapes, embodying the depth of New Orleans's woes.

Early in August, as the number of deaths climbed daily, cemeteries overflowed, bringing mass death into plain view citywide. With few people willing or able to dig shallow graves, corpses literally piled up in the streets. The Fourth District Cemetery, where many of New Orleans's indigent dead were buried, hosted some of the worst calamities. On Friday, August 4, workers lugged seventy-one corpses to the cemetery, where six men struggled to keep pace interring bodies. Overwhelmed, the men finally gave up, leaving forty coffins sitting out in the heat over the weekend. In a scathing exposé, one journalist reported that "the action of the sun, through the frail enclosures, produced a rapid decomposition of the bodies, several of which swelled so as to burst the coffins." The smell of rotting corpses, an "unusually violent and offensive effluvia," attracted people from the surrounding neighborhood, who reported the awful scene to the board of health.[63] In other instances, rushed and weary laborers buried coffins beneath only a light sprinkling of soil, "in the manner of potato ridges," and with the first rains the coffins floated back above ground, funereal rafts navigating the city's streets.[64]

Repelled yet apparently fascinated by these spectacles of public death, editors at the *Daily Delta* took "a visit to the cemetery" and reported their findings in lurid fashion, worthy of the dime novels of the day. As the *Delta*'s writers entered the graveyard they were appalled to see "several little children engaged in the most joyous merriment, and an old woman vending ice cream to passers-by, who had to hold camphor to their noses to avoid fainting from the odor." The authors then employed a vast array of adjectives, recounting rows of coffins, the clouds of flies circling them, and the foul odors in the air. Two days later, the *Daily Crescent* outdid the *Delta* for sheer horror. In the *Crescent*'s story, the sinister gravediggers made "haste with another morsel contributed to the

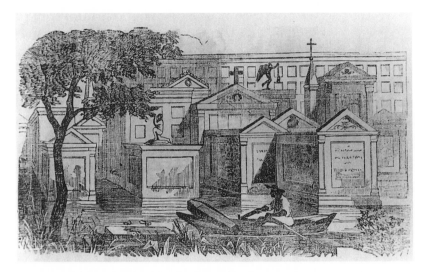

Figure 13. New Orleans's cemeteries, composed of burial vaults and crypts, often filled with water during hard rains (image dated 1853). Courtesy of the Special Collections Division, Tulane University.

grand banquet of death"; the lone woman by the gates had multiplied into groups of "old and withered crones and fat huckster women, fretting in their own grease, dispensing ice creams and confection"; and the insects had transformed into swarms of "green bottle-flies that hovered on their merchandise, and that anon buzzed away to drink dainty inhalations from the green and festering corpses."[65]

Beyond mere sensationalism, the stories' implications were clear: the epidemic had sullied even the most sacred of rituals in New Orleans. This theme was best expressed in a detail that both papers included in their articles. Due to a shortage of able-bodied men, African-American slaves dug graves for white victims of the pestilence. Confronted with the prospect of a series of disasters similar to the one taking place at the Fourth District Cemetery, New Orleans's government had turned to African-American slaves and free people of color to dig graves. First, the city deployed convict labor—chain gangs composed of slaves—to cemeteries requiring assistance. The board of health then offered the unheard-of sum of five dollars per hour, as well as food and drink, for hauling coffins and digging graves. When more than fifteen hundred people died from yellow fever in the week leading to August 14, still more African-Americans were impressed into the ranks of the gravediggers, while others willingly seized the opportunity to make relatively large sums of quick money.[66]

The public image of African-Americans burying the dead discomfited many New Orleanians, because it proved that yellow fever had altered the city's social, as well as its spatial and economic, orders. Typically, funerals in New Orleans were holy events, sanctified and segregated rituals. The presence of African-Americans crossing a color line, therefore, seemed profane. Although the press reported that the "half naked negroes, who superintended the burials, observed a proper solemnity and performed their disagreeable duties in a becoming manner," many New Orleanians likely remained upset by the breakdown in social and spatial segregation at gravesites.[67] Ultimately, however, few people had any choice. Either African-Americans would bury white bodies, or corpses would continue decaying aboveground. Eventually, white New Orleanians reconciled themselves to this turn of events by acknowledging that digging graves was depressing, taxing in August's heat, and thought to be dangerous due to constant exposure to miasms—and thus, many white people argued, inhuman work ideally suited to African-Americans.

In part, expediency and the antebellum South's social and racial caste system explain why New Orleanians finally accepted African-Americans digging graves during the epidemic.[68] Another reason, however, proved even more compelling for many people: African-Americans were reputedly immune to yellow fever. Throughout the first half of the nineteenth century, the South's medical community observed that slaves and free people of color rarely succumbed to yellow fever. Over time, many of the region's physicians began arguing that African-Americans were resistant or immune to the disease. Dr. Samuel Cartwright, among others, gained fame for studies of the "physical peculiarities of the negro race."[69] Passing over acclimation, Cartwright and his peers posited other sources for African-American immunity, pointing instead to a host of "natural" attributes, such as skin pigmentation and an enlarged liver, all ostensibly unique to the bodies of slaves and free people of color. Cartwright wrote that "the difference in the organic or physical characters imprinted by the hand of Nature on the two races" accounted for African-American immunity.[70] Other physicians concurred, arguing that slaves and free people of color were "naturally" immune to the disease, both because of physical traits and their continent of origin.[71]

Thus, while New Orleans's Creoles proudly wore their reputed immunity as a badge of honor, African-American resistance to the disease carried social stigma. Because of the theory of acclimation, immunity among Creoles represented permanence in New Orleans. For whites generally, immunity and good health connoted upper-class standing or membership in the city's public, while New Orleanians typically viewed susceptibility to disease as symptomatic of impurity, transience, and poverty. For slaves and free people of color, however, immunity symbolized bodily difference and ties to the untamed nature found on the "dark continent" of Africa. Cartwright and his colleagues therefore insisted that the "primitive" condition of slaves and free people of color insulated them from disease; that they emitted odors which repelled sickness; and that they sweated copiously, flushing yellow fever from their bodies even if they somehow contracted the disease.[72] Extrapolating wildly, these physicians argued that African-Americans were "perfect non-conductors of yellow fever," going so far as to suggest that during the summer months, New Orleans should array a phalanx of slaves along its riverfront, a human levee designed to keep back a flood of pestilence.[73]

And yet, although white pseudoscientists naturalized reputed African-American immunity to yellow fever, resistance to the disease among slaves and free people of color still caused racial anxiety during the epidemic of 1853. Early in the summer, in fact, as doctors were treating the first cases of yellow fever at Charity Hospital, rumors of a planned slave insurrection had surfaced. Sensational reports on June 14 had suggested that on the previous night an unnamed free person of color had alerted local police that more than twenty-five hundred well-armed slaves were conspiring to seize the city's arsenals and the U.S. mint. Once safe within these beachheads, the informant had claimed, the rebels would set fire to New Orleans as a signal to waves of co-conspirators lurking outside the city. Although the turncoat had never said as much, local papers had intimated that a slaughter had been planned. With yellow fever threatening the vulnerable city, it would not do to have immune slaves planning a revolt. And so, although incredulous, the chief of police had sounded the alarm. In the ensuing shakedown, no evidence had turned up substantiating the allegations. Still, in the following days, as the local papers reassured their readers that yellow fever no longer posed any threat to the city, they had called for more stringent laws restricting the freedom of movement and assembly for the city's African-American population during the dangerous summer months.[74]

Perhaps as a way of further placating anxious New Orleanians who felt threatened during the epidemic by the sight of African-Americans burying the city's dead, Cartwright and his cohort conscripted nature into what they deemed a holy war, employing their findings as rotting planks in the proslavery platform. Practicing "states-rights medicine," these quacks looked to environmental determinism, arguing that "nature" had gifted the South with an African-American population immune to yellow fever.[75] Facing off with abolitionists who viewed the epidemic as the cleansing hand of God, Cartwright sneered and turned such arguments topsy-turvy, noting that "nature scorns to see the aristocracy of the white skin...reduced to drudgery under a Southern sun, and has issued her fiat."[76] Capitalizing on the fears that people had about the mechanics of suntans, Cartwright raged that white men, and immigrants particularly, who engaged in menial labor "waged war against Nature by making negroes of themselves in laboring in the sun." The editors at the *Daily Delta* joined the chorus, observing that whites who had succumbed to yellow fever had done "work in the hot noon-day summer's sun, that the negroes ought to do." Going a step further, the *Delta* claimed that "negroes who have masters to take care of them, never die with yellow fever....If they do die, it is because they have been practicing the abolition theory."[77] The epidemic thus might have been avoided entirely, the *Delta* reasoned, if African-Americans had done the city's heavy lifting, as nature intended, leaving whites to do work that better suited them.

The question of whether African-Americans were or are immune to yellow fever remains unanswered. Many epidemiologists argue that what appears to be inherent immunity is actually a product of high levels of acquired immunity. Other experts insist that prolonged exposure to the disease over generations in Africa yielded genetic resistance. If African-American resistance to yellow fever is biologically founded, still other scholars suggest, the disease acted as another kind of biological revenge for the slave trade, laying waste to European-Americans while African-Americans enjoyed genetic resistance.[78] Ironically, this revenge only increased the Euro-American hunger for slaves by devastating pools of Native- and Euro-American workers in the South, thus supporting the contention of "scientific" racists like Cartwright and his cohort that "nature" had "formed" African-Americans to work in the region's heat and humidity by rendering them immune to yellow fever.[79] Though this sounds like a recipe for environmental racism—and indeed it sometimes was—some African-Americans took advantage of their alleged immunity, at least during the epidemic of 1853, challenging New Orleans's social and spatial order as they worked for high pay in public.

The case of African-Americans using the demand for gravediggers to their own advantage is an example of how the epidemic offered disfranchised New Orleanians some occupational and spatial mobility. The experience of female nurses offers another such instance. In an era when the medical community's professional credibility often faced challenges, the city's physicians' inability to offer even palliative care in 1853 proved especially damaging to their reputations.[80] And doctors' misplaced faith in brutal, heroic treatments like cathartics and bloodletting ultimately lowered their prestige to its antebellum nadir. Many New Orleanians, choosing between death at yellow fever's hands or agonizing therapies prescribed by physicians, turned away from the city's exclusively male doctors and instead sought out nurses. As a result, the epidemic altered gender relations in the city, as men lost their chokehold on the medical arts, while female nurses received recognition and high pay for work done in public. The example of these nurses illuminates surprising mobility for women in New Orleans, though often couched in dominant concepts of female nurturing and moral authority.[81]

In 1853, most New Orleanians frowned on women seeking roles in public. With *Uncle Tom's Cabin* the country's most talked-about book, and news of Harriet Beecher Stowe's travels in Europe plastered across the city's headlines, New Orleans's powerful slaveholders felt besieged by movements that seemed like mirror-image twins to them: abolitionism and women's rights. One reporter wrote that "Women's Rights" had "allied itself to abolitionism and almost every other rickety crazy ism." Another claimed that "Lucy Stone, Antoinette Brown, and Lucretia Mott" were "in cahoots with Greeley, Channing, Burleigh, and Garrison."[82] The language that the city's press used in describing the epidemic—laden with gender images—also provides a telling glimpse at gender ideology in the city. The virus was uniformly masculine, terror in its face always feminine. People who stayed in the city during the epidemic displayed "manly courage," those who contemplated flight succumbed to "Madam Rumor."[83] In 1853, courage was manly, cowardice womanly, the seemingly omnipotent virus masculine, and ostensibly dangerous discussion of its presence in the city feminine.

In the face of such entrenched attitudes about gender, nursing provided some women with occupational opportunity and financial gain, while advancing them into the public sphere. The female nurses that blazed a trail others followed in New Orleans were the Sisters of Charity. Often seen working in "infirmaries, hospitals, and rickety tenements...fearless of contamination, dressing loathsome wounds and inhaling the most nauseating odors the presence of the Sisters of Charity in part debunked the myth of the frail Southern Belle."[84] Yet, due to their Catholicism, asceticism, and nurturing work falling within the parameters of the "cult of true womanhood," the changes that they wrought in the city's gender dynamics often went unnoticed.[85] Even conservative New Orleanians could accept nuns working in public, because they gave care to the sick and devoted their lives to the Church, both acceptable extensions of a woman's "proper" domain. Therefore, when the Sisters of Charity forayed into public, it often was not deemed an overtly political act. Still, even as the Sisters of Charity seemed to reinforce concepts of female purity, they paved the way for nurses who followed them, women who worked not for God or the Church, but for a wage in public.

As male doctors fell from favor during the epidemic of 1853, demand for female nurses steadily increased. In late August, an observer noted that "nurses are very difficult to be obtained," and "the very highest wages are in many cases offered without success."[86] By the month's end, experienced female nurses earned more than ten dollars per day, while even neophytes received half that. At the same time, with the death rate during the epidemic half as great for women as for men, many people recognized that female bodies, often denigrated as weak or infirm, were sometimes hardier than those of males.[87] Looking back, a relief worker who lived through the epidemic wrote about advances women made in 1853. "To designate the weakness or cowardice of men as effeminacy," he insisted, "is a reproach to women not supported by experience or facts. Women are far superior to men in moral courage and physical endurance."[88] Ultimately, because they worked so hard and bravely, female nurses challenged dominant gender roles in the city as they improved their lot financially. For the duration of the epidemic they drew high wages and transcended traditional gender barriers, emerging from the pestilence with an expanded role in the public sphere and the city's medical community.

PRAYING FOR FROST

Although many New Orleanians believed that the epidemic had reached its zenith with the horrors at the Fourth District Cemetery, the death toll rose still higher throughout each week in August. Helpless in the face of such desolation, the mayor, A. D. Crossman, and the board of health resorted to a show of artillery, hopeful that a public display of military force would banish the disease from the city, or at least renew people's shaken faith in municipal government. On Thursday, August 18, New Orleanians woke suddenly at sunrise, startled by the echoing booms of cannons fired in the city's public squares near the waterfront.[89] Alas, to many critics the fireworks seemed only to have driven the outbreak to new heights, especially when approximately three hundred people died on the so-called "black day" of Sunday, August 21, leaving more than fifteen hundred people dead from yellow fever during the third week of the month.[90] With the entire "city almost wholly at a stand," a depressed newspaper commentator ventured to the levee to take New Orleans's economic pulse, reporting that the riverbanks stood almost completely empty in the late-summer sun.[91] When news came out that an additional sixteen hundred people had died in the month's final week, morale in the city sank to new depths.[92]

At the end of August, after every terrestrial effort to control the epidemic had failed, New Orleanians looked to the heavens, as they grappled with their frailties. In the month's last week, each of the city's major religious denominations sponsored a series of public prayer meetings. Collectively, supplicants sank to their knees before a "God" they hoped would be "merciful," acknowledging that they had "grievously sinned," provoking divine wrath.[93] The mayor, still anxious over his powerlessness during the epidemic, then used the city's pious mood to his advantage by casting the pestilence not as a failure of government, but as an act of God.[94] He set aside September 2 as a day of fasting and prayer, during which people would "close their stores, offices, shops and public places" in order to placate the "Supreme Being" who had chosen "to lay the heavy hand of Pestilence on" New Orleans.[95] So seriously did New Orleanians take the day of reverence that, amazingly, in a city renowned for its taverns and its citizens' prodigious consumption of alcohol, "even the bar rooms were closed." As one cleric suggested when he noted that "the science of the doctors is powerless against God," the epidemic had undermined New Orleanians' belief in human efficacy when compared to the terrible power of the nonhuman world, whether "God" or "nature."[96]

Following the day of public prayer, the weekly death toll finally began declining. Although many New Orleanians believed that the city's entreaties had been answered by a benevolent deity, it is more likely that the epidemic receded for epidemiological and environmental reasons. Based on the number of deaths reported in the city, by mid-September at least eight thousand people had succumbed to yellow fever. Even assuming a remarkably high ratio of deaths to recoveries, it is likely that at least fifteen thousand more people had contracted and survived the virus, leaving those individuals immune to future attacks. After accounting for the vast horde of migrants who fled the city—one source guessed that only seventy-five thousand people remained in New Orleans throughout the summer—and the portion of the city's population that had acquired immunity during previous epidemics, it is fair to conclude that by the beginning of September, the available reservoir of hosts for yellow fever had fast begun to evaporate. With autumn's approach, the virus's vector, too, began disappearing. In the second week of September, low temperatures in the city fell into the fifties, and the cooler weather limited the remaining mosquitoes' efficiency as disease couriers. The result was fewer than a thousand deaths for the month: a fearful total in past epidemics, but cause for celebration in 1853.[97]

In September's second week, when only four hundred people died, many New Orleanians took stock of how yellow fever had changed the city.[98] Their reactions highlight ways in which the epidemic had shifted people's perceptions of what they called nature generally and the Mississippi particularly. For many onlookers it seemed that the epidemic had come at an especially inopportune time, a cruel joke played on the city by its dynamic environs. For these observers, the epidemic was not a product of either human action or inaction, nor was it an act of God; instead it was a natural disaster. For more than a century, New Orleanians had pointed to the fifteen thousand miles of the Mississippi system as evidence that theirs was nature's chosen city. And for most of the first half of the nineteenth century, especially after steamboats arrived on the river system, those predictions seemed prescient. Only the construction of canals and railroads, powerful technologies diminishing the importance of so-called natural trade routes, threatened New Orleans's control of the valley's commerce. Still, except for a few relatively isolated dissenters, the city's commercial elites had ignored that threat leading to 1853, because even as new technologies captured a growing share of the valley's trade, New Orleans had been enjoying its finest business seasons ever. As a result, boosters had bragged louder than ever about the city's "natural advantages," claiming that trade preferred the "natural" route to market over inferior "artificial" paths.[99]

These characterizations of New Orleans's privileged place in nature were marked by strains of environmental determinism as crude as those espoused by Dr. Cartwright and his peers when discussing African-American physiology. In the boosters' reading, nature, embodied by the layout of the Mississippi system, was a benevolent force that would *inevitably* carry trade to New Orleans and the city to greatness. But if history offers its students any lessons, one is that people who wait for the inevitable are almost always disappointed. New Orleanians were no exception, because their confidence that nature had destined the city to be the capital of a commercial empire either ignored or underplayed the dynamism of the delta's environment. With the epidemic of 1853, the river, for instance, seemed to betray the city. In normal years, September signaled the start of the busy autumn trade season. In mid-September 1853, however, as the epidemic waned, commentators surveyed the open sweep of alluvial soil at the empty levee, mourning that there was "no improvement...in the general business of our city." Faced with this turn of events, Judah Benjamin, at the time among the most powerful of the city's commercial elites and later secretary of the Confederate treasury, commented on the slow pace of trade, lamenting that "there is no need of our taking any action now to curtail expenditures—Nature has done that for us by the epidemic."[100]

The most obvious result of these shifts in people's attitudes could be found in loud calls for additional technological innovation in the city. When New Orleanians realized that the river alone could or would not sweep them on its waters to empire, and that nature might continue to bring pestilence to the city in the future, in mid-September stories began appearing in the local papers demanding that the city discipline its environment further by draining local wetlands and sponsoring the construction of railroads. In other words, critics insisted that the city embrace artifice that would diminish people's reliance on the fickle environment and, particularly, the river. For example, though editors at the *Delta* still trumpeted New Orleans's "great natural advantages," they also suggested that the city's "afflictions are our best monitors and teachers." The lesson that they had learned during the epidemic was clear: the river had been kind to New Orleans in the past, but the city would nonetheless require railroads to "drive away all the dark remembrances of the pestilence."[101] An article in the *Picayune* went further, arguing that the Mississippi itself was to blame for the city's woes. The author granted that "in natural advantages...New Orleans is, as has been so often said, superior to any other place on the globe." Yet, he opined, the city's relationship with the river had "lulled her into an unwise security from which she has at length been unpleasantly aroused." Again, the cure for New Orleans's ills could be found only in the healing "hand of art."[102]

What accounted for this change? After all, New Orleans had faced environmental hardships throughout its history: floodwaters in its streets, storms beating down its buildings, and pestilence claiming thousands of its citizens. The epidemic of 1853, however, was different because of its scale and timing. Never before had a disaster of such magnitude occurred at so critical a juncture, with the railroad boom crescendoing in the North and the city facing challenges from commercial rivals throughout the valley. The epidemic also caught New Orleanians off guard, as they felt most confident about their ability to control their surroundings. The era of steam had been marked by the order that people had imposed on the river and the city's waterfront. When confronted with their environment's lingering and potentially destructive dynamism, many New Orleanians became furious. The sense of betrayal ran so deep that eventually some people called for moderation, asking that the Mississippi's critics "do justice...to our noble river: a wide pervading influence for evil has been attributed to our great benefactor—that restless stream so pregnant with blessings."[103] But a shift had taken place; some members of the community insisted that the river could never be trusted again.

In September 1853, as New Orleanians accepted that the Mississippi was not bringing trade to the levee as "nature" intended, that instead the river carried only additional "non-immunes" or "fuel," which kept the epidemic smoldering, the board of health belatedly imposed a quarantine on the city's port.[104] So profoundly had the epidemic shaken people's faith in nature and the Mississippi that, despite the city's entrenched commercial ideology, even some newspaper editors and local physicians publicly supported the quarantine. Other journalists and doctors, still unconvinced of the merits of such a drastic step, nonetheless worked to keep the riverfront closed, if not by law then in effect, cautioning people who contemplated returning to the city to wait until well into the cooler fall business season.[105] Although one angry critic scoffed that these efforts came far too late, "like shutting the stable door after the horse was stolen," the quarantine did limit the arrival of additional unacclimated hosts, further drying up the virus's shrinking reservoir and hastening the final end of the epidemic of 1853.[106]

Ironically, as New Orleanians cursed the river and nature's capriciousness, the delta's unpredictable climate brought the city an unexpected gift: an early killing frost on October 24. This frost demonstrated again the power of the weather in mid-nineteenth-century life. To many urban Americans living today in centrally heated and air-conditioned homes, autumn's first frost hardly merits a second thought. We typically ignore such subtle seasonal markers because they have so little impact on our daily lives. During epidemic summers in antebellum New Orleans, however, waking to the sight of frost glazing the city signaled yellow fever's departure, though nobody knew exactly why. As unseasonably cool temperatures lingered through October's end and into November 1853, providing relief for New

Orleanians who had boiled during the summer, the weather wiped out any *Aedes aegypti* mosquitoes still serving as vectors in the city. Weeks earlier, the board of health had announced the epidemic's end, but many New Orleanians had waited for the arrival of frost before celebrating.[107]

In 1853, frost also served as a harbinger for the revival of the city's economy. As the waterfront drew crowds of traders in mid-October, New Orleanians could look to the Mississippi's banks to see that the epidemic had ended. A writer from the *Delta* read the waterfront landscape when he noted, with some exaggeration, that "all signs of the late pestilence have been obliterated by the waves of prosperity that roll along the levee."[108] Crowds of returning people flocked not only to the riverfront, but to all of the city's public places, including its streets, which had been filled only with funeral corteges a month earlier. On October 24, at midday, a "constant tide of humanity" flowed along Canal Street, "the main artery of New Orleans."[109] The combination of cool weather, a crowded levee, and people out in public offered New Orleanians signs that the epidemic of 1853 had ended and hope had returned to their city.

For all that had changed in New Orleans during the epidemic of 1853, much remained the same, particularly the heated contests raging over definitions of the public and control of the waterfront. In November, well after the first frost, many New Orleanians began experiencing chills and fever again. Because mostly immigrants suffered from a mysterious ailment that had killed 177 people by the end of the month, the local papers quelled news of an epidemic, scolding that "no prudent or temperate person need entertain any doubt but that at the present time he can abide in New Orleans as safely and healthily as anywhere in the Union."[110] With the quarantine at the city's port recently lifted, and business returning to normal, even after word spread that the killer was cholera, journalists still insisted that "New Orleans is not afflicted with any epidemic, or any disease which threatens even remotely to be an epidemic."[111] As far as New Orleans's papers were concerned, no cholera epidemic occurred in the winter of 1853–54. The press never even reported the death toll, likely in an effort to revive the city's commercial reputation and because those who died in the city fell outside of the parameters of a public deemed worthy of mourning. More than 600 documented deaths from the disease, however, later contradicted the papers' spurious claims.[112]

Although some New Orleanians apparently learned little from the yellow-fever epidemic of 1853, the episode offers modern readers many lessons about the interactions of a city and its surroundings. As the epidemic changed New Orleans demographically, socially, culturally, geographically, and economically, it highlighted the difficulty of trying to separate where the natural environment ends and the built begins. Pathogens hidden aboard ships brought disease to a city where clouds of mosquitoes, so numerous because of characteristics of New Orleans's climate *and* urban fabric, waited to serve as vectors. An epidemic began and then raged out of control, fostered by crowds, cultural misconceptions, and commercial practices. Race and gender castes ossified and broke before being repaired and reinforced by the city's elites. Yellow fever emptied some spaces and filled others, redefining the way New Orleanians used and viewed their public landscapes. Events that can not be labeled and explained as entirely urban or natural all were part of an episode that resisted such rigid categories. In this lies the ultimate lesson of the epidemic of 1853: cities and their surroundings should not be seen in opposition to each other. Instead we find the built and the natural mingling as part of the complex narrative of New Orleans's urban-environmental history.

In 1853, such lessons were still more than half a century away for most New Orleanians. Only at the start of the twentieth century, after the advent of germ theory and the discovery that *Aedes aegypti* mosquitoes served as the disease's vector, did the city weather the last of its major yellow-fever epidemics. In 1905, yellow fever arrived in New Orleans, only to be banished by medical professionals who viewed urban space economically, socially, *and* ecologically. In that year, New Orleanians learned that they could not completely separate one section of the city from the next based on social class or ethnic categories, because mosquitoes and pathogens easily crossed such flimsy boundaries. At the same time, health officials, who knew that when it came to halting the transmission of communicable diseases all people were included in the "public," applied an expanded definition of that word and a relatively sophisticated understanding of urban space in New Orleans. Only then did the city free itself from yellow fever.[113]

But at the end of 1853 the dawn of such a modern understanding was still a long way off. In the interim, New Orleanians were to cope with lingering dynamism in the delta by further disciplining the river and the waterfront. Almost immediately after the epidemic of 1853, elites in New Orleans, including Judah Benjamin, began sponsoring railroad construction in Louisiana. Although laborers laid very little track before the Civil War began, in the postbellum period New Orleanians succeeded in luring railroads to the city by offering large sections of the waterfront as incentives to trunk lines that agreed to come to town. Those land grants were to reignite long-simmering debates about the public status of the waterfront, as many New Orleanians bristled when they found their access to the river blocked by out-of-town corporations. Ultimately, the city reclaimed the riverbanks in the name of the public, building a modern port at the waterfront, based on the most up-to-date ideas about the rational use of urban space. That landscape, with its networks of storage facilities and miles of railroad track, would have seemed like a dream to members of the city's commercial community in the fall of 1853.

CHAPTER 4

Triumphs in the Cause of Advancement and Progress

RAILROADS ON THE WATERFRONT

On February 12, 1864, a reporter spent the afternoon strolling New Orleans's waterfront with a friend. The two men were stunned by what they saw: "acres of unoccupied space." Disgusted, the scribe recounted that "all is dull and dreary where we have looked upon a picture of commercial activity unexcelled. We came for relaxation and pleasure. We returned oppressed with melancholy."[1] The men should not have been surprised at finding the waterfront unoccupied: when Union flag officer David Farragut had sailed his fleet past the forts guarding the lower reaches of the Mississippi in April 1862, he had effectively closed the river; and when New Orleans had fallen to Northern troops, the city's dreams of empire had evaporated. With the federal embargo diverting commerce from the Mississippi, in the first year of the Union occupation of New Orleans, trade at the city's port had barely exceeded receipts from the early days of the era of steam. A year later, business had slumped still further. The value of goods traded at the levee, not quite thirty million dollars, had dipped below that of any year after the Louisiana Purchase. By the end of the war, New Orleans's most prominent commercial journal estimated that between 75 and 90 percent of the valley's trade was finding its way to other markets.[2] For observers in the city, the silence at the waterfront (figure 14) told the story of economic hard times born of years of civil war.

Figure 14. In the years immediately before and after the Civil War, the waterfront remained open, with few structures standing between the city's front row
of buildings and the Mississippi (photograph ca. 1850s). Courtesy of The
Historic New Orleans Collection.

Renewed expectations of prosperity arrived in tandem with peace in
New Orleans, as the city's commercial community anticipated a return
of business lost during the war. These optimists were soon disappointed,
when traders who had shipped goods to market in the city on the north-
to-south river route during the antebellum period continued their
wartime practice of utilizing more direct west-to-east routes via railroads.
In the year after the Federal blockade ended, receipts at the city's port
ballooned over one hundred million dollars. But hundreds of thousands
of cotton bales that Confederates had hoarded in dusty barns during the
war swelled that number, blunting the impact of the rerouted trade in
New Orleans. And even in that unusually profitable year—by postbellum standards—goods such as flour, pork, and wheat, which had flowed
to the city prior to the war, were almost entirely absent at the waterfront.[3] Valley traders, it seemed, had grown relatively comfortable with
railroads during the war. As one contemporary study of the internal commerce of the United States noted: "Thanks to the embargo of war, the

railroads had gained in four years an advance on the Mississippi which under ordinary favorable circumstances it would have taken them twenty years to have secured."[4]

Despite the shifting landscape of trade in the United States after the war, some New Orleanians still clung to the myth that "nature" intended for trade necessarily to travel down the "great river, which," they claimed, had "been carved out by Nature's God as the natural outlet for the products of the West."[5] Realists like George Washington Cable, on the other hand, later scoffed at such nonsense. Recalling the city's woebegone postwar commercial climate, he said that "the moment East and West recognized the practicability of taking straighter courses [to market]...the direct became the natural route, and the circuitous the unnatural."[6] In other words, long before the language of cultural relativism became popular, Cable recognized that "nature" was conceptually fluid, and though New Orleanians had long believed it immutable and absolute, a reliable guarantor of future earnings, it actually shifted with the behavior of valley traders.

After the war, few of those traders weighed the relative merits of "natural" versus "artificial" routes to market. Instead they contemplated bottom-line issues such as efficiency, safety, and shipping costs. In each case railroads typically bested the Mississippi system, and ironically the rivers' "naturalness" often accounted for their shortcomings. Railroads could run year-round, whereas riverboats required high water, especially on the Mississippi's smaller tributaries. While waiting for a stream to reach flood stage, shippers often watched, helpless, as perishables rotted, varmints consumed their wares, or market prices plummeted. Additionally, traders enjoyed lower insurance rates on railroads, rates that fell further as underwriters recognized that trains did not have to contend with the Mississippi system's snag-filled waters. Railroads were also relatively unhindered by the valley's layout. Engineers could lay track most anywhere, while steamboats remained bound by the channels of the streams they navigated. Trains, therefore, could travel the most direct route between trade centers, servicing, sometimes even creating, the boom towns sprouting throughout the West in the postwar years. In short, shipping via rail was cheaper, faster, more reliable, and generally viewed as safer than the river route.[7] The rivers never stood a chance in competition with railroads, comparatively isolated from the vagaries of climate and geography.

During the era of Reconstruction, even the river route's most diehard defenders recognized that railroads had diminished the significance of the valley's watercourses, the "natural advantages" that boosters had long counted on for vaulting New Orleans to empire. The city's hinterland, which had once been defined by what New Orleanians called nature, now could be redefined again, by artifice. As environmental historian William Cronon has noted, the sway of geography could be overwhelmed by the logic of capital.[8] Consequently, converts cried out that the city now required the service of railroads if it was to compete for trade. Although a few stalwart entrepreneurs had begun building rail lines in Louisiana before the war, their efforts had been hindered by distrust of an industry that threatened the Mississippi system's status, as well as by environmental obstacles, such as epidemics, and by the enormous cost of laying track through the swampy bayou country of the southern portion of the state. As a result, when the Civil War began, less than three hundred miles of track crossed Louisiana, leaving New Orleanians little choice late in the 1860s but to follow the national trend of offering railroads attractive grants of land, among other incentives, to come to the city.[9]

Those land grants represented the first steps in a process that was to play out over the course of more than thirty years. From the era of Reconstruction through the turn of the twentieth century, New Orleans repeatedly reconfigured its waterfront to compete for trade in an era of industry and new technologies that would have been unimaginable just decades earlier. At a moment when mechanical innovators—amateur inventors as well as professional scientists and engineers—became national heroes, and the technologies emerging from their workshops and labs seemingly held out utopian promises, New Orleans industrialized its port and the Mississippi River in an effort to recapture trade and the dream of empire lost during the war. First, state and municipal officials granted portions of the waterfront piecemeal to railroad corporations while clamoring for the federal government to engineer some of the lingering dynamism out of the river. Then, near the turn of the twentieth century, confronted with the disappointing results of profligate waterfront giveaways and federally sponsored river improvements, reformers in the city proposed various endeavors they labeled progressive. These self-styled progressives, trading in the cultural currency of science and rationality, reclaimed the waterfront in the name of the public by building a system of municipally owned docks, enormous warehouses, and miles of rails along the city's border with the Mississippi.

Throughout this process, people's shifting perceptions of nature and the river coupled with the impact of the stream's geomorphology to influence the production of space in New Orleans, yielding dramatic changes in the city's relationship with the Mississippi. In these years, as land-based transportation technologies supplanted those bound to the river, railroads made their own spatial demands on the city, forcing municipal officials and business interests, still committed to a commercial ideology, to respond. Accordingly, as much of the nation became enraptured by sublime landscapes, popularized by painters such as Thomas Moran and Albert Bierstadt who labeled them natural, New Orleans distanced itself from the Mississippi, erecting what amounted to walls along the waterfront. And as New Orleanians overhauled the riverbanks, the number of people who could access that space shrank, recasting one measure of the waterfront's public status. The results were mixed. By the start of World War I, many residents of the city hailed the remade port as the fruit of rational, scientific planning, catering to the needs of trade and technology. Other observers, however, mourned the city's lost spatial connection with the river, certain that New Orleans had sacrificed the feature that had made it special—its urban-riparian sense of place— on the altar of commercial gain, mistakenly likened to the public good.

The first major change at the riverfront took place in 1867, when the city council gave the New Orleans, Opelousas, and Great Western Railroad 125 feet of the waterfront opposite the French Quarter for "freight and ferry purposes."[10] Soon afterward, the state legislature granted the New Orleans, Mobile, and Chattanooga line the right to build a terminal on the riverbanks, beginning at Canal Street and extending four blocks upriver, across land that had once formed a part of Edward Livingston's batture property. The legislature also allowed that line to lay double track along much of the waterfront. At nearly the same time, the city council made a similar grant to the New Orleans, Jackson, and Great Northern line, meaning that a second set of double track was to run along the waterfront. Whereas the riverbanks had always mostly been open on the city side of the levee, a vast tract of alluvial soil between the front row of the city's buildings and the Mississippi, in the wake of these grants structures of commerce sprouted up along the waterfront.[11]

Why were legislators willing to grant portions of the riverfront, long the city's most valued public space, to private railroad interests? The answer is complicated. First, commerce remained king in the city, and many lawmakers believed that New Orleans needed railroads if it was to regain its antebellum economic status. This conviction accompanied a belief, prevalent in the nation's legal community, characteristic of much public policy enacted in Gilded Age New Orleans: unproductive public resources should be turned over to the private sector to maximize their efficient use.[12] Building on these positions, neither the legislature nor the council believed that they were simply giving away the waterfront; instead they saw the railroads as agents of development, ostensibly servants of the public's interests, much as their predecessors had viewed the Fulton group before agreeing to grant its monopoly on the river system at the start of the era of steam. Finally, these grants took place during the period of Reconstruction, when some legislators, especially so-called carpetbaggers, may not have been as familiar with the state's civil code of laws, including the riparian servitude guaranteeing the public's rights along the waterfront.

Elected officials' unfamiliarity with the law does not explain the relatively muted criticism that initially greeted these grants in New Orleans. To understand this, one must look at the widespread belief at that time that only railroads could salvage the city's economy, and also at issues of urban aesthetics. By the late 1860s, few residents of the city valued the river for its beauty; for too long New Orleanians had seen the Mississippi only as a commercial highway or an alimentary canal, filled with raw waste and decaying animal carcasses. Also, during the Civil War, the waterfront had fallen into such disrepair that in the postbellum years it no longer served as the municipal showplace that it once had. In 1866, a journalist reported that the "wharves have gone to decay and ruin" and that the "levee itself is full of holes and chasms that make it in many places, almost impassable for vehicles, and dangerous for pedestrians."[13] By the war's end, many people believed that the riverfront was an outdated and potentially hazardous relic of their city's past. The notion that the waterfront had become dangerous then gained wider currency when the city's dockworkers engaged in a series of strikes on the levee between 1865 and 1867.[14] The waterfront was decrepit, archaic, and the locus of labor unrest. So it was hardly surprising that many New Orleanians turned their back on the city's link with the Mississippi after the war, watching without complaint as railroads began building permanent structures along the riverbanks.

Trains, however, did not arrive entirely without controversy, as river interests clung to their decreasing power at the waterfront. For instance, in 1870, riverboat pilots lodged protests with the city, claiming that the new division of space made it "impossible to discharge the cargoes of the steamboats at the points on the levee designated as their landing places."[15] Drawing on a worldview that they did not realize was outdated in a postwar era of technological innovation, the pilots cautioned that railroads were New Orleans's enemy and a threat to the city's commercial future. In response, the council coldly assigned a new, less desirable docking location to the steamboats, "anticipating that a large portion of the river landing would be encroached upon and occupied by railroad companies."[16] In doing so, the council showed the riverboatmen the same offhand disrespect that it once had showered on dated transportation technologies when steamboats arrived on the Mississippi. From favored sons to stepchildren: so far had river interests plummeted in New Orleans with the railroads' arrival.

Still, the riverboat pilots did not loose their grip on the riverbanks without a fight. Thomas Leathers, who captained the famed *Natchez*, railed that if the waterfront grants continued, "the steamers would be driven from New Orleans." He warned that New Orleanians "would wake up to a realization of their error when they found trade entirely diverted to other channels, their Levee deserted and their streets grass-grown."[17] Despite his passion, Leathers's pleas fell on deaf ears. Although controversies over the grants did not end there—years of legal wrangling about the railroads' right to build in the city's public spaces followed—most concerned parties echoed the sentiments of a state supreme-court judge, who, after hearing protests from several riverboatmen seeking to overturn the original grant to the New Orleans, Mobile, and Chattanooga line, responded that "the testimony of witnesses has been referred to show that the use of the batture by the railroad company will be injurious to the commerce of this city. In my judgment this testimony only proves that the witnesses are about a quarter of a century behind the age in which they live."[18] In the justice's words, one senses that power had shifted in the city. The railroad grants were justified and legally upheld as a necessary addition to the urban landscape if New Orleans hoped to compete for the valley's trade. Privatization of urban space had become public-spirited in an age of industry. A move toward private planning was gathering momentum in New Orleans.

The riverbanks told the story of a city captivated by the potential of technological innovation and uncertain about the value of its once hallowed natural advantages. Just as New Orleans had built wharves along the riverfront in the 1830s to serve steamboats and capitalize on the Mississippi's commercial potential, postbellum legislators, with the courts' sanction, remade the riverfront again to accommodate the needs of railroads. As a result, for the first time in the city's history, tracks, depots, and trains divided New Orleans from the river (figure 15). Trains traveled the riverfront's length, challenging horse carts and pedestrians for

Figure 15. Railroad tracks running between the city and the waterfront (image ca. early twentieth century). Courtesy of the Special Collections Division, Tulane University.

primacy in the city's most important public space.[19] One reporter observed the hazardous contests taking place over use of the riverfront. On the double tracks shadowing the river, he found a clash of transportation technologies. "Teams drive recklessly," he explained, "on the same tracks on which in-coming trains are drawn by rapidly moving locomotives."[20] Railroads, with their speed, power, and spatial requirements were transforming the waterfront, and, for the moment at least, most New Orleanians looked on approvingly from a safe distance.

The railroad grants also represented a transition in New Orleans's relationship with the river. For the first time, a cross section of the city's populace acknowledged that New Orleans could not float on the Mississippi to empire. Still, although the waterfront railroads represented the river's diminished status, it would be wrong to conclude that the city had forsaken the Mississippi entirely. The remade waterfront suggested instead that New Orleanians sought to augment, not abandon, their natural advantages, which they recognized could not alone recapture the valley's trade. In doing so, they hoped to secure the best of both worlds for their city: a metropolis connected to its hinterland by artificial trade routes, railroads, and by so-called natural avenues of commerce, the Mississippi system. Served by both river and rail, New Orleans's people of commerce felt certain that they could regain their standing in the valley.

PRYING OPEN THE MISSISSIPPI'S MOUTH

In the winter of 1869, for the first time in many years, a sense of optimism pervaded New Orleans's commercial community. The previous year, the city had received more than six hundred thousand bales of cotton, a meager figure during the era of steam but cause for celebration compared to the war years, when dockworkers had seldom handled more than a hundred thousand bales annually.[21] At the city's waterfront, a vitality missing since before the war was afoot again. The bellow of steam whistles, the clank of construction, and a new sound—the chugging of trains—banished the depressing silence that had shrouded the levee for more than seven years. Pedestrians who crossed freshly laid railroad tracks to get to the river saw steamers piled high with cotton bales. The presence of both river and rails led boosters, meeting at a commercial convention in New Orleans, to claim, "Recognizing the fact that 'Westward the Star of Empire has taken its way,' we declare in favor of the Crescent City as the seat of a commercial empire, whose scepter shall rule the world."[22] For the first time since before the war, New Orleans seemed perched on the brink of greatness. Then bad news filtered up the river in mid-February, halting the city's half-uttered self-congratulatory rhetoric.

On February 18, as New Orleanians scanned their morning newspapers, they read with horror that the river was blockaded again. This time Union gunboats were not to blame; instead a sand bar had formed at the river's mouth, choking off trade. Unaware of the danger, a steamship had run aground the previous night. The river's current had then pivoted the vessel at the point where it clung to the bar, leaving it resting, perpendicular to the channel, with no room for vessels "trying to creep around her stern."[23] A logjam of ships had quickly formed on both sides of the trapped steamer, creating the impression that somebody needed only to pop a cork to unleash a gush of commerce. After more than two weeks, one reporter estimated that the "damage done to the commerce of New Orleans by the detention of vessels at the bar…is incalculable."[24] Unseasonably warm days, high humidity, and heavy rain soon caused panic in the city, as traders scampered to salvage produce stored at the waterfront. Goods lying in the holds of vessels stranded on the river also rotted or served as snacks for shipboard rodents. All the while, New Orleanians worried that the crisis would divert trade away from their already beleaguered markets. As the blockade dragged on for a month, the *Daily Picayune* likened New Orleans's commercial community to a "hedged in animal."[25]

The dilemma facing the city was not new. The Mississippi carries more than 275 million cubic yards of sediment to the gulf annually, material which stains the river a deep brown. If gathered together, this load could form a structure approximately a mile square and twenty-five stories high. Ninety miles below New Orleans, at the so-called Head of the Passes, the river divides into several distinct and smaller outlets, including South Pass and Southwest Pass. From above, these passes resemble a bird's foot, splayed out into the gulf (figure 16). Because a stream's ability to carry material in suspension is directly proportional to its current—the faster the current the more material can be carried—when the Mississippi empties into the gulf, as its current diminishes, the river is unable to support the sediment that it has carried from throughout its valley. Consequently, the river deposits its bed load there, sometimes creating sandbars. Early efforts at overcoming silting at the river's mouths included a variety of remedies that succeeded in degrees varying from a little to not at all. For the most part, though, New Orleanians recognized that they could do little about the fickle passes.[26]

In 1869, however, the city's businessmen knew that they stood at a crossroads in the nation's economic history. In an era of steel rails, valley shippers refused to gamble that the river would remain open as commerce required. So New Orleanians demanded unprecedented action. Having already lured railroads to the city, they again sought a technological fix for their problems. With the Mississippi apparently spurning its chosen city, frustrated observers derided the river as "defective," abandoning the "natural route" by calling for a canal circumventing the unpredictable passes.[27] Business interests hoped that an artificial outlet for the river would do for the city what the Erie Canal had done for Manhattan decades earlier: guarantee New Orleans a stable connection with its hinterland.[28] A canal, like the railroads, would not depend on favorable climatic conditions or the whims of the capricious Mississippi. A canal would offer the city the predictability that the river lacked. In short, a canal promised the city's commercial community the control over its environment that it had always craved.

After the blockade of 1869, New Orleans's elites lobbied the federal government to control the river mouth. In one memorial to Congress, frustrated New Orleanians explained that "nature, so prodigal of her gifts in this fertile and prosperous valley, has interposed an impediment to its freedom of commerce."[29] For years, such pleas went unanswered, as leaders at the U.S. Army Corps of Engineers, charged with keeping the passes open, deemed a canal too costly to build. Instead, the Corps

Figure 16. The Mississippi winds through lower Louisiana until it reaches its
outlets at the Gulf of Mexico. Note the mouths of the Mississippi *(lower right)*
at the "bird-foot" delta in this map detail (1885; republished 1900). Courtesy
of the Special Collections Division, Tulane University.

deployed a dredge boat, the *Essayons* (French for "let us try"), to deepen
the passes. Again and again, the *Essayons* tried and failed. Finally, in
March 1873, as another blockade threatened trade in the city, Charles
Howell, the Corps officer working the passes at the time, lost patience
with dredging. He decided, after much prompting from members of New
Orleans's chamber of commerce, that a canal was the only way to guarantee navigation and trade on the river. Howell had grown tired of struggling with the Mississippi, while technology seemingly offered a solution
to problems at the river's mouth.[30] With the Corps reversing its position,
and powerful interests in New Orleans behind the project, it seemed that
the city would have its canal—until James Eads arrived on the scene.

Eads was one of the great success stories of his day. A self-taught engineer, he made a fortune in a variety of river-related businesses, ranging from underwater salvage operations, to supplying the Federal government with gunboats during the Civil War, to spanning the Mississippi
at St. Louis with a steel bridge that still bears his name.[31] Although Eads
was a great apostle of progress and technology, above all he loved the
river and found the idea of a canal at its mouth repulsive. In the spring
of 1873, as river interests met in St. Louis to discuss future improvements
on the Mississippi, Eads held court. The majority at the gathering supported a canal; an artificial outlet, they thought, provided the best hope
for permanently fixing the river's mouth. On the second day of the meeting, however, Eads addressed the throng. Over a buzz of protests, he
claimed to have the cure for canal fever. A system of jetties—artificial
riverbanks designed to narrow a stream, keeping its current powerful
and channel deep—Eads promised, would pry open the river mouth
without desecrating the Mississippi.[32]

For another year Eads squared off with canal proponents, including
members of New Orleans's commercial community and the chief of the
Army Corps of Engineers, Andrew Humphreys, who was eager to maintain the Corps's dominance on the lower river. Humphreys insisted that
only he and his subordinates, trained military engineers, could be trusted
to reshape the plastic landscape to serve human endeavors. Eads countered that the river should not be abandoned. Drawing on a rhetoric of
artifice, the civilian engineer promised to complete nature's good work
by applying the hand of man. The two men sparred often, each donning
the mantle of science and expertise to lend legitimacy to his cause. Then,
in February 1874, Eads thought that he had ended the conflict when he
offered Congress a deal that it could not refuse: he would build his system of jetties at Southwest Pass and collect payment only if the works

maintained a channel deep enough to keep trade flowing on the river. Eads immediately drew fire from elites in New Orleans because of his "no cure, no pay" deal.[33]

New Orleanians, committed to an artificial opening for the river, begged Eads to abandon his pursuit of jetties. In one missive, twenty-seven of the city's leading businessmen accused the engineer of being an "outsider" on the river. Worse still, they suggested that his motives were unsavory, that he served St. Louis in its quest for commercial dominance in the valley by offering New Orleans the jetties as a Trojan horse at the river mouth, untested technology that would inevitably fail when confronted with the Mississippi's power.[34] Other New Orleanians, lobbying at the time in Washington for a canal, criticized Eads for underestimating the depths of the river's malfeasance. Whereas the civilian engineer promised order on the Mississippi, they insisted that he would deliver chaos instead. Certain that the Mississippi could not be tamed by the hand of man, they suggested that if Eads believed otherwise, he misread the dangers of entrusting New Orleans's economic future to the devious river. Returning to the theme that Eads did not fully comprehend the environment that he proposed to improve, they asked Congress to ignore "the half insane propositions of strangers" on the river. They pleaded with the legislators not to "permit us to be destroyed" by Eads's ill-fated jetties. And they explained that the Mississippi had taught them humility, leaving them confident that Eads's hubris was misplaced on the great stream.[35]

After convening a commission to study the problems at the Mississippi's mouth and then deliberating over the panel's findings, Congress finally granted Eads the jetties contract on March 3, 1875.[36] But the deal was not as attractive as the civilian engineer had hoped, especially because Eads would have to build his works at the smaller and shallower South Pass, rather than at Southwest Pass, as he had wished. For Eads, who, like so many other engineers of his time, had posterity in his sights, working at South Pass seemed short-sighted, because he suspected that deep-drafted, ocean-going vessels would soon outgrow the smaller outlet. Still, Eads recognized that Congress was offering him a chance to make good on the river's promise to the valley, to create a landscape in which human ingenuity prevailed over the vagaries of the untamed environment. And so, when presented with the chance to stamp his mark on one of the great engineering dilemmas of the day, Eads finally accepted.

In 1875, South Pass was a wet wilderness, threatening to onlookers. One traveler gasped that she had "never beheld a scene so utterly desolate as this entrance to the Mississippi. Had Dante seen it, he might have drawn images of another Bolgia from its horrors."[37] Another writer, struck by the setting's prehistoric mood, noted, "One would not, in fact, be much surprised to behold a bepaddled ichthyosaurus floundering in the river; to see a monstrous plediosaurus sporting on its surface; or to hear a colossal iguanodon crashing with heavy tramp, through yon cypress-brake."[38] In his account of the jetties' construction, even Eads's assistant, E. L. Corthell, also an engineer and man of science, admitted that his mind had reeled when first confronted with the desolate sight of South Pass. "The whole country," he wrote, was nothing but "a low, flat marsh of mud, reeds, and grasses, which, in long narrow strips, is thrust out into the gulf." As Corthell scanned the horizon for any topographical feature, he found "not even a background of high land to relieve the monotony of the scene."[39] On that canvas, Eads worked from a palette of technologies to paint an image of progress and civilization, hoping to reassure New Orleanians and people around the nation that the river, even at its wildest, could be shaped by powerful artifice and human expertise.

In the summer of 1875, Eads dispatched workers to South Pass, where they sank parallel lines of piles, the jetties' spine, into the river and gulf floor and then connected them with willow mattresses, the works' muscle, sinew, and flesh. After just a year, long walls stretched from South Pass far into the gulf, amplifying the river's scour and carving out a deeper channel. By May 1876, Eads had become so sure of success that he invited a steamship, the *Hudson,* to navigate the jetties. The deep-drafted vessel steamed to South Pass on May 16, arriving at low tide, and after getting caught on the bar overnight, it cleared the jetties the following morning. Eads and his crew celebrated, certain that the spectacle had proven that the river was open for good.[40]

In midsummer 1879, after numerous setbacks, including a yellow-fever epidemic during the summer of 1878 that rivaled the terrible scourge of 1853, Eads and his crew of sun-baked, sweat-soaked laborers completed the jetties.[41] By transforming the landscape at the river's mouth (figure 17), Eads and his crew offered observers a symbol of the seemingly limitless power of human ingenuity and technology. After centuries of unpredictability, South Pass remained consistently deep enough for steel-hulled vessels to enter and exit the river. A small village of neat buildings stood next to the jetties, providing further evidence, when juxtaposed with their surroundings, of people's apparent ability to control the environment. New Orleanians, who had been skeptical about Eads and the river, soon claimed the jetties as part of their municipal land-

Figure 17. James Eads's laborers transformed the landscape at South Pass into a tableau of progress. Port Eads, a symbol of civilization, stands amid the wetlands on the right in this image (1885). Order, embodied by the vessels entering the river in a linear progression, was ostensibly imposed on the Mississippi by the jetties. Courtesy of The Historic New Orleans Collection.

scape and the Mississippi as their benefactor again. Popular junkets ran from the city to South Pass, jammed with people eager to see technology taming the river.[42] Eads's own assessment of the jetties reveals the scene greeting New Orleanians when they arrived. "They [the jetties] constitute a remarkable illustration of how completely the immense forces of nature may sometimes be controlled," he suggested.[43]

By the time that Eads's workers had finished the jetties, railroads had crossed the country, Alexander Graham Bell had summoned his assistant over the world's first working telephone, fantastic inventions had begun pouring forth from Thomas Edison's lab at Menlo Park, and the Roeblings neared completion on the Brooklyn Bridge. The nation rode a wave of unprecedented technological advance, and to many onlookers the jetties epitomized the power of engineers and inventors to overcome environmental obstacles. It seemed that nature was knowable and pliant, another tool in the hands of brilliant men armed with inspiration, data, and artifice to reshape the continent. Writers at the *New York Tribune,* for instance, marveled of the jetties that "genius, persistence and practical skill have seldom won so great a triumph over the forces of nature."[44] When confronted with the transformation of South Pass, Mark Twain, a noted skeptic, nonetheless gushed that "Captain Eads, with his jetties, has done a work at the mouth of the Mississippi which seemed clearly impossible; so we do not feel full confidence now to prophesy against like impossibilities."[45] In Twain's words lay the meaning of the jetties for many observers: human beings had demonstrated apparent dominion over even the most intractable problem on the river. As for New Orleanians, Eads had not just redeemed South Pass, but the Mississippi's reputation, altering its meaning for the city again.

Yet, few New Orleanians pondered the jetties as a metaphor or symbolic landscape; they were too busy celebrating because valley traders had resumed shipping their wares to the city. In 1876, Eads's first year of work at South Pass, New Orleans had received barely three hundred thousand bushels of grain.[46] By 1878, that number had climbed over four million bushels, and huge piles of corn, wheat, rye, and oats at the waterfront heralded the return of the region's trade. When grain receipts the next year climbed by more than 110 percent, New Orleans's press corps reopened discussions of empire. The *Daily Picayune* guessed that soon "the entire grain product of the Northwest, beyond the Missouri, and much of that grown between the Mississippi and the Missouri, now controlled by Chicago, must find its way down the Mississippi to our city." Such predictions seemed accurate, after an average of more than eleven million bushels of grain arrived at the levee annually between 1880 and 1883, prompting one traveler to note that New Orleans "seemed like a city rising from the dead."[47] The jetties had performed another miracle: they had breathed life into an urban corpse.

With the grain trade booming, ships navigating the jetties, and railroads traversing the waterfront, members of New Orleans's revitalized commercial community searched for ways to advertise that their city was open for business. In the winter of 1884–85, they settled on hosting a world's fair, the Industrial and Cotton Centennial Exposition, on a huge parcel of land today known as Audubon Park. The fairgrounds stood in the midst of the city's up-and-coming uptown district, fronted on one side by the Mississippi, with St. Charles Avenue and its rows of stately mansions, on the other.

On December 16, 1884, the fair opened, a spectacle composed of didactic landscapes designed to show that New Orleans typified what people were soon to call the New South—a land of racial harmony, burgeoning industry, and economic diversity, far removed from the discord of civil war.[48] To accomplish such a complex goal, the fair, like others in the nineteenth century, housed a dizzying array of goods and services, art and architecture, agricultural produce and industrial output, high culture and pop kitsch. The exposition boasted huge crowds, neoclassical buildings, ethnographic displays, colossal steam engines, temples made of soap, cathedrals crafted from cracker boxes, costumed pigs, anatomy exhibits drawn from Civil War battlefields, and towers of sugar cane. But, what may have been even more revealing was what was almost entirely absent from the Cotton Exposition: cotton. Although Louisiana offered a folksy exhibit of the staple, "an old man and woman and their dog, composed of ginned cotton," one visitor was stunned to see "the supremacy of King Cotton audaciously challenged here in the chief city of his dominions by the new State of Nebraska, which proclaims on an enormous screen in letters of golden ears, that 'Corn is King,' and shows a huge portrait of the rival sovereign formed of red and yellow kernels."[49]

Throughout the fair, grain seemed ascendant, perhaps because the event's planners were reluctant to focus on cotton, the crop of the past, favoring instead grain, the harvest of Eads's triumph, the South Pass jetties. For New Orleanians, the fair offered a chance to showcase their city's bright future, and they blanched at the thought of appearing backwards. Whereas cotton reeked of the antebellum era, of slavery and secession, grain smacked of progress, of the ascendant West and harsh environments controlled by powerful artifice, such as the railroads and jetties that served the city. Awash in a sea of profits for the first time in years, New Orleanians used the fair to celebrate their rejuvenated economy and the innovations upon which it rested. As Louisiana's governor, S. D. McEnery, had explained at the fair's opening, credit for the exposition belonged to "the genius of Eads presiding over the Mississippi River."[50] The presence of so much grain at the fair narrated New Orleans's rise from the ashes of war, the arrival of railroads at the waterfront, and the power of the jetties to impose order on the Mississippi. In an era of boom and bust, New Orleans's future seemed relatively secure in 1884, as visitors sidled up to exhibits at the fair.

RECONSIDERING THE WATERFRONT

For all of the optimism that New Orleanians evinced at the fair, their reborn dreams of empire soon proved fleeting. Even as tourists flocked to the city, admiring the sights at the Cotton Exposition, the grain trade began declining. In 1883, New Orleans had received more than eleven million bushels of grain, as valley traders had identified the river as a cheaper route to market than the railroads. In 1884, however, that number plummeted to six and a half million bushels.[51] What, New Orleanians asked, was wrong? After all, the jetties still kept the river open. The answer to this question was simple: it was the valley's landscape of trade that had shifted again. By the time the fair opened, railroads had adjusted their rates to recapture the region's grain. Once more, New Orleans's commercial community was left wondering what to do. The river finally seemed to be under control, but railroads ran roughshod through their city. New Orleanians turned, as they had in the past, to the waterfront, rethinking changes made there in the years following the war.

When the city and state had begun offering land grants to railroads after the war, the assumption had been that the lines would bring development and efficiency to the waterfront. Legislators had reasoned that private corporations would impose discipline at the riverbanks, lowering costs at the city's port and bringing trade back to New Orleans.[52] Despite their passion for privatizing public spaces, though, and the logic of capitalism's invisible hand, their plan had gone awry. With several railroads competing for control of the waterfront, inefficiency at the port had persisted. Then, railroads in the upper valley had jeopardized the city's economic rebirth by manipulating their fee structures to take back the region's grain. As a result, in part because people's hopes for the railroads had been unrealistic, and also because the lines were not in business to prop up the city's economy, New Orleanians, including the city's commercial community, grew frustrated and then angry about the decision to give the waterfront away. In sum, as distant corporate power began to seem threatening, locals demanded that the city reclaim the Mississippi's banks.

As early as 1882, some people began framing their misgivings about the waterfront grants in spatial and aesthetic terms. After the railroads had arrived, these critics noted profound differences between ways of seeing the corporations: on paper, promising commercial gain, and as physical entities, altering the landscape and occupying space at the waterfront. When the Louisiana and Texas line began building a depot at the riverfront, across from Jackson Square, the *Daily States* called the structure "unsightly" and a "profanation." The paper warned that the building was "cutting the square off from the river, and thus destroying in great measure, the charm and beauty of...New Orleans."[53] By 1885, with five sets of double track dividing New Orleans from the river, and trains traveling the riverbanks to their depots at all hours, it became clear that the railroads had not arrived without a price; they had ushered in an era of industrial spatial order at the waterfront, altering the city's relationship with the Mississippi.[54] As western historian William Deverell has noted of Californians' reactions to the railroads, excitement about the lines in theory and accommodation to them in practice were very different things.[55]

While some scolds carped about the spatial impact of the railroads, others noted that the lines were causing social problems in the city, particularly after "tramps" who rode the rails to New Orleans began squatting at the levee. Eventually, hundreds of "barefooted urchins" built a tent city on the batture, beneath the municipal wharves (figure 18). New Orleanians, terrified of these transients, labeled them "wharf rats" and blamed them for unsolved crimes in the city. Frightened gossips told "tales of murder and robbery which fairly make the blood curdle in one's veins," claiming that the "wharf rats" were responsible for several unidentified corpses, "floaters found in the river" early in the decade.[56] Other angry New Orleanians complained that "gangs...frequently made raids not only on vessels in port, cargoes on the wharves, but even upon vehicles passing in the streets." The railroads abetted the thieves, who often leapt from hiding as passersby waited for a train to pass.[57] Because of the waterfront's increasingly squalid condition, many New Orleanians refused to visit the levee, unwilling to accept homeless people living there as part of the public that had a legitimate right to use that space.

Figure 18. Homeless children and adults squatted beneath the municipal wharves in the postbellum period, generating tremendous class anxiety in New Orleans (image dated 1873). Courtesy of The Historic New Orleans Collection.

    People who indicted the railroads on social and spatial grounds were relatively rare compared to those who expressed outrage because the lines had apparently failed the city commercially. Not only was New Orleans's economy unpredictable in the 1880s—prone, like the rest of the nation's, to sudden shifts—but railroads often seemed to be at fault. Loss of confidence in railroads around the country helped spark a national economic downturn in 1884, and the lines' reputations suffered in the aftermath. In New Orleans, the railroads received more bad press that spring when the Texas and Pacific line reneged on a deal one of its corporate predecessors had cut with the city. The council responded by revoking the line's right to use the riverbanks. Faced with losing its portion of the waterfront, the Texas and Pacific sued the city, spurring a group of businesspeople to seek reform along the Mississippi's banks.[58]
    In 1885, with the waterfront a confusing web of rails, a group of elite reformers insisted that the city's economic woes could be traced to two factors: inefficient management of the port, and the political machine—known locally as the Democratic Ring—which they held accountable for giving away the riverfront to out-of-town railroad corporations. Like other machines nationwide, the Ring relied on immigrant and working-

class voters who looked to its ward bosses for basic municipal services and jobs. Consequently, commercial elites, used to controlling the waterfront and other matters of public policy in the city, had relatively little power during the Ring's reign. Chafing because of their diminished status, the commercial community used the city's lagging economy as a springboard back to power in the spring of 1885. At the time, elites formed the so-called Committee of One Hundred. Although it failed to topple the Ring, in 1888, another elite organization, the Young Men's Democratic League, succeeded, when New Orleanians elected Joseph Shakespeare as their reform mayor.[59]

With Shakespeare in office, New Orleans's people of commerce began trying to reclaim both the waterfront and political power for themselves. They formed the Public Belt Railroad Commission, hoping to lay a ring of municipally owned rails around the city. The commission argued that if the project were completed, when private railroads arrived at New Orleans's borders, they would transfer their rolling stock to the public line, which would haul the cars to their destinations in the city. The commission members hoped to increase efficiency by limiting delays and costs attendant to transferring freight from one carrier to another, which, in turn, would decrease fees at the port. At the same time, a second, unspoken goal underlay the proposal: the belt line would return control of the waterfront to local businesspeople, diminishing the power of the Ring and out-of-town corporations that were slipping from favor in the city.

To gain support for their cause, the commission used language fusing themes traditionally associated with the waterfront—its status as a public space—and ideas gaining popularity in cities nationwide as the Gilded Age ended—the superiority of rationally planned, urban spaces overseen by experts.[60] To blend these themes, in its publicity tracts the commission hailed the power and influence of "science," while still insisting that the waterfront "must remain a public thoroughfare." The public that the commission had in mind was quite specific: local experts devoted to promoting trade. Accordingly, the commission members revealed that they subscribed to a precedent set during the era of steam, claiming that the waterfront could "only be used in a public way, for the one object, Commerce." Finally, they blamed machine politicians and private out-of-state railroad corporations for confusion at the riverbanks, noting that the tangle of tracks at the waterfront had not brought the city prosperity.[61] In short, the commission members argued that the waterfront should be rationally planned by experts, public (guaranteeing local control), and devoted to commerce alone.

After the commission began lobbying, it quickly discovered how deeply the railroads had rooted themselves in the waterfront's alluvial soil. With the Texas and Pacific suit against the city still pending, the riverfront remained a contested and clogged space. So, while the commission members claimed the riverbanks for their version of the public, at an open hearing held in midsummer 1888, an official from the Southern Pacific Railroad reminded New Orleanians that the waterfront grants were not a privilege for the corporations alone, but for the city as well. An officer from the besieged Texas and Pacific then demanded that private rail lines have control over any belt railroad built at the waterfront in the future.[62] With the riverfront property's status uncertain, despite widespread support for the belt line, the idea foundered for some time.

As late as 1890, the railroads still had not given an inch. At the time, E. L. Corthell, who had been James Eads's lieutenant at South Pass, suggested a compromise: a belt line running on Claiborne Avenue, at the city's rear, controlled by Jay Gould's Louisville and Nashville road, which held a right of way there. B. M. Harrod, a belt-line advocate and powerful member of New Orleans's commercial community, countered that "the entire importance of this city is its location to the river and its great levee." If private lines would not relinquish their control of the waterfront, Harrod added, "the interests of the railroads are in direct antagonism to those of the city." Other belt-line supporters agreed, admitting that while "commerce demands great facilities, it should be our care in affording these facilities to see they are of a character to actually benefit commerce without trespassing upon the rights and comfort of the community."[63] In this way, local businesspeople used the waterfront's historically public character as both carrot and stick in their quest to regain power next to the Mississippi. Corthell retorted to such arguments by pointing to the meteoric rise of Chicago, intimating that New Orleans needed to emulate its competitor to the north if it wished to regain economic glory. The Windy City, like other metropolitan areas around the country, had recently given up part of its waterfront, granting railroads generous rights of way along the lakeshore.[64]

As the impasse dragged on, belt-line proponents confronted not only corporate greed, but also widespread not-in-my-backyard attitudes among New Orleanians fighting spatial battles usually confined to the waterfront. Many city residents' reactions to the belt-line proposal suggest that their interpretations of how New Orleans's public spaces should be produced, and who should control those spaces, differed from those of local commercial elites. With the belt line's location up for grabs, New

Orleanians confronted the perils of industrialism, spreading throughout the city's public spaces. For instance, homeowners on Louisiana Avenue, a proposed route for the line, demonstrated, clamoring about safety and property values. Claiborne Avenue's residents followed suit, as did Napoleon Avenue's property owners, in a "storm of protest." Nashville Avenue's denizens wasted no time protesting; they simply filed for an injunction to keep the belt line off their street. Confronted with such widespread self-interest, Harrod exclaimed that "there was no street on which the residents would not object to the belt road."[65] Then, with New Orleans splintering into factions, railroad representatives met in April. The corporations supported Corthell's plan, threatening to leave the city if they did not get their way at the waterfront. Finally, in June 1891, Louisiana's supreme court granted the Texas and Pacific its injunction against the city; pending the results of an appeal, the riverfront could not be reclaimed from the railroads.[66] Faced with such obstacles, the belt railway again sank to the bottom of the city's agenda.

Only in 1894 did the issue resurface, when the city council, attempting to broker a deal that would increase its power and influence at the waterfront, passed a belt-line ordinance.[67] But the city's trust in the council had plummeted during the Gilded Age, mirroring trends nationwide, and critics charged that corrupt legislators were behind the ordinance. Elite reformers claimed that the Ring, which had regained power two years earlier when John Fitzpatrick became mayor, had crafted the legislation, and that the council was in the Illinois Central's pocket—a charge that was to prove accurate. Other New Orleanians still complained that the line would lower their property values and make the streets unsafe. With the city in turmoil, on May 21, 1894, two mass protests took place, which the press described as among "the most remarkable incidents in municipal history" and an outpouring of "popular feeling which makes and unmakes the records of the day." At one of the demonstrations, three thousand people gathered uptown as darkness fell, their faces lit by huge bonfires and lanterns strung from the trees bordering St. Charles Avenue. Boisterous groups of protesters carried signs reading: "Defend Your Homes," "We Are Determined," and "Do Better or Get Out." The next day, the chastened council repealed the ill-fated public belt ordinance.[68]

Throughout the summer, controversy surrounding the belt line dominated the news. After the May protests, reformers spent months securing indictments against several council members for their involvement with the Illinois Central. Still, even with the belt railway temporarily discredited, many people remained committed to reclaiming the riverbanks from private corporations. But it was to be two more years before a coalition of city planners, urban professionals, and commercial elites banded together to hatch a plan for reorganizing the waterfront. Until then, railroads continued squabbling with one another and the city for control of the Mississippi's banks.

SEGREGATING SPACE BY USE

While New Orleanians unraveled the mess surrounding the belt line, organized laborers seized the waterfront in the fall of 1894 and spring of 1895. Both years, unions struck, as African-American and white dockworkers struggled for higher wages and more workplace control. In 1895, from March 9 to 13, the waterfront became a battleground, with gangs of armed white workers, hundreds strong, firing shots at rival African-Americans laborers and terrorizing anyone else in the vicinity. Directly across from picturesque Jackson Square, "bullets sang and whistled round the wharf like hail."[69] All told, at least six African-American workers were killed in the melee, while Mayor Fitzpatrick allowed the bloodletting to continue, apparently unwilling to alienate the Ring's white, working-class constituents.[70] Again, the complicated nature of public space had shaped events in the city. As whites and African-Americans struggled for workplace autonomy and better wages, they also had fought for control of the waterfront, eager to demonstrate that they were a legitimate part of the public in the city.

For New Orleans's commercial community, these riots encapsulated all that was wrong in the city. To lose control of the waterfront to the railroads was frustrating; to watch as organized labor set up armed camps along the riverbanks intolerable. But the elites' hands were tied so long as Fitzpatrick's police stood idly by. And so, facing mayhem in the city, Louisiana's governor, Murphy Foster, stepped in. Foster had long been a friend to New Orleans's people of commerce, and on March 13 he ordered the state militia to occupy the levee. For twelve days after that, state troops "kept the peace" next to the Mississippi, while the city's commercial exchanges pledged financial support to underwrite the effort.[71] By the end of the riots of 1895, New Orleans's elites found themselves with more power at the waterfront than they had enjoyed in years. As labor historian Eric Arnesen has noted, the city's unions retreated in the years following the riots, leaving commercial elites ascendant.[72] But other troubling issues also lingered in the city. Even with organized labor quiescent, the waterfront remained a chaotic and contested space. Private railroads still controlled the Mississippi's banks, and charges remained prohibitively high at the Port of New Orleans.

Once again, capitalizing on unrest in the city, elite reformers regained power in the political arena and at the waterfront in 1896. Pointing to debacles like the corrupt belt-line ordinance of 1894 and the riots of 1895, their man, Walter Flower, defeated the machine candidate in the mayoral election. Flower's supporters traded on fear in the city, warning that a class war had come to the waterfront. Racial anxiety also aided their cause, as images of African-American men, rioting next to the Mississippi, haunted New Orleanians who voted for order and a circumscribed and segregated public using and controlling the waterfront. A lawyer and former head of the city's cotton exchange, Flower soon demonstrated his commitment to serving commercial interests, fighting for a number of initiatives that would consolidate power for the city's elites, including shrinking the size of the Ring-dominated council and revamping the Port of New Orleans. And although he and Governor Foster had a chilly relationship, Flower found dedicated allies in the state government when it came to waterfront reform.[73]

In July 1896, the state legislature, at the urging of Flower and New Orleans's businessmen, touched off a comprehensive restructuring of the city's port. The legislators knew that valley traders increasingly avoided the Port of New Orleans, despite the railroads serving the city and the remarkable South Pass jetties. Identifying the port's high prices as the source of the problem, the state created a public administrative body charged with modernizing and overseeing the waterfront. Act 70 of 1896 empowered the newly created Board of Commissioners of the Port of New Orleans—known locally as the Dock Board—to "administer the public wharves," "construct new wharves," and "erect sheds thereon to protect merchandise in transit." The Dock Board was to draw its members from New Orleans's commercial community, so-called experts thought well suited to manage the waterfront and protect the public's interests by maximizing that resource's return for the city—regardless of the consequences.[74]

In creating the Dock Board, the legislature hoped to "expand commerce by removing many of the obstacles...placed in the way of its advancement."[75] Act 70 indicated which "obstacles" the legislators believed had stalled growth and the means by which they hoped to clear those hurdles. First, the legislators consolidated control of the waterfront under a body of elite experts, diminishing the power of organized labor, the railroads, and the Ring. Second, the legislature insisted that the Dock Board construct a network of storage facilities at the waterfront to buffer goods stored there from the extremes of the delta's climate. These sheds would be the culmination of years of wild musings: a mediator between the market and the weather. After their construction, New Orleanians, at last, would have engineered some of the remaining dynamism out of the city's site by regulating the delta's climate. Finally, the legislators attempted to alleviate spatial confusion at the waterfront by instructing the Dock Board to create a complete system there, integrating all of the port's services. In sum, the legislators hoped to impose order at the port— spatial, economic, environmental, and political discipline next to the Mississippi, the enduring dream of the city's commercial community.

Although the Dock Board assumed its duties amid much fanfare in 1896, private interests with a stake at the waterfront challenged Act 70's constitutionality, treating the board's members like claim-jumpers. Then, even after Louisiana's courts legitimated the Dock Board's authority, the commissioners accomplished little, because years earlier, during the Gilded Age, the city had been convinced that "private individuals can execute almost any kind of work at less cost than if done by the municipal government" and accordingly had leased out the administration of its wharves to a private corporation through May 1901.[76] With the wharves out of reach through the start of the next century, the board admitted that it would have to wait until the leases expired before beginning its real work. In the interim, the commissioners contemplated the best designs for updating the waterfront. The board consulted with shippers, planners, engineers, and architects. After gathering extensive data, the commissioners chose to construct a riverfront landscape based on the most up-to-date ideas about the scientific use of urban space. The new port would be a comprehensive system, with erosion-resistant wharves to thwart the voracious river, a modern switching apparatus to facilitate the exchange of goods, huge commodities elevators to sort produce into saleable units, and a host of massive steel warehouses to render the delta's unpredictable climate comparatively powerless.[77]

With its dependence on expertise and system building, the board's blueprint for the waterfront provides an early example of reform initiatives that were to be dubbed "progressive" in New Orleans.[78] For the Dock Board, efficiency was beautiful; it was modern, the product of professional planning. And the commissioners were certain that the remade port would be a model of efficiency, founded on segregating space into use-based categories. Looking back at the port's history, the board members saw a chaotic, mixed-use space, more hodgepodge than system. Impressed by contemporary time-motion studies and notions about rationalizing urban landscapes, the commissioners thus argued that a single-use space would be easier to regulate, more efficient, and would better serve the public in the city by catering to the demands of commerce. Unlike the state legislators and city council members, however, who only recently had insisted that the private sector could maximize the benefits of public resources like the waterfront, the Dock Board's members argued that trained experts such as themselves were best able to revamp and administer the Port of New Orleans.

Ironically, as the board contemplated how to circumscribe the waterfront's uses and users, it turned to the civil code's riparian servitude, justifying its decisions by arguing that the modernized waterfront would be public because it would be redeemed from the railroads. This rhetoric, too, smacked of progressive reform. Founded in a simple dualism—with a righteous "public," citizens of New Orleans, on one side, and greedy "interests," private corporations becoming ever more bloated in an era of runaway mergers, on the other—such morally righteous language obscured far more than it revealed. The people of New Orleans, divided by race, class, gender, and ethnic differences, among other things, were not a unified lot; they lacked a single vision of the best way to develop and use the waterfront. At the same time, as scholars have demonstrated of many of the era's reformers, the Dock Board, regardless of its claims, would serve business interests in the city.[79] So who was included in the public for whom the waterfront was intended? Certainly not organized labor. But what about people who used the riverbanks for recreation or as a spot to contemplate the city's relationship with the Mississippi? Such questions would have seemed pointless to Dock Board members, who believed that an industrial era demanded urban space segregated by use and that the waterfront should be a landscape dedicated to commerce alone.

In 1901, with the question of how the Dock Board defined the public still unasked and unanswered, workers constructed the first of the proposed storage warehouses, directly across from Jackson Square. That shed, and others like it built later, offered a glimpse of how the city's perceptions of the Mississippi had changed after the Civil War. The warehouses lacked adornment, any effort to beautify otherwise dull buildings occupying space next to the river. This aggressively utilitarian architecture is revealing, because for decades, but especially in the wake of the World's Columbian Exposition, held in Chicago in 1893, landscape ar-

chitects and planners nationwide had attempted to uplift urbanites by
enlivening their surroundings with lush parks, inspiring monuments, and
neoclassical buildings. Then, at the beginning of the twentieth century,
the so-called City Beautiful movement, in which reformers nationwide
had called for comprehensive urban planning, had taken off around the
country. Also during those years, preservationists—accused by some critics of belonging to a wilderness cult—popularized the notion that the
nonhuman world could be valued on its own terms, just as conservationists, committed to science and efficiency, forced business interests to
rethink the ways that they traditionally had used natural resources.[80]

And so, as cities such as Chicago and Manhattan created magnificent
waterfront parks that still serve them, New Orleans was plopping huge
rectangles of steel on the Mississippi's banks. As national-parks advocate John Muir fought to protect streams in the Sierra Nevada, New Orleanians hid the greatest of the nation's rivers behind a row of drab warehouses. Why, as people around the country were getting "back to nature"
or enlisting in an army of urban-environmental reformers, were New Orleanians turning their backs on the Mississippi?[81] The answer is that the
river was not the right kind of nature. Too dynamic, too dirty, too hard
to appreciate, too commercial for too long, the Mississippi did not seem
to have healing or spiritual qualities, and its waterfront was not the sort
of Arcadian landscape favored at the time. In other words, the river, at
least in the eyes of most New Orleanians, was not sublime; they looked
at it in the same way that we might view an interstate highway today.

With enthusiasm for its projects running high in the city, in 1903, the
Dock Board issued a two-million-dollar bond earmarked for port improvements. Flush with the proceeds from that offering, the next year
the board's laborers completed two more warehouses at the waterfront
and began working on ten others that were to "embrace" approximately
seventy-five hundred feet of the riverbanks. When workers completed
those buildings, the board's structures covered more than two linear
miles of the Mississippi's waterfront.[82] The Dock Board had left its mark
on the landscape, and it argued that the new port reasserted the riverfront's public standing. Many New Orleanians agreed. In 1902, a reporter called the Henderson Street shed "the most material improvement
of a public character made on the river in many a year," and "splen-
did."[83] It did not matter to the journalist that the warehouse stood between the city and the river or that it lacked architectural charm. The
Dock Board, he believed, had reclaimed the waterfront from out-of-state

corporations, and its structures, because they smacked of efficiency and promoted commercial growth, were, in their own way, beautiful.

And yet, even as the city celebrated the riverfront's redemption, private railroads still fought to maintain their hold on the Mississippi's banks. As a result, in the shadows cast by the Dock Board's warehouses, disorder claimed space at the waterfront. Trains, traveling without an integrated schedule, menaced the board's laborers, and prices at the port remained high. Reformers consequently realized that their comprehensive system remained incomplete and demanded that the city take a final step in reclaiming the riverfront; they insisted that New Orleans finally build a public belt railroad.

After the corrupt ordinance of 1894, the belt railroad had continued its circuitous path through the city's history. In 1898, belt-line advocates rejoiced when the state supreme court overturned the Texas and Pacific grant, opening a stretch of the waterfront. In 1900, the council passed another belt-line ordinance, but it lacked funds for construction. In 1903, the council granted the New Orleans and San Francisco line—the Frisco—a parcel of the riverfront in exchange for assistance with the belt railroad. But Mayor Paul Capdevielle, who had been elected on a "municipal ownership" platform, vetoed the measure. The council, tired of losing power at the waterfront, then passed the ordinance over his veto, and Capdevielle in turn sued the council. In May 1903, the state supreme court ruled for the defendants. The council went on to grant another piece of the riverfront to the Louisiana Railway and Navigation Company, again in exchange for help with the belt line.[84] Infuriated, Capdevielle turned to the Dock Board for assistance in 1904.

The belt line was a final piece in the puzzle that the Dock Board was assembling at the waterfront. The combined power of the private, out-of-town railroads and the council threatened the board's plans, so, at Capdevielle's urging, the commissioners sued the Frisco, justifying their decision by pointing to the public character of the waterfront, which they ostensibly guarded in their capacities as board members. In its decision, the state supreme court explained that the case boiled down to who had the right to shape the waterfront: the council or the Dock Board? Pointing to Act 70 and the waterfront's public designation, the court ruled for the board, insuring that private railroads would have little to do with the belt line's future. Less than six months later, the council capitulated when it passed an updated ordinance creating a new Public Belt Railroad Commission—composed of members of the city's commercial community—with the Dock Board's approval.[85] The city would finally have its belt line.

On July 1, 1905, the belt-railroad commission celebrated breaking ground at the riverfront. With almost a thousand people gathered beneath one of the Dock Board's warehouses, Mayor Martin Behrman drove the line's "golden spike."[86] Almost immediately, the commission faced off with disgruntled rail interests, unwilling to give up their portions of the waterfront without a fight. Throughout the summer, the Illinois Central (IC) dispatched armed thugs to thwart the belt line's work crews. On August 20, isolated skirmishes erupted into a "war" when the belt line's laborers found the IC's goons at the waterfront, entrenched behind overturned rail cars, waiting to defend their terrain. For a time, "open riot prevailed," until the police began "to arrest every man who tried to interfere."[87] That evening, as Mayor Behrman ate his dinner at home, the IC's superintendent called to find out how long his men would be locked up. Behrman, sending a signal to private rail interests, coolly asked the superintendent why the police had not arrested him as well. Almost fifty of the IC's workers went to jail that day, only to be released after signing a statement guaranteeing no further interference with the belt line's construction.[88] Behrman's message had arrived.

Although controversy still plagued the belt line, construction progressed quickly, and it opened on August 3, 1908.[89] Over a celebratory feast, boasting a heart-rending array of meats—hare, veal, salami, beef, mutton, ham, and turkey—Louisiana's governor, Jared Sanders, hailed the triumphant march of progress in New Orleans. Waxing nostalgic for a lost golden age of natural advantages, Sanders acknowledged that "while there are these great natural outlets, commerce seeks the channel of least resistance." Using rhetoric from the era of steam, he warned that "distance has been practically annihilated, and if New Orleans wished to enjoy its great advantages, man must come to its assistance." Such sentiments resurrected the theme of completing nature's work, lingering from the antebellum era. People would have to finish what the river had started, and in New Orleans, such actions would be undertaken by public-spirited bodies of experts charged with administering the waterfront. The city, Sanders concluded, would still realize its quest for empire because of innovations like the belt line. The following day, under a banner headline reading "PUBLIC BELT RAILROAD FORMALLY OPENED," writers at the *Daily Picayune* noted that New Orleans had finally "realized the dream of years."[90] Less than two years later, the belt line was to traverse more than twelve miles of the riverfront (figure 19). And in 1910, it handled

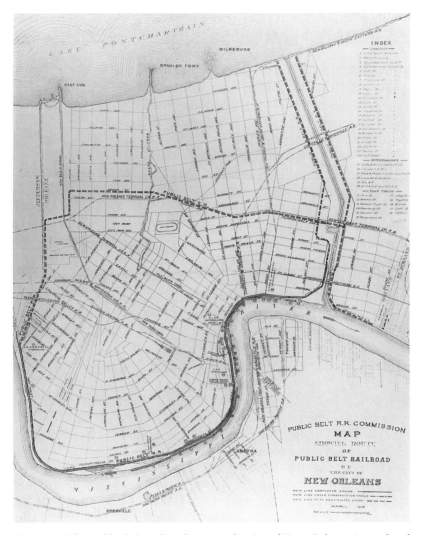

Figure 19. The public belt railroad ringing the city of New Orleans (map dated April 1919). Courtesy of the Special Collections Division, Tulane University.

more than a hundred thousand cars, forming a crucial part of the city's port system.[91]

In that year, federal commissioners visited the waterfront, calling it "the greatest heritage which the people of New Orleans possess" and "the most perfect terminal coordination in the country."[92] The commission included a map of the waterfront in its report. On it, the belt line's tracks lay between the front row of New Orleans's buildings and

the Dock Board's warehouses, like sutures binding the city and port together. Sixteen sheds stood beyond the tracks—covering four linear miles
of the waterfront—like a huge scar. From above, this is what the port
looked like: rails and warehouses linking the city and river.[93] But maps
hide social and political discord, as well as environmental complexity.
They are simplified, rational, typically idealized representations of what
is often much more complicated and messy terrain.[94] On the ground, at
the Crescent City's waterfront, the scene was different; the belt line and
storage warehouses blocked access to the riverbanks, walling New Orleanians off from the river. The waterfront had undergone a sweeping
transition: from an open space, economically inefficient and disorganized, parceled out to private corporations, to a modern, sophisticated
system, a progressive landscape integrated under the control of a single
body of elite experts. Those administrators had produced space rationally, rebuilt dilapidated wharves, and covered the riverbanks with huge
sheds to protect the valley's trade. What impact were their efforts to have
on the city's relationship with the Mississippi? And, regardless of the
Dock Board's claims, would the waterfront be more public or less public than it had been in the past?

WAREHOUSES AS WALLS ON THE WATERFRONT

For years, New Orleans's reformers bragged about their achievements,
justifiably claiming that they had revitalized the city's economy. In 1904,
goods exported at the port had been worth approximately 150 million
dollars and imports a paltry 34 million. By 1922, those numbers had
grown to more than 600 million and 300 million dollars respectively.
Buoyed by the city's improving fortunes, in 1913 Mayor Behrman noted
that "one of the greatest incentives to civic development is found in our
incomparable Public Belt system."[95] Two years later, the Dock Board's
president, Ernest Loeb, concurred, lamenting that "for 200 years, it has
been dreamed that New Orleans would some day be the Metropolis of
the Union and for these 200 years the people of New Orleans have talked
natural advantages but did little else." Loeb argued that his cohort was
different: "Talk has given way to action—action based on scientific
knowledge."[96] For Loeb, progressive ideals had liberated New Orleans
from constraints that corrupt politicians, rapacious corporations, even
the delta's climate and geography had imposed on the city's economy.
The port demonstrated the immense power of rational planning, of science and expertise.

In the years after the port's renovation, commercial reformers gloated not only about economic gains, but also because they had ostensibly returned the waterfront to the public. In 1912, W. B. Thompson, then chair of the belt line, recalled that only recently corporations had monopolized the riverbanks before a new era had dawned. "The great prolific privileges which minister to the needs and make for the prosperity of all the people" he promised, would no longer be "summarily grabbed by the private few." Instead, the waterfront would be "held by the people and operated for the general advancement of trade." Thompson's point was clear: because trade could thrive at the waterfront, that space finally served the public. Linking the public's interests with commerce was nothing new; elites had done the same thing throughout the city's history. What had changed was that such an equation had been institutionalized, built into the waterfront landscape, a "public" space devoted to commerce alone.[97]

So how public was the riverfront? No doubt, as Behrman, Loeb, and Thompson suggested, a booming economy served people throughout the city. Yet the waterfront best represented an elite perspective of urban space: orderly, single-use, and commercial. In contrast, competing interests, including organized labor, found little room to express their views there. For decades, workers had claimed space at the waterfront, using the levee as a platform on which they asserted their status as citizens. By the end of the nineteenth century, however, following events such as the Haymarket riot and the Homestead strike, many Americans associated unions with violent upheavals.[98] New Orleanians were no exception, and few complained as the revitalized waterfront placed the city's dockworkers behind walls, administered under an industrial regimen. Whereas observers had long associated New Orleans with commerce, and commerce with labor at the waterfront, for the first time in the city's history most people could not get to the riverbanks to see either the Mississippi or the workers who toiled there.

Changes in the waterfront's administration also allowed New Orleans's elites to cloak antilabor policies behind public-spirited rhetoric. Dock Board and public-belt-railroad employees became entangled in complicated definitions of the public when they tried to organize or strike at the waterfront after 1910. In 1913, for example, the belt-railroad commission insisted that because it was an agent of the municipal government, a strike by its employees would be a "menace to the public welfare," a position suggesting that somehow its workers were not part of the public in the city. Two years later, the Dock Board informed its laborers that, as an arm of the state, it could not negotiate with unions. Waterfront workers thus found themselves without much of the power they had wielded in recent years. As Eric Arnesen has noted, "an important and dangerous precedent against union labor had been established."[99] Commercial elites had leveraged their control of the port into grounds for union busting, making it clear that if the waterfront was a public space, then organized laborers were not part of the public.

In effect, after more than a century of battles, commercial interests in the city had definitively seized control of the riparian servitude. This became especially clear after a state supreme court decision of 1912 gave the Dock Board broad discretionary powers at the waterfront for the "purpose of maintaining and developing...commerce."[100] Years later, businesspeople pointed to this decision as the one which had "firmly fixed the principle of the servitude upon the river frontage for the purposes and uses of commerce, until at this time the matter is no longer in dispute."[101] Not only had linking the public's interests with those of commerce found spatial representation at the waterfront, but the state supreme court had lodged that principle in judicial precedent as well.

The rebuilt waterfront had an impact not just on laborers, but on all people who hoped to visit the riverbanks. Although the belt railroad eliminated some dangers at the waterfront by coordinating trains there under a single administrative body, crossing the belt line's tracks remained hazardous. At the same time, the port's reorganization turned people who came to promenade next to the river, individuals who might have called themselves tourists in the nineteenth century, into trespassers, misplaced in a space designated not for recreation but for trade alone. In short, the waterfront had become what a scholar of the American landscape, John Stilgoe, calls a "metropolitan corridor," the area abutting railroad rights of way around the nation. Stilgoe notes that these landscapes typically are located on the margins of cities, in out-of-the-way places.[102] And, over time, changes at the port had removed the waterfront from the city's core to its periphery, where few people dared to go unless authorized to do so.

The waterfront's marginalization did not go entirely unnoticed or unchallenged, as some observers mourned the city's new spatial priorities. Upon returning to New Orleans after a long absence, Ernest Peixotto, a former resident, recounted that "the levees that I remember, with their throngs of negroes and whites, their acres of cotton bales baking in the sun; their river packets like floating palaces...all have departed." His memories had been "supplanted in a wave of improvement," by "warehouses that, one after another in endless succession, effectually screen the charming Crescent City that used to string its houses and plazas along the river bank."[103] Other travelers noticed similar trends. After a visit in 1915, Mildred Cram reflected that her hosts had skirted the French Quarter and Mississippi, viewing them as musty antiques. Cram had been aghast when she had found the river flowing hidden behind sheds (figure 20). Disappointed, she huffed that "we spent hours in the steel and concrete warehouses and gazed lovingly at big ships lying like passive Prometheuses while the giant claws of snorting derricks dived into their vitals." She summed up her visit by noting she had been "deafened by the rattle and clamour of commerce."[104] While Cram understood that the port's reorganization had spurred economic growth, she wondered if the new waterfront landscapes represented progress, particularly because the French Quarter had begun a steady decline in the years after the Dock Board had severed the city's link with the river. Reformers, it seemed, had traded the city's unique charms for anonymous efficiency.

So, while most New Orleanians approved of the revamped waterfront, critics such as Peixoto and Cram regretted that the interactions between the city and river, intimate across two hundred years, had evolved into something colder—a business deal. How was it possible that the nation's quintessential river city had cut ties with the Mississippi with so little protest from the people living there? The answer, again, is that reformers had framed the waterfront's modernization in public-spirited terms. But it was equally significant that, at the same time, other spatial developments in the city had abetted the process of revamping the waterfront. In other words, as reformers created the modern waterfront landscape, spatial distractions drew people's attention away from the riverbanks. As a result, the process of disassociating the city from the Mississippi and limiting access to the waterfront drew less attention than it might have otherwise.

Perhaps the most far-reaching of those spatial changes was a modern drainage system built for New Orleans around the turn of the century, as cities nationwide engaged in sanitary reform.[105] From its founding, New Orleans had been bound to the high ground flanking the Mississippi, atop of the river's natural levee, a thin sliver of dry land amid the delta's swamps. Terrain suitable for urban construction had extended less than two miles from the waterfront, to just beyond Claiborne Avenue. After that, the so-called backswamp began, a cypress wetland stretching for miles, interrupted only occasionally by bayou ridges, to Lake Pontchartrain's shore. Throughout the nineteenth century, numer-

Figure 20. The Mississippi, to the left, is walled off from the city by the Dock
Board's sheds and several rows of double track (photograph ca. mid-twentieth
century). Courtesy of the Special Collections Division, Tulane University.

ous efforts at keeping New Orleans dry and reclaiming the backswamp
had failed, leaving much of the city soggy. In 1887, author Charles Dudley Warner had visited New Orleans to write a travel piece. Warner was
stunned by the sight of "open gutters green with slime...in which the
cat became the companion of the crawfish, and the vegetables in decay
sought a current to oblivion."[106] Then, in 1895, sanitary engineers believed that they had devised a plan that would wring the water out of
New Orleans. The backbone of the system would be miles of canals and
multiple sets of huge electric pumps designed to keep water flowing out
of the city at all times. A year later, the state legislature had created the
Drainage Commission of New Orleans—later folded into the Sewerage
and Water Board—to build that system.[107]

By 1914, the drainage system consisted of nearly seventy miles of
canals and seven pumping stations. The next year, reformers noted that
"practically the whole of the 25,000 acres of the City is now available
for development."[108] Growth in assessed property told part of the story

of the expansion. In 1890, the city's tax rolls had included 132 million dollars in property; by 1914 that number had nearly doubled. Mayor Behrman, thrilled by the brimming municipal coffers and caught up in the era's passion for draining wetlands, summed up the system's impact: "land, before worthless, became at once available for agriculture and city development." Amazed by the changes, George Washington Cable, a committed critic of New Orleans, still wrote that "the curtains of swamp forest are totally gone. Their sites are drained dry and covered with miles of gardened homes." In time, builders began including cellars in new structures, features "hitherto unknown in the architectural scheme of New Orleans and never dreamed of in the wildest imaginings of her citizens."[109] Even the dead enjoyed better conditions due to improved drainage. With New Orleans's water table lowered by more than ten feet in places, burials, once nearly impossible in the city's saturated soil, became common. As for the city's relationship with the Mississippi, people moved away from the levee and river. The urbanization of the backswamp, therefore, may have accounted in part for the limited protest surrounding changes taking place at the waterfront.

In those same years, New Orleanians were distracted by other new spaces as well, including a park built on the former site of the Cotton Exposition. Audubon Park, as it was called, served many people who had once promenaded at the waterfront. Unlike the riverbanks, though, it was neatly packaged urban nature, confined within clear boundaries. In short, the park was what one scholar of American culture, Leo Marx, has called a "middle landscape," offering the sanctity of nature and the safety of civilization.[110] And New Orleanians loved it, especially because its designer, John Olmsted (nephew of landscape architect Frederick Law Olmsted), had crafted an "urban Eden" out of what had been an untamed landscape. In 1904, one journalist noted that the park grounds had evolved from an "unkempt pasture overgrown with wild weeds, where no one ever went," into "beautiful gardens, with smooth lawns, clear lakes, and flower beds."[111] Here, in New Orleans, one could find the influence of urban-environmental reform and the City Beautiful movement. Beneath canopies of massive oaks draped with Spanish moss, New Orleanians strolled amid a form of Arcadian nature, benign, romantic, with urbanity cast to its margins. Because of its beauty, the park became a more desirable space than the waterfront; for most observers, the park even seemed to conform more closely to what they thought of as nature.

Like many planned, green spaces that were being constructed around the country at the time, Audubon Park was also an instrument of order.

It offered New Orleanians a healthy recreational environment, "lungs for the city," while assisting in the process of compartmentalizing urban spaces into zones for commerce and recreation, work and residence, nature and culture. At first, the park served as an accidental boundary between the city and river, keeping New Orleanians away from the waterfront, an unintended consequence of spatial reform. In time, though, the park's planners chose actively to separate their "pristine" environment from the industrial activities at the waterfront, planting tall shrubs to serve as "natural" borders, hiding the unsightly belt line's tracks at the park's rear.[112] The waterfront would be the locus of commerce in the city, while the park would offer an antidote for the hardships of urban living. People visiting the park were content to feel far removed from the waterfront, even though they stood only a stone's throw from Mississippi and the city's port.

By the beginning of World War I, the Dock Board's sheds, the belt railroad, and Audubon Park formed obstacles between the city and the river. And the waterfront, which always had been a multiuse open space—market, port, and promenade—was the domain of commerce alone. At the same time, new drainage technologies allowed settlement on terrain that decades earlier had formed part of the city's backswamp. Consequently, few people came into contact with the Mississippi, historically part of their daily lives. Reformers had reclaimed the riverbanks from private railroads and then built walls between the city and river. The result was that the waterfront was both more and less public, depending on one's perspective and priorities, than it had been for half a century, and New Orleans and the Mississippi were farther from each other than ever before. But the Mississippi was soon to reintroduce itself to the city during seasons of catastrophic flooding, again raising questions, still unanswered, about who controlled the riverbanks. Ironically, those floods were in part a product of another progressive spatial reform effected in the city and valley after the Civil War: the construction of massive artificial levees lining the Mississippi.

CHAPTER 5

An Act of God

GOOD FRIDAY

On April 15, 1927, which was Good Friday that year, New Orleans's large Catholic community shuffled through the stations of the cross. Steady rain falling from a dark sky made the holy day seem even more somber than usual, as priests urged their flocks to pray for the Mississippi Valley. Storms had buffeted the region for months, leaving it soaked in one of the worst flood years in history. By January 1, 1927, the valley's soil had saturated and its water tables had filled. The ground could absorb no more precipitation, which then had discharged into the Mississippi system instead. Streams, normally low in their banks so early in the year, had spread out into surrounding flood plains. All winter, heavy snow had fallen in the valley's northlands, blanketing the area from the Alleghenies to the Rockies, while downpours had continued farther south. In early spring, air heavy with moisture had swirled up from the Gulf of Mexico, causing more rain and adding to the flow of the region's already swollen rivers. By Good Friday, more than fifty thousand valley residents had been forced from their homes by raging water, a terrifying statistic with peak flood season still weeks away on the cloudy horizon.[1]

As New Orleanians dropped to their knees on Good Friday, they probably did not think about their own plight. For even as the Mississippi system funneled the valley's flood waters toward them, most New Orleanians believed that they were completely safe behind the massive artificial levee standing sentinel between the city and the rising river—a confidence that soon proved misplaced. Few people in New Orleans realized that sometime the previous night a stray bolt of lightning had struck the central power station that provided the current for the city's vaunted drainage system. Without electricity, the enormous centrifugal pumps keeping the city dry had spun slowly to a halt. Without the pumps working, New Orleans began filling with water.[2]

In part, the city suffered because of its odd topography. For millennia, the Mississippi had left its bed annually, depositing its natural levee with the greatest volume of sediment near its banks, and leaving the adjacent land sloping down, away from the stream. Then, throughout the city's history, people had built the levee up, corralling the Mississippi during its flood stages but also raising it higher above New Orleans. A tourist visiting the city in the late nineteenth century had remarked that "it was a fearful sight to see the vast river, more than a mile wide, rising inch by inch until it reached the top of the levee, when hundreds of ships and steamers were floating far above the level of the streets—as high, indeed as the roofs of the houses in the back streets of town." Another visitor, bemused by the sight of the city lying "lower than the river," had noted that "the situation is strange and dramatic. It stirs the imagination and arouses the interest, and when one thinks of New Orleans, the Mississippi and the stout wall of earth flanking it seem the most vital features of the place."[3] Even today, people are amazed to look up and find an ocean-going vessel, seemingly levitating over the city but actually floating on the Mississippi, its waters high above the surrounding landscape.

By 1927, the levee had grown so tall that a sightseer walking from the river into the city would slowly have descended nearly forty feet of elevation over a mile and three quarters. Except for relatively precipitous terrain immediately adjacent to the river, the grade was so gentle as to seem almost imperceptible. The tourist then would have stood on ground several feet below sea level, and any further hiking would have traversed what had been a wetland—the backswamp—reclaimed by the city's drainage system early in the twentieth century. Finally, after traveling five more miles over nearly flat terrain, the sightseer would have climbed Lake Pontchartrain's levee at the city's rear. Like the river's, Pontchartrain's waters are elevated above New Orleans, held in check only by a levee. In sum, the city resembles a bowl floating in a massive cauldron. Only a rim of raised edges keeps water from flowing into a sunken center (figure 21).[4]

Despite the city's precarious position, river or lake overflows rarely occurred throughout New Orleans's history. Instead, inundations of an-

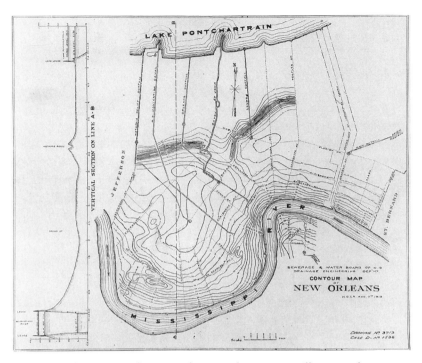

Figure 21. This topographic map of New Orleans (1919) illustrates the recessed terrain at the city's center. The cross section featured on the left side of
the page runs from point A, on the bottom, to point B, on the top. Courtesy of
the Special Collections Division, Tulane University.

other origin plagued locals, due in part to unintended consequences stem-
ming from the city's artificial levees and powerful drainage system. In
most metropolitan areas, rainwater flows out of town, into nearby
streams or bodies of water, but in New Orleans runoff travels away from
the river and lake levees into the recessed terrain between. One guide-
book related that a "stranger is at once struck by the novel sight of the
surface water running from the river." This oddity, coupled with a high
water table—often less than two feet below ground—made flooding a
threat during heavy rains. A frustrated booster noted that "into the New
Orleans area, then, all the water in the world could flow, but not one
gallon could flow out naturally. Nor could it sink into the ground and
so lose itself, because of the height of the water level of the ground."[5]
New Orleans's drainage system, which lifted water over the levees surrounding the city, went far toward alleviating flooding from the gulf
storms that often buffeted the delta. But in the early twentieth century,
by draining the backswamp and paving a great deal of terrain that for-

merly had been wetlands—actions celebrated at the time as the reclamation of wasted land in the city—New Orleanians unwittingly created
the potential for even more catastrophic flooding than in the past. If the
city's drainage system failed, even with the surrounding levees keeping
lake and river water out, a heavy rain could fill the city to its brim.

That was exactly what happened on April 15, 1927. After power out-
ages during the deluge halted the municipal drainage apparatus, storm
water began collecting in New Orleans. The irony of the situation was
lost on people at the time: the levees had been built to keep New Orleans
dry, but without the pumps they helped trap water within the city.
Throughout the day, as heavy rain fell, workers struggled in vain to repair the damaged power station. As the sun went down behind thick
clouds, boats navigated Canal Street, the main thoroughfare of the city's
commercial district. All told, more than fourteen inches of rain fell in
New Orleans on Good Friday—more rain in a single *day* than the city
usually received on average in its wettest *month*.[6]

The downpour's impact in the city was immediate and far-reaching.
New Orleanians had remained calm for months while the upper valley's
residents watched muddy torrents sweep away their homes. Now the city
faced a flood of its own, albeit of a different kind. One local business-
man, L. B. Keiffer, recalled that although the levee remained intact and
the river had not risen appreciably over the course of a single day, the
Good Friday flood caused panic in the city. Keiffer noted that "from the
moment this inundation occurred...people began to realize—they had
never thought before what was staring them in the face, what could happen to us if we really had a flood." New Orleanians, worried that the
river might actually break free of its pen and destroy the city, grew restless behind the levee. In short, the Good Friday flood presented people
with "an actual picture of what would happen...if the levee broke."
Faced with such a terrifying prospect, many of the city's residents began
contemplating the river's unchecked power and human culpability in creating calamities that most New Orleanians had always explained away
as beyond control, as "natural disasters."[7]

For some people in the city, the Good Friday deluge was the first in a
series of events in 1927 that forced them to reexamine flood control policies on the Mississippi system. Although many New Orleanians were
certain that flooding throughout the valley was "natural" or an "act of
God," others, questioning such fatalistic views, eventually learned that
humans—especially engineers, as well as commercial elites and the politicians they influenced—had played an important role in causing the high

water. As a result, after Good Friday, New Orleanians grappled with their role in what was labeled the worst "natural" disaster in U.S. history.[8] The dawning realization that they shared responsibility for creating such a catastrophe shook the city's residents, yielding changes in the ways that they thought about technology, urban space, environmental disasters, and their relationship with the Mississippi River.

Predictably, as New Orleanians contemplated the disaster's origins, they studied the waterfront. Even before the city had flooded, a group of powerful businessmen, local professionals, and city-service commissioners had formed a committee dedicated to averting the impending financial and environmental apocalypse they feared was bearing down on them. On Good Friday, with water hip-deep in the city's streets, that group, later named the Citizens Flood Relief Committee (CFRC), gathered to discuss New Orleans's levee. Marcel Garsaud, the Dock Board's manager, explained that unless a "crevasse" (breach) occurred somewhere upriver, the Mississippi would surpass any flood height on record, and the city's levee would inevitably give way under the strain. Other businesspeople at the meeting, including two local bank presidents, warned that even if the levee somehow survived, the city would be ruined. Already, they complained, investors were pulling out of local markets, consumers were fleeing, shops were closing their doors, and commerce was grinding to a halt.

The committee also discussed the impact that a flood would have on the city's commercial front, including the recently revamped port and public belt railroad. The CFRC's members decided that New Orleans had sunk too much time, energy, and, above all, money into its waterfront to see the river sweep that landscape away. The waterfront, which belonged to the public, would have to be protected at all costs. New Orleans's investment, which happened to serve the city's commercial community, including several people attending the meeting, was too great to be sacrificed to the Mississippi. After reaching consensus, the committee's members resolved to pursue a drastic solution: they would sponsor the destruction of the levee roughly twelve miles downstream, creating a man-made crevasse to relieve pressure along the city's waterfront.[9]

LEVEES-ONLY

In New Orleans the levee is more than just a barrier protecting the city from river flooding; it is a municipal icon and symbolic landscape, embodying countless battles against a dynamic urban-riparian environment.

Inextricably woven into New Orleans's history and urban fabric, it provided the foundation on which the city was built, when French colonists constructed a colonial outpost on high ground provided by the river's natural levee. Then, after the Mississippi flooded repeatedly in the city's early years, New Orleanians augmented the natural levee, confining the river behind a low earthen wall. By 1727, an artificial embankment, eighteen feet wide and a yard high, stretched for approximately one mile fronting the city. Later, throughout the colonial period, people further improved the levee until, just after the Louisiana Purchase, it snaked from north of Baton Rouge to south of New Orleans.[10]

In the antebellum era of the city's American period, although the levee continued growing, it was steeped in controversy, like all features of the waterfront landscape. Recriminations followed most floods, with people wondering what had caused the levee's failures.[11] Often, the culprit was development throughout the Mississippi Valley. Every stand of trees cleared for agriculture or acre of grassland paved for urban expansion channeled more water into the Mississippi system, increasing the likelihood of floods. In other words, not only trade knit the distant reaches of the valley together, but ecology did so as well. In time, New Orleanians recognized that local oversight of a regional problem made little sense. They argued that Congress should construct levees with federal funds, employing key words to frame river improvements as a national issue. Lobbyists described the Mississippi system as an "inland sea" vital for "interstate commerce." More, wider, and higher, they cried, regarding the levees, hoping to reach distant ears in Washington.[12]

New Orleanians did not get their wish until after the Mississippi flooded in 1849. In that year, the levee just upriver from the city gave out, at the Sauve plantation. Water and mud flowed into New Orleans, drenching more than two hundred city blocks for weeks and driving twelve thousand people from their homes. The calamity captured national attention. And in its wake, Congress passed the Swamp Land Act of 1850, offering valley states immense tracts of wetlands in exchange for guarantees that they would reclaim the terrain by building levees to keep the Mississippi system contained and under control.[13] At the same time, the federal government commissioned two surveys of the Mississippi to provide guidance in formulating future flood control policy, one undertaken by an army engineer, Andrew Humphreys, the other by a civilian, Charles Ellet.

Although the Swamp Land Act had little impact on New Orleans's levees, the two river surveys were to help reshape the city's waterfront in the future. In 1850, Ellet published his *Report on the Overflows of the Delta of the Mississippi River.*[14] His findings, though impressionistic, were nonetheless breathtaking, particularly his recognition that humans had exacerbated the Mississippi's inundations by confining floodwaters behind levees. In highlighting people's ability to alter the environment, Ellet presaged the work of George Perkins Marsh, who was to publish *Man and Nature* fourteen years later. Marsh is hailed as one of the first modern environmentalists, because he recognized that humans had an impact on processes previously labeled natural.[15] But Ellet arrived at such findings first, writing that "the difficulty in protecting the delta from overflow is produced by the artificial embankments along the borders of the Mississippi, and the cultivation of the praeries."[16] In short, levees and development could be hazardous; they could shape the Mississippi's behavior.

The solution to flooding was relatively simple, in Ellet's opinion: to balance changes made by settlers in the valley's land- and waterscapes, engineers needed to mimic the river and "nature" by implementing a multitiered flood-control plan. Such a plan should include "higher and stronger levees," outlets, or spillways, to shunt floods from the trunk stream, enlarged distributaries along the lower river, and huge reservoirs to keep rain water from running off into the system.[17] Flood-control engineers adopted few of Ellet's revolutionary concepts until long after his death, in large measure because he was so far ahead of his time in recognizing the futility of trying to control the river without accounting for the impact that humans had on the environment.

Policy makers spurned Ellet for another reason as well: when Humphreys finished his survey (co-authored with H. L. Abbot)—known as *Physics and Hydraulics*—in 1861 he savaged the civilian engineer's credibility. In an era marked by a growing faith in the power of data, Humphreys, a proud empiricist, loathed Ellet's intuitive style. The civilian's good reputation also threatened Humphreys's beloved Army Corps of Engineers, as West Point was losing its standing as one of the profession's few domestic training schools. As a result, Humphreys rebutted almost all of his rival's conclusions, arguing that reservoirs were "chimerical" and outlets "disastrous." He scoffed at augmenting distributaries, worrying, presciently, that the Mississippi might be captured by a smaller stream. With outlets, reservoirs, and distributaries ruled out, Humphreys left himself only levees. Accordingly, he argued that "an organized levee system must be depended upon for the protection against floods in the Mississippi valley." Levees alone, he claimed, "may be relied upon for protecting all the alluvial bottom lands liable to inundation."[18]

Humphreys's findings exemplified what environmental historian Donald Worster, writing about the history of ecological ideas, labels an "imperial" approach to nature. In Worster's telling, the emergence of a Darwinian worldview, with its emphasis on competition and extinction, caused many scientists to reevaluate the natural world, calling for a liberal application of the ostensibly civilizing influence that humans had on their surroundings. For engineers working in the United States, this imperial view not only typified their intellectual culture but also served their professional interests. As one historian of engineering has written, "their reputations depended on the utilization of nature, rather than its glorification."[19] And as Americans increasingly looked to engineers to mediate between people and their surroundings—to control nature, in other words—the profession's prestige grew. Consequently, Humphreys gained enormous authority not only because he promised that military engineers could solve the problem of river flooding, but also because of the empirical foundation on which he rested his claims. His survey of the delta acted as a kind of inventory of the unknown in an era obsessed with discovery, and thus provided him with the imprimatur of science and reason, leaving Ellet an afterthought at the time.[20]

Without a doubt, Humphreys's advocacy of levees-only proved influential. After ascending to chief of the Army Corps of Engineers, Humphreys dispatched proponents of other flood-control initiatives from his lofty post. Because of his vigilance, scholars have demonized him as the most important, sometimes even the lone, architect of the valley's levees, a brilliant man who grew bitter and power-mad, wielding his office's prerogatives with venom and impunity.[21] Although there is much truth in this perspective, other factors contributed to the rise of the enormous levees on the river system, including the role played by James Eads—often glorified as a hero in the valley's mythology—and the power of local political and economic interests consistently pushing for levees, even as the floods they faced rose higher each year.

Humphreys retired almost immediately after Congress created the Mississippi River Commission (MRC) in 1879, because that body diminished the power of military engineers, while Eads, flush with his jetties' success, joined the commission and became an important proponent of levees-only. In 1880, the MRC's annual report reflected Eads's influence, suggesting that levees, like jetties, deepened the river's channel, thus lowering flood heights on the Mississippi.[22] The next year, after several commission members disavowed those findings, Eads apparently pitched a fit, refusing to sign the commission's annual report and publishing a document of his own explaining the benefits of levees-only.[23] Two years later, Eads silenced all dissent when the MRC's report stated unequivocally: "It is obvious that for secure protection of the valley from overflow there is necessary a system of levees high and strong enough to withstand the greatest flood. *No other means of protection is practicable or even possible.*"[24]

So, as an era of federally sponsored flood control on the Mississippi dawned, the men who shaped that policy pushed for levees-only. Their position reflected the day's reverence for science and technologies promising to control the river. Eads, for example, had once explained that "what I know of the Mississippi are facts, and facts are the uncut jewels which grind false theories to powder."[25] Had Humphreys not made a career of disagreeing with civilian engineers, he would have appreciated such faith in the power of objective observation. Only Ellet might have demurred, warning his colleagues about the dangers of overconfidence as he reviewed the consequences of human action on the river. But Ellet's day would not come for decades.

Despite Humphreys's and Eads's support, levees-only was not just a case of elite engineers handing down public policy from above. The actions of New Orleans's municipal government and commercial community, consistently demanding levees, debunked such a top-down analysis. Even in 1871—after a crevasse just north of the city, at Bonnet Carré (pronounced "bonney carrey"), indicated that spillways could lower floods when the river dropped quickly after the breach opened—New Orleanians still called for more levees. Economics and spatial politics girded their stance. Levees were easier and far cheaper to construct than spillways and huge reservoirs, which required that the city or state acquire and set aside vast tracts of land for inundation. Both alternatives were costly and angered proponents of private-property rights and apostles of progress who viewed undeveloped land as a wasted commodity.[26] Levees, meanwhile, were cost-efficient, provided tangible evidence of improvement, enjoyed the MRC's support, and used relatively small quantities of land.

Local interests working with the MRC soon revamped New Orleans's waterfront. With the MRC serving as a technical clearinghouse and providing two-thirds of the construction costs, the levee reached new heights. Then, at the nineteenth century's end, uncoordinated efforts in New Orleans that were geared toward imposing order along the riverbanks fused into comprehensive planning, rooted in the city's commercial ideology. Starting in 1890, the city's flood control fell under the rubric of the newly formed Orleans Levee District, a progressive organization created during the reform era that saw the Dock and Drainage Boards established. The so-called Levee Board also drew members from within the ranks of the city's commercial community, placing power in the hands of "experts" charged with guarding an undefined public's interests. Within two years, the board had brought much of the city's levee up to the MRC's exacting standards: rising three feet above any flood on record, four to ten feet across at the crown, and between six and seven times as wide as that at the base (figure 22). Workers also had built almost five linear miles of new levees. All told, laborers had added more than five hundred thousand cubic yards of earth to the levees, an incredible amount of material, but just a few clods of dirt compared to the construction that followed.[27]

Although the levees-only policy enjoyed broad local support, the works themselves were sometimes controversial additions to the waterfront, demonstrating that environmental hazards can become social problems when they undermine powerful human institutions, such as property rights. Throughout the first half of the 1890s, riparian proprietors, concerned about their land values, filed numerous suits against the Orleans Levee Board. The state courts, after deliberating, typically held for the board's right to build on the city's waterfront.[28] These decisions mirrored other legal rulings of the period, in which the judiciary found for the state's right to seize property and build public works on the riverbanks, such as the warehouses for the revamped Port of New Orleans. The full extent of the Levee Board's power, however, remained unclear until the U.S. Supreme Court ruled on the case *Eldridge v. Trezevant* in 1896. With its decision in *Eldridge,* the court fleshed out the law of takings in Louisiana, delineating the rights of riparian proprietors and the levee boards throughout the state.

The dispute began when William Eldridge tried to stop municipal workers from building a levee on his property. After local judges rejected his plea, Eldridge appealed to the U.S. Supreme Court, which ruled on how the Orleans Levee Board could acquire land for its works. The question of takings is complicated nationwide, but nowhere more so than in Louisiana. The most common method of seizing property in the United States is expropriation via eminent domain, which carries a burden of payment on the state's part. In Louisiana, though, another method exists: appropriation, which has no such burden because of the civil law's riparian servitude.[29] As one legal scholar has noted, by the nineteenth

Figure 22. Pedestrians atop the artificial levee, as tall as the neighboring rooftops (photograph dated 1899). Courtesy of The Historic New Orleans Collection.

century's end, the servitude's significance lay "in the powers that it" granted "the state and its political subdivisions to regulate the public use of the banks, and to appropriate the banks for themselves for the construction of works serving the general interest."[30] The state then saw levee building as an ideal application of the servitude, while Eldridge thought his property rights were being buried under an earthen embankment.

In January 1896, the court denied Eldridge's appeal, stating that in Louisiana, "the provisions of the Fourteenth Amendment of the Constitution do not override public rights, existing in the form of servitudes."[31] In other words, the court ruled that levee construction constituted an appropriate extension of the public's rights at the waterfront, as guaranteed by the civil law's riparian servitude. The decision's significance was staggering: the state could take property without compensating riparian land owners, making levees even cheaper and more

enticing than ever before in Louisiana. Eventually, the state began offering riparian proprietors in New Orleans, where waterfront land had
enormous value, an ambiguous "right of action" against the levee
board, but in the meantime, the Orleans Levee Board enjoyed a moment
of free rein at the waterfront, and it celebrated by going on a building
binge.[32]

The *Eldridge* decision sealed the city's Faustian bargain with the levees-only policy. The embankment eventually grew into a monument to
Eads, Humphreys, legislators and local interests sympathetic to the policy, and the justices who had ruled on *Eldridge*. From 1892 to 1896 the
Levee Board added more than one million cubic yards of earth to the
levee, leaving New Orleans looking like a walled village, barricaded
against impending invasion. Then, after 1907, the board began using
mechanical earth-moving equipment, cutting construction costs by more
than 50 percent. Over the next twenty years, the board's workers added
almost fifteen million more cubic yards of earth to the artificial embankment. New Orleans's levee, once elevated only three feet above the
adjacent terrain, towered over the city that it ostensibly protected.[33]

Strangely, as the levee grew the river kept rising just enough to over-
top its banks during flood stages. Flood assessment on the lower Mississippi is based on two features: height, a measurement calibrated to a
scale known as Cairo datum, which refers to the mean level of the Gulf
of Mexico at Biloxi, Mississippi; and volume, the cubic feet per second
of water in the river's channel. Flood readings are taken at gauges at numerous spots along the Mississippi, including one at the Carrollton river-
bend in uptown New Orleans, where St. Charles Avenue runs into Carrollton Avenue, in the shadow of the levee. In 1897, with the city's levees
newly improved, the river climbed more than a foot and a half feet higher
than ever before. To proponents of levees-only in New Orleans, advocates with an ironclad faith in technology and human efficacy, the high
water proved only one thing: the city required larger and taller levees
"that will remain impregnable against any flood."[34] If the river had
reached new heights, these people reasoned, the levees would have to be
built up as well to protect New Orleans.

During an era of progressive reform in the city, many New Orleanians believed that experts could solve any environmental problem, including flooding. After all, the city was still enthralled by the triumph of
Eads's jetties, the reclamation of the backswamp, and the modernization
of the port. So, while skeptics echoed Ellet's warning that levees raised
the river, most people considered such a view defeatist.[35] As floods rose,

engineers insisted that levees-only promised a future in which "the protection against overflow will be perfect." Smith Leach, an Army Corps
of Engineers officer, summed up such hubris in his article "The Mississippi River—What It Needs and Why It Needs It." He explained that
"what nature has failed to do, and what remains for man to accomplish
in order to fit the Mississippi river to his wants and uses, is summed up
in one word, control." Even after the 1903 flood broke records on the
river gauges, Louisiana's chief engineer insisted that "the greatest need
of the levees...is enlargement."[36] The levee had become a landscape
demonstrating people's apparent dominion over the river; to turn away
from it would be admitting defeat in a centuries-old battle with the delta's
dynamic environment.

In this context, New Orleans built up its levee, despite mounting evidence linking the bulwark to increasing flood heights. For instance, in
the springs of 1912 and 1913 the river set new high-water marks on its
gauges, before smashing levees upstream of the city. Canny observers
noted an odd and disturbing feature of the floods in those years: their
volume had been smaller than past inundations whose heights had been
much lower. This combination of diminished volume and greater height
unnerved some New Orleanians who had steadfastly supported the
levees-only policy through the years. In 1913, George Maxwell, director of the National Reclamation Society, a flood-control reform organization in the city, warned that "the levee system alone, supplemented by
nothing else, never has been a safeguard and never will."[37] But bureau-
cratic inertia on the part of the Corps, MRC, and Congress proved too
powerful to overcome. Unmoved by growing unrest about the levees-
only policy, the federal government based a sweeping flood-control act
in 1917 entirely on that ill-conceived policy.[38]

In 1922, another flood reached new heights on the river gauges, raising still more questions about the levees-only policy (figure 23). On April
14 of that year, the river climbed over the twenty-one-foot mark at the
Carrollton gauge. Two weeks later, the levee twelve miles downstream
of the city, at Poydras, gave way. The Mississippi rushed through the crevasse, relieving pressure on the city's levee. As a result, New Orleans
stayed dry during the flood, but the reasons why highlighted problems
with levees-only. To a growing coalition of spillway advocates, it seemed
clear that confining floods within levees raised the river, ultimately causing more catastrophic inundations than in the past. Outlets of any kind,
such as the one created at Poydras, could relieve pressure on the levees
and lower flood heights. Organizations such as the Safe River Commit-

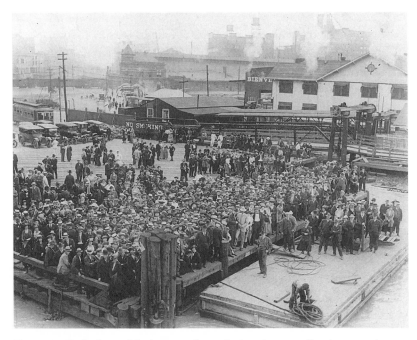

Figure 23. Onlookers visit the waterfront during the 1922 flood, measuring the high water as it laps against the top of the levee. Courtesy of the Louisiana State Museum.

tee of 100 formed in New Orleans, arguing that the episode at Poydras had proven that levees exacerbated flooding on the river, a problem only spillways could solve.[39]

To these reformers, it appeared that Ellet had been right. New Orleans faced increasingly grave danger, as runoff from throughout the valley, flowing into the Mississippi system and confined behind levees, roared toward the city each spring. Once again, though, Congress, influenced by levees-only lobbyists, ignored history and the Poydras crevasse when it passed another flood-control act in 1923, based exclusively on a program of levee building. The following year, the MRC reiterated its intractability on the subject in its annual report, blindly insisting that "levees afford the only practicable means for flood control in the lower Mississippi Valley."[40] With that, the MRC proved that its policies had not shifted over the course of more than thirty years, three decades in which the levees flanking the Mississippi had grown taller each year, while flood heights on the river had also steadily climbed. The stage was set for the events that unfolded, beginning in New Orleans on Good Friday, 1927.

THE CITIZENS FLOOD RELIEF COMMITTEE

By 1927, most New Orleanians took the levee for granted. It had always been a part of the city's landscape, and it seemed that if the Levee Board, the MRC, the Corps, and Congress had their way, it would be a fixture at the waterfront in the future. After the 1927 flood, one longtime resident of the city proudly recalled, "I was born in the State of Louisiana back of these levees, and in my boyhood I could get on my Shetland pony and see over the levees." But things had changed: "to-day I would have to get on top of the roof of the very home where I lived as a boy to see over the levees." The protective embankments, he suggested, had become "miniature mountains."[41]

His words suggest that some New Orleanians had naturalized the artificial levee by 1927, that it had become such an accepted part of the waterfront that observers could almost believe that it predated human settlement of the region. This reading of the landscape made sense for a number of reasons. It served the Orleans Levee Board's interests if New Orleanians saw the embankment as natural, rather than as a human artifact whose failings could be blamed on its sponsors. To encourage this perception, the board had planted grass along the levee, lending it the look of an uninterrupted hill ringing the city. Additionally, the levee had grown so large by 1927 that it seemed fixed in space, looming high above its surroundings. It was by far the most prominent topographical feature in the city. And as the levee had grown more massive physically, its presence had become deeply ingrained in the minds of those who saw it, a crucial point of reference on many New Orleanians' cognitive maps, often at the expense of the Mississippi flowing behind. In large measure this was a function of the levee's scale. As it rose higher (as shown in figure 24), it became the greatest obstruction standing between the city and river.

Because of its size, onlookers at the waterfront often saw just the levee; to view the river required climbing the embankment. A tourist named John Hammond recalled his first sight of the levee, when, overwhelmed by the size of the rampart, he momentarily forgot that the Mississippi flowed behind. "There towered before me a great mound of earth that somehow made me think of the Pyramids," he wrote. Only after he "ascended a long incline in the half light of evening" did Hammond recall the river's presence. "After reaching the top," he noted, "suddenly there came to my view the muddy waters of the Mississippi." The scene shifted: "The city lay back of me, far beneath the level of the mighty river

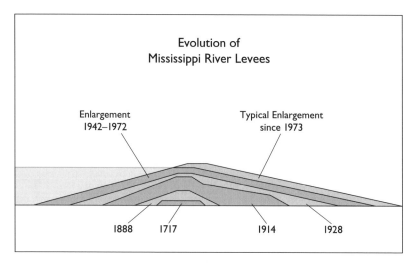

Figure 24. This scale of levee heights offers a sense of the embankment's evolution, from small mound to massive rampart. Adapted from scale courtesy of the U.S. Army Corps of Engineers, New Orleans District.

upon whose brink I stood. It seemed so easy for the river to dash away the barrier of earth, imposing as that had seemed a few minutes ago."[42] By 1927, most observers believed that the levee had become an impregnable border separating the river and city; only those who scaled the embankment were reminded of the river's power. Then, the Good Friday flood offered all New Orleanians such a glimpse.

In the weeks leading to the Good Friday flood, members of the city's commercial community had conspired to maintain confidence in the levee by squashing news of the flooding upriver. Their actions serve as a frightening reminder of the epidemic of 1853, when elites in the city had engaged in similar behavior in the name of the public's interests, which they had equated with commercial advance. In both cases, censors, downplaying environmental hazards, exposed New Orleanians to grave danger to protect business interests in the city. In March and early April 1927, Isaac Cline, the meteorologist who headed the U.S. Weather Bureau office in New Orleans, had distributed flood warnings to the press: "PLEASE POST THIS WARNING TO RECEIVE THE WIDEST POSSIBLE NOTICE." Cline's strident tone emerged out of an intimate personal history with floods. He had been in charge of the weather bureau in Galveston, Texas, in 1900, when a devastating hurricane had hit the city, bringing with it a storm surge that had killed at least three thousand people, including his wife.[43]

Because of his experience with disaster, Cline was infuriated when the press ignored him in 1927. On Thursday, April 14, he sent a dramatic dispatch to the city papers, warning that "recent heavy and frequent rains over the middle Mississippi valley and western tributaries have augmented the flood waters and increased the seriousness of the situation. If the levees hold, the stages of 1922 will be exceeded along the Mississippi below Vicksburg." When he received no response even to that dire report, Cline demanded answers from the local press corps. A group of reporters admitted that a propaganda committee, rooted in the city's commercial community, was working to keep news of the flood out of the papers. Enraged, Cline excoriated the journalists, noting that "the greatest flood in history is approaching and your action is suppressing flood information and warnings."[44] His rage accomplished little. Once again, New Orleans's commercial community had taken it upon itself to decide the public's best interests, choosing to expose people to environmental danger rather than allowing trade to be slowed.

The next day, as water gathered in the streets, the members of the Citizens Flood Relief Committee realized that to convince people that the city's levee would hold, the embankment downstream, near Poydras, would have to go. Their strategy was based on precedent; New Orleans had long built its levees higher than its poorer neighbors could afford. Following the floods of 1912 and 1913, one local advocate of spillways had sheepishly admitted as much. "The city," he said then, "has maintained a differential of safety in the matter of flood control by reason of the fact that concentrated wealth there enables it to build and maintain stronger and better levees than any other section of the valley." The result was that "when large floods come, some other levees go before the strain on our levees reaches the maximum."[45] In 1927, however, the CFRC's members could not afford to wait for that likely eventuality. In part, they feared that before the levee failed elsewhere, the city's economy would already have faltered. They also worried that if the levees did not break elsewhere and failed in the city—regardless of how unlikely that might be—New Orleans would never recover from the disaster.

The CFRC's decision to destroy the levee at Poydras was a revolutionary act. That a local ad-hoc committee with no formal ties to Louisiana's political structure tried to reverse federal policy without seeking public approval demonstrated the self-conscious power of New Orleans's commercial community. The CFRC held no referendum or hearing to discuss its decision, which was to have consequences not only in the city, but in Plaquemines and St. Bernard parishes. For if the levee were dynamited at Poydras, those so-called river parishes would be flooded. And although they were sparsely settled—the vast majority of the area was made up of interconnected wetlands—there were towns there, including Arabi, home to stockyards and a sugar refinery employing thousands of workers.[46] Farther south, in the marsh, lay the nation's richest fur-producing regions. Countless people made their living off the land in those wetlands, either trapping or fishing. Demolishing the levee at Poydras would destroy Arabi, the region's muskrat and fish stocks, as well as the levees-only policy. Yet, following the CFRC's decision, its members spent little time contemplating such outcomes; they focused instead on marshaling the support needed to achieve their goal.

After the CFRC met on Good Friday, Garsaud and New Orleans's mayor, Arthur O'Keefe, asked the MRC for permission to dynamite the levee. At first, they received a chilly reception, likely because they were suggesting that the MRC jettison decades of policy and admit culpability in raising the river. And yet, the Mississippi was impossibly swollen, and the MRC knew that it was not a question of *if* the levee would fail but *where* and *when*. If the breach happened in New Orleans, one of Louisiana's congressmen later suggested, it would have been "an interesting sight for those who love to picture to themselves the flames of hell."[47] So, although the MRC's members believed that it was unlikely that the levee would fail in the city, the question remained: could they take that gamble? Deciding that the answer was no, they hedged their bets by insisting that the CFRC also secure approval from the War Department and the State of Louisiana as well as promise compensation for the proposed artificial crevasse's victims. Elated, Garsaud and O'Keefe accepted the conditions.[48]

Meanwhile, events unfolding upriver added to the sense of dread in the city. On April 19 and 20, storms dumped still more rain on the valley. Then, the levee at Mound Landing, Mississippi, gave way, releasing the engorged river. Water did not surge from the crevasse, as images of the Johnstown Flood might suggest. Instead, the river spread from the gap slowly, at approximately fourteen miles per hour. Despite its languid pace, the unleashed flood had immense power. One account relates that the water gouged a trough a hundred feet deep into the soil and that the flood's volume was 470,000 cubic feet per second—more than double Niagara Falls'. Soon an area fifty miles wide and a hundred miles long lay under twenty feet of water.[49] The crevasse could have relieved New Orleanians had the flood found an outlet to the gulf other than the Mississippi. But no such outlet existed, and because the delta's soil was too saturated to absorb much water, the torrent ran off into the river system, flowing again toward the city.

If the Good Friday flood had caused panic in the city, headlines on April 22—the day after the Mound Landing crevasse—pushed many New Orleanians beyond their breaking point. That day, the *Times Picayune* offered its first extensive coverage of the flood, drowning the press's code of silence beneath breaking waves of sensational descriptions and images. With news from Mound Landing splashed all over the city's papers, more than twenty thousand locals began reinforcing the levee between Baton Rouge and New Orleans (figure 25). Armed foremen patrolled communities adjacent to the embankment, impressing able-bodied men into service if they had no proof that they held other jobs.[50] Back inside the city, a correspondent from the Associated Press explained that "the assurance that the flood could not reach the city had disappeared and anxiety had taken its place. Every unusual steamboat whistle in the harbor sounded like the dreaded four long blasts which means the levee has given way."[51]

As the AP reporter indicated, one by-product of the mood in New Orleans was that the waterfront reemerged as a much-discussed public space, crowded with anxious residents of the city, all keeping close tabs on the rising Mississippi. With a river flood apparently threatening their homes, New Orleanians, as they had throughout the city's history at such times, reconnected with the Mississippi, long hidden behind railroad tracks, the Dock Board's warehouses, and the massive levee. In his memoir of the flood, Lyle Saxon recalled that "going down to the levees became the great civic enterprise. All day long, especially during the lunch hour and in the evenings, it looked as if half the cars in town were parked along the city's river front, and the levees were so thronged that it finally became necessary to station armed guards in the most accessible spots."[52] For the first time in decades, a cross section of the city's population congregated near the Mississippi, pondering its relationship with the river.

The waterfront gatherings in 1927 shed light on how the production of space in the city and people's perceptions of the river sometimes intersected, often reinforcing each other. For decades leading up to the great flood, New Orleanians had found the riverbanks nearly inaccessible because of the growing artificial levee and the commercial structures standing there. From the end of Reconstruction through 1927, the Mississippi had flowed by the city, effectively walled off from its residents. Except during periods of unusually high water, many New Orleanians had forgotten the Mississippi's significance in those years, only to be re-

Figure 25. African-Americans, forced to improve the levee during the 1927
flood, as overseers look on. Courtesy of the U.S. Army Corps of Engineers,
New Orleans District.

minded of its power when they returned to the waterfront to find the
river straining against the levee, threatening the city.

Even as New Orleanians became fascinated by the spectacle of impending disaster on display at the riverfront, the CFRC's members
wasted no time gazing at the river; they were far too busy trying to meet
the Mississippi River Commission's conditions. With water spreading
through the Mound Landing crevasse, James Thomson, a CFRC delegate in Washington, met with Secretary of War Dwight Davis, Chief of
the Army Corps of Engineers Edgar Jadwin, and President Calvin
Coolidge. Thomson made an impassioned plea, hoping to win support
for the CFRC's plan. Each man, though, uneasy about abandoning the
levees-only policy and aware of the chaos that would ensue in the river
parishes, remained skeptical. They wondered if such a drastic measure
would be needed if the levee failed again above New Orleans. None of
the three, however, ruled out the CFRC's request, and that was enough
for Thomson, who returned to the city.[53]

Not all the news was so positive for the CFRC. On April 23,
Louisiana's governor, Oramel Simpson, also expressed reservations about
whether the river parishes should be destroyed. In effect, the CFRC was
asking Simpson to choose between his constituents, to determine where

the more worthy portion of the public resided, in the city or the countryside. Although he hoped to protect New Orleans's residents and vulnerable commercial front, Simpson wondered aloud if the upstream levees would hold, suggesting that the city might be safe long before it became necessary to demolish the embankment, and with it the river parishes. The next morning, Isaac Cline's prediction, finally a fixture in the papers, suggested that Simpson was likely right to be so skeptical. Cline noted that the city would face peril only if the levees held upriver, an unlikely turn of events in his estimation. The CFRC faced a crisis. If Simpson did not capitulate, all was lost. He had to be convinced to choose the CFRC's version of the public's welfare over any broader definition that he may have held. So on April 24, the CFRC lured Simpson to New Orleans, aware that he would agree to destroy the levee only after receiving word from an engineer saying that such a course was necessary, a legal brief assuring him that he had the right to make the decision, and a written guarantee that the city would fully compensate the planned crevasse's victims.[54]

When the governor arrived in New Orleans on Monday, April 25, the CFRC's members spirited him to a meeting where H. Generes Dufour, a prominent local attorney serving on the committee, reassured Simpson that he had the authority to sanction the levee's destruction. Next, George Schoenberger, Louisiana's chief engineer, and John Klorer, the commissioner of public property and a longtime advocate of spillways, made their pitch for dynamiting the levee. Finally, Dufour produced a telegram from Charles Potter, the head of the MRC, stating that Simpson should decide where he wished to cut the levee, convey his decision to the MRC, and expect quick approval. The group then made its way to a larger meeting next door, where the state attorney general, Percy Saint, promised Simpson that he had the "police power to act in an emergency of this character." Saint then explained that he believed that it was the governor's "duty . . . to sacrifice a small percentage of the property value of the State in order to safeguard and protect greater interests."[55] In other words, Saint, like the CFRC, had decided that the city and its commercial community merited more protection than the people of the river parishes. This stand revealed that while the artificial crevasse's proponents based their definitions of the public's interests in part on numbers—population and economic productivity—apparently they also were considering questions of social class.

Simpson then turned the floor over to two rebuttal witnesses, Simon Leopold and John Dymond, representatives from the river parishes. Per-

haps never in the nation's history had the interests of city and countryside clashed so clearly. On one side of the dispute stood New Orleanians, embodying classic images of American urban life, dating back at
least to Thomas Jefferson's era, including wealth, power, and deca-
dence.[56] New Orleanians were all too willing to sacrifice their rural
neighbors to protect the city's interests, which, the urbanites argued, really were the state's or public's interests. On the other side of the conflict
stood the representatives of the river parishes, the ostensibly virtuous
and humble countryside, where thrift and hard work formed the community's bedrock. After steeling themselves, Leopold and Dymond suggested that if destroying a section of the levee proved necessary, it would
be best to make the cut *above* the city, allowing the released water to
flow harmlessly into Lake Pontchartrain. In sum, the two men appealed
to the CFRC's better angels, asking the New Orleanians not to be short-
sighted. They hoped that the committee would look beyond 1922, when
the Poydras crevasse had relieved pressure on the city's levees, and instead focus on 1871, when a crevasse at Bonnet Carré, upstream from
the city, had yielded a similar outcome.[57]

Sadly for the river parishes, the CFRC was not looking only for results, but for a spectacle. If the committee had hoped just to relieve pressure on the city's levees, an upriver cut would have fit the bill. The CFRC,
however, needed to inspire confidence locally and nationwide that New
Orleans was safe and ready for business. A crevasse upstream, therefore,
risked enhancing doubts about whether the flood waters would flow into
the city, disrupting business. A crevasse downstream of New Orleans,
on the other hand, would reassure interested observers around the country that the city had weathered another major flood, dry and eager for
investment. Leopold and Dymond quickly realized their plight and
changed course midstream, asking only that the CFRC guarantee repa-
rations for the proposed crevasse's victims. The committee signed a document promising as much, and the meeting adjourned.[58]

As news of the deal leaked downstream, community leaders and residents of the river parishes gathered at a large public meeting. The day
before, angry armed guards had begun patrolling Poydras's levee around
the clock, firing shots at a photojournalist and reporter who ventured
too close to the embankment. That kind of bitterness and anxiety pervaded at the meeting, as participants asked why their representatives had
settled so cheaply with the city.[59] Finally, Judge Leander Perez, one of
the most powerful men not only in the river parishes, but in politics state-
wide, drafted a scathing telegram to the CFRC, raging that the aggrieved

"citizens and tax payers of St. Bernard and Plaquemines...vigorously protest against the action taken towards cutting the levee at Poydras." Perez believed that it was illegal and antidemocratic that the decision had been made behind closed doors and without a public hearing. He closed by noting that the "provision for compensation" was "utterly insufficient."[60] Perez and his neighbors confronted a powerful realization: domination of the environment can lead to social domination of one group of people over other less privileged people.

Even the residents of the river parishes—indignant, united, organized, seemingly with justice on their side—could not stop the events that had begun in New Orleans on Good Friday. On April 26, the CFRC cleared its last hurdle when its members received a wire from Chief Engineer Jadwin, who "interposed no objection to the creation of a temporary break in the Mississippi River levee near the site of the old Poydras crevasse." Governor Simpson immediately began preparing the order to cut the levee, declaring "that a public emergency exists, and, in order to deal with this situation, an artificial break in the levee of the Mississippi River is hereby ordered to be created at or near Poydras plantation in the Parish of St. Bernard, Louisiana, at twelve o'clock noon, on Friday, April 29, 1927." At 9:45 P.M. on Tuesday, April 26, 1927, Simpson signed the order. The people of the river parishes had less than three days to collect their possessions and leave their homes.[61] The levees-only policy had less than three days, too, before it disappeared beneath a flood that it was designed to contain.

WHEN THE FLOOD WATERS RECEDE, THE POOR FOLKS ALONG THE RIVER START ALL OVER AGAIN

After Simpson authorized the levee's destruction, events accelerated in the area surrounding the city. Rumors had caused more than four thousand people to leave the river parishes on April 26, in an "endless caravan which streamed out of the doomed area."[62] The exodus conjured up images of refugees fleeing an impending invasion, and, in retrospect, served as a grim harbinger of things to come, of the tens of thousands of folks who were to take to the nation's roads after the Depression began, just two years later. One reporter wrote that the residents of the river parishes walked with "bundles and packs on their shoulders" or "rode in small cars, wheels touching fenders under the strain of the load, many in open trucks mountainously high and bulging out on all sides with chairs, bedsteads and kitchen stoves...every earthly possession that could be saved, even the faithful old dog." Some member of New Orleans's press corps amplified the class prejudice which seemingly underlay the CFRC's decision, minimizing the horror by noting that the people of the river parishes were just "glad to be well paid."[63]

Not all of the refugees accepted their plight so readily. Many of the area's well-armed trappers still stalked the levee, protecting their land and livelihood. These were people who held views of the river, levee, and the public's interests very different from those of the members of the CFRC. The trappers believed that the local landscape was theirs; it was their home and the source of their sustenance. They were not willing to stand by as urban elites destroyed the river parishes to protect the city's investment in its waterfront and economic future. In response to the trappers' actions, National Guardsmen arrived in the river parishes to keep the peace. Despite their presence, as Secretary of Commerce Herbert Hoover, then in charge of flood relief in the Mississippi Valley, arrived with Chief Engineer Jadwin to inspect the Poydras levee, angry locals fired shots at them. Then, after news spread that a mob would march on New Orleans to cut its levee, saving the river parishes, the Guard began patrolling the city as well, only to find New Orleanians, armed with shotguns, already protecting the waterfront.[64]

In the midst of the turmoil, the CFRC dispatched its propaganda arm, the Emergency Clearing House Publicity Committee (ECHPC), to begin spreading the news that the city was safe and economically viable. Composed of members drawn from the city's press corps, Association of Commerce, and Advertising Club, on April 27 the ECHPC "flashed" an optimistic story nationwide over the wire services, reading in part, "TRADE BRISK, STOCKS JUMP, AFTER CRISIS—Immediately following the issuance of Governor Simpson's proclamation…announcing that the levee at Poydras would be cut Friday noon, thus assuring entire safety to New Orleans, business in the city after a few days' decline, resumed normalcy." The committee then wired additional memos to 350 of the nations' largest papers, claiming that the city was thriving. One section of this tract stated that "New Orleans never has been flooded by the Mississippi River and in our judgment never will."[65] It seemed that both journalistic integrity and the lessons of history would be sacrificed on the altar of commerce.

With less than twenty-four hours left before the levee's destruction, people state-wide engaged in a flurry of final preparations. Vehicles, pedestrians, and livestock clogged the road to New Orleans, as evacuation efforts in the river parishes continued. Officials hoped to clear all of the approximately ten thousand people who resided in the area. To shelter the refugees, they outfitted New Orleans's army-supply base with rows of cots. In keeping with the era's racial climate, one floor was to house whites and another African-Americans, two very different publics in the eyes of the state. The flood itself was going to be massive: 250,000 cubic feet per second of water emitting from a crevasse below the Poydras plantation, at Caernarvon, twenty-two miles downstream from the Carrollton river gauge, and thirteen and a half miles from Canal Street. Engineers estimated that water would eventually cover approximately seventy thousand acres of land. As daylight on Thursday waned, planes flew over the river parishes seeking stragglers, while officials deployed trucks to assist families still in the area. Finally, at 4:00 A.M. on Friday, armed guards blocked the roads leading to the river parishes, and state officials issued special air-traffic-control regulations before closing the Mississippi to all unauthorized vessels. An eerie silence fell over the Caernarvon levee.[66]

The CFRC was not satisfied simply with securing the city's safety. It insisted on turning the crevasse into a landscape of power, demonstrating New Orleans's once-and-future control over its environment and the city's commitment to its supposed destiny as a commercial metropolis. As a result, the CFRC invited reporters from around the country to what promised to be a gala event. At 7:15 A.M., dynamite arrived on the scene in an armored car. At high noon, the time scheduled for the explosion, troops still scrambled to ensure that the surrounding area was deserted. By 1:00 P.M. the crowd of sweating journalists grew surly, but few were willing to risk missing the explosion. Finally, at 2:18 P.M., a demolitions expert received a signal from a surveillance plane flying above. The first blast went off, sending dirt fifty feet into the air (figure 26), and then nothing. Five minutes later, another roar, but still no sign of the river. Three more minutes passed before a third explosion went off. Water finally emerged from the levee, and soon a stream fifteen feet wide lapped at the porches of homes standing nearby (figure 27).[67]

Disappointment hung in the air after the blasts. One journalist wrote that "they dynamited the levee, all right...a governor, a major general, a brace of brigadier-generals, colonels and majors galore...all were there." He explained that "as an engineering feat, the operation is pronounced a success by those who issued the official communiqués. As a military maneuver...the affair was also a success. As a spectacular show, your correspondent, back from the battle front, announces that it was a flop." The hype and the outcome had nothing in common, leaving re-

Figure 26. Dirt flies into the air as charges are detonated at Caernarvon (photograph dated 1927). Courtesy of The Historic New Orleans Collection.

porters hot, weary, and frustrated. The writer noted that "they had come from all over America to see something approximating the end of the world...flame and smoke and a thundering detonation heard for miles." The reality was far different: "There was to be a mighty wall of water suddenly unleashed, Niagara-like, ripping, tearing all before it; whirling down toward the Gulf of Mexico like the onrush of Attilla's horde of Huns. Was there? There was not."[68]

As water flowed from the crevasse, the St. Bernard Parish sheriff, L. A. Mereaux, offered running commentary to the assembled group of reporters, suggesting that urban elites had imposed their version of the public's welfare on the river parishes. Mereaux was a huge presence, even standing next to the levee. He measured over six feet tall and weighed more than two hundred pounds. He wore knee-high boots, olive-drab riding breeches, a khaki shirt, a felt hat, and a kerchief around his neck. An imposing Colt six-shooter rode on his hip. Mereaux understood the scene far better than the reporters gathered around to hear his folksy wisdom. He growled that "this ruins us," because "the Parish of St. Bernard...supplies more furs to the world than Canada and Russia put together. The trapping will be ruined for from three to five years. We've

Figure 27. Water flows from the artificial crevasse at Caernarvon, flooding the parishes below New Orleans (photograph dated 1927). Courtesy of the Library of Congress.

got the best oysters in the world. The oyster trade will be ruined. The truck farms are gone. The cattle and caning industries will be wrecked." Three weeks earlier Mereaux had been offered 250 dollars per acre for land soon to be flooded. He promised to sell that land for 10 dollars per acre. Nobody accepted. Mereaux walked to the crevasse's edge and concluded: "Gentlemen, you have seen today the public execution of this parish."[69] With that, he spun on his heel and left, disgusted by the carnival atmosphere surrounding the levee's destruction and the inundation of land that he knew and loved.

Few shared Mereaux's sense of outrage in New Orleans, where, in the coming days, giddiness spread as quickly as water poured from the crevasse. Anxious inquiries almost immediately stopped coming into one local newspaper, whose phones had very nearly been "destroyed by the pressure of such calls." A shrewd car dealer promised a replacement for any vehicle purchased from him if it were ever damaged by the Mississippi. "Forget the River. Let's get down to business," his ad suggested.[70] But New Orleanians could not forget the river. Many still checked on the Mississippi during visits to the waterfront, or traveled to see the crevasse firsthand aboard a steamer departing the city's levee twice daily for sightseeing junkets.[71]

By May 1, it seemed that the crevasse had eliminated any further threat of river flooding in the city, if such a threat had ever existed. The CFRC, though, still was not satisfied: its members believed that they were not getting enough bang for their buck. From the first, the levee had been far more durable than the engineers charged with its demolition had anticipated. And so, on May 3, the CFRC complained that "we have placed ourselves in a position of putting up a large amount of money, and we are entitled to more than we are getting."[72] Butler then decided that more charges would have to be detonated at Poydras in an additional show of force. Through May's first week, almost forty tons of dynamite opened the crevasse, which had originally been only six hundred feet wide, to almost two thousand feet across. The emerging flood eventually was "roaring like Niagara."[73]

While the river soon dropped at the Carrollton gauge, assuaging concerns even within the skeptical ranks of the CFRC, the increased flow prompted indignation and outrage among other observers, for whom the crevasse always had reeked of urban and upper-class privilege. Immediately after the levee's demolition, the national media suggested that the city had sacrificed its rural neighbors to the river. Selfish and greedy, as these stories saw it, New Orleans embodied people's worst fears about cities. Of even greater concern to the CFRC, some of these articles claimed that the crevasse had backfired, that the city still faced grave danger, while others accused New Orleans's commercial community of trying to "soft pedal" the out-of-town media. The *Memphis Commercial Appeal* was especially biting in its coverage, printing a bold headline reading: "N'ORLEANS BABBITS TRY TO COLOR NEWS." The accompanying article astutely argued that some New Orleanians feared "unfavorable publicity for their town far more than they dreaded the mad, muddy waters of the flooded Mississippi River."[74]

Facing this brewing crisis, the ECHPC began, in early-twenty-first-century terms, trying to control the spin. The committee sent additional press releases to newspapers around the country and broadcast upbeat reports during the Red Cross's radio coverage of relief efforts. The most influential committee members then contacted their colleagues at newspapers in other cities, calling in favors, and sealing gentlemen's agreements over the phone. A. G. Newmayer, the committee's chair, reached out to his friend Victor Hanson, the *Birmingham News*'s editor. Newmayer asked "Vic" to retract harsh coverage of the events in New Orleans; Hanson complied. The committee enjoyed similar successes in other instances as well, so much so, that by the end of the first week of May, at a meeting to plan future strategy its members distributed favorable news coverage gathered from around the country, congratulating themselves on a job well done.[75]

Other problems proved more difficult to solve than public-relations woes. Environmental consequences from the artificial crevasse were evident immediately, as the river parishes' farmers lost a growing season to the flood. At the time, some experts predicted that crop outputs would be diminished for years.[76] Still, while farmers suffered, the most obvious losers were the trappers who had worked the area's backwaters. As the river rushed from the crevasse, it flooded a large portion of the state's muskrat habitat. In response, trappers worked with the State Conservation Agency to save animals, constructing approximately fifteen hundred "life rafts for muskrats," which they anchored to trees.[77] The conservationists then transported thousands of muskrat nests onto the rafts, hoping the animals would float safely above the flood. Soon afterward, observers celebrated because as many as three hundred animals scrambled around on each raft. As one amused journalist reported, people were "throwing life preservers to muskrats."[78] More than that, trappers were trying to save their way of life from the flood.

Unfortunately, efforts to protect the animals often backfired. Muskrats are nocturnal critters, and many went blind in the daylight or died of exposure on the rafts. Others starved, as the grasses on which they fed were submerged for months. One account estimated that 85 percent of the inundated area had been "swept clean of muskrats." The next fall a two-hundred-thousand-acre survey of the river parishes turned up "very little wild life." Then, in January 1928, an official lamented that "the Caernarvon crevasse country was as clear of muskrats as a chicken's mouth of teeth." Eventually, even conservative estimates admitted that as much as 50 percent of the state's muskrat population had perished as a result of the artificial crevasse.[79]

The muskrats' destruction typified the crevasse's results: the catastrophe outstripped all predictions. Although the CFRC's members had tried to minimize havoc by planning a crevasse—a revealing look at their faith in the ability of engineers to control the river—the outcome proved far more chaotic. This was especially true of the flood's refugees. Four days after the levee's destruction, an office opened in the city, promising "every claimant would be given prompt action and would receive 100 percent of the claims as adjusted."[80] The rhetoric sounded promising, but behind the scenes the CFRC was organizing for a fight by putting together a legal team to protect its interests. On May 12, the committee buckled under the strain of the refugees' demands, and its lawyers sprang into action. Food disbursements to people left homeless by the flood were more costly than expected, so the committee began deducting relief allotments from final settlements. A week later, the CFRC guessed that the final claims would not exceed two million dollars. The actual figure was to be more than fifteen times that number.[81]

As disputes with refugees devolved into court battles, the CFRC's dealings with the trappers illustrated the shady deals and double crosses that the city's elites employed in negotiations. The CFRC did not want to honor claims from trappers for animals that could not be counted, for which no receipts existed, and whose numbers might not have been depleted as drastically as claimed. Consequently, the CFRC's lawyers, working closely with representatives from the state, asked to see the account books for fourteen fur dealers who had conducted their business in cash as a way of hiding profits from authorities. The CFRC hoped that the trappers, facing a choice between prosecution, for tax evasion, and small settlements, would pick the latter. The trappers did neither. They sued the commission, claiming that the audit was unconstitutional. Two months later, the court ruled against the trappers, providing the CFRC with leverage in future negotiations. The defeated trappers then forged a quick settlement with the CFRC.[82]

In the wake of the flood, the crevasse's impact could be judged in the contrasting economic and spatial climates in the city and river parishes. While New Orleans's markets recovered relatively quickly, the parishes' economy foundered for years. With the fur season wiped out by the flood and their negotiating position undermined, many trappers went hungry in the winter of 1927–28. The next year, despite a state-sponsored muskrat restocking program, trappers still took approximately one million fewer pelts than they had in years prior to the crevasse. At the same time, while the city remained dry during the river flood, the parishes' public and private spaces, including parks, factories, and homes, were soaked.[83] The levee in Louisiana existed to protect the public; it rested on the riparian servitude which stated that the Mississippi's banks belonged to all of the state's citizens. Consequently, the CFRC and organizations that had sanctioned the levee's destruction had made a clear choice, at least partly class-based, between publics. They had sacrificed the people of the poorer river parishes so that New Orleanians, and particularly the city's commercial community, could thrive.

A NATURAL DISASTER?

As the high water from the 1927 flood finally receded, survivors throughout the valley began cleaning up. At its peak, the flood had stretched over a thousand miles long and eighty miles wide, covering more than sixteen million acres of land, or approximately twenty-six thousand square miles (figure 28). At least 250 victims had died during the catastrophe, and more than 160,000 families had been driven from their homes. In Louisiana alone, in excess of a million acres of crops and head of livestock had been destroyed, and nearly six hundred houses had been razed.[84] When people from north of Cape Girardeau, Missouri, to south of New Orleans dug out from beneath the muck, they searched for not only their possessions but for answers. For years, the Mississippi River Commission and local levee districts had promised that the line of defenses was impregnable. Then the Mississippi had overwhelmed the levees again. Who, or what, was responsible?

Answering that question by calling the flood a natural disaster, or an act of God, absolved people of any responsibility, suggesting that the river or an angry deity had caused the inundation. And as environmental historian Ted Steinberg argues, labels such as "natural disaster" and "act of God" often have been used by powerful segments of society to maintain social and economic order during moments of uncertainty and stress.[85] This was certainly the case in New Orleans, as the MRC, levee boards, politicians, and commercial community had relied on such language for decades, implying that despite their best efforts, nature, and the river especially, remained unpredictable at times and could be controlled only with additional funding and new investments in technology. After 1927, such explanations rang false for many bitter observers throughout the Mississippi Valley, particularly for those who surveyed the human-induced damage near New Orleans. It took little time for aggrieved refugees of the Caernarvon crevasse, for example, to echo the sentiments of an angry trapper who had raged shortly after the levee's demolition that the "deliberate inundation of two Parishes is not an act of God—it is an act of man, inspired by a spirit of self-preservation."[86]

The trapper's sentiments quickly entered the popular consciousness: just as the crevasse downstream of New Orleans had not been an entirely natural disaster, neither had the whole of the 1927 flood. Alarmed onlookers realized that these events had resulted from of a volatile mix of environmental and social factors—unprecedented short-term precipitation and long-term development throughout the valley and years of

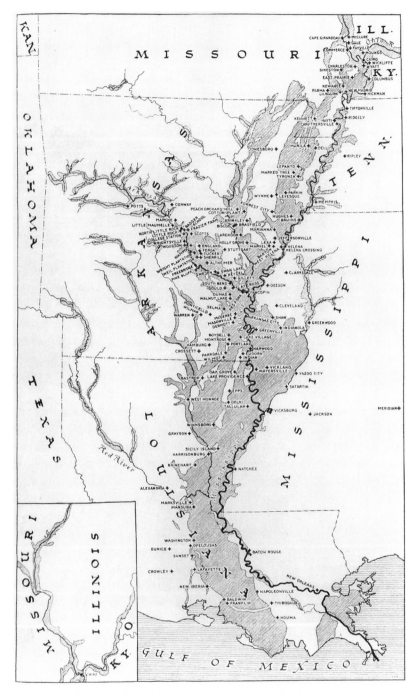

Figure 28. The 1927 flood stretched from Illinois to the Gulf of Mexico. Courtesy of the Special Collections Division, Tulane University.

flawed public policy and faith in technology's ability to control the river, as well as the power of the Crescent City's commercial community. As it became impossible to explain away the disaster as natural or as an act of God, the valley's residents, and New Orleanians especially, were forced to rethink their relationship with the Mississippi, at least in the short term, as they realized that human actions had helped create the flood.

Scrutiny of people's involvement in the disaster hinged on examining the role that levees had played in raising the river. In the days leading to the Caernarvon crevasse, the National Geographic Society had observed of the Mississippi's levees that "man's modern devices, contrived to give him greater comforts, have turned upon him."[87] Then, after the flood, a bandwagon filled with critics eager to tear down the levees-only policy on the river system. Senator Joseph Ransdell of Louisiana, a lifelong levee man, penned a revealing letter to President Coolidge, admitting that "the flood seems to demonstrate the necessity of revision by the Mississippi River Commission of the ideas and plans for flood control developed by it since its creation."[88] At first glance, Ransdell's about-face apparently suggests that people's attitudes had changed, that the days of an imperial view of nature on the river were numbered, and that engineers would begin to work with the Mississippi instead of simply trying to dominate it.

President Coolidge agreed with Ransdell, promising that he would initiate a new era of flood control on the Mississippi system. And with Coolidge's announcement, analysts and lobbyists began assessing past policy failures and offering alternatives sometimes marked by new visions of the river. Walter Parker, the head of the Safe River Committee of 100, enjoyed swimming with the stream of public opinion, rather than bucking the current. Of "the levees-only people," he gloated, "when they fail, as they always do, they blame their failure on acts of God, on too much water, or too much wind."[89] James Kemper, another spillways advocate, suggested that "the flood of 1927 was necessary to show everybody, what some of us have known for a long time, that the valley is the victim of the most ruthless, obstinate, and monumental blundering engineering policy ever known in America." Another time, Kemper went further: "Man wants to take the river's natural storage reservoir and make no compensation for it. The river contends it is against Natural Law and cannot be done. The river is right."[90] In sum, a heightened appreciation for what people called nature, including the Mississippi's regimen, apparently emerged after the flood, accompanied by the realization in some quarters that controlling the river completely might be impossible, and that past efforts to that end had proved disastrous.

When Congress held hearings in the winter of 1927–28 to discuss two new flood-control proposals, one offered by the Army Corps of Engineers, the other by the MRC, expert witnesses lined up to testify about the river's power and the folly of levees-only. Much of the testimony echoed Ellet's prophecies from three-quarters of a century earlier. For instance, W. B. Greely, the chief of the U.S. Forest Service, spoke about the direct correlation between deforestation in the valley and flooding.[91] E. A. Sherman, his subordinate, expanded on the point, discussing all development in his presentation. Sherman explained regarding precipitation in the valley that "every building that has a waterproof roof put on it, every square yard of concrete that is laid down for the establishment of an impervious highway [means] it does not go down into the soil, but it goes immediately into run-off."[92] The foresters suggested, as Ellet had, that the valley's environment needed to be conceptualized holistically. The Mississippi and flood-control policies on the river could no longer be considered in isolation from the region's landscapes and the millions of people who had helped produce them.

It was left to the renowned conservationist Gifford Pinchot to sum up the flaws of levees-only. When Pinchot spoke, he commanded attention. His exploits as a forester were legendary and his reputation as a man unwilling to suffer fools unrivaled. Months earlier, he had called "the levees-only policy...the most complete engineering blunder and failure...in the history of the civilized world."[93] At the hearings, Pinchot offered his audience a history lesson, explaining in his self-aggrandizing style that he and Theodore Roosevelt had tried to view the river as a complete system, but that entrenched bureaucrats at the Corps and MRC had thwarted them. As a result, Pinchot scoffed that "the most serious danger to adequate and permanent flood control and river utilization in the Mississippi Basin is the intractable attitude of officials who, having taken a position, demand (the forces of nature to the contrary notwithstanding) that their view, once expressed, shall always be right." Pinchot could have been talking about Eads, Humphreys, or any of countless others who had vouched for the efficacy of levees-only through the decades. He insisted on a revised view of the Mississippi system and the valley in which "nature" would be allowed more leeway.[94]

Donald Worster has written that the Dust Bowl years of the 1930s sparked an intellectual revolution in the United States, as farmers, scientists, and government bureaucrats came face-to-face with the consequences of ignoring complex relationships that account for disasters they called natural. Dust storms in the country's midsection, Worster suggests, gave rise to what we now might call an ecological view of the environment, a holistic way of conceptualizing the interactions of humans and their nonhuman surroundings.[95] The Dust Bowl no doubt played a critical role in spurring this shift, but the congressional hearings held after the 1927 flood suggest that an earlier environmental disaster also served as a catalyst for the rise of an ecological worldview in some sections of the nation's scientific and engineering communities. And in the years after 1927, experts charged with flood control on the Mississippi began promising that they would treat the river, its tributaries, and its floodplain as an integrated system, as a whole, not as discrete parts that could be manipulated by technology.

The MRC's and the Corps's flood-control plans provided the best evidence that people's perceptions of nature and the river had shifted, if only slightly. Although both organizations still rejected reforestation and reservoirs as prohibitively expensive, they abandoned the levees-only policy in favor of plans based on levees *and* spillways, ostensibly incorporating elements of what they called the Mississippi's natural behavior into their flood-control initiatives. Secretary of War Davis boasted of the Corps's ideas: "The plan conforms to the natural tendencies of the river when in flood. The river is led rather than driven or forced." Chief Engineer Jadwin agreed, explaining that "man must not try to restrict the Mississippi River too much in extreme floods. The river will break any plan which does this. It must have the room it needs." The MRC also granted that it had always been "satisfied that any flood…could be carried between levees…and it was therefore unnecessary to provide diversions or other auxiliary methods of relief." The events of 1927, though, had finally "demonstrated that such auxiliaries should receive due consideration in any flood control project."[96] In some ways a cycle had been completed. Nearly seventy years after Ellet's death, the Corps and the MRC appeared ready to embrace ideas that he had originally put forth in the years leading to the Civil War.

And yet, the inclusion of spillways in the Corps's and MRC's plans does not indicate that the imperial view of nature and the flood-control engineers' faith in technological fixes had been completely supplanted in a wave of ecological revelations. Although engineers from the Corps, MRC, and elsewhere recognized that the levees-only policy had failed, they were still convinced that the river could be tamed, given the right tools. In the wake of the 1927 flood, a journalist asked Secretary Hoover, an engineer and technocrat, if it was "possible to *control* the Mississippi River." Without hesitation, Hoover responded: "Sure! If we can take care of a normal flood, we also can take care of a super-flood. To control the Mississippi is not a difficult engineering job. It's merely a matter of financing."[97] Other engineers around the country shared Hoover's optimism, and their attitude characterized future flood-control efforts on the Mississippi. The flood of 1927 had not changed their goals, nor had it shaken their faith in the possibility of subduing the river. What had changed was the means that engineers were going to employ as they attempted to control the Mississippi.

Ultimately, Congress drafted a bill amalgamating the two flood-control proposals, and President Coolidge signed the Jones-Reid Act on May 15, 1928, ending the era of levees-only on the Mississippi.[98] Despite all of the rhetoric about allowing the river to behave naturally, however, the Jones-Reid Act still sought to control the Mississippi using technology. The difference from past plans was not in hard choices made to allow nature to run its course, but in a grudging accommodation to the Mississippi's intransigence best exemplified by the spillways included in the new initiative. Spillways, long anathema to the Corps and MRC, suggested that those organizations had finally realized that a multitiered approach to flood control offered them the best chance of taming the river. For decades, engineers, politicians, local businesspeople, and valley citizens, spurred not only by faith in human innovation, but also by economic interests, had ignored evidence that levees raised river levels. Although the floods of 1912, 1913, and 1922 had changed some critics' minds, the valley's allegiance to levees-only had remained intact through those disasters. Only the flood of 1927 had forced people to reexamine their loyalties. And, as the region's residents discovered that they were not being served by levee construction, policy makers finally heeded new demands from the valley. As a result, spillways were to be part of new flood-control plans.

For New Orleanians, the most important feature of the Jones-Reid Act was an outlet slated for construction at Bonnet Carré, approximately thirty miles upriver, and the site of a crevasse in 1871 that had relieved pressure on the city's levee. By 1927, the expense of closing the port and public belt railroad, coupled with the city's geology, often precluded further levee augmentation. Because the riverbanks are composed of loose, alluvial deposits, they provide an unstable foundation on which to build—thus the city's levee typically could not be raised higher without risking a catastrophic waterfront collapse. In other words, the levees had reached their maximum height in most places, meaning that the city could no longer afford to build its embankment higher than its neighbors. Thus, in the future, New Orleans would not have its safety valve, its guarantee that the city would remain dry during river floods. Once again, New Orleans's investment in waterfront infrastructure had rendered it less nimble in dealing with the delta's dynamic environment, another example of how the production of space in the city could be shaped by the nonhuman world. And so, New Orleanians had lobbied hard for a spillway.[99]

Fortunately for the city, Bonnet Carré provided a near-perfect location for an outlet from the Mississippi. The proposed spillway's entrance, at the river, stood just over five miles from its exit, at Lake Pontchartrain. The site was typical of the delta. The terrain sloped gently down from the river, descending approximately twenty feet to the lake. Farmers had cultivated the land nearest the river, but the rest of the area remained a wetland, interspersed with cottonwood, cypress, and ash trees. The Corps planned to construct a seven-thousand-foot weir at the river, designed to control the amount of water in the spillway. From there, the water, confined by high levees on either side, was to flow through cleared land. The levees closest to the river were to be constructed just over a mile apart and then spread like a fan, until the spillway stretched to more than two miles wide at the lakeshore. The proposed weir could be opened when the river reached twenty feet on the Carrollton gauge in New Orleans and remain closed at all other times. The maximum output of the spillway was to be approximately 250,000 cubic feet per second, similar to the final figure for the crevasse at Caernarvon.[100]

On January 2, 1929, the Corps sponsored a festive event to celebrate the start of construction at Bonnet Carré and the end of flooding in New Orleans.[101] Despite the project's popularity, though, the outlet was immediately plagued by land-use controversies, because the Corps had to acquire almost eight thousand acres of land for its spillway, uprooting property owners standing in the way of technological advance. Consequently, the people who were to be displaced sought an injunction to halt work in late summer 1929. The court quickly ruled for the Corps, but it insisted that the land be expropriated, insuring compensation for the aggrieved proprietors. With that ruling acting as a cornerstone, the Corps poured concrete on October 21, 1929. Construction moved forward at a furious pace. By early 1931, the Corps had completed the spillway's weir, and in summer 1932, it finished the levees flanking the outlet. Four years later, workers announced that the bridges over the spillway were done. Finally, in December 1936, the Corps pronounced the Bonnet Carré Spillway operational.[102] The project's completion proved timely; a month later a flood began moving downstream toward New Orleans.

Reports indicate that New Orleanians remained jittery about river flooding as late as a decade after the Good Friday disaster. On January 27, 1937, with the flood crest still hundreds of miles upstream, W. F. Mc-Donald, Isaac Cline's successor at the weather bureau, noted widespread panic in the city. In a report published in the *Times Picayune*, McDonald advised people to "go quietly and confidently about their regular business, secure in the knowledge that their defenses against flood danger are well nigh impregnable." But New Orleanians had heard about impregnable defenses before, and they had learned that the river did not respect such boasts. Then, on January 30, the Corps opened the Bonnet Carré Spillway. McDonald reported a sudden shift in the city's mood, as the rush of water through the outlet calmed New Orleanians. "We may fear some of Nature's moods," he wrote, "but not the Mississippi River." The following day, spectators jammed the roadway above the outlet. As Mardi Gras drew near, one observer likened the throng to a "crowd of Carnival proportions." The spillway performed admirably, prompting the head of the Army Corps of Engineers, Edward Markham, to label it "perfect." Flood water coursed through the outlet at Bonnet Carré until March 16, when the spillway closed, marking the flood's end.[103]

With the spillway's success, the Corps transformed a threatening flood, a moment when the river seemed wild and chaotic, into a benign spectacle (figure 29). Unlike in 1927, when people had flocked to the city's levee to witness the power and dynamism of the river for themselves, in 1937 onlookers traveled upstream to Bonnet Carré to see the technology that finally had ostensibly brought order to the Mississippi. On a bridge high over the muddy water rushing through the spillway, New Orleanians celebrated their apparent control of nature. And the impression that engineers definitively had imposed their will on the river found further expression when the Corps determined that the flood was over by closing the spillway. Humans ended the 1937 flood, not the Mississippi.

During the 1937 flood, the spillway undoubtedly proved itself a technological marvel. Yet, judged by other standards, it was a failure. Just as levees had throughout the nineteenth and the beginning of the twentieth centuries, the spillway provided a false, even dangerous, sense of security in New Orleans. That engineers could open an outlet, releasing a flood into Lake Pontchartrain while eliminating pressure on New Orleans's levee, as easily as one might pull the plug in an overfilled bath-

Figure 29. Sightseers watch as floodwaters rush through the Bonnet Carré Spillway. Courtesy of the Special Collections Division, Tulane University.

tub, maintained the illusion that experts could discipline the river with technology. As the spillway diverted the flood in 1937, Markham gloated that "New Orleans is the safest place on the lower river." In the city, he claimed, the "problem is not controlling the river but rumors." "Old Man River," he promised, "is tamed at last."[104] But the contention that the river was under control was nonsense, inflated rhetoric like that used by levees-only proponents in the years leading to the 1927 flood. In that regard nothing had changed.

Another thing had not changed: the attitude of flood-control engineers. After the 1927 flood, the Corps and MRC, admitting that past policy had been "unnaturally" rigid, had pledged to work in harmony with the Mississippi in the future. Spillways, they had suggested, mirrored the river system's layout and thus were a far more "natural" alternative to levees. But spillways were neither more nor less natural than artificial levees. Both were human creations, elaborate and expensive artifice designed to control the river. And both had unintended consequences. Spillways were just another step toward making the Mississippi into what Richard White, referring to the Columbia River, has called an "organic machine," located at the crossroads of the human and non-human.[105] Furthermore, spillways treated a flood's symptoms, not its cause, which was development throughout the valley. On that issue, the Corps and MRC still ignored Ellet's findings. Deforestation and urbanization in the valley accelerated after 1927, resulting in more water than ever running off into the river system and more people living in harm's way on its flood plain. Consequently, disasters—whether "natural," human-constructed, or "acts of God"—became more catastrophic over time, leading to the massive floods of 1993 and beyond.

Finally, one last thing did not change. New Orleans never filled with river water after 1927. The Corps's engineering genius kept the city dry no matter how high the Mississippi ran after the completion of the Bonnet Carré Spillway. And because of that, because of landscapes of power fronting the city—the levee—and at Bonnet Carré, because the city remained isolated from the river spatially, many New Orleanians became confident again that the Mississippi did not threaten them. Some people even forgot the river looming high above the city, as the CFRC in 1927 hoped that they and others around the country might. The spillway had accomplished what the Caernarvon crevasse had not been able to: it apparently had insulated New Orleans from the river once and for all. But, while the Mississippi seemed comparatively docile, it still played a role in producing space in the city, as New Orleanians discovered in the 1950s when they contemplated building a riverfront expressway fronting the French Quarter. At that time, the Mississippi's unpredictable geomorphology worked with human perceptions of the river, leading to a popular uprising that ultimately left the waterfront more open and accessible than it had been since the late nineteenth century.

EPILOGUE

The Simple Needs
of Automobiles

On November 19, 1958, Louis Bisso, the director-secretary of the City
Planning Commission of New Orleans, gaveled to order an important
public hearing held to decide the fate of a proposed riverfront expressway. Proponents of the project believed that the highway would not only
revitalize New Orleans's urban core of businesses, but also relieve traffic
congestion on the narrow streets of the city's Vieux Carré, or French
Quarter. In short, the meeting's participants wanted to perform major
surgery on New Orleans: they would add a new artery for commerce,
clear obstructions from older blocked channels, and give the city a facelift
in the process. Bisso explained that the six-lane highway would shadow
the Mississippi and be elevated approximately forty feet above the river's
crescent-shaped meander fronting the French Quarter (figure 30).[1]

After hearing Bisso's presentation, numerous local businesspeople, including members of the Dock Board and chamber of commerce, embraced the plan without reservation. They were certain that cars—the
latest in a long succession of transportation technologies promising sal-
vation to the city's commercial interests—would improve New Orleans's
economic standing. Then, many of the normally cautious and protective
members of the French Quarter's influential preservation community surprisingly agreed that the highway would improve conditions in the Vieux
Carré by diverting cars, trucks, and buses from the historic district's interior. The majority of the assembled preservationists asked only that the
roadway be built at grade level rather than looming above the river,

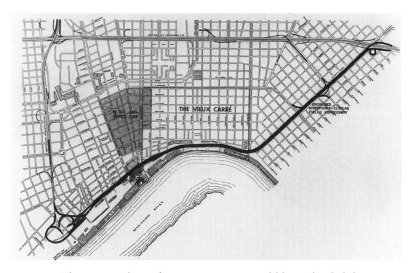

Figure 30. The proposed riverfront expressway would have divided the city from the river (1981). Courtesy of the Special Collections Division, Tulane University, and William Borah.

where it might quickly become an eyesore. Their position was based in part on an understanding of the city's geology, another example of the nonhuman world playing a role in producing space in New Orleans. Because the Vieux Carré sits entirely on loose, alluvial soil, which transmits vibrations over great distances, the prospect of diminished motor-vehicle traffic promised less wear and tear on the buildings responsible for the district's national architectural reputation. The preservationists thus reckoned that decreased traffic congestion in the historic district's heart merited support for the highway, despite the project's potential aesthetic shortcomings.[2]

Finally, as the meeting concluded, two dissenting voices struggled to be heard over the din of boosterism. Martha Robinson, a local activist prominent in the city's preservation community, first admitted that the expressway might relieve crowding in the Quarter, but then cautioned that "the automobile is a Frankenstein" that might destroy the Vieux Carré if allowed to run amok. Joseph Burke, a merchant whose shoe store stood on Elysian Fields Avenue, the proposed freeway's eastern leg, followed Robinson. Burke came armed with a petition signed by 150 residents and businesspeople who worried that the roadway would turn their neighborhood into a "slum."[3]

Robinson's words—likening cars to the monstrous antihero from
Mary Shelley's classic Romantic novel—were not merely glib; the preser-
vationist tapped into key themes emerging in some quarters of American culture in the years after World War II. Following the detonation of
the atomic bombs at Hiroshima and Nagasaki, as frightened observers
realized that people had it in their power to end the world, technology,
which for generations had been widely venerated in New Orleans and
around the country as a panacea, suddenly appeared to be an instrument
of destruction as well.[4] Accordingly, Robinson warned that cars, no matter how benevolent their original purposes, could be counted on to carry
with them unintended consequences. Like steamboats and railroads before them, automobiles, she seemed to be suggesting, would not arrive
in New Orleans without making demands on the city. And so, with apoc-
alyptic intellectual currents swirling around New Orleans and the nation, although for most observers the automobile remained a powerful
symbol of liberation, of the good that technology could do, for others,
like Robinson, cars demanded close scrutiny lest they lay waste to the
urban environment.

Despite the mild protests voiced at the meeting by skeptics such as
Robinson and Burke, less than a week later, the City Planning Commission placed the riverfront expressway on New Orleans's Major Street
Plan.[5] This decision indicated that the commission expected that there
would soon be a new highway located between the city and the Mississippi. Its members did not realize that they had started what was to be
a decade-long battle forcing New Orleanians to ask age-old questions
about the waterfront, mirroring and updating disputes that had captivated the city for almost two centuries: How could the Mississippi best
serve New Orleans? Who should control the riverbanks? Should that
space be recreational or commercial, public or private, mixed- or single-
use? Could it be all of those things at once? The answers to those questions were to have a profound impact on not only New Orleans's reciprocal relationship with the Mississippi but on the placement of highways
in urban areas nationwide.

For most people, the name "New Orleans" calls up soft-focus mental images of the nation's quintessential river city, in which pedestrians
stroll the banks of the continent's most famed and largest watercourse
as graceful riverboats ply the Mississippi. Although such visions are de-
cidedly idealized and romantic, they are also accurate representations of
the city's waterfront, at least to a point. As this book has demonstrated,

for much of New Orleans's history, the river and city enjoyed a close relationship, with the waterfront serving as a public space, though the
exact nature of that designation shifted over time. Throughout the eighteenth and most of the nineteenth centuries, local custom, litigation, and
legislation combined to keep the riverfront free of structures limiting access to the Mississippi. For instance, the batture dispute led directly into
debates about the construction of steamboat wharves in the 1820s and
1830s, a conflict that ultimately divided the city into thirds. Through the
end of the Civil War, then, the waterfront remained a permeable boundary between the city and river.

Only during the era of Reconstruction did municipal officials, amid
lingering controversy, entice railroads to the city with grants of riverfront land. For the first time, depots, train tracks, and terminals separated New Orleans and the Mississippi, both physically and in the imaginations of the city's residents. Then, as the nineteenth century ended,
self-described progressive reformers rationalized space at the waterfront,
building huge artificial levees to protect the city from river flooding, and
warehouses to keep goods stored at the Port of New Orleans safe from
the delta's climate. By 1910, massive sheds covered almost four linear
miles of the riverfront, including the area directly across from the French
Quarter, leaving that once-open, public, multiuse space covered with
structures, off-limits to most New Orleanians and visitors to the city, and
almost exclusively commercial. Finally, in the early 1950s, the Army
Corps of Engineers built a twelve-and-a-half-foot-high floodwall along
the length of the waterfront.[6] If the levee, railroads, and warehouses had
not entirely severed the city's spatial link to the river, this floodwall
finished the job. Consequently, by the middle of the twentieth century,
the waterfront had become a stark border between the city and the river.
The Mississippi churned on to the Gulf of Mexico behind barriers composed of rails, depots, storage warehouses, the massive levee, and a concrete floodwall (figures 31 and 32).

So it was that by 1958, standing in long shadows cast by these structures, most New Orleanians, even the city's dedicated preservationists,
did not view the proposed highway as a threat. The waterfront had undergone a sweeping transformation across two centuries, and few people remembered when that landscape had served as anything but the domain of commerce. Throughout its history, the city had most often
produced space near the river to accommodate transportation technologies rather than public access or use. Reshaping the waterfront for
automobiles thus followed a long tradition of planning and development

in the city. In fact, the idea for a riverfront expressway had first surfaced in 1946, when Robert Moses, New York's notorious freeway builder, had suggested building a roadway along the Mississippi's banks, but funding for such a project had not been available at the time. Then, when Congress passed the Federal Highway Act of 1956—the largest public-works program in U.S. history—money for such initiatives had become plentiful, rekindling local interest in a riverfront expressway and leading eventually to the decision of 1958.[7]

For four years after that, city and state officials had struggled to secure the clearances needed to begin constructing the freeway. Then, with workers finally poised to break ground, the river had reasserted its role in shaping New Orleans's landscapes, clouding the roadway's future. Early in 1962, after officials noticed the riverfront shifting beneath their feet, geologists warned that the storage structures (figure 33) standing across from Jackson Square weighed too much for the alluvial soil below. The city had ignored this environmental constraint when building the waterfront wharves and warehouses, but it could do so no longer. If the problem was not addressed immediately, a bank might cave into the river, leading to a catastrophic flood. Facing this looming threat, the city reluctantly destroyed the structures opposite the French Quarter.[8] Following the demolition, for the first time in more than fifty years New Orleanians could access and see the river from Jackson Square, rekindling local interest in the Mississippi's place in the city and in opening the waterfront for recreational use (figure 34).

At nearly the same time that the Mississippi reintroduced itself to New Orleans, intellectual developments nationwide fomented opposition to the highway. In 1961, Jane Jacobs published *The Death and Life of Great American Cities*, generating popular interest in the negative consequences of urban renewal. Among her arguments, Jacobs criticized the impact that cars and highways had on metropolitan areas, and particularly "expressways that eviscerate cities." She also insisted that mixed-use, public spaces kept urban areas healthy, and that "nature" should be an important part of cities.[9] A year later, Rachel Carson's *Silent Spring* came out, a call for vigilance regarding the nation's fragile environment and the clearest articulation to that point of ecological principles such as the interdependence of all organisms and ecosystems.[10] Much like *The Death and Life of Great American Cities*, *Silent Spring* did not begin a social movement. Instead it lent environmentalists credibility and the common vocabulary of popular ecology, while at the same time spreading the movement's message to thousands of readers who had never considered

Figure 31. By the middle of the twentieth century, railroad tracks and the Dock Board's sheds loomed between New Orleans and the river. Café du Monde stands in the middle of the frame in this photograph (ca. mid-twentieth century). Jackson Square is to the left in the foreground, just out of the frame. Courtesy of the Special Collections Division, Tulane University.

such issues before, many of whom resided in cities like New Orleans. In the early 1960s, environmentalists, who often had concerned themselves only with conservation or wilderness preservation, began contemplating urban landscapes as well. And urban activists, who only occasionally to that point had considered the nonhuman world—for example, in the work of the pathbreaking landscape architect Ian McHarg—began rethinking the ongoing power of nature in shaping cities.[11]

Late in 1962, preservationists and environmentalists working in New Orleans, worried about degradation in the city, coalesced around their shared concerns. These two groups of reformers found that they shared conceptual footing, including an ironclad faith in the application of lay ecological ideas, such as holism and interdependence, in the city's future planning process. Later labeled "freeway fighters," when these activists

Figure 32. The Army Corps of Engineers floodwall, standing between the French Quarter and the waterfront (photograph ca. late twentieth century). Courtesy of the U.S. Army Corps of Engineers, New Orleans District.

Figure 33. A storage facility, standing between Jackson Square and the river, limits access to the Mississippi (photograph ca. mid-twentieth century). Courtesy of the Southeastern Architectural Archive, Tulane University.

gazed at the Mississippi's banks they saw an opportunity to take a stand. For many years, some of the city's visionary preservationists had suggested that a parcel of the riverfront should be redeveloped as a public plaza, a landscape where New Orleanians could reconnect with the Mississippi, drawing the river back into their daily lives. The area left empty after the removal of the Dock Board's structures seemed like an ideal location for such a promenade. And so, with the expressway plan blocking their way, the freeway fighters, some of whom had recently supported the highway, mounted the first organized attacks on the proposal.[12]

From the pages of a local paper, the *Vieux Carré Courier,* activists began rallying support for their cause, firing broadsides at the expressway's boosters. For instance, William Long, the *Courier*'s editor, revealed a fondness for Jacobs when he wrote that the city should not "mortgage all to the automobile and its many planning problems." A local historian, Harnett Kane, then demonstrated that although individuals living in New Orleans may not have witnessed a time when the city had enjoyed a close spatial relationship with the river, collective memories—shared sets of recollections, often contested and highly contingent—of that era lingered. In his article, Kane capitalized on the Mississippi's evocative power, warning that the expressway would "forever shut out the Vieux Carré from the river, which gave it its birth and vitality." Architectural historian Dolores Hayden has argued that "urban landscapes are storehouses for these social memories, because natural features such as hills or harbors, as well as streets, buildings, and patterns of settle-

Figure 34. New Orleanians renewed the link between Jackson Square and the Mississippi when they removed the storage shed that had divided the two (photograph dated 1970). Courtesy of The Historic New Orleans Collection.

ment, frame the lives of many people and often outlast many lifetimes."[13] With the Mississippi riverfront serving as a huge mnemonic device, Kane conjured up images of a past and future levee promenade.

Kane was among the first of the freeway fighters to suggest revitalizing the city's spatial tie to the river, a goal that was to become the movement's signature. In 1962, however, many people scoffed at this idea. What later was to be called the "freeway war" was just beginning around the country, and the expressway's opponents initially were outgunned in one of the conflict's first skirmishes. Although many of the activists had battled developers in the past, in 1962 they also fought the powerful highway lobby, government officials, and the city's commercial community. Those groups pushed hard for the road, accompanied by urbanists influenced by the French planner Le Corbusier, who insisted that highways could revive dying cities.[14] As Jacobs noted at the time: "The simple needs of automobiles are more easily understood and satisfied than the complex needs of cities, and a growing number of planners and designers have come to believe that if they can solve the problems of traffic, they will thereby have solved the major problems of cities."[15] So, as the freeway fighters railed against chaining New Orleans's future to the automobile, thereby touching off a "modern-city catastrophe," many proponents of urban renewal in Louisiana still maintained that a riverfront expressway would begin a renaissance in the city's core while protecting the Quarter.[16]

Consequently, even as the *Courier* printed its antiexpressway rhetoric, the city moved ahead, budgeting 2.1 million dollars to secure a riverfront right of way in 1962. Two years later, the U.S. Bureau of Public Roads included the expressway in its massive interstate highway system. This meant that the project would be eligible for federal funds, guaranteeing that the city could recoup 90 percent of its construction costs from Washington. New Orleans's mayor, Victor Schiro, was already counting the federal dollars flowing into the city's coffers when he hailed the decision, predicting that the expressway would fuel growth and development.[17] On the other hand, celebrated architectural critic Lewis Mumford, who published a scathing critique of urban planning in the automobile age that year, disagreed. Mumford lumped the expressway's many boosters with other scoundrels who used "extravagant federal subsidies to forward their obsolete highway plans and destroy the cities they supposedly serve."[18]

With the initiative gathering momentum, environmentalists and urban activists staked out additional common ground at a public meeting held on January 29, 1965. More than seven hundred people attended the gathering that night, including community organizers, faculty and students from Tulane University, professionals, and preservationists. As a result of the size and diversity of the crowd, fresh perspectives marked the hours of speeches, with the growing cadre of freeway fighters influenced by popular ecological concepts. The activists, enthralled by the possibility of integrating what they called nature into New Orleans, expressed a holistic view of the riverfront's place within the urban form. Technology was a fragmenting agent, they believed, threatening to cut the city off from the Mississippi. Accordingly, many of the speakers were loathe to allow only the Quarter's interior to be preserved, while the roadway sullied the district's periphery. Finally, at the meeting's end, the assembly voted to ask city and state officials to seek alternate routing for the highway, away from the waterfront.[19]

The rising tide of antiexpressway sentiment washed over another public hearing, held two months later by Louisiana's highway department. As students protested outside, a parade of speakers consumed more than

seven hours at the meeting. The night's highlight arrived when Thomas
Nicholls, vice chairman of the Vieux Carré Commission (VCC)—the
state-sanctioned preservation committee charged with protecting the
Quarter—spoke out. Nicholls stated that a year earlier, Louisiana's
supreme court had upheld the VCC's right to regulate all construction
in the Quarter. And because the road would fall within the district's limits, he argued, "the appropriate public authority to authorize construction of any structure in the established limits of the Vieux Carré is the
Vieux Carré Commission." He then announced that the VCC opposed
any "structure that tends to separate Jackson Square and the rest of the
Quarter from the river." Such a structure, Nicholls explained, would "inevitably destroy the historic identification of the Vieux Carré with the
activities on the wharves."[20]

Nicholls's proclamation signaled changes in how the VCC viewed the
French Quarter. Since 1936, when the state had created the VCC, the organization had been a leader in national preservation circles. Rather than
relying on antiquated "monumental" preservation standards, in which single buildings were saved for their architectural or historic value, regardless of their surroundings, the VCC had worked district-wide, saving networks of structures. As a result, the Quarter, along with Charleston, South
Carolina, had served as model preservation efforts. Still, though the VCC
had been relatively progressive, it had focused almost exclusively on the
built environment, sometimes at the expense of the city's relationship with
the river.[21] The river was choked with pollution and commercial barges;
its banks were littered with rails, warehouses, wharves, and a floodwall.
Because members of the VCC had reasoned that the industrial waterfront
was not, indeed could not possibly be, a part of one of the nation's great
historic districts, they had used the riverbanks as a dumping ground, occasionally shunting additional commercial development there, while preserving the Quarter's interior—at least until 1965.

At the highway-department hearing, Nicholls took a new position, a
more inclusive view of the Quarter's environs, which wove the riverbanks
into the historic district's fabric. He indicated that rather than abandoning or further marginalizing the waterfront, as it sometimes had in the
past, the VCC would claim the river and wharves as part of the Quarter's
future. This view of the urban landscape, again apparently influenced by
ecological concepts, allowed room for the Vieux Carré's built *and* riparian environments, even suggesting that the two were symbiotic.

Emboldened by Nicholl's stand, several freeway fighters began lobbying in Washington, where the secretary of the interior, Stewart Udall, had

recently published a book about the nation's environmental problems, *The Quiet Crisis*. Udall proved sympathetic to the activists, suggesting that the entire Quarter, including the waterfront, might be designated a national historic landmark. Facing the prospect of federal intervention, expressway proponents went on the attack, arguing that, because of the floodwall, the highway would not harm any of the historic district's buildings and would thus be completely removed from the Vieux Carré. This position suggested that the Corps's wall could serve as a kind of Maginot Line, keeping modern, commercial development, albeit much needed, out of the Quarter's romantic core. The pro- and antiexpressway views had completely diverged. Profreeway interests still saw the riverfront as a separate entity from the historic district. Freeway fighters rejoined that the city and river *were* linked. Although the riverfront lacked the wrought-iron balconies, the eighteenth-century Spanish-style buildings, and the quaint charm of the Quarter's interior, they argued that the waterfront remained the district's heart.[22]

As the battle raged on in New Orleans, the federal highway administrator, Rex Whitton, approved the proposed expressway, designated Interstate 310, on January 24, 1966.[23] The freeway fighters, refusing to submit, responded by campaigning nationwide to drum up renewed support for their cause. Their efforts paid quick dividends, as several prominent urban newspapers published articles skewering the highway, signaling that multiple fronts had opened in the freeway war by that time. The *New York Times,* for instance, added its voice to a growing chorus of discontent, fretting that cars and trucks had "ceased to be man's servants and became his masters." Highways, the *Times* warned, "march—imperially, relentlessly, inexorably—across stream, meadow, and woodland, through parks and nature preserves.... As neighborhoods are sliced in two and cemeteries are relocated, neither the quick nor the dead are safe."[24]

Buoyed by support from the national media, the freeway fighters again lobbied the federal government to reexamine its transportation policies, and spirited debate raged in Congress about the impact of highway construction on cities. This conflict revealed a growing consciousness among federal legislators about the environmental costs of freeways. In response to the shifting political climate, Congress passed three laws in 1966, each designed in part to change the criteria by which federally funded highways were approved. The Federal Highway Act, the Department of Transportation Act, and the National Historic Preservation Act all contained provisions insuring that historic sites and parklands were to be protected from future freeway construction.[25] In time, those pieces of legislation were to provide freeway fighters around the country with powerful artillery to continue battling the highway lobby and poorly planned roads.

As expressway opposition mounted nationally, the Bureau of Governmental Research (BGR), a political watchdog organization in New Orleans, announced that it would conduct an environmental-impact assessment of the roadway. Before it began its research, however, the pro-commerce and prodevelopment BGR asserted its nonpartisan standing, explaining that its report would not suggest routes removed from the riverfront, or condemn the roadway, but would offer suggestions about how to limit any negative impact the expressway might have on the French Quarter. Therefore, New Orleanians were shocked when, two months after the BGR began work, a draft of its findings leaked to a local television station. For a week in November, as they gathered to watch the evening news, the city's residents learned that the highway would increase noise levels in the Quarter while also limiting future development opportunities at the waterfront. Newscasters also warned that the expressway's shadow, coupled with noise from passing cars, would dramatically alter the scene near Jackson Square, a municipal treasure.[26]

With many locals confused about the roadway, the BGR released the full text of its study. Planners, engineers, architects, environmentalists, and preservationists all collaborated on the project, which was marked by an expansive, perhaps even ecological, view of the urban form. Roadway boosters nonetheless took solace in several sections of the document that predicted that the project would benefit the Quarter by decreasing the number of vehicles in the district's fragile interior. The freeway fighters rejoiced also, because the report raised numerous questions about the expressway's potential effects on the city's connection with the river. The researchers summed up their concerns by describing the "genius of the Quarter" as the district's "tout-ensemble," or "sum total effect, buildings plus environment."[27] In short, the BGR's researchers suggested that the relationship between the river and city, between what local residents had traditionally labeled the urban and natural, often assuming an inherent opposition between the two, was crucial in creating New Orleans's charm and needed to be guarded.

The tout-ensemble concept epitomized the freeway fighters' goal of highlighting the interdependent nature of space in New Orleans. The city and river were linked at the waterfront, and although that connection had become tenuous through the years, it could and should be strengthened by reconstructing the riverfront landscape as a vibrant public space open for recreation as well as commerce. The BGR report lamented that "the elevated expressway, because of its great massiveness and length through the Vieux Carré, will create a visual and physical barrier that will separate the historic core from the river." That " 'barrier effect' will tend to thwart future efforts to redefine the river once more as the natural physical boundary of the Vieux Carré."[28] Although the road might have many benefits, it would also threaten the Quarter's tout-ensemble by sacrificing the city's relationship with the river (figure 35).

The study's release shifted the debate about the expressway in New Orleans. When the probusiness BGR critiqued the roadway, it gave some project boosters and undecided community members pause. It proved especially important that the BGR cast the highway as a threat to future waterfront development. Throughout the twentieth century, and especially after the VCC's creation, New Orleans had increasingly built its economy not only on trade, but also on tourism. In those years, the city had capitalized on the Quarter's historic charms, using the district to attract visitors. In short, New Orleanians had crafted a "usable past" in the Quarter, which they had sold to visitors seeking sanitized and romantic Old South ambience, usually without any unpleasant allusions to slavery.[29] The BGR then suggested that a reopened waterfront, opposite the French Quarter, would be a valuable commodity; it could be transformed from a site of production into a landscape of consumption for tourists, eager to surround themselves with prepackaged versions of the past *and* with representations of the natural world growing in popularity at a time described by Donald Worster as the "Age of Ecology."[30] The BGR's argument thus demonstrated that some New Orleanians' views of the river had shifted: the Mississippi could serve the city as a commercial highway, as it had for more than two hundred years, and also as a historical artifact, recreational amenity, and aesthetic treasure. But only if the city found another site for the expressway.[31]

Suddenly, fighting the freeway did not seem necessarily countercultural; there was comfortable middle ground available between the roadway and a waterfront public park, an appealing position for probusiness moderates in the city to claim. Ironically, the BGR seemed to be saying that *not* building the expressway might be the best development initiative for the city—no growth as progrowth. Consequently, many powerful members of the New Orleans's upper-middle and upper classes joined the antiexpressway forces, especially after the state highway department recommended extending the roadway to join a proposed Mississippi River bridge slated to enter the city through the affluent, uptown Gar-

Figure 35. The expressway looms above the river, fronting the French Quarter. St. Louis Cathedral, on Jackson Square, stands on the lower right in this model (ca. 1960s). Courtesy of the Special Collections Division, Tulane University.

den District neighborhood. As elites who lived near that span's proposed route worried about their property values and urban aesthetics—echoing the sentiments of New Orleanians who had fought the earliest public belt railroad initiatives in the 1880s—the freeway fighters rejoiced because the bridge's association with the expressway linked French Quarter environmentalism with uptown NIMBYism.[32] One journalist noted that the BGR report "broke through the Magnolia Curtain, that curious combination of indolence and political self-interest which has settled so charmingly over the First Families of New Orleans."[33]

Shortly after the BGR report's publication, a group of freeway fighters again traveled to Washington, this time to lobby Lowell Bridwell, the new federal highway administrator. The activists hoped that Bridwell, faced with compelling facts, would withhold final approval of the expressway because it failed to meet standards set for federally sponsored construction in historically sensitive areas. After meeting with the freeway fighters, Bridwell decided that he needed to travel to New Orleans, and on June 19, 1967, he held a public hearing in the city. As the meeting ended, he promised a recommendation within three months. Late that summer, the Bureau of Public Roads released a plan for a riverfront expressway built at grade level. Although the project's proponents mourned their defeated elevated road, by December 1968 they had accepted the planned grade-level highway. The freeway fighters had not.[34]

On January 9, 1969, the New Orleans City Council held yet another public hearing, a forum to discuss the grade-level expressway proposal.

The project's proponents argued that a grade-level road offered a much-needed compromise, serving the city's commercial interests while preserving the Quarter's tout-ensemble. Freeway fighters, sensing blood in the water, circled for the kill. No expressway suited the city's needs, they contended. If one had to be built, it should be depressed below grade level, out of sight, regardless of cost. With the city more divided than ever, at the meeting's end the council narrowly approved the grade-level expressway by a vote of four to three.[35] The expressway had weathered its greatest challenge in New Orleans. Although it had descended from its elevated perch to a more stable position at grade level, the roadway's final fate lay in the hands of the secretary of transportation, John Volpe, an engineer and staunch advocate of highway construction nationwide.

Volpe, perhaps attempting to stay above the fray, sent one of his senior staffers, James Braman, the assistant secretary for urban systems and environment, to New Orleans in the summer of 1969. Braman arrived in the city on June 6 and held a meeting with the expressway's boosters. After hours of presentations, in which the road's supporters rehashed well-worn arguments, Braman then met with the freeway fighters. There, too, he suffered through rhetoric, gone stale with age. With his day nearing an end, Braman assured the activists that he would return to Washington and give his assessment to Volpe, who would make the "awesome decision" within two months. It did not take Volpe anywhere near that long. Just three weeks later, he announced that the roadway was dead.[36] He justified his decision with language nearly identical to that used by the BGR in its report published in 1966. Volpe explained that the federal government could not support the project, because "the Riverfront Expressway would have separated the French Quarter from its Mississippi River levee, and waterfront."[37] In other words, he had accepted that the Quarter's identity was in part an outgrowth of its relationship with the river, as the freeway fighters had suggested for years.

Even after Volpe announced the expressway's cancellation, the controversy did not end. Freeway fighters boldly predicted that a new era had dawned at New Orleans's waterfront, a time in which the city would celebrate its spatial, cultural, and historical relationship with the Mississippi.[38] In their memoir of the conflict, two of the leading activists, Richard Baumbach and William Borah, recall that "the heretofore invincible Highway Gang had been stopped dead in its tracks on the banks of the Mississippi River in New Orleans. It was a great victory for the little people." The expressway's boosters, on the other hand, moaned that the city had sacrificed millions of dollars in federal funds, an opportunity to revitalize its waterfront for commercial purposes, and the chance to clear traffic from the Quarter's fragile streets. One resident of the historic district complained that the activists were a "small, but very vocal group." He warned that cars would soon destroy the district, and that "the same group of headline seekers will be found beating their breasts and doing nothing about it."[39]

In the days following the highway's demise, commentators around the country ruminated about the potential fallout from Volpe's choice. According to *Business Week,* the Department of Transportation admitted that cancellation of the riverfront expressway marked the "first time any segment of the 42,500 mile Interstate System had been rejected for purely environmental reasons." The article also suggested that "new trends" were gaining support nationwide, offering "greater weight to social and environmental needs when building urban expressways."[40] Indeed, Volpe's decision seemed to signal that an ecological idea, adopted in the French Quarter by New Orleans's freeway fighters, had captured the national imagination: the concept of the tout-ensemble—the notion that a city could not be broken down into compartmentalized zones, but should be viewed as an interdependent whole—had helped sink a major freeway initiative.

For two centuries New Orleanians had typically constructed urban spaces in obeisance to emerging transportation technologies, often conflating the waterfront's public designation with commercial gain. Beginning in 1958, however, the freeway fighters had sought a new path. After applying a broad view of public space and urban nature to the city's waterfront landscape, they had taken on entrenched business interests, government officials, and the powerful highway lobby. Along the city's border with the Mississippi, those activists had looked beyond the floodwall, the levee, the train tracks, the warehouses, and the wharves, into the depths of collective memory, and then toward the city's future. There, they had seen a vibrant connection with one of the continent's greatest environmental wonders. As a result, the freeway fighters had demanded a place for the Mississippi in New Orleans, and a place for New Orleanians on the Mississippi's banks. They had called for an apposition of a river and its city.

It turned out that the years during which I wrote this book were good ones to take on a project such as this. As our cities have gobbled up millions of acres of previously wild lands, either growing at a reasonable rate or sprawling, depending on your perspective, the nation has become increasingly fascinated with the apparently strained intersection of what most people still insist on calling the urban and the natural. Nature, in general, has remained one of our passions, as the baby boomers raise the eco-boomers and the environmental movement attains a status akin to civic religion in many quarters. For decades, readers and television watchers have consumed a constant stream of books and programs focused on animal attacks, mountaineering, and environmental disasters, to name just a few popular subjects, all focused on conflicts falling within the boundaries of what my tenth-grade English teacher would have labeled Man versus Nature—further evidence that the nonhuman world has achieved remarkable cultural influence. And urban space, too, has generated seemingly endless discussions in recent years, as more relatively affluent people, tired of commuting hours each way to work, or perhaps eager for exposure to what they think of as culturally rich environs, return to cities only to find themselves wondering what makes for livable metropolitan surroundings. As a result, we have witnessed a renewed interest in public landscapes and urban architecture, subjects often thought dead as recently as the 1980s.

In these same years, cities around the nation, indeed throughout the world, have continued to embark on a process that dates back to the late 1950s: they have rediscovered their watery edges. This book, then, has been written and published at a time when hundreds of metropolitan areas, ranging from Amsterdam to Vancouver, from Boston to Seattle, joined what some urbanists are calling a "new waterfront" movement.[41] It seems that for a host of reasons, modern urbanites, like people throughout human history, have a passion for water. And so, responding to market forces and citizen demands, many cities that once hid their waterfronts behind commercial structures are now following the lead of New Orleans, among other places, reopening those spaces for development, using local riverbanks, lakesides, and oceanfronts as magnets to attract investment, and in the process encouraging people to reacquaint themselves with the water sources that typically spurred urban settlement in the first place. These projects vary. Some of the new waterfronts are recreational, residential, or commercial; others are educational, environmental, or historical. But all are an attempt to relate a place more closely to a neighboring body of water, and all are a product of a cultural moment in which many city dwellers wish to interact with something that they call nature.

This book, therefore, appears to arrive at an opportune time, just as there is a popular appetite for its key themes. Still, a question demands attention: what can this study tell us, or what lessons are to be learned from reading about two centuries of New Orleans's relationship with the Mississippi River? To me, at first this seems like a troubling question because of a sign standing on the outskirts of New Orleans. Every time I land at the Crescent City's airport, after walking past the rows of ringing and whistling slot machines and then bypassing the shops promising "authentic Cajun food, packed for shipping," I finally emerge in the damp air, and then rent a car before merging onto Interstate 10 for the half-hour drive into the city. Just beyond the airport, a nondescript placard confronts me, reading, innocently enough: "Welcome to America's Most Interesting City." Okay, this seems fine—unless you are trying to make an argument that uses New Orleans as a representative example. Should that be the case, the words "America's Most Interesting City" point to what might be a serious problem: New Orleans has always stood apart in our national discussions. Too French, too Spanish, too ethnically diverse, too many good times, too corrupt, too Deep South, the northernmost Caribbean port, a tripartite racial system, and so on and so on. The point is clear: this place is not like the rest of the country; it is unique, sui generis, if you prefer.

No doubt, there is much truth to this point of view. Still, I think that study of the city's relationship with the river is valuable. Most urban areas in the United States have experienced protracted land-use disputes, nagging questions about how much and what kind of space to allocate to transportation technologies, and dilemmas about how to cope with disasters, whether "natural" or human-constructed. And most cities in this country have also grappled with questions of how best to administer or produce public spaces: how should such spaces be used, and who should be allowed to use them? In other words, who is part of the public in the city, and what kinds of behavior can lead to exclusion from this often ill-defined category? New Orleans, then, may be unusual, but it is not unique. The city's past therefore provides insights for an audience interested in urban morphology, planning history, the history of technology, and environmental history—especially for readers seeking an antidote to the last discipline's persistent Western bias. For these reasons, I believe that it makes sense to revisit the riverbanks in New Orleans in the years after the expressway controversy, when the city decided to reopen its waterfront, for a final summation of this book's arguments.

The landscape produced at the waterfront instead of the expressway is frustrating to many critics of urban space. The scene there includes an ultramodern aquarium, the tourist-driven French Market and Café du

Monde, two indoor shopping plazas, and riverboat gambling casinos
that are supposed to ply the river but often find excuses to cling to the
more profitable shoreline (figure 36). Of such "festival marketplaces,"
architectural historian M. Christine Boyer sneers, "open-air bazaars and
storehouses of heterogeneity, where one can buy anything from anywhere, have so concentrated geographical space and historical time that
the uniqueness of place and the specifics of context have been erased
completely."[42] In part, she is right. The city's waterfront is more a commercial carnival than an idealized public space or riparian wilderness.
In some ways, this landscape typifies what urban critics call the "geography of nowhere," a place without place, a homogenous urban landscape that blends into others like it nationwide.[43] In short, New Orleanians have used history, scrubbed of its unseemly elements, as an anchor
store in a preservation mall. In this way the waterfront again has become
what the city's commercial elites have always wanted: a landscape of
power, order, and discipline, a tableau of progress.

I would even argue that some of the well-intentioned freeway fighters
unwittingly cleared the way for the waterfront's commercialization, that
their perceptions of nature and the public abetted redevelopment of that
space while allowing other parts of the city to be blighted by highways.
For instance, during the expressway controversy, as the activists, most of
whom were white and relatively well off, fought for the riverbanks, workers built an elevated stretch of Interstate 10 through a predominantly low-
income neighborhood at the Quarter's rear, bisecting Claiborne Avenue,
a traditional route for the city's largest African-American Mardi Gras parade. In doing so, those workers also uprooted the "longest single stand
of oak trees" in the country (figures 37–39).[44] Consequently, the I-10 construction raises questions about the fallout from the freeway fighters'
definitions of nature and the public. Were the oak trees not natural
enough to fight for? Was Claiborne Avenue not a public enough space to
be worth saving, or were the people who typically used that landscape
not a sympathetic enough part of the public in the city? In fairness, some
of the freeway fighters did try to keep the I-10 spur off of Claiborne, but
many of the activists arrayed against the riverfront expressway were far
more comfortable appealing to people's positive associations of the Mississippi, while another group with far less power, the city's African-Americans, watched the destruction of a promenade that they deemed as valuable as the waterfront, but that could not lay claim to the moral and
cultural weight associated at the time with nature.

Figure 36. The waterfront, despite its shortcomings, is a mixed-use space again today: a park, a port, and promenade (photograph ca. 1990s). Courtesy of Richard Nowitz.

And yet, in light of the waterfront's controversial history, one might read the landscape along the riverbanks very differently. Just behind the commercial buildings' facades lurk far more complex tales. For the first time since the end of the nineteenth century, pedestrians can cross the railroad tracks still dividing the city and river, climb steps to the top of the protection levee standing opposite Jackson Square, and promenade at a park similar to the one that freeway fighters called for in 1962.[45] This landscape reveals volumes about not only the riverfront expressway controversy but about how non-elite New Orleanians have struggled for control of the waterfront for more than two centuries. For students of landscape history, the modern waterfront echoes with shouts from the batture riots, conflicts over the construction of the city's steamboat wharves, and the controversies surrounding the waterfront grants to railroads following the Civil War. After spending nearly a century behind walls, the riverbanks are once more available for people to use, a

Figure 37. The oak trees that once lined Claiborne Avenue (ca. 1960s). Courtesy of William Borah.

Figure 38. Construction workers clear trees from Claiborne Avenue (ca. 1960s). Courtesy of William Borah.

Figure 39. An elevated spur of Interstate 10 now looms above Claiborne Avenue (photograph ca. 1970s). Courtesy of William Borah.

functioning part of the city's tout-ensemble, and a symbol of countless battles over the control of urban landscapes.

Critics can still argue that the waterfront is not a true public space, that it is open to paying customers by invitation only. Again, there is truth to this perspective as well, but the full story is more elaborate than that, because many non-elites also claim space near the river. In 1972, shortly after the city opened the waterfront park, some onlookers began complaining about "hippies" strumming guitars while gazing at the Mississippi's turbid waters.[46] And "undesirables" continue using the waterfront today, including so-called street waifs—homeless children—whom business interests in the Quarter worry drive away skittish tourists. New Orleans's commercial community occasionally calls for rigid vagrancy laws that would define these individuals as outside the public by stripping them of their right to use the waterfront.[47] In occupying space at the riverbanks, though, non-elites in the city still reassert their citizenship, in some ways mirroring the actions of New Orleanians who, throughout much of the nineteenth century, used the waterfront as they saw fit. In short, the heterogeneous population found at the waterfront today offers another illustration that corporate control of that space is not absolute, and that the public still remains a tangled and contested concept.

At the same time, although developers have undoubtedly written a narrative of consumption onto the waterfront, other stories are also inscribed on that space. Because of the river's shape, people can gaze up- and downstream for miles, taking stock of the city's ties to the Mississippi. The malls, tacky steamboats, and aquarium are all there. But so too are freight trains, clattering along the riverbanks, laden with cargo, and the multicolored warehouses and wharves of the nation's second busiest port. While the public belt railroad and Dock Board's structures can be read as evidence of the power that commercial elites have wielded at the waterfront throughout the city's history, those places and the people who work at them also might remind bystanders of labor's importance in building a commercial metropolis. For this reason, it is important that onlookers can see that the waterfront remains a functioning port, a landscape of both production and consumption. Just as it was in the eighteenth and nineteenth centuries, the waterfront is again a multi-use space—market, port, and promenade.

As significantly, the Mississippi itself, rolling by the city that it helped create, is now accessible to onlookers at the waterfront. And so, although New Orleans's waterfront does have much in common with commodified public spaces like Baltimore's Inner Harbor, Boston's Quincy Market, and New York's South Street Seaport, the landscape along the Crescent City's riverbanks is evidence of the Mississippi's role in shaping urban space.[48] Whether as a wellspring for public memories, motivating the freeway fighters to battle the riverfront expressway, or through the power of fluvial tectonics, eroding and depositing terrain in the city, the Mississippi has played a profound role in producing space in New Orleans. The waterfront, then, might remind observers of some of the many meanings that the river has held for the city and of the Mississippi's enduring power. The levee, for instance, symbolizes not only technological sophistication and engineering prowess, but also environmental peril; for people familiar with the city's history, it is a sign that the river is never entirely under control. And the waterfront's openness today can reveal the significance of geology, the impact of an unstable urban foundation built by the river over millennia.

Too often, urban space and landscapes are portrayed exclusively as socially produced, as products of only human efforts.[49] As long as this remains the case, as long as cities are seen only as social artifacts, we will ignore the importance of urban nature, maintaining a false and destructive dichotomy between nature and culture. For this reason, we need to appreciate the depth of history embedded in landscapes such as the waterfront; doing so provides a useful corrective, a reminder of the non-human or ecological dimension of urban space. As I have struggled to portray it, the river's relationship with the city rebuts Lewis Mumford's contention that "nature, except in a surviving landscape park, is scarcely to be found near the metropolis."[50] This is a final story that one can read at the waterfront: a reminder to look carefully to find and understand nature, in all of its confusing guises, where it exists in urban areas. In the words of Jane Jacobs: "Nature, sentimentalized and considered as the antithesis of cities, is apparently assumed to consist of grass, fresh air and little else, and this ludicrous disrespect results in the devastation of nature."[51] New Orleans's waterfront suggests that Jacobs is right, that nature and public space are more complicated and resilient than we typically assume. The two are often intertwined, sometimes inextricably so.

Notes

ABBREVIATIONS

ASP, PL	*American State Papers, Public Lands*, vol. 2 (Washington, D.C.: Gales and Seaton, 1834)
Caplan Papers	Caplan Papers, Mississippi River Flood, record group no. 44, Louisiana State Museum Historical Center, New Orleans
CDV	Conseil de Ville Records, New Orleans City Archives, Louisiana Division, New Orleans Public Library
CFC, HR	*Hearings Before the Committee on Flood Control, House of Representatives, on the Control of Destructive Flood Waters of the United States,* multiple dates (Washington, D.C.: Government Printing Office)
Claiborne Letters	Dunbar Rowland, ed., *The Official Letter Books of W. C. C. Claiborne,* multiple vols. (Jackson, Miss.: State Department of Archives and History, 1917)
Dock Board Report	Board of Commissioners of the Port of New Orleans, *Annual Reports of the Board of Commissioners of the Port of New Orleans,* multiple years (New Orleans: n.p.)
NOB	*New Orleans Bee*
NODD	*New Orleans Daily Delta*
NODP	*New Orleans Daily Picayune*
NOI	*New Orleans Item*
NOIT	*New Orleans Item-Tribune*

NOMSJ	*New Orleans Medical and Surgical Journal*
NOMT	*New Orleans Morning Tribune*
NOS	*New Orleans States*
NOTD	*New Orleans Times Democrat*
NOTP	*New Orleans Times Picayune*
RSE	Louisiana Board of State Engineers, *Report of the Board of State Engineers to the General Assembly of Louisiana,* multiple dates (New Orleans: n.p.)
SBNOP	Second Battle of New Orleans Papers, Historic New Orleans Collection, Williams Research Center, New Orleans
SCR	Sanitary Commission of New Orleans, *Report of the Sanitary Commission of New Orleans on the Yellow Fever Epidemic of 1853* (New Orleans: Picayune Office, 1854)
VCC	*Vieux Carré Courier*

PROLOGUE. NATURE'S HIGHWAY TO MARKET

The title of this prologue is drawn from George Washington Cable, The Creoles of Louisiana *(New York: Charles Scribner's Sons, 1884), 217.*

1. Tom Weil, *The Mississippi River* (New York: Hippocrene Books, 1992), 21, 31; Willard Price, *The Amazing Mississippi* (New York: John Day, 1963), 4.

2. Ralph K. Andrist, *Steamboats on the Mississippi* (New York: American Heritage Publishing, 1962), 37; *The Mississippi River: A Short Historic Description of Flood Control and Navigation* (Vicksburg, Miss.: Mississippi River Commission, 1940), 1; D. O. Elliot, *The Improvement of the Lower Mississippi River for Flood Control and Navigation* (Vicksburg, Miss.: U.S. Army Corps of Engineers Waterways Experiment Station, 1932), 1: 24; Lyle Saxon, *Father Mississippi* (New York: Century, 1927), 253.

3. Price, *The Amazing Mississippi,* 102.

4. Weil, *The Mississippi River,* 244.

5. Roger T. Saucier, *Geomorphology and Quaternary Geologic History of the Lower Mississippi Valley* (Vicksburg, Miss.: U.S. Army Corps of Engineers Waterways Experiment Station, 1994), 136–41.

6. Charles R. Kolb and Jack R. Van Lopik, "Depositional Environments of the Mississippi River Deltaic Plain," in Martha Lou Shirley, ed., *Deltas in Their Geologic Framework* (Houston: Houston Geologic Society, 1969), 17.

7. Timothy Flint, *The History and Geography of the Mississippi Valley* (Cincinnati: E. H. Flint and L. R. Lincoln, 1832), 1: 103.

8. Albert Cowdrey, *The Delta Engineers: A History of the U.S. Army Corps of Engineers in the New Orleans District* (New Orleans: U.S. Army Corps of Engineers, 1971), iv.

9. Baron Marc de Villiers, "A History of the Foundation of New Orleans," *Louisiana Historical Quarterly* 3 (April 1920): 158; Pierre LeMoyne D'Iberville,

Iberville's Gulf Journals, ed. and trans. Richebourg Gaillard McWilliams (Tuscaloosa: University of Alabama Press, 1981), 57.

10. Price, *The Amazing Mississippi,* 4.

11. Peirce F. Lewis, *New Orleans: The Making of an Urban Landscape* (Cambridge, Mass.: Ballinger Publishing, 1976), 17.

12. Ibid.

13. Mathé Alain, *Not Worth a Straw: French Colonial Policy and the Early Years of Louisiana* (Lafayette, La.: Center for Louisiana Studies, 1988), 66–73; Gwendolyn Midlo Hall, *Africans in Colonial Louisiana: The Development of Afro-Creole Culture in the Eighteenth Century* (Baton Rouge: Louisiana State University Press, 1992), 2–14; Daniel H. Usner, *Indians, Settlers, and Slaves in a Frontier Exchange Economy: The Lower Mississippi Valley before 1783* (Chapel Hill: University of North Carolina Press, 1992), 16–24.

14. Francois Xavier Charlevoix, *Journal of a Voyage to North America,* ed. and trans. Louise Phelps Kellog (Chicago: Caxton Club, 1923), 2: 272, 258; Henry Murray, *Lands of the Slave and the Free* (London: John Parker and Son, 1855), 248.

15. John G. Clark, *New Orleans, 1718–1812* (Baton Rouge: Louisiana State University Press, 1970), 11.

16. Kevin Lynch, *The Image of the City* (1960; reprint, Cambridge, Mass.: MIT Press, 1998), 7; Amos Rapoport, *The Meaning of the Built Environment: A Nonverbal Communication Approach* (1982; reprint, Tucson: University of Arizona Press, 1990), 7–13; Yi-fu Tuan, *Topophilia: A Study of Environmental Perception, Attitudes, and Values* (Englewood Cliffs, N.J.: Prentice-Hall, 1974), 16–57.

17. Raymond Williams, *Keywords: A Vocabulary of Culture and Society* (1976; reprint, Oxford: Oxford University Press, 1983), 219; See William Cronon, introduction to William Cronon, ed., *Uncommon Ground: Toward Reinventing Nature* (New York: W. W. Norton, 1996), 23–56.

18. Edward Soja, *Postmodern Geographies: The Reassertion of Space in Critical Social Theory* (London: Verso, 1989), 1–18, 76–93; Michel Foucault, "Questions on Geography," in Colin Gordon, ed., *Power Knowledge: Selected Interviews and Other Writings, 1972–1977* (New York: Pantheon, 1980), 63–77.

19. Raymond Williams, *The Country and the City* (Oxford: Oxford University Press, 1973), 1–12; Neil Smith, *Uneven Development: Nature, Capital, and the Production of Space* (Oxford: Basil Blackwell, 1984), 2, 31, 55–58; William Cronon, *Nature's Metropolis: Chicago and the Great West* (New York: W. W. Norton, 1989), 7; Christine Meisner Rosen and Joel Arthur Tarr, "The Importance of an Urban Perspective in Environmental History," *Journal of Urban History* 30 (May 1994): 301–4; Eric Monkonnen, *America Becomes Urban: The Development of U.S. Cities and Towns, 1780–1980* (Berkeley: University of California Press, 1988), 3; Lewis Mumford, *The Culture of Cities* (1938; reprint, San Diego: Harcourt, Brace, 1970), 253.

20. Cronon, *Nature's Metropolis,* xix.

21. Henri Lefebvre, *The Production of Space,* trans. Donald Nicholson-Smith (Oxford: Basil Blackwell, 1998), 68–168; Mark Gottdiener, *The Social Production of Urban Space* (Austin: University of Texas Press, 1994), 25–69, 116–56, 195–228, 263–91.

22. D.W. Meinig, ed., *The Interpretation of Ordinary Landscapes: Geographical Essays* (New York: Oxford University Press, 1979), 2, 6, 164.

23. Anne Whiston Spirn, *The Language of Landscape* (New Haven, Conn.: Yale University Press, 1998), 17.

24. Jürgen Habermas, *The Structural Transformation of the Public Sphere* (Cambridge, Mass.: MIT Press, 1991), 32–43; Mike Davis, *City of Quartz: Excavating the Future in Los Angeles* (New York: Vintage, 1992), 226–86; Michael Sorkin, ed., *Variations on a Theme Park: Scenes from the New American City and the End of Public Space* (New York: Hill and Wang, 1992), xiii; Sam Bass Warner, *The Private City: Philadelphia in Three Periods of Its Growth* (Philadelphia: University of Pennsylvania Press, 1968), 62; Sharon Zukin, *Landscapes of Power: From Detroit to Disney World* (Berkeley: University of California Press, 1991), 11–14.

25. Don Mitchell, "The End of Public Space? People's Park, Definitions of the Public, and Democracy," *Annals of the American Association of Geographers* 85 (1995): 115.

26. Roy Rosenzweig and Elizabeth Blackmar, *The Park and the People: A History of Central Park* (Ithaca, N.Y.: Cornell University Press, 1992), 4–7; Susan Ruddick, "Constructing Difference in Public Spaces: Race, Class, and Gender as Interlocking Systems," *Urban Geography* 17 (1992): 137; Michael Schudson, "Was There Ever a Public Sphere? If So, When? Reflections on the American Case," in Craig Calhoun, ed., *Habermas and the Public Sphere* (Cambridge, Mass.: MIT Press, 1992), 147.

27. Dolores Hayden, "Urban Landscape History: The Sense of Place and the Politics of Space," in Paul Groth and Todd W. Bressi, eds., *Understanding Ordinary Landscapes* (New Haven, Conn.: Yale University Press, 1997), 113–14; Michel de Certeau, *The Practice of Everyday Life,* trans. Steven Rendall (Berkeley: University of California Press, 1984), 91–110.

28. Peter C. Baldwin, *Domesticating the Street: The Reform of Public Space in Hartford, 1850–1930* (Columbus: Ohio State University Press, 1999), 7–10; Mary P. Ryan, *Civic Wars: Democracy and Public Life in the American City During the Nineteenth Century* (Berkeley: University of California Press, 1997), 7–18; Richard Sennett, *The Fall of Public Man* (New York: W.W. Norton, 1974), 297; William H. Whyte, *City: Rediscovering the Center* (New York: Doubleday, 1988), 6, 7, 24.

29. John McPhee, *The Control of Nature* (New York: Farrar, Straus, and Giroux, 1989), 3–92.

30. John Brinckerhoff Jackson, *American Space: The Centennial Years, 1865–1876* (New York: W.W. Norton, 1972), 132.

31. M. Christine Boyer, *Dreaming the Rational City: The Myth of American City Planning* (Cambridge, Mass.: MIT Press, 1983), 6.

CHAPTER 1. A BATTURE LAID OUT FOR THE
PARTICULAR USE OF THE PUBLIC

This chapter title is from Julien Poydras, A Defense of the Right of the Public to the Batture of New Orleans (Washington, D.C.: Julien Poydras, 1809), 15.

1. *ASP, PL,* 13; Joseph E. Tregle, Jr., "Creoles and Americans," in Arnold R. Hirsch and Joseph Logsdon, eds., *Creole New Orleans* (Baton Rouge: Louisiana State University Press, 1992), 135–37; John A. Lovett, "Batture, Ordinary High Water, and the Louisiana Levee Servitude," *Tulane Law Review* 69 (December 1994): 574.

2. John Anthony Caruso, *The Mississippi Valley Frontier* (Indianapolis: Bobbs-Merrill, 1966), 159–236; Frederic Austin Ogg, *The Opening of the Mississippi: A Struggle for Supremacy in the American Interior* (New York: Macmillan, 1904), 71–639; Francis S. Philbrick, *The Rise of the West, 1754–1830* (New York: Harper and Row, 1965), 4–331; Arthur Preston Whitaker, *The Mississippi Question, 1795–1803* (New York: D. Appleton, 1934), 3–256; Arthur Preston Whitaker, *The Spanish-American Frontier, 1783–1795* (Boston: Houghton Mifflin, 1927), 1–221.

3. Harold Fisk, *Geological Investigation of the Alluvial Valley of the Lower Mississippi River* (Vicksburg, Miss.: Mississippi River Commission, 1944), 71; Charles R. Kolb and Jack R. Van Lopik, "Depositional Environments of the Mississippi River Deltaic Plain," in Martha Lou Shirley, ed., *Deltas in Their Geologic Framework* (Houston: Houston Geologic Society, 1969), 27.

4. J. O. Snowden, J. R. J. Studlick, and W. C. Ward, *Geology of Greater New Orleans* (New Orleans: New Orleans Geological Society, 1980), 1–22.

5. *ASP, PL,* 2–17.

6. Edward Livingston, *An Answer to Mr. Jefferson's Justification of His Conduct in the Case of the New Orleans Batture* (Philadelphia: William Fry, 1813), 11.

7. CDV, vol. 1, bk. 1, 227.

8. Joseph Modeste Sweeney, "Tournament of Scholars over the Sources of the Civil Code of 1808," *Tulane Law Review* 46 (Spring 1972): 585–602.

9. Quote from Shael Herman, *The Louisiana Civil Code* (New Orleans: Louisiana Bar Foundation, 1993), 50; see also A. N. Yiannopoulos, "The Public Use of the Banks of Navigable Rivers in Louisiana," *Louisiana Law Review* 31 (June 1971): 563–82.

10. *New Orleans in 1805: A Directory and a Census* (New Orleans: n.p., 1936), 11; Samuel Wilson, Jr., *The Vieux Carré, New Orleans: Its Plan, Its Growth, Its Architecture* (New Orleans: Bureau of Governmental Research, 1968), 53–70.

11. Marcel Giraud, *A History of French Louisiana* (Baton Rouge: Louisiana State University Press, 1987), 5: 206.

12. Christian Schultz, *Travels on an Inland Voyage* (New York: Isaac Riley, 1810), 2: 193.

13. Francis Bailey, *Journal of a Tour in Unsettled Parts of North America in 1796 and 1797* (London: Bailey Brothers, 1856), 301; Dell Upton, "The New Orleans Levee: Street of the World," in Zeynep Celik, Diane Favro, and Richard Ingersoll, eds., *Streets: Critical Perspectives on Public Space* (Berkeley: University of California Press, 1994), 277.

14. Timothy Flint, *The History and Geography of the Mississippi Valley* (Cincinnati: E. H. Flint and L. R. Lincoln, 1832), 1: 265.

15. Kolb and Van Lopik, "Depositional Environments," 23.

16. *State Papers and Correspondence Bearing upon the Purchase of the Territory of Louisiana* (Washington, D.C.: Government Printing Office, 1903), 58–63; William B. Hatcher, *Edward Livingston: Jeffersonian Republican and Jacksonian Democrat* (Baton Rouge: Louisiana State University Press, 1940), 26–99.

17. George Dargo, *Jefferson's Louisiana: Politics and the Clash of Legal Traditions* (Cambridge, Mass.: Harvard University Press, 1975), 75.

18. *ASP, PL,* 23–26.

19. *ASP, PL,* 26.

20. *ASP, PL,* 33.

21. *ASP, PL,* 22, 14; Thomas Jefferson, *The Proceedings of the Government of the United States, in Maintaining the Public Right to the Beach of the Mississippi, Adjacent to New Orleans, Against the Intrusion of Edward Livingston* (New York: Ezra Sargent, 1812), 17.

22. *Courier de la Louisiane,* November 4, 1807; *ASP, PL,* 80.

23. CDV, vol. 2, bk. 1, 84–85; *ASP, PL,* 80.

24. Quote from *ASP, PL,* 80; Edward Livingston, *Address to the People of the United States on the Measures Pursued by the Executive with Respect to the Batture at New Orleans* (New Orleans: Bradford and Anderson, 1808), 1: xi.

25. *ASP, PL,* 80.

26. CDV, vol. 1, bk. 3, 201; CDV, vol. 2, bk. 1, 82; CDV, vol. 2, bk. 1, 84–85; Jean Baptiste Simon Thierry, *Examen des droits de Etats-Unis et des pretensions de Mr. Edouard Livingston sur la batture en face du Faubourg Ste. Marie* (New Orleans: Thierry, 1808), 5; *ASP, PL,* 99.

27. Hatcher, *Edward Livingston,* 156–65; Dumas Malone, *The Sage of Monticello* (Boston: Little, Brown, 1981), 55–57; Dargo, *Jefferson's Louisiana,* 78.

28. John May to Samuel Beall, April 15, 1780, May Papers, Filson Club Historical Society, Louisville, Kentucky.

29. David Wood Meriwether to anonymous person, September 14, 1785, Meriwether Papers, Filson Club Historical Society, Louisville, Kentucky.

30. John Jay to Congress, August 3, 1786, in *Secret Journals and Acts and Proceedings of Congress* (Boston: Thomas B. Wait, 1821), 4: 53; Thomas Green to the governor of Georgia, December 23, 1786, in *Secret Journals of Congress,* 4: 315.

31. First quote from Harry Innes to John Brown, December 7, 1787, in Innes Collection, Kentucky Historical Society, Manuscripts and Archives Division, Frankfort, Kentucky; second, a memorial sent to Congress by a convention held in Kentucky on Monday, November 3, 1788, in William Littel, ed., *Political Transactions in and Concerning Kentucky* (Frankfort, Ky.: William Hunter, 1806), 104.

32. James Madison to Thomas Jefferson, August 20, 1784, in Julian P. Boyd, ed., *The Papers of Thomas Jefferson* (Princeton, N.J.: Princeton University Press, 1953), 7: 406.

33. List dated August 2, 1790, in ibid., 17: 113–16; Thomas Jefferson to William Carmichael, August 2, 1790, in *American State Papers, Foreign Relations* (Washington, D.C.: Gales and Seaton, 1832), 1: 247.

34. Thomas Jefferson to William Short and William Carmichael, March 18, 1792, in *ASP, PL,* 254.

35. E. Merton Coulter, "The Efforts of the Democratic Societies of the West to Secure Navigation of the Mississippi," *Mississippi Valley Historical Review* 9 (December 1924): 378–88.

36. James Madison to Thomas Pinckney, Washington, D.C., November 27, 1802, in *State Papers and Correspondence*, 63; *Kentucky Gazette*, November 30, 1802.

37. Charles A. Miller, *Jefferson and Nature: An Interpretation* (Baltimore: Johns Hopkins University Press, 1988), 229.

38. Ogg, *Opening of the Mississippi*, 514–16; Mary Kay Phelan, *The Story of the Louisiana Purchase* (New York: Thomas Y. Cromwell, 1979), 48–110; Marshall Sprague, *So Vast, So Beautiful a Land* (Athens: Ohio University Press, 1974), 276–313.

39. Thomas Jefferson to Robert Livingston, Washington, D.C., April 18, 1802, in *Old South Leaflets* (Boston: Director of the Old South Work, n.d.), 6: 126–50.

40. Pierre Derbigny, *Case Laid Before Counsel for Their Opinion on the Claim to the Batture, Situated in Front of the Suburb St. Mary* (New Orleans: n.p., 1807), xvii.

41. Ibid., vi.

42. Dargo, *Jefferson's Louisiana*, 110–57.

43. Derbigny, *Case Laid Before Counsel*, ii.

44. Ibid., ii–iii, xxvii.

45. *ASP, PL*, 43–53.

46. *ASP, PL*, 43, 47; Edward Livingston to Thomas Jefferson, May 5, 1808, in *ASP, PL*, 34; Livingston to James Madison, May 6, 1808, in *ASP, PL*, 34; Madison to Livingston, May 20, 1808, in *ASP, PL*, 35.

47. Livingston to Madison, July 13, 1808, in *ASP, PL*, 35.

48. Livingston, *Address to the People of the United States*, xxviii.

49. Hendrik Hartog, *Public Property and Private Power: The Corporation of the City of New York in American Law, 1730–1870* (Chapel Hill: University of North Carolina Press, 1983), 45–68.

50. Charles M. Haar and Lance Liebman, *Property and Law* (Boston: Little, Brown, 1977), 35–74; C. B. Macpherson, ed., *Property: Mainstream and Critical Positions* (Toronto: University of Toronto Press, 1978), 1–14; Carol M. Rose, "Possession as the Origin of Private Property," *University of Chicago Law Review* 52 (Winter 1985): 73–88; William B. Scott, *In Pursuit of Happiness: American Conceptions of Property from the Seventeenth to the Twentieth Century* (Bloomington: Indiana University Press, 1977), 5–114; A. W. B. Simpson, *A History of Land Law* (Oxford: Clarendon Press, 1986), 1–46; Kenneth J. Vanvelde, "The New Property of the Nineteenth Century: The Development of the Modern Concept of Property," *Buffalo Law Review* 29 (Winter 1980): 325–67.

51. *Acts Passed at the First Session of the Second Legislature of the Territory of Orleans* (New Orleans: n.p., 1808), 120–29.

52. *Digest of the Civil Laws Now in Force in the Territory of Orleans, with Alterations and Amendments, Adapted to Its Present System of Government* (New Orleans: n.p., 1808), bk. 2, tit. 1, art. 6, 8.

53. *Documents in Support of the Right of the Inhabitants of the City of New Orleans to the Alluvion in Front of the Suburb St. Mary Contested by Jean Gravier* (Washington, D.C.: A. and G. Way, 1809), 3, 5, 7, 9, 16, 23, 24.

54. Julien Poydras, *Speech of Julien Poydras, Esq. the Delegate from the Territory of Orleans, in Support of the Right of the Public to the Batture in Front of the Suburb of St. Mary* (Washington, D.C.: A. and G. Way, 1810), 23.

55. Ibid., 16, 21; Poydras, *A Defense,* 9.

56. Poydras, *Speech of Julien Poydras,* 8.

57. Ibid., 8, 19–21; Julien Poydras, *Further Observations in Support of the Right of the Public to the Batture of New Orleans* (Washington, D.C.: A. and G. Way, 1809), 12.

58. John Agnew, *Place and Politics: The Geographical Mediation of State and Society* (Boston: Allen and Unwin, 1987), 5; Tony Hiss, *The Experience of Place* (New York: Alfred A. Knopf, 1990), 12, 26, 118; John Brinckerhoff Jackson, *A Sense of Place, a Sense of Time* (New Haven, Conn.: Yale University Press, 1994), 90–91; Doreen Massey, *Space, Place, and Gender* (Minneapolis: University of Minnesota Press, 1994), 3, 20.

59. Poydras, *Speech of Julien Poydras,* 23.

60. B. Lafon, *Plan of the City and Environs of New Orleans,* engraving, 1816, Historic New Orleans Collection, Williams Research Center, New Orleans; Rolinson Tanesse et al., *Plan of the City and Suburbs of New Orleans,* engraving, 1817, Historic New Orleans Collection, Williams Research Center, New Orleans; map attachment in Livingston, *An Answer to Mr. Jefferson; ASP, PL,* 75, 77; *Livingston v. D'Orgenois,* 6 Mart. 87, o.s. (1819). Title of this section drawn from Poydras, *A Defense,* 9.

61. Hatcher, *Edward Livingston,* 156–65; Malone, *The Sage of Monticello,* 55–57; *Livingston v. Jefferson,* 15 Fed. 8411 (1811); CDV, vol. 2, bk. 4, 115.

62. CDV, vol. 2, bk. 4, 118, 121, 134; CDV, vol. 2, bk. 5, 15; W. C. C. Claiborne to Julien Poydras, August 16, 1813, in *Claiborne Letters,* 5: 260–61; Claiborne to Thomas B. Robertson, September 4, 1813, in *Claiborne Letters,* 6: 264.

63. CDV, vol. 2, bk. 5, 15.

64. CDV, vol. 2, bk. 5, 11, 100, 101.

65. CDV, vol. 2, bk. 6, 37, 71, 131; CDV, vol. 3, bk. 1, 105, 149; CDV, vol. 3, bk. 2, 167; CDV, vol. 3, bk. 3, 108, 116.

66. Mark Gottdiener, *The Social Production of Urban Space* (Austin: University of Texas Press, 1994), 163.

67. Poydras, *A Defense,* 9.

68. See, for example, Anne Whiston Spirn, *The Granite Garden: Urban Nature and Human Design* (New York: Basic Books, 1984), xi, 4–34.

CHAPTER 2. HUMAN GENIUS, ORGANED WITH MACHINERY

The title of this section is drawn from William Milburn, Ten Years of Preacher Life *(New York: Derby and Jackson, 1859), 214.*

1. H. Dora Stecker, "Constructing a Navigation System in the West," *Ohio Archeological and Historical Quarterly* 22 (1913): 18–22.

2. Charles Sealsfield, *The Americans as They Are* (London: Hurst, Chance, 1828), 53.

3. Leland D. Baldwin, *The Keelboat Age on Western Waters* (Pittsburgh: University of Pittsburgh Press, 1941), 64.

4. Captain Basil Hall, *Travels in North America, in the Years 1827 and 1828* (Edinburgh: Cadell, 1829), 3: 323.

5. John Halley Journal, in King Library Special Collections, University of Kentucky, Lexington; George Rogers Taylor, *The Transportation Revolution, 1815–1860* (White Plains, N.Y.: M. E. Sharpe, 1951), 143.

6. Louis Hunter, *Steamboats on the Western Rivers* (Cambridge, Mass.: Harvard University Press, 1949), 8.

7. *Claiborne Letters,* 5: 185.

8. William Claiborne to Robert Livingston, March 26, 1811, in *Claiborne Letters,* 5: 192; chap. 26, *Acts of the Second Session of the Third Legislature of the Territory of Orleans,* April 19, 1811 (New Orleans: n.p., n.d.), 112.

9. Ruth Schwartz Cowan, *A Social History of American Technology* (Oxford: Oxford University Press, 1997), 109–10.

10. Leo Marx, *The Machine in the Garden: Technology and the Pastoral Ideal in America* (Oxford: Oxford University Press, 1964), 5–9.

11. *Louisiana Gazette,* January 11, 1812; Robert C. Reinders, *End of an Era: New Orleans, 1850–1860* (New Orleans: Pelican Publishing, 1964), 7.

12. Langdon Winner, *The Whale and the Reactor: The Search for Limits in an Age of Technology* (Chicago: University of Chicago Press, 1986), 10, 17, 47.

13. *Heirs of Fulton and Livingston v. Henry M. Shreve,* accession 70A–006, file 1003, box 449452, Federal Records Center, Forth Worth, Tex.; Edith McCall, *Conquering the Rivers: Henry Miller Shreve and the Navigation of America's Inland Waterways* (Baton Rouge: Louisiana State University Press, 1984), 11–17.

14. *Niles' Weekly Register* 5 (December 18, 1813): 272; "Political Portraits with Pen and Pencil: Henry Miller Shreve," *The United States Magazine, and Democratic Review* 22 (February 1848): 170.

15. *Niles' Weekly Register* 8 (July 1, 1815): 320.

16. James Lloyd, *Lloyd's Steamboat Directory* (Cincinnati: James T. Lloyd, 1856), 44.

17. *Niles' Weekly Register* 10 (July 20, 1816): 348; "Political Portraits with Pen and Pencil," 169; *Korby and Fosdick v. Henry Miller Shreve,* docket 1392, Civil Court Collection, First District Court, Louisiana Division, New Orleans Public Library.

18. Records of the New Orleans Collector of Levee Dues, register of flatboats, barges, rafts, and steamboats in the port of New Orleans, 1806–23, New Orleans City Archives, Louisiana Division, New Orleans Public Library; *Louisiana Gazette,* March 13, 1817; *Louisiana Courier,* March 5, 1817; *Heirs of Fulton and Livingston v. Shreve.*

19. Henry M'Murtrie, *Sketches of Louisville and Its Environs* (Louisville, Ky.: Parsons, 1819), 202; Lloyd, *Lloyd's Steamboat Directory,* 45.

20. *Heirs of Fulton and Livingston v. Shreve; Louisiana Gazette,* May 6, 1817; *Louisville Journal,* April 19, 1817; Ari Kelman, "Forests and Other River

Perils," in Craig Colten, ed., *Transforming the Mississippi and Its Environs* (Pittsburgh: University of Pittsburgh Press, 2000), 45–63.

21. Timothy Flint, *A Condensed Geography and History of the Western States* (Cincinnati: E. H. Flint, 1828), 238; Henry Reynolds Journal, in King Library Special Collections, University of Kentucky, Lexington.

22. Records of the New Orleans Collector of Levee Dues, 1806–23; *Niles' Weekly Register* 33 (November, 17, 1827): 181; Senate, Ex. Doc. 42, 32nd Cong., 1st sess., 15; House, Ex. Doc. 6, pt. 2, 50th Cong., 1st sess., 199, 213, 221.

23. Charles Olliffe, *American Scenes* (1854; reprint, Painesville, Ohio: Lake Erie College Press, 1964), 25.

24. Lester B. Shippe, *Bishop Whipple's Southern Diary, 1843, 1844* (Minneapolis: University of Minnesota Press, 1937), 95.

25. House, Ex. Doc. 6, 191, 199, 215.

26. Ibid., 191, 201–2.

27. Charles Murray, *Travels in North America* (London: Richard Bentley, 1839), 2: 189.

28. Shippe, *Southern Diary,* 95.

29. Erik Friso Haites, "Ohio and Mississippi River Transportation, 1810–1860" (Ph.D. diss., Department of History and Economics, Purdue University, 1969), 45; Thomas S. Berry, *Western Prices Before 1861* (Cambridge, Mass.: Harvard University Press, 1943), 53, 55.

30. Lloyd, *Lloyd's Steamboat Directory,* 292–93.

31. Robert Baird, *View of the Valley of the Mississippi* (Philadelphia: H. S. Tanner, 1834), 340.

32. Ibid., 280.

33. Henry Tudor, *Narrative of a Tour of North America* (London: James Duncan, 1834), 2: 36.

34. *Niles' Weekly Register* 72 (July 31, 1847): 346.

35. James Hall, *Notes on the Western States* (Philadelphia: Harrison Hall, 1838), 217.

36. John Kasson, *Civilizing the Machine: Technology and Republican Values in America, 1776–1900* (New York: Viking, 1976), 114–22, 183; Marx, *Machine in the Garden,* 197; David E. Nye, *American Technological Sublime* (Cambridge, Mass.: MIT Press, 1994), 60–66, 133–34; Wolfgang Schivelbusch, *The Railway Journey: The Industrialization of Time and Space in the Nineteenth Century* (1977; reprint, Berkeley: University of California Press, 1986), 2, 23, 40.

37. Timothy Flint, "A Condensed Geography and History of the Western States," in John Francis McDermott, ed., *Before Mark Twain* (Carbondale: Southern Illinois University Press, 1968), 12.

38. Senate, Ex. Doc. 42, 113; F. Terry Norris, "Where Did the Villages Go?" in Andrew Hurley, ed., *Common Fields* (St. Louis: Missouri Historical Society, 1997), 81.

39. Richard White, *The Organic Machine* (New York: Hill and Wang, 1995), 4.

40. Baird, *View of the Valley,* 339; Zadok Cramer, *The Navigator: Containing Directions for Navigating the Monongahela, Allegheny, Ohio, and Mississippi Rivers* (Pittsburgh: Cramer, Spear, and Eichbaum, 1817), 7–213.

41. Mark Twain, *Life on the Mississippi* (1883; reprint, New York: First Vintage, 1991), 67.

42. Ibid.

43. House, Ex. Doc. 35, 17th Cong., 2nd sess., 21.

44. Twain, *Life on the Mississippi*, 68.

45. CDV, vol. 2, bk. 5, 298; CDV, vol. 2, bk. 6, 98; CDV, vol. 3, bk. 1, 187, 195.

46. CDV, vol. 3, bk. 2, 2; CDV, vol. 4, bk. 1, 327–36; CDV, vol. 4, bk. 2, 90; minutes of the meeting of the Louisiana House of Representatives, March 5, 1835, in *NOB*, April 6, 1835; *Digeste des ordonnances, resolutions, et reglemens de la Corporation de la Nouvelle-Orléans, et recueil de lois de la legislature relatives a la dite ville* (New Orleans: Gaston Brusle, 1836), 209.

47. *Digeste des ordonnances*, 209.

48. Minutes of the city council meeting of April 4, 1835, in *NOB*, April 7, 1835.

49. *NOB*, May 14, 21, 1835; John Smith Kendall, *History of New Orleans* (Chicago: Lewis Publishing, 1922), 1: 137; Samuel Jarvis Peters, "The Autobiography of Samuel Jarvis Peters," in George C. H. Kernion, "Samuel Jarvis Peters—The Man Who Made New Orleans of To-Day and Became a National Personality," *Publications of the Louisiana Historical Society* 7 (1913–14): 76.

50. Minutes of the city council meeting of August 13, 1835, in *NOB*, August 18, 1835.

51. *NOB*, October 19, 1835.

52. *NOB*, October 20, 1835.

53. Minutes of the city council meeting of October 27, 1835, in *NOB*, October 28, 1835.

54. *NOB*, February 13, 18, 19, 1836, March 2, 3, 10, 1836; Kendall, *History of New Orleans*, 1: 137–39.

55. Morton J. Horowitz, *The Transformation of American Law, 1780–1860* (Cambridge, Mass.: Harvard University Press, 1977), 1–3.

56. *Municipality No. 1 v. Municipality No. 2*, 12 La. 49 (March 1838), 83.

57. Ibid., 49.

58. See, for example, *Pulley and Erwin v. Municipality No. 2*, 18 La. 278, 278–85.

59. J. D. B. DeBow, "The Crescent City," *Commercial Review of the South and West* 3 (March 1847): 240.

60. H. Moellhausen, *Norman's Plan of New Orleans and Environs*, hand-tinted engraving, 1845, Historic New Orleans Collection, Williams Research Center, New Orleans; S. Pinistri, *New Orleans General Guide and Land Intelligence*, engraving, 1841, in Historic New Orleans Collection, Williams Research Center, New Orleans; W. Thornton Thompson, *Plan of Municipality No. 2 Showing Wards and Squares,* hand-colored lithograph, 1845, in Historic New Orleans Collection, Williams Research Center, New Orleans.

61. DeBow, "The Crescent City," 240–41.

62. Ibid.

63. House, Ex. Doc. 6, 205.

64. Taylor, *Transportation Revolution,* 158–65; Emory R. Johnson et al., *History of Domestic and Foreign Commerce of the United States* (Washington, D.C.: Carnegie Institution, 1915), 1: 345; House, Ex. Doc. 6, 215.

65. Carol Sheriff, *The Artificial River: The Erie Canal and the Paradox of Progress, 1817–1862* (New York: Hill and Wang, 1996), 11; "New Orleans: Its Present Situation and Future Prospects," *Commercial Review of the South and West* 2 (July 1846): 58.

66. *NOB,* December 27, 1850.

67. John G. Clark, "New Orleans and the River," *Louisana History* 8 (Spring 1967): 118–33.

68. *Acts Passed at the Second Session of the Second Legislature of the State of Louisiana* (New Orleans: n.p., n.d.), 8; Judith Kelleher Schafer, *Slavery, the Civil Law, and the Supreme Court of Louisiana* (Baton Rouge: Louisiana State University Press, 1994), 90–126.

69. *Goldenbow v. Wright,* 13 La. 371 (April 1839).

70. *Acts Passed at the First Session of the Twelfth Legislature of the State of Louisiana* (New Orleans: Jerome Bayon, 1835), 152–53; *Acts Passed at the First Session of the Fourteenth Legislature of the State of Louisiana* (New Orleans: J. C. De St. Romes, 1839), 118–20; *Acts Passed at the Second Session of the Fourteenth Legislature of the State of Louisiana* (New Orleans: Bullitt, Magne, 1840), 89–90; *Acts Passed at the Second Session of the Fifteenth Legislature of the State of Louisiana* (New Orleans: J. C. De St. Romes, 1842), 308–14.

71. *Samuel T. Williamson v. Alexander Norton, Master, et al.,* 7 La Ann. 393 (1854).

72. House, Ex. Doc. 21, 25th Cong., 3rd sess., 377.

73. Senate, Ex. Doc. 18, 30th Cong., 2nd sess., 46.

74. Quote from Lloyd, *Lloyd's Steamboat Directory,* 225–27; *NOB,* November 16, 1849.

75. First quote from *NOB,* November 17, 1849; second, from *NODP,* December 15, 1850; third, from *NOB,* December 18, 1850.

CHAPTER 3. THE NECROPOLIS OF THE SOUTH

The title of this chapter is drawn from "Health of the City," NOMSJ 8 (July 1851): 135.

1. *SCR,* 7.

2. First quote: *NODD,* May 1, 1853; second quote: *NODP,* May 13, 1853.

3. Robert C. Reinders, *End of an Era: New Orleans, 1850–1860* (New Orleans: Pelican Publishing, 1964), 7–9.

4. "Health, Mortality, Etc.," *NOMSJ* 10 (September 1853): 275.

5. *SCR,* 22–25.

6. John Duffy, *Sword of Pestilence: The New Orleans Yellow Fever Epidemic of 1853* (Baton Rouge: Louisiana State University Press, 1966), vii.

7. Jo Ann Carrigan, *Saffron Scourge: A History of Yellow Fever in Louisiana, 1796–1905* (Lafayette, La.: Center for Louisiana Studies, 1994), 55, 33.

8. Lawrence Lacey and Bruce Orr, "The Role of Biological Control of Mosquitoes in Integrated Vector Control," *American Journal of Tropical Medicine and Hygiene,* supplemental, 50 (1994): 107.

9. Correspondent's report from Kingston, Jamaica, in *NODD,* June 1, 1853.

10. *SCR,* 21.

11. Margaret Humphreys, *Yellow Fever and the South* (New Brunswick, N.J.: Rutgers University Press, 1992), 3–23.

12. Henry Tudor, *Narrative of a Tour of North America* (London: James Duncan, 1834), 2: 64.

13. *SCR,* 22.

14. Charles Rosenberg, *Explaining Epidemics* (Cambridge: Cambridge University Press, 1992), 297.

15. Marcel Spletsoser, "Back Door to the Land of Plenty: New Orleans as an Immigrant Port, 1820–1860" (Ph.D. diss., Louisiana State University, 1978), app.

16. P.F. Mattingly, *The Biology of Mosquito-Borne Disease* (London: Allen and Unwin, 1969), 21–24.

17. A.N. Clements, *The Physiology of Mosquitoes* (New York: Macmillan, 1963), 302; Jack C. Jones, "The Feeding Behavior of Mosquitoes," *Scientific American* 238 (June 1978): 138.

18. K. David Patterson, "Yellow Fever Epidemics and Mortality in the United States, 1693–1905," *Social Science and Medicine* 34 (1992): 863.

19. Jean Slosek, "*Aedes Aegypti* Mosquitoes in the Americas: A Review of Their Interactions with the Human Population," *Social Science Medicine* 23 (1986): 252.

20. *SCR,* 354.

21. Mosquitoes darkening skies: *NODD,* June 16, 1853; quote: L.H. Webb Diary, June 1, 6, 1853, record group 49, Louisiana State Museum Historical Center, New Orleans.

22. *NODD,* June 29, 1853.

23. *SCR,* 21. Title of this section is drawn from Charles E. Rosenberg, *The Cholera Years* (1962; reprint, Chicago: University of Chicago Press, 1987), 26.

24. *NODP,* June 23, 1853.

25. Conevery Bolton Valencius, "The Geography of Health and the Making of the American West," in Nicolaas Rupke, ed., *Medical Geography in Historical Perspective* (London: Wellcome Trust Centre for the History of Medicine at UCL, 2000), 122–27.

26. B. Dowler, "On the Necropolis of New Orleans," *NOMSJ* 7 (November 1850): 277.

27. Carrigan, *Saffron Scourge,* 80.

28. "Health of the City," *NOMSJ* 8 (July 1851): 135.

29. E.D. Fenner, *History of the Epidemic Yellow Fever at New Orleans, La., in 1853* (New York: Hall, Clayton, 1854), 4.

30. First quote from M. Morton Dowler, "On the Reported Causes of Yellow Fever and the So Called Sanitary Measures of the Day," *NOMSJ* 11 (July 1854): 44; second, from *NODD,* October 6, 1853.

31. Carrigan, *Saffron Scourge,* 80.

32. John McKowen, *Murder as a Money Making Art* (Baton Rouge, La.: Benton, 1901), 3, 59.

33. *New Orleans Daily Crescent,* June 22, 1853; "History and Incidents of the Plague in New Orleans," *Harper's* 7 (November 1853): 797.

34. Fenner, *History of the Epidemic,* 4.

35. Suzanne E. Hatty and James Hatty, *The Disordered Body: Epidemic Disease and Cultural Transformation* (Albany: State University of New York Press, 1999), 43.

36. *NODP,* July 30, 1853.

37. John Higham, *Strangers in the Land: Patterns of American Nativism, 1860–1925* (New Brunswick, N.J.: Rutgers University Press, 1955), 5–13; Judith Walzer Leavitt, *Typhoid Mary: Captive to the Public's Health* (New York: Beacon Press, 1997), 11–32.

38. *NODD,* July 22, 1853; *SCR,* unpaginated map insert.

39. *NODD,* July 22, 1853.

40. Samuel A. Cartwright, "Review of the Meteorology, Vital Statistics, and Hygiene of the State of Louisiana," *NOMSJ* 8 (September 1851): 238–49.

41. Patterson, "Yellow Fever Epidemics and Mortality," 855.

42. Reinders, *End of an Era,* 7; *NODP,* June 28, 1853; *NOB,* June 30, 1853; *NODD,* July 30, 1853.

43. George Washington Cable, *The Creoles of Louisiana* (New York: Charles Scribner's Sons, 1884), 292.

44. *New Orleans Price-Current, Commercial Intelligencer, and Merchants' Transcript,* July 23, 30, 1853; *NODP,* July 20, 1853.

45. Fenner, *History of the Epidemic,* 45.

46. *NODD,* July 24, 1853.

47. *NOB,* July 23, 1853; Zachary Robertson to Decius Beebe, July 27, 1853, Beebe Family Papers, record group 46, Louisiana State Museum Historical Center, New Orleans.

48. *NODD,* July 23, 26, 1853; *NODP,* August 3, 1853.

49. First quote from "Health, Mortality, Etc.," 275; second, from *NODD,* July 25, 1853.

50. Robertson to Beebe, July 27, 1853, Beebe Family Papers.

51. *NODP,* July 30, 1853; *NOB,* July 29, 1853; Cable, *The Creoles of Louisiana,* 298.

52. *NOB,* July 27, 28, 1853.

53. Ray Bellande, *Hotels and Tourist Homes of Ocean Springs, Mississippi* (Ocean Springs, Miss.: Ray Bellande, 1994), 2–7.

54. Raymond Williams, *The Country and the City* (Oxford: Oxford University Press, 1973), 1–9.

55. *NODP,* July 26, 29, 1853.

56. *NODD,* September 10, 1853.

57. *NODD,* July 23, 24, 1853.

58. *NODD,* August 1, 1853.

59. William Robinson, *Diary of a Samaritan* (New York: Harper and Brothers, 1860), 161, 150. Title of this section is drawn from "The Plague in the South-

west," *De Bow's Review of the Southern and Western States,* n.s., 15, no. 1 (December 1853): 622.

60. Thomas Keelah Wharton Diary, August 22, 1853, Manuscripts and Rare Books Division, New York Public Library; Robinson, *Diary of a Samaritan,* 150.

61. *NODD,* August 1, 8, 1853.

62. Robertson to Beebe, August 22, 1853, Beebe Family Papers.

63. *NODD,* August 8, 1853.

64. "Plague in the Southwest," 619.

65. *NODD,* August 9, 1853; *New Orleans Daily Crescent,* August 11, 1853.

66. *NODD,* August 9, 1853; Fenner, *History of the Epidemic,* 38.

67. *NODD,* September 1, 1853.

68. John Blasingame, *Black New Orleans, 1860–1880* (Chicago: University of Chicago Press, 1973), 1–27.

69. Samuel A. Cartwright, "Report on the Diseases and Physical Peculiarities of the Negro Race," *NOMSJ* 7 (May 1851): 701.

70. Ibid., 187.

71. A. Hester, "Medical History of Two Epidemic Yellow Fevers," *NOMSJ* 7 (July 1850): 82; J. C. Nott, "The Epidemic of Yellow Fever in Mobile in 1853," *NOMSJ* 10 (March 1854): 577.

72. Hester, "Medical History," 82.

73. Cartwright, "Prevention of Yellow Fever," *NOMSJ* 10 (November 1853): 316.

74. *NODD,* June 14–19, 1853; *NODP,* June 14–21, 1853; Mayor A. D. Crossman to Major General D. E. Twiggs, June 14, 1853, in New Orleans Office of the Mayor, Letter Books, 1811–1920, New Orleans City Archives Collection, New Orleans Public Library.

75. Marie Louise Marshall, "Samuel A. Cartwright and States' Rights Medicine," *NOMSJ* 93 (August 1940): 75.

76. *NODP,* September 29, 1853; *NODD,* September 23, 1853; Cartwright, "Prevention of Yellow Fever," 312.

77. Cartwright, "Meteorology, Vital Statistics, and Hygiene," 246; *NODD,* August 14, 1853.

78. Kenneth F. Kiple and Virginia H. Kiple, "Black Yellow Fever Immunities, Innate and Acquired, as Revealed in the American South," *Social Science History* 1 (Summer 1977): 420; K. David Patterson, "Disease Environments of the Antebellum South," in Ronald L. Numbers and Todd Savitt, eds., *Science and Medicine in the Old South* (Baton Rouge: Louisiana State University Press, 1989), 164.

79. Hester, "Medical History," 82.

80. John Harley Warner, *The Therapeutic Perspective: Medical Practice, Knowledge, and Identity in America, 1820–1885* (Princeton, N.J.: Princeton University Press, 1997), 4, 12–19.

81. John Duffy, ed., *The Rudolph Matas History of Medicine in Louisiana* (Baton Rouge: Louisiana State University Press, 1962), 174–206; Mary P. Ryan, *Cradle of the Middle Class* (Cambridge: Cambridge University Press, 1981), 12.

82. *NODD,* June 5, September 15, 1853.

83. *NODD,* July 28, 1853; *NODP,* June 23, 1853.

84. Robinson, *Diary of a Samaritan,* 195.

85. Barbara Welter, "Cult of True Womanhood," *American Quarterly* 18 (Fall 1966): 151–79.

86. Robertson to Beebe, August 27, 1853, Beebe Family Papers.

87. "Table of the Deaths in New Orleans During the year 1853," in *SCR*, unpaginated.

88. Robinson, *Diary of a Samaritan*, 168.

89. *NODP*, August 19, 1853.

90. *NODD*, August 23, 1853; Fenner, *History of the Epidemic*, 38.

91. *New Orleans Price-Current, Commercial Intelligencer, and Merchants' Transcript*, August 27, 1853.

92. Fenner, *History of the Epidemic*, 38.

93. *NODP*, August 24, 1853.

94. Theodore Steinberg, *Acts of God: The Unnatural History of Natural Disaster in America* (Oxford: Oxford University Press, 2000), 19.

95. Proclamation of the Mayoralty of New Orleans, August 30, 1853, New Orleans Office of the Mayor, Letter Books, 1811–1920.

96. Robertson to Beebe, September 3, 1853, Beebe Family Papers; Edward E. Legendre to Archbishop Anthony Blanc, August 11, 1853, Correspondence Collection, Archives of the Archdiocese of New Orleans.

97. *New Orleans Daily Crescent*, September 26, 1853; "Meteorological Register for New Orleans," *SCR*, unpaginated table; *NODD*, October 1, 1853.

98. *NOB*, September 19, 1853.

99. "New Orleans, Its Present Situation and Future Prospects," *Commercial Review of the South and West* 2 (July 1846): 58.

100. *New Orleans Price-Current, Commercial Intelligencer, and Merchants' Transcript*, September 17, 1853; Judah P. Benjamin to James Robb, September 8, 1853, Judah P. Benjamin Letters, MSS 265, folder 173, Historic New Orleans Collection, Williams Research Center, New Orleans.

101. *NODD*, September 11, 1853.

102. *NODP*, September 14, 1853.

103. *SCR*, 442.

104. *NODP*, September 4, 1853.

105. *NODP*, September 14, 1853; *New Orleans Price-Current, Commercial Intelligencer, and Merchants' Transcript*, September 17, 1853.

106. "Plague in the Southwest," 614.

107. *NODD*, October 13, 1853; *NODP*, October 26, 1853.

108. *NODD*, November 26, 1853.

109. *NOB*, October 25, 1853.

110. *NODD*, November 25, 1853.

111. *NODP*, December 8, 1853.

112. Duffy, *Sword of Pestilence*, 114.

113. Carrigan, *Saffron Scourge*, 170–202.

CHAPTER 4. TRIUMPHS IN THE CAUSE OF ADVANCEMENT AND PROGRESS

This chapter's title is drawn from Facts About the Port of New Orleans *(New Orleans: Picayune Job Print, 1912), 1.*

1. *NODP,* February 13, 1864.

2. James M. McPherson, *Battle Cry of Freedom: The Civil War Era* (New York: Ballantine Books, 1988), 420; House, Ex. Doc. 6, pt. 2, 50th Cong., 1st sess., 224, 227.

3. House, Ex. Doc. 6, 225–26.

4. Ibid., 227.

5. *Proceedings of the Commercial Convention Held in New Orleans, May 24th, 27th, 28th and 29th, 1869* (New Orleans: L. Graham, 1869), 9.

6. George E. Waring and George Washington Cable, "History and Present Condition of New Orleans, Louisiana," *Tenth Census, Report on the Social Condition of Cities,* vol. 19, pt. 2 (Washington, D.C.: Government Printing Office, 1887), 252.

7. Louis Hunter, *Steamboats on the Western Rivers* (Cambridge, Mass.: Harvard University Press, 1949), 585; George Rogers Taylor, *The Transportation Revolution, 1815–1860* (White Plains, N.Y.: M.E. Sharpe, 1951), 71–72.

8. William Cronon, *Nature's Metropolis: Chicago and the Great West* (New York: W.W. Norton, 1989), 84.

9. Edwin Dale Odom, "Louisiana Railroads, 1830–1880" (Ph.D. diss., Department of History, Tulane University, 1961), 98.

10. Louisiana General Assembly, Ordinance 799, n.s., art. 70, *Jewell's Digest of the City Ordinances, Together with the Constitutional Provisions and Acts of the General Assembly, Relative to the Government of the City of New Orleans* (New Orleans: Edwin L. Jewell, 1887), 188.

11. Louisiana General Assembly, Act 67 of 1869, *Jewell's Digest of the City Ordinances* (1882), 495; *New Orleans, Mobile, and Chattanooga Railroad Company v. City of New Orleans et al.,* 26 La. Ann. 517; *New Orleans City Ordinances Relating to the New Orleans, Jackson, and Great Northern Railroad Co.; New Orleans, St. Louis, and Chicago Railroad Co.; Chicago, St. Louis, and New Orleans Railroad Co., and to the New Orleans Belt Co. from May 17th, 1852 to August 15th, 1881* (New Orleans: A.W. Hyatt, 1881), 8.

12. Bonnie J. McCay, *Oyster Wars and the Public Trust: Property, Law, and Ecology in New Jersey History* (Tucson: University of Arizona Press, 1998), 33, 38; Roy Rosenzweig and Elizabeth Blackmar, *The Park and the People: A History of Central Park* (Ithaca, N.Y.: Cornell University Press, 1992), 156; Theodore Steinberg, *Nature Incorporated: Industrialism and the Waters of New England* (Amherst: University of Massachusetts Press, 1991), 177, 203.

13. *New Orleans Daily Crescent,* January 15, 1866.

14. Eric Arnesen, *Waterfront Workers of New Orleans: Race, Class, and Politics, 1863–1923* (Champaign: University of Illinois Press, 1994), 22–31.

15. City Council of New Orleans, minutes from the city council meeting of October 11, 1870, *Official Proceedings of the City Council of New Orleans, 1870–71* (New Orleans: Republican Publishing, 1870), 39.

16. Minutes from the city council meeting of December 6, 1870, *Official Proceedings,* 144.

17. *NODP,* December 18, 1870.

18. *Mobile and Chattanooga Railroad Company v. City of New Orleans,* 537. *William C. Harrison et al. vs. New Orleans Pacific Railway Company,* 34 La. Ann. 462; *Mrs. S.D.A. Werges vs. St. Louis, Chicago, and New Orleans*

Railroad Company, 35 La. Ann. 641; *F. W. Tilton et al. vs. New Orleans City Railroad Company,* 35 La. Ann. 1062; *Alexander Hill vs. Chicago, St. Louis, and New Orleans Railroad Company,* 26 La. Ann. 478.

19. W. H. Coleman, *Historical Sketch Book and Guide to New Orleans* (New York: W. H. Coleman, 1885), 30–31, 40–41; E. H. Robinson and R. H. Pidgeon, *Atlas of the City of New Orleans* (New York: E. Robinson, 1883), index map, pls. 1, 2, and 6; Sanborn Fire Insurance Company, *Maps of New Orleans, 1876,* 2: 31, Southeastern Architectural Archive, Tulane University; Sanborn Fire Insurance Company, *Maps of New Orleans, 1885,* 2: 37, 41–42, Southeastern Architectural Archive.

20. "The Great South," *Scribner's* 7 (December 1873): 136.

21. "Review of the New Orleans Market," *De Bow's Review,* ATW, 5 (September 1868): 883.

22. *Proceedings of the Commercial Convention Held in New Orleans,* 43.

23. *NODP,* February 18, 1869.

24. *NODP,* March 6, 1869.

25. *NODP,* March 17, 1869.

26. E. L. Corthell, *A History of the Jetties at the Mouth of the Mississippi River* (New York: John Wiley and Sons, 1881), 15; Luna B. Leopold, *A View of the River* (Cambridge, Mass.: Harvard University Press, 1994), 26–44; Walter M. Lowerey, "Navigational Problems at the Mouth of the Mississippi River, 1698–1880" (Ph.D. diss., Vanderbilt University, 1956), 32–99.

27. Albert Stein, "Improvement of the Mississippi River," *DeBow's Review,* ATW, 7 (December 1869): 1065.

28. Carol Sheriff, *The Artificial River: The Erie Canal and the Paradox of Progress, 1817–1862* (New York: Hill and Wang, 1996), 10, 68.

29. *NODP,* December 21, 1870.

30. *NODP,* April 16, 1871, March 22, 1873.

31. Florence L. Dorsey, *Road to the Sea: The Story of James B. Eads and the Mississippi River* (New York: Rinehart, 1947), 15, 53, 99.

32. *Proceedings of a Congressional Convention on River Improvement, St. Louis, May 1873* (St. Louis: Woodward, Tiernan, and Hale, 1873), 3; *NODP,* May 6, 10, 1873.

33. John Barry, *Rising Tide* (New York: Simon and Schuster, 1996), 61–75; quote from James Eads to Senator Carl Schurz, January 24, 1874, in Estill McHenry, ed., *Addresses and Papers of James B. Eads* (St. Louis: Slawson, 1884), 130.

34. Businessmen of New Orleans to James Eads, March 18, 1874, in McHenry, ed., *Addresses and Papers,* 146.

35. Corthell, *History of the Jetties,* 40.

36. Ibid., 261.

37. Francis Trollope, *Domestic Manners of the Americans* (London: Whittaker, Treacher, 1832), 2.

38. "The Mississippi River," *De Bow's Review,* ATW, 5 (May 1868): 457.

39. Corthell, *History of the Jetties,* 69.

40. Ibid., 75–80, 108–9.

41. Ibid., 212.

42. *NODP,* May 2, 27, 1877.

43. Corthell, *History of the Jetties,* 184.

44. *New York Tribune,* July 15, 1879, in Dorsey, *Road to the Sea,* 216.

45. Mark Twain, *Life on the Mississippi* (1883; reprint, New York: First Vintage, 1991), 182.

46. House, Ex. Doc. 6, 163.

47. *NODP,* May 20, 1881; House, Ex. Doc. 6, 163; last quote from Laurence Oliphant, *Episodes in a Life of Adventure; or, Moss from a Rolling Stone* (Edinburgh: William Blackwood and Sons, 1887), 112.

48. *NODP,* December 17, 1884; Harry Grady, *The New South* (New York: Robert Bonner's Sons, 1890), 146.

49. Donald Clive Hardy, "The World's Industrial and Cotton Exposition" (master's thesis, Tulane University, 1964), 37; Henry McElderry, *Description of Selected Specimens from the Medical and Surgical Sections of the Army Medical Museum* (New Orleans: n.p., 1884–85), 11–15, 17; C.J. Barrow, *Report of the U.S. Commissioner, and a List of the Collective Exhibit of the State of Louisiana, at the World's Industrial and Cotton Centennial Exposition* (New Orleans: A.W. Hyatt, 1885), 11; Edward C. Bruce, "The New Orleans Exposition," *Lippincott's Magazine of Popular Literature and Science,* o.s., 35 (April 1885): 417; Herbert S. Fairhall, *The World's Industrial and Cotton Centennial Exposition* (Iowa City: Republican Publishing, 1885), 19; Robert W. Rydell, *All the World's a Fair: Visions of Empire at American International Expositions, 1876–1916* (Chicago: University of Chicago Press, 1984), 73–98; first quote from A. de G. de Fonblanque, "Report by Consul Fonblanque on the World's Cotton Centennial Exhibition at New Orleans," in *Reports by Her Majesty's Diplomatic and Consular Officers Abroad on Subjects of Commercial and General Interest* (London: Harrison and Sons, 1885), 2: 36; second quote from Eugene Smalley, "In and Out of the New Orleans Exposition," *Century Magazine* 30 (June 1885): 14.

50. Fairhall, *Cotton Centennial Exposition,* 20.

51. House, Ex. Doc. 6, 163.

52. House, Ex. Doc. 1, pt. 2, 40th Cong., 3rd sess., 345.

53. *New Orleans Daily States,* April 20, 1882.

54. Sanborn Fire Insurance Company, *Maps of New Orleans, 1885,* 2: 2.

55. William Deverell, *Railroad Crossing: Californians and the Railroad, 1850–1910* (Berkeley: University of California Press, 1994), 2.

56. *NODP,* July 29, 1881.

57. *NODP,* December 23, 1884.

58. Samuel P. Hays, *The Response to Industrialism, 1885–1914* (Chicago: University of Chicago Press, 1957), 5; *New Orleans v. Texas and Pacific Railway Company,* 171 U.S. Rep. 312, 327–28.

59. Arnesen, *Waterfront Workers,* 78; Jon C. Teaford, *The Unheralded Triumph: City Government in America, 1870–1900* (Baltimore: Johns Hopkins University Press, 1984), 34; Joy Jackson, *New Orleans in the Gilded Age* (Baton Rouge: Louisiana State University Press, 1969), 27–33, 82–98.

60. John D. Fairfield, *The Mysteries of the Great City: The Politics of Urban Design, 1877–1937* (Columbus: Ohio State University Press, 1993), 2–7.

61. Untitled circular issued by the Public Belt Railroad Commission (1888), in "Public Belt Railroad," folder 1, vertical file, Special Collections, Tulane University; *NODP*, January 12, 1889.

62. *NOTD*, June 16, 1888.

63. *NOTD*, January 19, 1890.

64. *NOTD*, January 25, 1890; Ann Buttenwieser, *Manhattan Water-Bound: Manhattan's Waterfront from the Seventeenth Century to the Present* (Syracuse, N.Y.: Syracuse University Press, 1999), 62–64.

65. *NODP*, February 1, 5, 1890; *NOTD*, June 28, August 12, 1890; Harrod quote from *NOTD*, June 28, 1890.

66. *NODP*, April 6, 8, 1890; *New Orleans v. Texas and Pacific Railway Company*, 330.

67. *NODP*, May 16, 1894.

68. *NODP*, May 22, 24, 1894.

69. *NOTD*, March 10–14, 1895; Arnesen, *Waterfront Workers*, 140.

70. Arnesen, *Waterfront Workers*, 128, 134.

71. *NOTD*, March 14, 26, 1895.

72. Arnesen, *Waterfront Workers*, 141–43.

73. William Ivy Hair, *Carnival of Fury: Robert Charles and the New Orleans Race Riot of 1900* (Baton Rouge: Louisiana State University Press, 1976), 95–108; John Smith Kendall, *History of New Orleans* (Chicago: Lewis Publishing, 1922), 2: 507–9, 511–29.

74. Louisiana General Assembly, Act 70, *Acts Passed by the General Assembly of the State of Louisiana at the Regular Session, Begun and Held in the City of Baton Rouge on the Eleventh Day of May, 1896* (Baton Rouge, La.: Advocate, 1896), 103.

75. Ibid., 102.

76. Board of Commissioners of the Port of New Orleans, *First Annual Report of the Board of Commissioners of the Port of New Orleans* (New Orleans: Mauberret Printing, 1897), 7 (hereafter, Dock Board Report, preceded by ordinal number); *John Duffy et al. vs. City of New Orleans et al.*, 49 La. 114; Fourth Dock Board Report, 7; *NODP*, March 10, 1881.

77. Third Dock Board Report, 7; Sixth Dock Board Report, 2–11.

78. William M. Deacon, *Martin Behrman Administration Biography* (New Orleans: John J. Weighing, 1917), 47–55; Daniel Rodgers, "In Search of Progressivism," *Reviews in American History* 10 (December 1982): 113–32; John Buenker, John Burnham, and Robert Crunden, *Progressivism* (Rochester, Vt.: Schenkman, 1977), 3–29, 71–103.

79. Samuel P. Hays, *Conservation and the Gospel of Efficiency* (Cambridge, Mass.: Harvard University Press, 1959), 2–4.

80. David Schuyler, *The New Urban Landscape: The Redefinition of City Form in Nineteenth-Century America* (Baltimore: Johns Hopkins University Press, 1986), 186–96; William H. Wilson, *The City Beautiful Movement* (Baltimore: Johns Hopkins University Press, 1989), 2–86; Hays, *Gospel of Efficiency*, 2–8; Stephen Fox, *The American Conservation Movement: John Muir and His Legacy* (Madison: University of Wisconsin Press, 1981), 139–47; Roderick Nash, *Wilderness and the American Mind* (New Haven, Conn.: Yale University Press, 1967), 161–80.

81. Buttenwieser, *Manhattan Water-Bound*, 126; Robert L. Dorman, *A Word for Nature: Four Pioneering Environmental Advocates, 1845–1913* (Chapel Hill: University of North Carolina Press, 1998), 166–70; Peter J. Schmitt, *Back to Nature* (Baltimore: Johns Hopkins University Press, 1990), 3–10, 56–83.

82. Sixth Dock Board Report, 7–11; Seventh Dock Board Report, 11, 15; Eighth Dock Board Report, 1; Ninth Dock Board Report, 6–11.

83. *New Orleans Daily States*, August 31, 1902.

84. *NODP*, February 11, 1903; *NODP*, September 1, 1900, in *Ordinance of the City of New Orleans Providing for a Belt Railroad Board for the City of New Orleans, and a Public Belt Railroad System* (New Orleans: Allied Printers, 1900), unpaginated; *New Orleans v. Texas and Pacific Railway Company*, 344; City Ordinance 147, n.c.s., in *Ordinance Providing for a Belt Railroad; Capdevielle, Mayor v. New Orleans and S.F.R. Co. et al.*, 110 La. 904, 34 So. 868, 868–69, 872; *Behrman v. Louisiana Ry. and Nav. Co.*, 127 La. 775, 54 So. 25, 27–29.; *NODP*, February 11, 1903.

85. *Board of Com'rs for Port of New Orleans v. New Orleans and S.F.R. co. et al.*, 112 La. 1011, 36 So. 837; *NODP*, May 24, 1904.

86. *NODP*, July 2, 1905; "Behrman Tells," *NOI*, December 5, 1922.

87. *New Orleans Daily States*, August 21, 1905.

88. "The Romance of the New Orleans Public Belt Railway," in *NOTP*, magazine section, August 1, 1915; "Behrman Tells," *NOI*, December 6, 1922.

89. *Behrman v. Louisiana Ry. and Nav. Co.; Louisiana Railway and Navigation Company v. Behrman, Mayor of the City of New Orleans*, 235 U.S. 164.

90. *NODP*, August 20, 1908.

91. Deacon, *Martin Behrman Administration Biography*, 28.

92. *Report of the Commissioner of Corporations on Transportation by Water in the United States*, vol. 3, *Water Terminals* (Washington, D.C.: Government Printing Office, 1910), 148, 151.

93. Ibid., unpaginated map.

94. Susan Schulten, *The Geographical Imagination in America, 1880–1950* (Chicago: University of Chicago Press, 2001), 1–7, 239–42.

95. Kendall, *History of New Orleans*, 2: 552; Martin Behrman, *Civic Development* (New Orleans: n.p., 1913), 12.

96. Ernest M. Loeb, *Common Cause of the Mississippi Valley* (New Orleans: n.p., 1915), 1.

97. W.B. Thompson, "Address of Mr. W.B. Thompson Before the Liberal Institute, March 31, 1912: On Public Ownership, Control, and Operation of Terminal Facilities at the Port of New Orleans," in *Facts About the Port of New Orleans*, 46.

98. Paul Krause, *The Battle for Homestead, 1880–1892: Politics, Culture, and Steel* (Pittsburgh: University of Pittsburgh Press, 1992), 350–56; Carl Smith, *Urban Disorder and the Shape of Belief: The Great Chicago Fire, the Haymarket Bomb, and the Model Town of Pullman* (Chicago: University of Chicago Press, 1995), 168–72.

99. Arnesen, *Waterfront Workers*, 214.

100. *Warriner et al. v. Board of Com'rs of Port of New Orleans et al.*, 62 So. 157.

101. J. F. Coleman, "Physical Aspects of the Port of New Orleans," *World Ports* 11 (May 1923): 63.

102. John R. Stilgoe, *Metropolitan Corridor: Railroads and the American Scene* (New Haven, Conn.: Yale University Press, 1983), 3, 81, 170.

103. Ernest Peixotto, *Our Historic Southwest* (1916), 6–7, in "Description 1912–1913," vertical file, Special Collections, Tulane University.

104. Mildred Cram, *Old Seaport Towns of the South* (New York: Dodd, Mead, 1917), 288.

105. Martin V. Melosi, *Garbage in the Cities: Refuse, Reform, and the Environment, 1880–1980* (College Station: Texas A&M University Press, 1981), 16–29.

106. Charles Dudley Warner, "New Orleans," *Harper's* 24 (1887): 186.

107. Advisory Board of New Orleans, *Report on the Drainage of the City of New Orleans, by the Advisory Board, Appointed by Ordinance No. 8327* (New Orleans: T. Fitzwilliam, 1895), 23–28; Act 114, in *Acts Passed by the General Assembly of the State of Louisiana*, 162–65.

108. Martin Behrman, *New Orleans: A History of Three Great Public Utilities. A Paper Read by Martin Behrman, Mayor of New Orleans, Before a Convention of League of American Municipalities, Milwaukee, Wisconsin, September, 29, 1914* (New Orleans: Brando, 1914), 3; quote from *Thirty-second Annual Report of the Sewerage and Water Board of the City of New Orleans* (New Orleans: American, 1915), 65.

109. Behrman, *History of Public Utilities*, 11; George Washington Cable, "New Orleans Revisited," *Book News Monthly* 27 (April 1909): 564; Behrman, *History of Public Utilities*, 5.

110. Leo Marx, *The Machine in the Garden: Technology and the Pastoral Ideal in America* (Oxford: Oxford University Press, 1964), 22.

111. Ronald Forman, *Audubon Park: An Urban Eden* (New Orleans: Friends of the Zoo, 1985), xi; *NOTD*, September 1, 1904.

112. "Audubon Park, New Orleans: Sketches Illustrating Certain Ideas Touched upon in the Report of Olmsted Brothers, Landscape Architects," Brookline, Mass., December 13, 1897, in Audubon Park Commission Collection, Archives and Manuscripts, Special Collections Department, Earl K. Long Library, University of New Orleans; *NOTP*, July 10, 1899.

CHAPTER 5. AN ACT OF GOD

This chapter's title is drawn from CFC, HR, November 7 to November 22, 1927, pt. 1, 255.

1. John Barry, *Rising Tide: The Great Mississippi Flood of 1927 and How It Changed America* (New York: Simon and Schuster, 1996), 173–88; Pete Daniel, *Deep'n as It Come: The 1927 Mississippi River Flood* (New York: Oxford University Press, 1977), 3–12; Arthur DeWitt Frank, *The Development of the Federal Program of Flood Control on the Mississippi River* (New York: Columbia University Press, 1930), 187–89; Lyle Saxon, *Father Mississippi* (New York: Century, 1927), 279–90.

2. *New York Daily Mirror*, April 27, 1927, in Caplan Papers, box 1.

3. First quote: T. L. Nichols, *Forty Years of American Life* (London: Longmans, Green, 1874), 132; second quote: Clifton Johnson, *Highways and Byways of the Mississippi Valley* (1906), 2, in "Description, 1906–1908," vertical file, Special Collections, Tulane University.

4. Map of New Orleans, in Sewerage and Water Board of New Orleans, *Twenty-eighth Semi-Annual Report of the Sewerage and Water Board of New Orleans* (New Orleans: American, 1913), unpaginated; Thomas Ewing Dabney, *The Indestructible City* (New Orleans: New Orleans Association of Commerce, 1928), 3, 4; Advisory Board of New Orleans, *Report on the Drainage of the City of New Orleans, by the Advisory Board, Appointed by Ordinance No. 8327* (New Orleans: T. Fitzwilliam, 1895), 15, 17, 34.

5. First quote from James Zacharie, *New Orleans Guide and Exposition Hand Book* (New Orleans: New Orleans New Company, 1885), 44; George C. Earl, *Sewerage, Water, and Drainage System of New Orleans* (New Orleans: Sewerage and Water Board of New Orleans, 1904), 1, in "Drainage," folder 1, vertical file, Special Collections, Tulane University; last quote from Dabney, *Indestructible City*, 7.

6. *New York Daily Mirror,* April 27, 1927, in Caplan Papers, box 1; CFC, HR, November 7 to November 22, 1927, pt. 1, 255.

7. CFC, HR, November 7 to November 22, 1927, pt. 1, 255, 257–58.

8. Ibid., 255.

9. Caplan Papers, box 1, 1.

10. House, Rep. 44, 42nd Cong., 2nd sess., 2; Benjamin G. Humphreys, *Floods and Levees of the Mississippi River* (Washington, D.C.: Mississippi River Levee Association, 1914), 19.

11. John Smith Kendall, *History of New Orleans* (Chicago: Lewis Publishing, 1922), 1: 167–69.

12. Senate, Rep. 410, 29th Cong., 1st sess; House, Rep. 741, 30th Cong., 1st sess.

13. Ann Vileisis, *Discovering the Unknown Landscape: A History of America's Wetlands* (Washington, D.C.: Island Press, 1999), 72–73, 77–79, 85–86; George E. Waring and George Washington Cable, "History and Present Condition of New Orleans, Louisiana," *Tenth Census, Report on the Social Condition of Cities,* vol. 19, pt. 2 (Washington, D.C.: Government Printing Office, 1887), 249; Albert Cowdrey, *Land's End: A History of the New Orleans District, U.S. Army Corps of Engineers, and Its Lifelong Battle with the Lower Mississippi and Other Rivers Wending Their Way to the Sea* (New Orleans: U.S. Army Corps of Engineers, 1977), 9; Robert W. Harrison, *Alluvial Empire* (Little Rock, Ark.: Pioneer Press, 1961), 1: 74.

14. Charles Ellet, *Report on the Overflows of the Delta of the Mississippi,* in Senate, Ex. Doc. 20, 32nd Cong., 1st sess., 1.

15. Robert L. Dorman, *A Word for Nature: Four Pioneering Environmental Advocates, 1845–1913* (Chapel Hill: University of North Carolina Press, 1998), 5–42; David Lowenthal, *George Perkins Marsh: Prophet of Conservation* (Seattle: University of Washington Press, 2000), 17.

16. Ellet, *Report,* 27–36; quote from Charles Ellet, *The Mississippi and Ohio Rivers* (Philadelphia: Lippincott, Grambo, 1853), 132.

17. Ellet, *Mississippi and Ohio Rivers,* 132.

18. Andrew A. Humphreys and H. L. Abbot, *Report upon the Physics and Hydraulics of the Mississippi River* (Washington, D.C.: Government Printing Office, 1867), 162, 176, 173, 155, 192.

19. Donald Worster, *Nature's Economy: A History of Ecological Ideas* (1977; reprint, Cambridge: Cambridge University Press, 1994), 114–77; second quote from Edwin T. Layton, Jr., *The Revolt of the Engineers* (Baltimore: Johns Hopkins University Press, 1986), 55–60; Raymond H. Merritt, *Engineering in American Society, 1850–1875* (Lexington: University Press of Kentucky, 1969), 132.

20. Edwin T. Layton, Jr., "Mirror Image Twins: The Communities of Science and Technology in Nineteenth Century America," *Technology and Culture* 12 (October 1971): 579.

21. Florence L. Dorsey, *Road to the Sea: The Story of James B. Eads and the Mississippi River* (New York: Rinehart, 1947), 147–218; Humphreys, *Floods and Levees,* 24–45; James P. Kemper, *Rebellious River* (1949; reprint, New York: Arno Press, 1972), 34–57; Martin Reuss, "Andrew A. Humphreys and the Development of Hydraulic Engineering," *Technology and Culture* 26 (January 1985): 2; Todd Shallat, *Structures in the Stream: Water, Science, and the Rise of the U.S. Army Corps of Engineers* (Austin: University of Texas Press, 1994), 99.

22. Senate, Ex. Doc. 58, 46th Cong., 2nd sess., 14.

23. Senate, Ex. Doc. 10, 47th Cong., 1st sess., 1, 3, 11; James B. Eads, *Minority Report of the Mississippi River Commission* (Washington, D.C.: Gibson Brothers, 1882), 1, 5, 7.

24. House, Ex. Doc. 37, 48th Cong., 1st sess., 19.

25. Correspondence with businessmen of New Orleans, April 6, 1874, in Estill McHenry, ed., *Addresses and Papers of James B. Eads* (St. Louis: Slawson, 1884), 154.

26. *RSE,* 1871, 17.

27. Frank, *Development of the Federal Program,* 44–47; *Act No. 93 Creating the Orleans Levee District* (New Orleans: Hyatt, 1891), 3; *RSE,* April 20, 1890, to April 20, 1892, 8.

28. *Ruch v. City of New Orleans,* 43 La. Ann. 275, 9 So. 473; *Hart v. Board of Levee Commissioners for Parish of New Orleans,* 54 Fed. 559; *Pontchartrain R. Co. v. Board of Levee Commissioners of Orleans Levee District,* 49 La. Ann. 570, 21 So. 765.

29. John A. Lovett, "Batture, Ordinary High Water, and the Louisiana Levee Servitude," *Tulane Law Review* 69 (December 1994): 562; Martin Mayer, "The Public and Private Domains of the State," *Tulane Law Review* 12 (1938): 429–31; Charles R. Schwartz, Jr., "Levees and Batture in the Law of Louisiana," *Tulane Law Review* 21 (1947): 652–65; Richard Wolfe, "The Appropriation of Property for Levees," *Tulane Law Review* 40 (February 1966): 233–82.

30. A. N. Yiannopoulos, "The Public Use of the Banks of Navigable Rivers in Louisiana," *Louisiana Law Review* 31 (June 1971): 574.

31. *Eldridge v. Trezevant,* 160 U.S. 452.

32. Wolfe, "Appropriation of Property," 254; Schwartz, "Levees and Batture," 653–54.

33. *RSE,* April 20, 1892, to April 20, 1894, 21; *RSE,* April 20, 1896, to April 20, 1898, 66, 119; *RSE,* April 20, 1908, to April 20, 1910, 127; *RSE,* April 20, 1910, to April 20, 1912, 37, 107–12; *RSE,* April 20, 1912, to April 20, 1914, 131–33; *RSE,* April 20, 1914, to April 20, 1916, 48; *RSE,* April 20, 1916, to April 20, 1918, 103; *RSE,* April 20, 1918, to April 20, 1920, 55; *RSE,* April 20, 1920, to April 20, 1922, 113; *RSE,* April 20, 1922, to April 20, 1924, 120; *RSE,* April 20, 1924, to April 20, 1926, 117; *RSE,* April 20, 1926, to April 20, 1928, 63.

34. *RSE,* April 20, 1896, to April 20, 1898, 22; *RSE,* April 20, 1896, to April 20, 1898, 119.

35. *RSE,* April 20, 1892, to April 20, 1894, 37.

36. First quote from H. St. L. Coppée, "The Lower Mississippi and Its Regulation," in Frank H. Thompkins, ed., *Riparian Lands of the Mississippi River, Past—Present—Prospective* (New Orleans: Frank H. Thompkins, 1901), 63; second quote from Smith S. Leach, "The Mississippi River—What It Needs and Why It Needs It," in Thompkins, ed., *Riparian Lands,* 94; final quote from *Annual Report of the Mississippi River Commission for the Fiscal Year Ending June 30, 1903* (Washington, D.C.: Government Printing Office, 1903), 58.

37. George Maxwell, "Control of Floods a National Problem," 3, in "Flood Control, M–Z," vertical file, Special Collections, Tulane University.

38. Kemper, *Rebellious River,* 100–102.

39. Barry, *Rising Tide,* 162–67; D. O. Elliot, *Improvement of the Lower Mississippi River for Flood Control and Navigation* (Vicksburg, Miss.: U.S. Waterways Experiment Station, 1932), 2: 319–20; "Report of Engineering Committee to the Safe River Committee of 100," in "Flood Control, M–Z."

40. Harrison, *Alluvial Empire,* 1: 158; Kemper, *Rebellious River,* 103–4; quote from U.S. Army Chief of Engineers, *Annual Report of the Mississippi River Commission for the Fiscal Year Ending June 30, 1924* (Washington, D.C.: Government Printing Office, 1924), pt. 1, 1893.

41. CFC, HR, November 7 to November 22, 1927, pt. 1, 223.

42. John Martin Hammond, *Winter Journeys in the South* (Philadelphia: J. B. Lippincott, 1916), 115.

43. "Flood Warnings, March 23–April 29, 1927," in Isaac Monroe Cline Papers, Record Group 44, Louisiana State Museum Historical Center; Erik Larson, *Isaac's Storm: A Man, a Time, and the Deadliest Hurricane in History* (New York: Crown Publishers, 1999), 188–249.

44. Dispatch for April 14, 1927, in Cline Papers; second quote from Isaac Monroe Cline, *Storms, Floods, and Sunshine* (New Orleans: Pelican Publishing, 1945), 198.

45. *Hearings Before the Committee on Flood Control, House of Representatives, 64th Congress, First Session on H.R. 13975* (Newlands-Broussard-Rainey River Regulation Bill), March 31, April 1, 2, and 4, 1916, pt. 1 (Washington, D.C.: Government Printing Office, 1916), 105.

46. Barry, *Rising Tide,* 234–36.

47. CFC, HR, January 27 to February 1, 1928, pt. 6, 4519.

48. CFC, HR, January 2 to January 17, 1928, pt. 4, 2069.

49. *Memphis Commercial Appeal,* April 20, 21, 1927; Daniel, *Deep'n as It Come,* 17; Barry, *Rising Tide,* 201–6.

50. *NOTP*, April 22, 1927; Saxon, *Father Mississippi*, 317.
51. Saxon, *Father Mississippi*, 322.
52. Ibid., 317.
53. Caplan Papers, box 1, 5.
54. *NOS*, April 24, 25, 1927; Caplan Papers, box 1, 6.
55. Caplan Papers, box 1, 7–9.
56. Thomas Bender, *Toward an Urban Vision: Ideas and Institutions in Nineteenth-Century America* (Baltimore: Johns Hopkins University Press, 1975), 22–28.
57. Caplan Papers, box 1, 14.
58. Ibid.
59. *New Orleans Times*, April 22, 1927; *NOTP*, April 25, 1927; *Baltimore Sun*, April 27, 1927.
60. Caplan Papers, box 1, 15.
61. *NOMT*, April 27, 1927; Caplan Papers, box 1, 20–22.
62. *Minneapolis Journal*, April 27, 1927. The title of this section is drawn from Richard Wright, "The Man Who Saw the Flood," in Richard Wright, *Eight Men* (New York: Thunder's Mouth Press, 1940), 110.
63. First reporter: *NOI*, April 27, 1927; second reporter: *NOS*, April 27, 1927.
64. *Los Angeles Times*, April 27, 1927; *Dallas Journal*, April 28, 1927; *NOMT*, April 28, 1927.
65. Caplan Papers, box 1, unpaginated.
66. *NOMT*, April 29, 1927; Caplan Papers, box 1, 31; *Minneapolis Journal*, April 27, 1927.
67. *New Orleans Evening Item*, April 29, 1927; *NOS*, Saturday, April 30, 1927; *NOTP*, April 30, 1927.
68. *NOS*, April 30, 1927.
69. *NOS*, April 30, 1927.
70. Inquiries: *NOI*, April 27, 1927; car dealer: *NOTP*, May 30, 1927.
71. *NOTP*, May 3, 1927; *NOI*, May 4, 1927; *NOS*, May 1, 1927.
72. Caplan Papers, box 2, 39.
73. Quote from *NOS*, May 1, 1927; see also *NOMT*, May 2, 1927; *NOI*, May 4, 1927.
74. *Baltimore Sun*, April 30, 1927; *Birmingham News*, April 30, 1927; *Los Angeles Times*, April 30, 1927, in Caplan Papers, box 2, unpaginated; *Memphis Commercial Appeal*, May 2, 1927.
75. Caplan Papers, box 1, 35, and box 2, unpaginated.
76. *Baltimore Sun*, April 27, 1927.
77. Louisiana Department of Conservation, *Eighth Biennial Report of the Department of Conservation of the State of Louisiana* (New Orleans: Department of Conservation, 1928), 232.
78. *NOI*, May 1, 15, 1927; Frederick Simpich, "The Great Mississippi Flood of 1927," *National Geographic* 52 (September 1927): 264; *NOMT*, May 5, 1927.
79. First quote from *St. Bernard Voice*, June 11, October 7, 1927; second quote from *NOS*, January 29, 1928; estimate from Frank, *Development of the Federal Program*, 193.

80. *NOI*, May 3, 1927.

81. Caplan Papers, box 2, 47, 67, box 3, 83; *NOMT*, May 12, 1927.

82. Caplan Papers, box 4, unpaginated; *NOTP*, August 19, 20, 21; *NOMT*, August 22, 1927.

83. *NOIT*, April 21, 1929; *St. Bernard Voice*, January 14, 1929.

84. *The Final Report of the Colored Advisory Commission* (Washington, D.C.: American Red Cross, 1929), 8; *The Mississippi River Flood Control Association, Losses and Damages Resulting from the Flood of 1927* (Memphis: Mississippi River Flood Control Association, 1928), 4, 70, 72; *The Mississippi Valley Flood Disaster of 1927* (Washington, D.C.: American Red Cross, 1929), 5–7.

85. Theodore Steinberg, *Acts of God: The Unnatural History of Natural Disaster in America* (Oxford: Oxford University Press, 2000), xx.

86. *St. Bernard Voice*, April 30, 1927.

87. *New Orleans Evening Item*, April 29, 1927.

88. *NOI*, May 1, 1927.

89. *NOMT*, May 5, 1927.

90. First quote: James P. Kemper, "The Mississippi River Flood Problem," *New Orleans Life* (August 1927): 16, in James P. Kemper Papers, record group 52, Louisiana State Museum Historical Center; second quote: James P. Kemper, *A.B.C. of the Flood Problem* (New Orleans: National Flood Prevention and River Regulation Commission, 1927), 1.

91. CFR, HR, November 28, 1927 to December 19, 1927, pt. 3, 1772.

92. CFC, HR, January 18 to January 26, 1928, pt. 5, 3129.

93. *NOTP*, May 20, 1927.

94. CFC, HR, January 18 to January 26, 1928, pt. 5, 3467–74.

95. Donald Worster, *Dust Bowl: The Southern Plains in the 1930s* (Oxford: Oxford University Press, 1982), 125–84; Worster, *Nature's Economy*, 253.

96. Davis and Jadwin quotes from House, Misc. Doc. 90, 70th Cong., 1st sess., 2, 4; second quote from House, Com. Doc. 1, 70th Cong, 1st sess., 49.

97. Dana Burnett, "Between Hoover and High Water," *Collier's* 80 (July 16, 1927): 9.

98. Frank, *Development of the Federal Program*, 205–47.

99. *NOMT*, June 1, 1927; Caplan Papers, box 6, unpaginated.

100. U.S. Army Chief of Engineers, *Annual Report of the Mississippi River Commission for the Fiscal Year Ending June 30, 1937* (Washington, D.C.: Government Printing Office, 1937), pt. 1, 1773; *RSE*, April 20, 1930, to April 20, 1932, 155; U.S. Army Corps of Engineers, *Bonnet Carré Spillway* (New Orleans: U.S. Army Corps of Engineers, n.d.), 3–16.

101. *NOTP*, January 3, 1929.

102. Corps of Engineers, *Bonnet Carré Spillway*, 7; *NOTP*, September 4, October 22, 1929; Cowdrey, *Land's End*, 48–49.

103. First and second McDonald quotes: *NOTP*, January 28, 31, 1937; observer's quote: *NOTP*, February 1, 1937; Markham's quote: *NOTP*, February 21, 1937; flood's end: *NOTP*, March 17, 1937.

104. *New Orleans Sunday Item Tribune*, February 21, 1937.

105. Richard White, *The Organic Machine* (New York: Hill and Wang, 1995), ix–xi, 108–11.

EPILOGUE. THE SIMPLE NEEDS OF AUTOMOBILES

The title of this epilogue is drawn from Jane Jacobs, The Death and Life of Great American Cities *(1961; reprint, New York: Vintage, 1992), 7.*

1. City Planning Commission of New Orleans, transcript of a public hearing concerned with placing the riverfront expressway on the major street plan of New Orleans, November 19, 1958, 2, in SBNOP.

2. Ibid., 2–8.

3. Ibid., 12, 14.

4. Donald Worster, *Nature's Economy: A History of Ecological Ideas* (1977; reprint, Cambridge: Cambridge University Press, 1994), 341–47.

5. Resolution of the City Planning Commission of New Orleans, December 23, 1858, in SBNOP.

6. *New Orleans States Item,* August 19, 1951, in Vieux Carré Commission Reports (ca. 1951–79), New Orleans City Archives, Louisiana Division, New Orleans Public Library, box 3.

7. Robert Moses, "Arterial Plan for New Orleans" (November 1946), in SBNOP; *Federal-Aid Highway Act of 1956,* ch. 462, § 108 (a), (e), (1), 70 Stat. 378.

8. *NOTP,* January 18, 1962.

9. Jacobs, *Great American Cities,* 4, 7, 14, 246, 258–68, 444.

10. Rachel Carson, *Silent Spring* (1962; reprint, New York: Houghton Mifflin, 1994), 5–13.

11. Adam Rome, *The Bulldozer in the Countryside: Suburban Sprawl and the Rise of American Environmentalism* (Cambridge: Cambridge University Press, 2001), 183.

12. *VCC,* January 27–February 2, 1962.

13. Long quote from *VCC,* March 10–16, 1962; Kane quote from *VCC,* April 21–27, 1962; Dolores Hayden, *The Power of Place: Urban Landscapes as Public History* (Cambridge, Mass.: MIT Press, 1995), 9; Simon Schama, *Landscape and Memory* (New York: Alfred A. Knopf, 1995), 61.

14. Clay McShane, *Down the Asphalt Path: The Automobile and the American City* (New York: Columbia University Press, 1994), 208–28.

15. Jacobs, *Great American Cities,* 7.

16. *VCC,* March 10–16, 1962; Tom Lewis, *Divided Highways: Building the Interstate Highways, Transforming American Life* (New York: Viking, 1997), 31–41, 86, 123.

17. *NOTP,* December 1, 1962, October 13, 1964.

18. Lewis Mumford, *The Highway and the City* (New York: New American Library, 1964), 244–56; *VCC,* February 5, 1965.

19. *VCC,* January 22, 1965; *NOTP,* January 30, 1965.

20. Transcript of public hearing concerned with placing the riverfront expressway on the federal interstate highway system, March 24, 1965, in SBNOP;

Vieux Carré Property Owners and Associates, Inc., v. City of New Orleans, 246 La. 788, 167 So. 2d 367.

21. M. Christine Boyer, *The City of Collective Memory: Its Historical Imagery and Architectural Entertainments* (Cambridge, Mass.: MIT Press, 1998), 383–88; William Murtagh, *Keeping Time: The History and Theory of Preservation in America* (New York: John Wiley and Sons, 1997), 28–32, 58; Mike Wallace, "Preserving the Past," in Mike Wallace, *Mickey Mouse History and Other Essays on American Memory* (Philadelphia: Temple University Press, 1996), 181–84; Norman Tyler, *Historic Preservation* (New York: W. W. Norton, 2000), 38; David Hamer, *History in Urban Places: The Historic Districts of the United States* (Columbus: Ohio State University Press, 1998), 7.

22. Howard R. Stagner, Assistant Director, National Park Service, U.S. Department of the Interior, to Mark Lowrey, July 21, 1965, in SBNOP; *VCC*, July 23, 1965; *NOTP*, July 25, 1965; Tulane University School of Architecture, "Study of the Proposed Riverfront and Elysian Fields Expressway and an Alternate Proposal" (October 1965), 13, in SBNOP.

23. *NOTP*, January 25, 1966.

24. *New York Times*, November 20, 1966.

25. *Congressional Record*, Senate, 89th Cong., 2nd sess., April 18, 1966, 112: 8222–23; June 2, 1966, 112: 12128–29; July 14, 1966, 112: 15670–71; July 11, 1966, 112: 15168–69; July 29, 1966, 112: 17630–39; *Federal Highway Act of 1966*, Pub. L. no. 89–574, §15(a), 80 Stat. 771, as amended 23 U.S.C. § 138 (Supp. V 1975); *Department of Transportation Act*, Pub. L. no. 89–670, §4(f), 80 Stat. 934 (1966), as amended 49 U.S.C. § 1653 (f) (Supp. V 1975); *National Historic Preservation Act of 1966*, Pub. L. no. 89–665, §101 (a) (1), 80 Stat. 916, codified at 16 U.S.C. §470 (a) (1) (Supp. V 1975).

26. *NOTP*, September 25, 1966; transcript of WDSU-TV newscast, November 17, 19, 20, 1966, in SBNOP.

27. Bureau of Governmental Research (BGR), "Evaluation of the Effects of the Proposed Riverfront Expressway" (December 1966), 9, 14, 24, 32, 53, 64, 102, 105, 108, in SBNOP.

28. Ibid., 102.

29. Warren I. Susman, "History and the American Intellectual: The Uses of a Usable Past," in Warren I. Susman, *Culture as History: The Transformation of American Society in the Twentieth Century* (New York: Pantheon Books, 1984), 7–26.

30. Worster, *Nature's Economy*, 306.

31. BGR, "Evaluation of the Effects," 8, 89.

32. *NOTP*, October 28, 1966, January 19, 1967; *VCC*, April 28, 1967.

33. Patricia Dunhill, "An Expressway Named Destruction," *Architectural Forum* (March 1967): 58, in SBNOP.

34. Wilmer, Cutler, and Pickering to Federal Highway Administrator Lowell K. Bridwell, April 11, 1967, in SBNOP; *NOTP*, June 20, 1967; *New Orleans States Item*, August 23, 1967; *NOTP*, December 12, 21, 1968.

35. *NOTP*, January 10, 1969.

36. *NOTP*, June 7, July 2, 1969.

37. U.S. Department of Transportation, *Department of Transportation News*, Office of the Secretary, July 9, 1969, in SBNOP.

38. *VCC*, July 4, 1969.

39. Richard Baumbach and William Borah, *The Second Battle of New Orleans: A History of the Vieux Carré Riverfront Expressway Controversy* (Tuscaloosa: University of Alabama Press, 1981), 193; *NOTP*, July 2, 5, 1969.

40. "Halting the Highway Men," *Business Week* (July 19, 1969): 37, in SBNOP.

41. Ann Breen and Dick Rigby, *The New Waterfront: A Worldwide Urban Success Story* (New York: McGraw-Hill, 1996), 8–25, 188–217; Blake Gumprecht, *The Los Angeles River: Its Life, Death, and Possible Rebirth* (Baltimore: Johns Hopkins University Press, 1999), 235–301.

42. Jon Goss, "Disquiet on the Waterfront," *Urban Geography* 17, (1996): 221–40; Boyer, *City of Collective Memory*, 423.

43. James Howard Kunstler, *The Geography of Nowhere: The Rise and Decline of America's Man-Made Landscape* (New York: Simon and Schuster, 1993), 7–36.

44. Lewis, *Divided Highways,* unpaginated illustration caption.

45. *NOTP*, February 7, 1974; all of the following in Vieux Carré Commission Records (ca. 1951–79), box 3: Burke and Associates, "Riverfront Boardwalk Extension" (March 1979); "Moonwalk Construction" press release (October 8, 1975); New Orleans Central Area Council, "Vieux Carré Promenades: A Development Concept Prepared for the Central Area Council of the Chamber of Commerce of the New Orleans Area, September 1970. Max Z. Conrad, Landscape Architect"; "Moonwalk Project Correspondence"; "Moonwalk History"; see also Vieux Carré Commission Reports (1970–74).

46. Cashio, Cochran, Sullivan, Inc., and Wayne A. Collier, Director, Vieux Carré Commission, "The Jackson Square, Washington Artillery Park, French Market Workshop" (October 12, 1972), in Vieux Carré Commission Reports (ca. 1951–79), box 3.

47. *NOTP*, January 11–25, 1997.

48. M. Christine Boyer, "Cities for Sale," in Michael Sorkin, ed., *Variations on a Theme Park: Scenes from the New American City and the End of Public Space* (New York: Hill and Wang, 1992), 182–202.

49. Hayden, *Power of Place*, 20.

50. Lewis Mumford, *The Culture of Cities* (1938; reprint, San Diego: Harcourt, Brace, 1970), 252.

51. Jacobs, *Great American Cities*, 444.

Works Cited

This list is divided into six sections, in the following order: Manuscript Sources, Maps, Court Cases, Periodicals, Published Primary Sources, and Secondary Sources.

MANUSCRIPT SOURCES

Audubon Park Commission Collection. Archives and Manuscripts, Special Collections Department, Earl K. Long Library, University of New Orleans.

Beebe Family Papers. Record group 46, Louisiana State Museum Historical Center, New Orleans.

Benjamin, Judah P. Letters. MSS 265, folder 173, Historic New Orleans Collection, Williams Research Center, New Orleans.

Caplan Papers. Mississippi River Flood. Record group 44, Louisiana State Museum Historical Center, New Orleans. Cited as Caplan Papers.

Cline, Isaac M. Papers. Record group 44, Louisiana State Museum Historical Center, New Orleans.

Conseil de Ville Records. New Orleans City Archives, Louisiana Division, New Orleans Public Library. Cited as CDV.

Correspondence Collection. Archives of the Archdiocese of New Orleans.

"Description, 1906–1908." Vertical file, Special Collections, Tulane University.

"Description, 1912–1913." Vertical file, Special Collections, Tulane University.

"Drainage." Folder 1. Vertical file, Special Collections, Tulane University.

"Flood Control, M–Z." Vertical file, Special Collections, Tulane University.

Halley, John. Journal. King Library Special Collections, University of Kentucky, Lexington.

Innes Collection. Manuscripts and Archives Division, Kentucky Historical Society, Frankfort, Ky.

Kemper, James P. Papers. Record group 52, Louisiana State Museum Historical Center, New Orleans.

May Papers. Filson Club Historical Society, Louisville, Ky.

Meriwether Papers. Filson Club Historical Society, Louisville, Ky.

New Orleans Office of the Mayor. Letter Books, 1811–1920. New Orleans City Archives, New Orleans Public Library.

"Public Belt Railroad." Folder 1. Vertical file, Special Collections, Tulane University.

Records of the New Orleans Collector of Levee Dues. Register of flatboats, barges, rafts, and steamboats in the port of New Orleans, 1806–23. New Orleans City Archives, Louisiana Division, New Orleans Public Library.

Reynolds, Henry. Journal. King Library Special Collections, University of Kentucky, Lexington.

Second Battle of New Orleans Papers. Historic New Orleans Collection, Williams Research Center, New Orleans. Cited as SBNOP.

Supreme Court of Louisiana Legal Archives. Archives and Manuscripts, Special Collections Department, Earl K. Long Library, University of New Orleans.

Vieux Carré Commission Reports. Multiple dates. New Orleans City Archives, Louisiana Division, New Orleans Public Library.

Wharton, Thomas K. Diary. Manuscripts and Rare Books, New York Public Library.

Webb, L. H. Diary. Record group 49, Louisiana State Museum Historical Center, New Orleans.

MAPS

Lafon, B. *Plan of the City and Environs of New Orleans*. Engraving, 1816. Historic New Orleans Collection, Williams Research Center, New Orleans.

Moellhausen, H. *Norman's Plan of New Orleans and Environs*. Hand-tinted engraving, 1845. Historic New Orleans Collection, Williams Research Center, New Orleans.

Pinistri, S. *New Orleans General Guide and Land Intelligence*. Engraving, 1841. Historic New Orleans Collection, Williams Research Center, New Orleans.

Robinson, E. H., and R. H. Pidgeon. *Atlas of the City of New Orleans*. New York: E. Robinson, 1883.

Sanborn Fire Insurance Company. *Maps of New Orleans, 1876*. Vol. 2. Southeastern Architectural Archive, Tulane University.

———. *Maps of New Orleans, 1885*. Vol. 2. Southeastern Architectural Archive, Tulane University.

Tanesse, Rolinson, et al. *Plan of the City and Suburbs of New Orleans*. Engraving, 1817. Historic New Orleans Collection, Williams Research Center, New Orleans.

Thompson, W. Thornton. *Plan of Municipality No. 2 Showing Wards and Squares*. Hand-colored lithograph, 1845. Historic New Orleans Collection, Williams Research Center, New Orleans.

COURT CASES

Alexander Hill v. Chicago, St. Louis, and New Orleans Railroad Company. 26 La. Ann. 478.
Behrman v. Louisiana Ry. and Nav. Co. 127 La. 775, 54 So. 25.
Board of Com'rs for Port of New Orleans v. New Orleans and S.F.R. co. et al. 112 La. 1011, 36 So. 837.
Capdevielle, Mayor, v. New Orleans and S.F.R. Co. et al. 110 La. 904, 34 So. 868.
Eldridge v. Trezevant. 160 U.S. 452.
F. W. Tilton et al. v. New Orleans City Railroad Company. 35 La. Ann. 1062.
Goldenbow v. Wright. 13 La. 371.
Hart v. Board of Levee Commissioners for Parish of New Orleans. 54 Fed. 559.
Heirs of Fulton and Livingston v. Henry M. Shreve. Accession 70A–006, file 1003, box 449452, Federal Records Center, Forth Worth, Tex.
John Duffy et al. v. City of New Orleans et al. 49 La. 114.
Korby and Fosdick v. Henry Miller Shreve. Docket 1392, Civil Court Collection, First District Court, Louisiana Division, New Orleans Public Library.
Livingston v. D'Orgenois. 6 Mart. 87, o.s. (1819).
Livingston v. Jefferson. 15 Fed. 8411 (1811).
Louisiana Railway and Navigation Company v. Behrman, Mayor of the City of New Orleans. 235 U.S. 164.
Mrs. S. D. A. Werges v. St. Louis, Chicago, and New Orleans Railroad Company. 35 La. Ann. 641.
Municipality No. 1 v. Municipality No. 2. 12 La. 49 (March 1838).
New Orleans, Mobile, and Chattanooga Railroad Company v. City of New Orleans et al. 26 La. Ann. 517 (1893).
New Orleans v. Texas and Pacific Railway Company. 171 U.S. Rep. 312.
Pontchartrain R. Co. v. Board of Levee Commissioners of Orleans Levee District. 49 La. Ann. 570, 21 So. 765.
Pulley and Erwin v. Municipality No. 2. 18 La. 278.
Ruch v. City of New Orleans. 43 La. Ann. 275, 9 So. 473.
Samuel T. Williamson v. Alexander Norton, Master, et al. 7 La. Ann. 393 (1854).
Vieux Carré Property Owners and Associates, Inc., v. City of New Orleans. 246 La. 788, 167 So. 2d 367.
Warriner et al. v. Board of Comm'rs of Port of New Orleans et al. 62 So. 157.
William C. Harrison et al. v. New Orleans Pacific Railway Company. 34 La. Ann. 462.

PERIODICALS

Baltimore Sun.
Birmingham News.
Courier de la Louisiane.
Dallas Journal.
DeBow's Review.
Kentucky Gazette.

Los Angeles Times.
Louisiana Courier.
Louisiana Gazette.
Louisville Journal.
Memphis Commercial Appeal.
Minneapolis Journal.
New Orleans Bee. Cited as NOB.
New Orleans Daily Crescent.
New Orleans Daily Delta. Cited as NODD.
New Orleans Daily Picayune. Cited as NODP.
New Orleans Daily States.
New Orleans Evening Item.
New Orleans Item. Cited as NOI.
New Orleans Item-Tribune. Cited as NOIT.
New Orleans Medical and Surgical Journal. Cited as NOMSJ.
New Orleans Morning Tribune. Cited as NOMT.
New Orleans Price-Current, Commercial Intelligencer, and Merchants' Transcript.
New Orleans States. Cited as NOS.
New Orleans States Item.
New Orleans Sunday Item Tribune.
New Orleans Times.
New Orleans Times Democrat. Cited as NOTD.
New Orleans Times Picayune. Cited as NOTP.
New York Daily Mirror.
New York Times.
New York Tribune.
Niles' Weekly Register.
St. Bernard Voice.
Vieux Carré Courier. Cited as VCC.

PUBLISHED PRIMARY SOURCES

Act No. 93 Creating the Orleans Levee District. New Orleans: A. W. Hyatt,
    1891.
*Acts Passed at the First Session of the Fourteenth Legislature of the State of
    Louisiana.* New Orleans: J. C. De St. Romes, 1839.
*Acts Passed at the First Session of the Second Legislature of the Territory of Or-
    leans.* New Orleans: n.p., 1808.
*Acts Passed at the First Session of the Twelfth Legislature of the State of
    Louisiana.* New Orleans: Jerome Bayon, 1835.
*Acts Passed at the Second Session of the Fifteenth Legislature of the State of
    Louisiana.* New Orleans: J. C. De St. Romes, 1842.
*Acts Passed at the Second Session of the Fourteenth Legislature of the State of
    Louisiana.* New Orleans: Bullitt, Magne, 1840.
*Acts Passed at the Second Session of the Second Legislature of the State of
    Louisiana.* New Orleans: n.p., n.d.
Acts Passed by the General Assembly of the State of Louisiana at the Regular

Session, Begun and Held in the City of Baton Rouge on the Eleventh Day of May, 1896. Baton Rouge, La.: Advocate, 1896.

Acts of the Second Session of the Third Legislature of the Territory of Orleans, April 19, 1811. New Orleans: n.p., n.d.

Advisory Board of New Orleans. *Report on the Drainage of the City of New Orleans, by the Advisory Board, Appointed by Ordinance No. 8327.* New Orleans: T. Fitzwilliam, 1895.

American State Papers, Foreign Relations. Vol. 1. Washington, D.C.: Gales and Seaton, 1832.

American State Papers, Public Lands. Vol. 2. Washington, D.C.: Gales and Seaton, 1834. Cited as *ASP, PL.*

Annual Report of the Mississippi River Commission for the Fiscal Year Ending June 30, 1903. Washington, D.C.: Government Printing Office, 1903.

Bailey, Francis. *Journal of a Tour in Unsettled Parts of North America in 1796 and 1797.* London: Bailey Brothers, 1856.

Baird, Robert. *View of the Valley of the Mississippi.* Philadelphia: H. S. Tanner, 1834.

Barrow, C. J. *Report of the U.S. Commissioner, and a List of the Collective Exhibit of the State of Louisiana, at the World's Industrial and Cotton Centennial Exposition.* New Orleans: A. W. Hyatt, 1885.

Baumbach, Richard, and William Borah. *The Second Battle of New Orleans: A History of the Vieux Carré Riverfront Expressway Controversy.* Tuscaloosa: University of Alabama Press, 1981.

Behrman, Martin. *Civic Development.* New Orleans: n.p., 1913.

———. *New Orleans: A History of Three Great Public Utilities. A Paper Read by Martin Behrman, Mayor of New Orleans, Before a Convention of League of American Municipalities, Milwaukee, Wisconsin. September 29, 1914.* New Orleans: Brando, 1914.

Board of Commissioners of the Port of New Orleans. *Annual Reports of the Board of Commissioners of the Port of New Orleans.* Multiple years. New Orleans: n.p. Cited as Dock Board Report.

———. *First Annual Report of the Board of Commissioners of the Port of New Orleans.* New Orleans: Mauberret Printing, 1897.

Boyd, Julian P., ed. *The Papers of Thomas Jefferson.* Vol. 7. Princeton, N.J.: Princeton University Press, 1953.

Bruce, Edward C. "The New Orleans Exposition." *Lippincott's Magazine of Popular Literature and Science,* o.s., 35 (April 1885).

Burnett, Dana. "Between Hoover and High Water." *Collier's* 80 (July 16, 1927).

Cable, George Washington. *The Creoles of Louisiana.* New York: Charles Scribner's Sons, 1884.

———. "New Orleans Revisited." *Book News Monthly* 27 (April 1909).

Carson, Rachel. *Silent Spring.* 1962. Reprint, New York: Houghton Mifflin, 1994.

Cartwright, Samuel A. "Prevention of Yellow Fever." *New Orleans Medical and Surgical Journal* 10 (November 1853).

———. "Report on the Diseases and Physical Peculiarities of the Negro Race." *New Orleans Medical and Surgical Journal* 7 (May 1851).

―――. "Review of the Meteorology, Vital Statistics, and Hygiene of the State of Louisiana." *New Orleans Medical and Surgical Journal* 8 (September 1851).

Charlevoix, Francois Xavier. *Journal of a Voyage to North America*. Vol. 2. Ed. and trans. Louise Phelps Kellog. Chicago: Caxton Club, 1923.

City Council of New Orleans. *Official Proceedings of the City Council of New Orleans, 1870–71*. New Orleans: Republican Publishing, 1870.

City of New Orleans. *Ordinance of the City of New Orleans Providing for a Belt Railroad Board for the City of New Orleans, and a Public Belt Railroad System*. New Orleans: Allied Printers, 1900.

Cline, Isaac Monroe. *Storms, Floods, and Sunshine*. New Orleans: Pelican Publishing, 1945.

Coleman, J. F. "Physical Aspects of the Port of New Orleans." *World Ports* 11 (May 1923).

Coleman, W. H. *Historical Sketch Book and Guide to New Orleans*. New York: W. H. Coleman, 1885.

Commissioner of Corporations on Transportation by Water. *Report of the Commissioner of Corporations on Transportation by Water in the United States*. Vol. 3, *Water Terminals*. Washington, D.C.: Government Printing Office, 1910.

Congressional Record. Senate, 89th Cong., 2nd sess., April 18, June 2, July 11, July 14, and July 29, 1966. Vol. 112.

Coppée, H. St. L. "The Lower Mississippi and Its Regulation." In Frank H. Thompkins, ed., *Riparian Lands of the Mississippi River, Past—Present—Prospective*. New Orleans: Frank H. Thompkins, 1901.

Corthell, E. L. *A History of the Jetties at the Mouth of the Mississippi River*. New York: John Wiley and Sons, 1881.

Cram, Mildred. *Old Seaport Towns of the South*. New York: Dodd, Mead, 1917.

Cramer, Zadok. *The Navigator: Containing Directions for Navigating the Monongahela, Allegheny, Ohio, and Mississippi Rivers*. Pittsburgh: Cramer, Spear, and Eichbaum, 1817.

Dabney, Thomas Ewing. *The Indestructible City*. New Orleans: New Orleans Association of Commerce, 1928.

Deacon, William. *Martin Behrman Administration Biography*. New Orleans: John J. Weighing, 1917.

DeBow, J. D. B. "The Crescent City." *Commercial Review of the South and West* 3 (March 1847).

de Fonblanque, A. de G. "Report by Consul Fonblanque on the World's Cotton Centennial Exhibition at New Orleans." In *Reports by Her Majesty's Diplomatic and Consular Officers Abroad on Subjects of Commercial and General Interest*. Vol. 2. London: Harrison and Sons, 1885.

Derbigny, Pierre. *Case Laid Before Counsel for Their Opinion on the Claim to the Batture, Situated in Front of the Suburb St. Mary*. New Orleans: n.p., 1807.

Digeste des ordonnances, resolutions, et reglemens de la Corporation de la Nouvelle-Orléans, et recueil de lois de la legislature relatives a la dite ville. New Orleans: Gaston Brusle, 1836.

Digest of the Civil Laws Now in Force in the Territory of Orleans, with Alterations and Amendments, Adapted to Its Present System of Government. New Orleans: n.p., 1808.

Documents in Support of the Right of the Inhabitants of the City of New Orleans to the Alluvion in Front of the Suburb St. Mary Contested by Jean Gravier. Washington, D.C.: A. and G. Way, 1809.

Dowler, B. "On the Necropolis of New Orleans." *New Orleans Medical and Surgical Journal* 7 (November 1850).

Dowler, M. Morton. "On the Reported Causes of Yellow Fever and the So Called Sanitary Measures of the Day." *New Orleans Medical and Surgical Journal* 11 (July 1854).

Eads, James B. *Minority Report of the Mississippi River Commission.* Washington, D.C.: Gibson Brothers, 1882.

Ellet, Charles. *The Mississippi and Ohio Rivers.* Philadelphia: Lippincott, Grambo, 1853.

Elliot, D. O. *The Improvement of the Lower Mississippi River for Flood Control and Navigation.* 2 vols. Vicksburg, Miss.: U.S. Army Corps of Engineers Waterways Experiment Station, 1932.

Facts About the Port of New Orleans. New Orleans: Picayune Job Print, 1912.

Fairhall, Herbert S. *The World's Industrial and Cotton Centennial Exposition.* Iowa City: Republican Publishing, 1885.

Fenner, E. D. *History of the Epidemic Yellow Fever at New Orleans, La., in 1853.* New York: Hall, Clayton, 1854.

The Final Report of the Colored Advisory Commission. Washington, D.C.: American Red Cross, 1929.

Flint, Timothy. *A Condensed Geography and History of the Western States.* Cincinnati: E. H. Flint, 1828.

———. "A Condensed Geography and History of the Western States." In John Francis McDermott, ed., *Before Mark Twain.* Carbondale: Southern Illinois University Press, 1968.

———. *The History and Geography of the Mississippi Valley.* Vol. 1. Cincinnati: E. H. Flint and L. R. Lincoln, 1832.

Grady, Harry. *The New South.* New York: Robert Bonner's Sons, 1890.

"The Great South." *Scribner's* 7 (December 1873).

Hall, Captain Basil. *Travels in North America, in the Years 1827 and 1828.* Vol. 3. Edinburgh: Cadell, 1829.

Hall, James. *Notes on the Western States.* Philadelphia: Harrison Hall, 1838.

Hammond, John Martin. *Winter Journeys in the South.* Philadelphia: J. B. Lippincott, 1916.

"Health, Mortality, Etc." *New Orleans Medical and Surgical Journal* 10 (September 1853).

"Health of the City." *New Orleans Medical and Surgical Journal* 8 (July 1851).

Hearings Before the Committee on Flood Control, House of Representatives, 64th Congress, First Session on H.R. 13975 (Newlands-Broussard-Rainey River Regulation Bill). March 31, April 1, 2, and 4, 1916. Pt. 1. Washington, D.C.: Government Printing Office, 1916.

Hearings Before the Committee on Flood Control, House of Representatives, on the Control of Destructive Flood Waters of the United States. Multiple dates. Washington, D.C.: Government Printing Office. Cited as CFC, HR.

Hester, A. "Medical History of Two Epidemic Yellow Fevers." *New Orleans Medical and Surgical Journal* 7 (July 1850).

"History and Incidents of the Plague in New Orleans." *Harper's* 7 (November 1853).

House, Com. Doc. 1, 70th Cong, 1st sess.

House, Ex. Doc. 35, 17th Cong., 2nd sess.

House, Ex. Doc. 21, 25th Cong., 3rd sess.

House, Ex. Doc. 1, pt. 2, 40th Cong., 3rd sess.

House, Ex. Doc. 37, 48th Cong., 1st sess.

House, Ex. Doc. 6, pt. 2, 50th Cong., 1st sess.

House, Misc. Doc. 90, 70th Cong., 1st sess.

House, Rep. 741, 30th Cong., 1st sess.

House, Rep. 44, 42nd Cong., 2nd sess.

Humphreys, A. A., and H. L. Abbot. *Report upon the Physics and Hydraulics of the Mississippi River.* Washington, D.C.: Government Printing Office, 1867.

Humphreys, Benjamin G. *Floods and Levees of the Mississippi River.* Washington, D.C.: Mississippi River Levee Association, 1914.

Jacobs, Jane. *The Death and Life of Great American Cities.* 1961. Reprint, New York: Vintage, 1992.

Jefferson, Thomas. *The Proceedings of the Government of the United States, in Maintaining the Public Right to the Beach of the Mississippi, Adjacent to New Orleans, Against the Intrusion of Edward Livingston.* New York: Ezra Sargent, 1812.

Jewell's Digest of the City Ordinances, Together with the Constitutional Provisions and Acts of the General Assembly, Relative to the Government of the City of New Orleans. New Orleans: Edwin L. Jewell, 1882 and 1887.

Kemper, James P. *A.B.C. of the Flood Problem.* New Orleans: National Flood Prevention and River Regulation Commission, 1927.

Leach, Smith S. "The Mississippi River—What It Needs and Why It Needs It." In Frank H. Thompkins, ed., *Riparian Lands of the Mississippi River, Past—Present—Prospective.* New Orleans: Frank H. Thompkins, 1901.

LeMoyne D'Iberville, Pierre. *Iberville's Gulf Journals.* Ed. and trans. Richebourg Gaillard McWilliams. Tuscaloosa: University of Alabama Press, 1981.

Littel, William, ed. *Political Transactions in and Concerning Kentucky.* Frankfort, Ky.: William Hunter, 1806.

Livingston, Edward. *Address to the People of the United States on the Measures Pursued by the Executive with Respect to the Batture at New Orleans.* Vol. 1. New Orleans: Bradford and Anderson, 1808.

———. *An Answer to Mr. Jefferson's Justification of His Conduct in the Case of the New Orleans Batture.* Philadelphia: William Fry, 1813.

Lloyd, James T. *Lloyd's Steamboat Directory.* Cincinnati: James T. Lloyd, 1856.

Loeb, Ernest M. *Common Cause of the Mississippi Valley.* New Orleans: n.p., 1915.

Louisiana Board of State Engineers. *Report of the Board of State Engineers to the General Assembly of Louisiana.* Multiple dates. New Orleans: n.p. Cited as *RSE.*

Louisiana Department of Conservation. *Eighth Biennial Report of the Department of Conservation of the State of Louisiana.* New Orleans: Department of Conservation, 1928.

McElderry, Henry. *Description of Selected Specimens from the Medical and Surgical Sections of the Army Medical Museum.* New Orleans: n.p., 1884–85.

McHenry, Estill, ed. *Addresses and Papers of James B. Eads.* St. Louis: Slawson, 1884.

McKowen, John. *Murder as a Money Making Art.* Baton Rouge, La.: Benton, 1901.

Milburn, William. *Ten Years of Preacher Life.* New York: Derby and Jackson, 1859.

"The Mississippi River." *De Bow's Review,* ATW, 5 (May 1868).

The Mississippi River: A Short Historic Description of Flood Control and Navigation. Vicksburg, Miss.: Mississippi River Commission, 1940.

The Mississippi River Flood Control Association, Losses and Damages Resulting from the Flood of 1927. Memphis, Tenn.: Mississippi River Flood Control Association, 1928.

The Mississippi Valley Flood Disaster of 1927. Washington, D.C.: American Red Cross, 1929.

M'Murtrie, Henry. *Sketches of Louisville and Its Environs.* Louisville: Parsons, 1819.

Mumford, Lewis. *The Culture of Cities.* 1938. Reprint, San Diego: Harcourt, Brace, 1970.

————. *The Highway and the City.* New York: New American Library, 1964.

Murray, Charles. *Travels in North America.* Vol. 2. London: Richard Bentley, 1839.

Murray, Henry. *Lands of the Slave and the Free.* London: John Parker and Son, 1855.

New Orleans City Ordinances Relating to the New Orleans, Jackson, and Great Northern Railroad Co.; New Orleans, St. Louis, and Chicago Railroad Co.; Chicago, St. Louis, and New Orleans Railroad Co., and to the New Orleans Belt Co. from May 17th, 1852 to August 15th, 1881. New Orleans: A. W. Hyatt, 1881.

"New Orleans: Its Present Situation and Future Prospects." *Commercial Review of the South and West* 2 (July 1846).

Nichols, T. L. *Forty Years of American Life.* London: Longmans, Green, 1874.

Nott, J. C. "The Epidemic of Yellow Fever in Mobile in 1853." *New Orleans Medical and Surgical Journal* 10 (March 1854).

Old South Leaflets. Vol. 6. Boston: Director of the Old South Works, n.d.

Oliphant, Laurence. *Episodes in a Life of Adventure; or, Moss from a Rolling Stone.* Edinburgh: William Blackwood and Sons, 1887.

Olliffe, Charles. *American Scenes.* 1854. Reprint, Painesville, Ohio: Lake Erie College Press, 1964.

Peters, Samuel Jarvis. "The Autobiography of Samuel Jarvis Peters." In George C. H. Kernion, "Samuel Jarvis Peters—The Man Who Made New Orleans of To-Day and Became a National Personality." *Publications of the Louisiana Historical Society* 7 (1913–14).

"The Plague in the Southwest." *De Bow's Review of the Southern and Western States,* n.s., 15, no. 1 (December 1853).

"Political Portraits with Pen and Pencil: Henry Miller Shreve." *United States Magazine, and Democratic Review* 22 (February 1848).

Poydras, Julien. *A Defense of the Right of the Public to the Batture of New Orleans.* Washington, D.C.: Julien Poydras, 1809.

———. *Further Observations in Support of the Right of the Public to the Batture of New Orleans.* Washington, D.C.: A. and G. Way, 1809.

———. *Speech of Julien Poydras, Esq., the Delegate from the Territory of Orleans, in Support of the Right of the Public to the Batture in Front of the Suburb of St. Mary.* Washington, D.C.: A. and G. Way, 1810.

Proceedings of a Congressional Convention on River Improvement, St. Louis, May 1873. St. Louis: Woodward, Tiernan, and Hale, 1873.

Proceedings of the Commercial Convention Held in New Orleans, May 24th, 27th, 28th and 29th, 1869. New Orleans: L. Graham, 1869.

"Review of the New Orleans Market." *De Bow's Review,* ATW, 5 (September 1868).

Robinson, William. *Diary of a Samaritan.* New York: Harper and Brothers, 1860.

Rowland, Dunbar, ed. *The Official Letter Books of W. C. C. Claiborne.* Multiple vols. Jackson, Miss.: State Department of Archives and History, 1917. Cited as *Claiborne Letters.*

Sanitary Commission of New Orleans. *Report of the Sanitary Commission of New Orleans on the Yellow Fever Epidemic of 1853.* New Orleans: Picayune Office, 1854. Cited as *SCR.*

Saxon, Lyle. *Father Mississippi.* New York: Century, 1927.

Schultz, Christian. *Travels on an Inland Voyage.* Vol. 2. New York: Isaac Riley, 1810.

Sealsfield, Charles. *The Americans as They Are.* London: Hurst, Chance, 1828.

Secret Journals and Acts and Proceedings of Congress. Vol. 4. Boston: Thomas B. Wait, 1821.

Senate, Ex. Doc. 18, 30th Cong., 2nd sess.

Senate, Ex. Doc. 20, 32nd Cong., 1st sess.

Senate, Ex. Doc. 42, 32nd Cong., 1st sess.

Senate, Ex. Doc. 58, 46th Cong., 2nd sess.

Senate, Ex. Doc. 10, 47th Cong., 1st sess.

Senate, Rep. 410, 29th Cong., 1st sess.

Sewerage and Water Board of New Orleans. *Annual Reports of the Sewerage and Water Board of the City of New Orleans.* New Orleans, n.p., n.d.

Shippe, Lester B. *Bishop Whipple's Southern Diary, 1843, 1844. 1845.* Reprint, Minneapolis: University of Minnesota Press, 1937.

Simpich, Frederick. "The Great Mississippi Flood of 1927." *National Geographic* 52 (September 1927).

Smalley, Eugene V. "In and Out of the New Orleans Exposition." *Century Magazine* 30 (June 1885).

State Papers and Correspondence Bearing upon the Purchase of the Territory of Louisiana. Washington, D.C.: Government Printing Office, 1903.

Stein, Albert. "Improvement of the Mississippi River." *DeBow's Review,* ATW, 7 (December 1869).

Thierry, Jean Baptiste Simon. *Examen des droits de États-Unis et des pretensions de Mr. Edouard Livingston sur la batture en face du Faubourg Ste. Marie.* New Orleans: Thierry, 1808.

Thompkins, Frank H., ed. *Riparian Lands of the Mississippi River, Past—Present—Prospective.* New Orleans: Frank H. Thompkins, 1901.

Trollope, Francis. *Domestic Manners of the Americans.* London: Whittaker, Treacher, 1832.

Tudor, Henry. *Narrative of a Tour of North America.* Vol. 2. London: James Duncan, 1834.

Twain, Mark. *Life on the Mississippi.* 1883. Reprint, New York: First Vintage, 1991.

U.S. Army Chief of Engineers. *Annual Report of the Mississippi River Commission for the Fiscal Year Ending June 30, 1924.* Pt. 1. Washington, D.C.: Government Printing Office, 1924.

———. *Annual Report of the Mississippi River Commission for the Fiscal Year Ending June 30, 1937.* Pt. 1. Washington, D.C.: Government Printing Office, 1937.

U.S. Army Corps of Engineers. *Bonnet Carré Spillway.* New Orleans: U.S. Army Corps of Engineers, n.d.

Waring, George E., and George Washington Cable. "History and Present Condition of New Orleans, Louisiana." In *Tenth Census, Report on the Social Condition of Cities,* vol. 19, pt. 2. Washington, D.C.: Government Printing Office, 1887.

Warner, Charles Dudley. "New Orleans." *Harper's* 24 (January 1887).

Wright, Richard. "The Man Who Saw the Flood." In Richard Wright, *Eight Men.* New York: Thunder's Mouth Press, 1940.

Zacharie, James. *New Orleans Guide and Exposition Hand Book.* New Orleans: New Orleans New Company, 1885.

SECONDARY SOURCES

Agnew, John. *Place and Politics: The Geographical Mediation of State and Society.* Boston: Allen and Unwin, 1987.

Alain, Mathé. *Not Worth a Straw: French Colonial Policy and the Early Years of Louisiana.* Lafayette, La.: Center for Louisiana Studies, 1988.

Andrist, Ralph K. *Steamboats on the Mississippi.* New York: American Heritage Publishing, 1962.

Arnesen, Eric. *Waterfront Workers of New Orleans: Race, Class, and Politics, 1863–1923.* Champaign: University of Illinois Press, 1994.

Baldwin, Leland D. *The Keelboat Age on Western Waters.* Pittsburgh: University of Pittsburgh Press, 1941.

Baldwin, Peter C. *Domesticating the Street: The Reform of Public Space in Hartford, 1850–1930.* Columbus: Ohio State University Press, 1999.

Barry, John. *Rising Tide: The Great Mississippi Flood of 1927 and How It Changed America.* New York: Simon and Schuster, 1996.

Bellande, Ray. *Hotels and Tourist Homes of Ocean Springs, Mississippi.* Ocean Springs, Miss.: Ray Bellande, 1994.

Bender, Thomas. *Toward an Urban Vision: Ideas and Institutions in Nineteenth-Century America.* Baltimore: Johns Hopkins University Press, 1975.

Berry, Thomas S. *Western Prices Before 1861.* Cambridge, Mass.: Harvard University Press, 1943.

Blasingame, John. *Black New Orleans, 1860–1880.* Chicago: University of Chicago Press, 1973.

Boyer, M. Christine. *The City of Collective Memory: Its Historical Imagery and Architectural Entertainments.* Cambridge, Mass.: MIT Press, 1998.

———. "Cities for Sale." In Michael Sorkin, ed., *Variations on a Theme Park: Scenes from the New American City and the End of Public Space.* New York: Hill and Wang, 1992.

———. *Dreaming the Rational City: The Myth of American City Planning.* Cambridge, Mass.: MIT Press, 1983.

Breen, Ann, and Dick Rigby. *The New Waterfront: A Worldwide Urban Success Story.* New York: McGraw-Hill, 1996.

Buenker, John, John Burnham, and Robert Crunden. *Progressivism.* Rochester, Vt.: Schenkman, 1977.

Buttenwieser, Ann. *Manhattan Water-Bound: Manhattan's Waterfront from the Seventeenth Century to the Present.* Syracuse, N.Y.: Syracuse University Press, 1999.

Carrigan, Jo Ann. *Saffron Scourge: A History of Yellow Fever in Louisiana, 1796–1905.* Lafayette, La.: Center for Louisiana Studies, 1994.

Caruso, John Anthony. *The Mississippi Valley Frontier.* Indianapolis: Bobbs-Merrill, 1966.

Clark, John G. *New Orleans, 1718–1812.* Baton Rouge: Louisiana State University Press, 1970.

———. "New Orleans and the River." *Louisiana History* 8 (Spring 1967).

Clements, A. N. *The Physiology of Mosquitoes.* New York: Macmillan, 1963.

Coulter, E. Merton. "The Efforts of the Democratic Societies of the West to Secure Navigation of the Mississippi." *Mississippi Valley Historical Review* 9 (December 1924).

Cowan, Ruth Schwartz. *A Social History of American Technology.* Oxford: Oxford University Press, 1997.

Cowdrey, Albert. *The Delta Engineers: A History of the U.S. Army Corps of Engineers in the New Orleans District.* New Orleans: U.S. Army Corps of Engineers, 1971.

———. *Land's End: A History of the New Orleans District, U.S. Army Corps of Engineers, and Its Lifelong Battle with the Lower Mississippi and Other Rivers Wending Their Way to the Sea.* New Orleans: U.S. Army Corps of Engineers, 1977.

Cronon, William. *Nature's Metropolis: Chicago and the Great West.* New York: W. W. Norton, 1989.

———, ed. *Uncommon Ground: Toward Reinventing Nature.* New York: W. W. Norton, 1996.

Daniel, Pete. *Deep'n as It Come: The 1927 Mississippi River Flood*. New York: Oxford University Press, 1977.

Dargo, George. *Jefferson's Louisiana: Politics and the Clash of Legal Traditions*. Cambridge, Mass.: Harvard University Press, 1975.

Davis, Mike. *City of Quartz: Excavating the Future in Los Angeles*. New York: Vintage, 1992.

de Certeau, Michel. *The Practice of Everyday Life*. Trans. Steven Rendall. Berkeley: University of California Press, 1984.

Deverell, William. *Railroad Crossing: Californians and the Railroad, 1850–1910*. Berkeley: University of California Press, 1994.

de Villiers, Baron Marc. "A History of the Foundation of New Orleans." *Louisiana Historical Quarterly* 3 (April 1920).

Dorman, Robert L. *A Word for Nature: Four Pioneering Environmental Advocates, 1845–1913*. Chapel Hill: University of North Carolina Press, 1998.

Dorsey, Florence L. *Road to the Sea: The Story of James B. Eads and the Mississippi River*. New York: Rinehart, 1947.

Duffy, John. *Sword of Pestilence: The New Orleans Yellow Fever Epidemic of 1853*. Baton Rouge: Louisiana State University Press, 1966.

———, ed. *The Rudolph Matas History of Medicine in Louisiana*. Baton Rouge: Louisiana State University Press, 1962.

Dunhill, Patricia. "An Expressway Named Destruction." *Architectural Forum* (March 1967).

Fairfield, John D. *The Mysteries of the Great City: The Politics of Urban Design, 1877–1937*. Columbus: Ohio State University Press, 1993.

Fisk, Harold. *Geological Investigation of the Alluvial Valley of the Lower Mississippi River*. Vicksburg, Miss.: Mississippi River Commission, 1944.

Forman, Ronald. *Audubon Park: An Urban Eden*. New Orleans: Friends of the Zoo, 1985.

Foucault, Michel. "Questions on Geography." In Colin Gordon, ed., *Power Knowledge: Selected Interviews and Other Writings, 1972–1977*. New York: Pantheon, 1980.

Fox, Stephen. *The American Conservation Movement: John Muir and His Legacy*. Madison: University of Wisconsin Press, 1981.

Frank, Arthur DeWitt. *The Development of the Federal Program of Flood Control on the Mississippi River*. New York: Columbia University Press, 1930.

Giraud, Marcel. *A History of French Louisiana*. Vol. 5. Baton Rouge: Louisiana State University Press, 1987.

Goss, Jon. "Disquiet on the Waterfront." *Urban Geography* 17 (1996).

Gottdiener, Mark. *The Social Production of Urban Space*. Austin: University of Texas Press, 1994.

Gumprecht, Blake. *The Los Angeles River: Its Life, Death, and Possible Rebirth*. Baltimore: Johns Hopkins University Press, 1999.

Haar, Charles M., and Lance Liebman. *Property and Law*. Boston: Little, Brown, 1977.

Habermas, Jürgen. *The Structural Transformation of the Public Sphere*. Cambridge, Mass.: MIT Press, 1991.

Hair, William Ivy. *Carnival of Fury: Robert Charles and the New Orleans Race Riot of 1900*. Baton Rouge: Louisiana State University Press, 1976.

Haites, Erik Friso. "Ohio and Mississippi River Transportation, 1810–1860." Ph.D. diss., Department of History and Economics, Purdue University, 1969.

Hall, Gwendolyn Midlo. *Africans in Colonial Louisiana: The Development of Afro-Creole Culture in the Eighteenth Century*. Baton Rouge: Louisiana State University Press, 1992.

"Halting the Highway Men." *Business Week* (July 19, 1969).

Hamer, David. *History in Urban Places: The Historic Districts of the United States*. Columbus: Ohio State University Press, 1998.

Hardy, Donald Clive. "The World's Industrial and Cotton Exposition." Master's thesis, Tulane University, 1964.

Harrison, Robert W. *Alluvial Empire*. Vol. 1. Little Rock, Ark.: Pioneer Press, 1961.

Hartog, Hendrik. *Public Property and Private Power: The Corporation of the City of New York in American Law, 1730–1870*. Chapel Hill: University of North Carolina Press, 1983.

Hatcher, William B. *Edward Livingston: Jeffersonian Republican and Jacksonian Democrat*. Baton Rouge: Louisiana State University Press, 1940.

Hatty, Suzanne E., and James Hatty. *The Disordered Body: Epidemic Disease and Cultural Transformation*. Albany: State University of New York Press, 1999.

Hayden, Dolores. *The Power of Place: Urban Landscapes as Public History*. Cambridge, Mass.: MIT Press, 1995.

———. "Urban Landscape History: The Sense of Place and the Politics of Space." In Paul Groth and Todd Bressi W., eds., *Understanding Ordinary Landscapes*. New Haven, Conn.: Yale University Press, 1997.

Hays, Samuel P. *Conservation and the Gospel of Efficiency*. Cambridge, Mass.: Harvard University Press, 1959.

———. *The Response to Industrialism, 1885–1914*. Chicago: University of Chicago Press, 1957.

Herman, Shael. *The Louisiana Civil Code*. New Orleans: Louisiana Bar Foundation, 1993.

Higham, John. *Strangers in the Land: Patterns of American Nativism, 1860–1925*. New Brunswick, N.J.: Rutgers University Press, 1955.

Hiss, Tony. *The Experience of Place*. New York: Alfred A. Knopf, 1990.

Horowitz, Morton J. *The Transformation of American Law, 1780–1860*. Cambridge, Mass.: Harvard University Press, 1977.

Humphreys, Margaret. *Yellow Fever and the South*. New Brunswick, N.J.: Rutgers University Press, 1992.

Hunter, Louis. *Steamboats on the Western Rivers*. Cambridge, Mass.: Harvard University Press, 1949.

Jackson, John Brinckerhoff. *American Space: The Centennial Years, 1865–1876*. New York: W. W. Norton, 1972.

———. *A Sense of Place, a Sense of Time*. New Haven, Conn.: Yale University Press, 1994.

Jackson, Joy. *New Orleans in the Gilded Age.* Baton Rouge: Louisiana State University Press, 1969.

Johnson Emory R., et al. *History of Domestic and Foreign Commerce of the United States.* Vol. 1. Washington, D.C.: Carnegie Institution, 1915.

Jones, Jack C. "The Feeding Behavior of Mosquitoes." *Scientific American* 238 (June 1978).

Kasson, John. *Civilizing the Machine: Technology and Republican Values in America, 1776–1900.* New York: Viking, 1976.

Kelman, Ari. "Forests and Other River Perils." In Craig Colten, ed., *Transforming the Mississippi and Its Environs.* Pittsburgh: University of Pittsburgh Press, 2000.

Kemper, James P. *Rebellious River.* 1949. Reprint, New York: Arno Press, 1972.

Kendall, John Smith. *History of New Orleans.* Vols. 1 and 2. Chicago: Lewis Publishing, 1922.

Kiple, Kenneth F., and Virginia H. Kiple. "Black Yellow Fever Immunities, Innate and Acquired, as Revealed in the American South." *Social Science History* 1 (Summer 1977).

Kolb, Charles R., and Jack R. Van Lopik. "Depositional Environments of the Mississippi River Deltaic Plain." In Martha Lou Shirley, ed., *Deltas in Their Geologic Framework.* Houston: Houston Geologic Society, 1969.

Krause, Paul. *The Battle for Homestead, 1880–1892: Politics, Culture, and Steel.* Pittsburgh: University of Pittsburgh Press, 1992.

Kunstler, James Howard. *The Geography of Nowhere: The Rise and Decline of America's Man-Made Landscape.* New York: Simon and Schuster, 1993.

Lacey, Lawrence, and Bruce Orr. "The Role of Biological Control of Mosquitoes in Integrated Vector Control." *American Journal of Tropical Medicine and Hygiene,* supplemental, 50 (1994).

Larson, Erik. *Isaac's Storm: A Man, a Time, and the Deadliest Hurricane in History.* New York: Crown Publishers, 1999.

Layton, Edwin T., Jr. "Mirror Image Twins: The Communities of Science and Technology in Nineteenth Century America." *Technology and Culture* 12 (October 1971).

———. *The Revolt of the Engineers.* Baltimore: Johns Hopkins University Press, 1986.

Leavitt, Judith Walzer. *Typhoid Mary: Captive to the Public's Health.* New York: Beacon Press, 1997.

Lefebvre, Henri. *The Production of Space.* Trans. Donald Nicholson-Smith. Oxford: Basil Blackwell, 1998.

Leopold, Luna B. *A View of the River.* Cambridge, Mass.: Harvard University Press, 1994.

Lewis, Peirce F. *New Orleans: The Making of an Urban Landscape.* Cambridge, Mass.: Ballinger Publishing, 1976.

Lewis, Tom. *Divided Highways: Building the Interstate Highways, Transforming American Life.* New York: Viking, 1997.

Lovett, John A. "Batture, Ordinary High Water, and the Louisiana Levee Servitude." *Tulane Law Review* 69 (December 1994).

Lowenthal, David. *George Perkins Marsh: Prophet of Conservation*. Seattle: University of Washington Press, 2000.

Lowerey, Walter M. "Navigational Problems at the Mouth of the Mississippi River, 1698–1880." Ph.D. diss., Vanderbilt University, 1956.

Lynch, Kevin. *The Image of the City*. 1960. Reprint, Cambridge, Mass.: MIT Press, 1998.

Macpherson, C. B., ed. *Property: Mainstream and Critical Positions*. Toronto: University of Toronto Press, 1978.

Malone, Dumas. *The Sage of Monticello*. Boston: Little, Brown, 1981.

Marshall, Marie Louise. "Samuel A. Cartwright and States' Rights Medicine." *New Orleans Medical and Surgical Journal* 93 (August 1940).

Marx, Leo. *The Machine in the Garden: Technology and the Pastoral Ideal in America*. Oxford: Oxford University Press, 1964.

Massey, Doreen. *Space, Place, and Gender*. Minneapolis: University of Minnesota Press, 1994.

Mattingly, P. F. *The Biology of Mosquito-Borne Disease*. London: George Allen and Unwin, 1969.

Mayer, Martin. "The Public and Private Domains of the State." *Tulane Law Review* 12 (1938).

McCall, Edith. *Conquering the Rivers: Henry Miller Shreve and the Navigation of America's Inland Waterways*. Baton Rouge: Louisiana State University Press, 1984.

McCay, Bonnie J. *Oyster Wars and the Public Trust: Property, Law, and Ecology in New Jersey History*. Tucson: University of Arizona Press.

McPhee, John. *The Control of Nature*. New York: Farrar, Straus, and Giroux, 1989.

McPherson, James M. *Battle Cry of Freedom: The Civil War Era*. New York: Ballantine Books, 1988.

McShane, Clay. *Down the Asphalt Path: The Automobile and the American City*. New York: Columbia University Press, 1994.

Meinig, D. W., ed. *The Interpretation of Ordinary Landscapes: Geographical Essays*. New York: Oxford University Press, 1979.

Melosi, Martin V. *Garbage in the Cities: Refuse, Reform, and the Environment, 1880–1980*. College Station: Texas A&M University Press, 1981.

Merritt, Raymond H. *Engineering in American Society, 1850–1875*. Lexington: University Press of Kentucky, 1969.

Miller, Charles A. *Jefferson and Nature: An Interpretation*. Baltimore: Johns Hopkins University Press, 1988.

Mitchell, Don. "The End of Public Space? People's Park, Definitions of the Public, and Democracy." *Annals of the American Association of Geographers* 85 (1995).

Monkonnen, Eric. *America Becomes Urban: The Development of U.S. Cities and Towns, 1780–1980*. Berkeley: University of California Press, 1988.

Murtagh, William. *Keeping Time: The History and Theory of Preservation in America*. New York: John Wiley and Sons, 1997.

Nash, Roderick. *Wilderness and the American Mind*. New Haven, Conn.: Yale University Press, 1967.

New Orleans in 1805: A Directory and a Census. New Orleans: n.p., 1936.

Norris, F. Terry. "Where Did the Villages Go?" In Andrew Hurley, ed., *Common Fields*. St. Louis: Missouri Historical Society, 1997.

Nye, David E. *American Technological Sublime.* Cambridge, Mass.: MIT Press, 1994.

Odom, Edwin Dale. "Louisiana Railroads, 1830–1880." Ph.D. diss., Department of History, Tulane University, 1961.

Ogg, Frederic Austin. *The Opening of the Mississippi: A Struggle for Supremacy in the American Interior.* New York: Macmillan, 1904.

Patterson, K. David. "Disease Environments of the Antebellum South." In Ronald L. Numbers and Todd Savitt, eds., *Science and Medicine in the Old South*. Baton Rouge: Louisiana State University Press, 1989.

———. "Yellow Fever Epidemics and Mortality in the United States, 1693–1905." *Social Science and Medicine* 34 (1992).

Phelan, Mary Kay. *The Story of the Louisiana Purchase.* New York: Thomas Y. Cromwell, 1979.

Philbrick, Francis S. *The Rise of the West, 1754–1830.* New York: Harper and Row, 1965.

Price, Willard. *The Amazing Mississippi.* New York: John Day, 1963.

Rapoport, Amos. *The Meaning of the Built Environment: A Nonverbal Communication Approach.* 1982. Reprint, Tucson: University of Arizona Press, 1990.

Reinders, Robert C. *End of an Era: New Orleans, 1850–1860.* New Orleans: Pelican Publishing, 1964.

Reuss, Martin. "Andrew A. Humphreys and the Development of Hydraulic Engineering." *Technology and Culture* 26 (January 1985).

Rodgers, Daniel. "In Search of Progressivism." *Reviews in American History* 10 (December 1982).

Rome, Adam. *The Bulldozer in the Countryside: Suburban Sprawl and the Rise of American Environmentalism.* Cambridge: Cambridge University Press, 2001.

Rose, Carol M. "Possession as the Origin of Private Property." *University of Chicago Law Review* 52 (Winter 1985).

Rosen, Christine Meisner, and Joel Arthur Tarr. "The Importance of an Urban Perspective in Environmental History." *Journal of Urban History* 30 (May 1994).

Rosenberg, Charles E. *The Cholera Years.* 1962. Reprint, Chicago: University of Chicago Press, 1987.

———. *Explaining Epidemics.* Cambridge: Cambridge University Press, 1992.

Rosenzweig, Roy, and Elizabeth Blackmar. *The Park and the People: A History of Central Park.* Ithaca, N.Y.: Cornell University Press, 1992.

Ruddick, Susan. "Constructing Difference in Public Spaces: Race, Class, and Gender as Interlocking Systems." *Urban Geography* 17 (1992).

Ryan, Mary P. *Civic Wars: Democracy and Public Life in the American City During the Nineteenth Century.* Berkeley: University of California Press, 1997.

———. *Cradle of the Middle Class.* Cambridge: Cambridge University Press, 1981.

Rydell, Robert W. *All the World's a Fair: Visions of Empire at American International Expositions, 1876–1916.* Chicago: University of Chicago Press, 1984.

Saucier, Roger T. *Geomorphology and Quaternary Geologic History of the Lower Mississippi Valley.* Vicksburg, Miss.: U.S. Army Corps of Engineers Waterways Experiment Station, 1994.

Schafer, Judith Kelleher. *Slavery, the Civil Law, and the Supreme Court of Louisiana.* Baton Rouge: Louisiana State University Press, 1994.

Schama, Simon. *Landscape and Memory.* New York: Alfred A. Knopf, 1995.

Schivelbusch, Wolfgang. *The Railway Journey: The Industrialization of Time and Space in the Nineteenth Century.* 1977. Reprint, Berkeley: University of California Press, 1986.

Schmitt, Peter J. *Back to Nature: The Arcadian Myth in Urban America.* Baltimore: Johns Hopkins University Press, 1990.

Schudson, Michael. "Was There Ever a Public Sphere? If So, When? Reflections on the American Case." In Craig Calhoun, ed., *Habermas and the Public Sphere.* Cambridge, Mass.: MIT Press, 1992.

Schulten, Susan. *The Geographical Imagination in America, 1880–1950.* Chicago: University of Chicago Press, 2001.

Schuyler, David. *The New Urban Landscape: The Redefinition of City Form in Nineteenth-Century America.* Baltimore: Johns Hopkins University Press, 1986.

Schwartz, Charles R., Jr. "Levees and Batture in the Law of Louisiana." *Tulane Law Review* 21 (1947).

Scott, William B. *In Pursuit of Happiness: American Conceptions of Property from the Seventeenth to the Twentieth Century.* Bloomington: Indiana University Press, 1977.

Sennett, Richard. *The Fall of Public Man.* New York: W. W. Norton, 1974.

Shallat, Todd. *Structures in the Stream: Water, Science, and the Rise of the U.S. Army Corps of Engineers.* Austin: University of Texas Press, 1994.

Sheriff, Carol. *The Artificial River: The Erie Canal and the Paradox of Progress, 1817–1862.* New York: Hill and Wang, 1996.

Simpson, A. W. B. *A History of Land Law.* Oxford: Clarendon Press, 1986.

Slosek, Jean. "*Aedes Aegypti* Mosquitoes in the Americas: A Review of Their Interactions with the Human Population." *Social Science Medicine* 23 (1986).

Smith, Carl. *Urban Disorder and the Shape of Belief: The Great Chicago Fire, the Haymarket Bomb, and the Model Town of Pullman.* Chicago: University of Chicago Press, 1995.

Smith, Neil. *Uneven Development: Nature, Capital and the Production of Space.* Oxford: Basil Blackwell, 1984.

Snowden, J. O., J. R. J. Studlick, and W. C. Ward. *Geology of Greater New Orleans.* New Orleans: New Orleans Geological Society, 1980.

Soja, Edward. *Postmodern Geographies: The Reassertion of Space in Critical Social Theory.* London: Verso, 1989.

Sorkin, Michael, ed. *Variations on a Theme Park: Scenes from the New American City and the End of Public Space.* New York: Hill and Wang, 1992.

Spirn, Anne Whiston. *The Granite Garden: Urban Nature and Human Design.* New York: Basic Books, 1984.

————. *The Language of Landscape*. New Haven, Conn.: Yale University Press, 1998.

Spletsoser, Marcel. "Back Door to the Land of Plenty: New Orleans as an Immigrant Port, 1820–1860." Ph.D. diss., Louisiana State University, 1978.

Sprague, Marshall. *So Vast, So Beautiful a Land: Louisiana and the Purchase.* Athens: Ohio University Press, 1974.

Stecker, H. Dora. "Constructing a Navigation System in the West." *Ohio Archeological and Historical Quarterly* 22 (1913).

Steinberg, Theodore. *Acts of God: The Unnatural History of Natural Disaster in America.* Oxford: Oxford University Press, 2000.

————. *Nature Incorporated: Industrialization and the Waters of New England.* Amherst: University of Massachusetts Press, 1991.

Stilgoe, John R. *Metropolitan Corridor: Railroads and the American Scene.* New Haven, Conn.: Yale University Press, 1983.

Susman, Warren I. *Culture as History: The Transformation of American Society in the Twentieth Century.* New York: Pantheon Books, 1984.

Sweeney, Joseph Modeste. "Tournament of Scholars over the Sources of the Civil Code of 1808." *Tulane Law Review* 46 (Spring 1972).

Taylor, George Rogers. *The Transportation Revolution, 1815–1860.* White Plains, N.Y.: M. E. Sharpe, 1951.

Teaford, Jon C. *The Unheralded Triumph: City Government in America, 1870–1900.* Baltimore: Johns Hopkins University Press, 1984.

Tregle, Joseph E., Jr. "Creoles and Americans." In Arnold R. Hirsch and Joseph Logsdon, eds., *Creole New Orleans.* Baton Rouge: Louisiana State University Press, 1992.

Tuan, Yi-fu. *Topophilia: A Study of Environmental Perception, Attitudes, and Values.* Englewood Cliffs, N.J.: Prentice-Hall, 1974.

Tyler, Norman. *Historic Preservation.* New York: W. W. Norton, 2000.

Upton, Dell. "The New Orleans Levee: Street of the World." In Zeynep Celik, Diane Favro, and Richard Ingersoll, eds., *Streets: Critical Perspectives on Public Space.* Berkeley: University of California Press, 1994.

Usner, Daniel H. *Indians, Settlers, and Slaves in a Frontier Exchange Economy: The Lower Mississippi Valley before 1783.* Chapel Hill: University of North Carolina Press, 1992.

Valencius, Conevery Bolton. "The Geography of Health and the Making of the American West." In Nicolaas Rupke, ed., *Medical Geography in Historical Perspective.* London: Wellcome Trust Centre for the History of Medicine at UCL, 2000.

Vanvelde, Kenneth J. "The New Property of the Nineteenth Century: The Development of the Modern Concept of Property." *Buffalo Law Review* 29 (Winter 1980).

Vileisis, Ann. *Discovering the Unknown Landscape: A History of America's Wetlands.* Washington, D.C.: Island Press, 1999.

Wallace, Mike. *Mickey Mouse History and Other Essays on American Memory.* Philadelphia: Temple University Press, 1996.

Warner, John Harley. *The Therapeutic Perspective: Medical Practice, Knowl-

edge, and Identity in America, 1820–1885. Princeton, N.J.: Princeton University Press, 1997.

Warner, Sam Bass. *The Private City: Philadelphia in Three Periods of Its Growth.* Philadelphia: University of Pennsylvania Press, 1968.

Weil, Tom. *The Mississippi River.* New York: Hippocrene Books, 1992.

Welter, Barbara. "Cult of True Womanhood." *American Quarterly* 18 (Fall 1966).

Whitaker, Arthur Preston. *The Mississippi Question, 1795–1803*. New York: D. Appleton, 1934.

———. *The Spanish-American Frontier, 1783–1795*. Boston: Houghton Mifflin, 1927.

White, Richard. *The Organic Machine.* New York: Hill and Wang, 1995.

Whyte, William H. *City: Rediscovering the Center.* New York: Doubleday, 1988.

Williams, Raymond. *The Country and the City.* Oxford: Oxford University Press, 1973.

———. *Keywords: A Vocabulary of Culture and Society.* 1976. Reprint, Oxford: Oxford University Press, 1983.

Wilson, Samuel, Jr. *The Vieux Carré, New Orleans: Its Plan, Its Growth, Its Architecture.* New Orleans: Bureau of Governmental Research, 1968.

Wilson, William H. *The City Beautiful Movement.* Baltimore: Johns Hopkins University Press, 1989.

Winner, Langdon. *The Whale and the Reactor: The Search for Limits in an Age of Technology.* Chicago: University of Chicago Press, 1986.

Wolfe, Richard. "The Appropriation of Property for Levees." *Tulane Law Review* 40 (February 1966).

Worster, Donald. *Dust Bowl: The Southern Plains in the 1930s.* Oxford: Oxford University Press, 1982.

———. *Nature's Economy: A History of Ecological Ideas.* 1977. Reprint, Cambridge: Cambridge University Press, 1994.

Yiannopoulos, A.N. "The Public Use of the Banks of Navigable Rivers in Louisiana." *Louisiana Law Review* 31 (June 1971).

Zukin, Sharon. *Landscapes of Power: From Detroit to Disney World.* Berkeley: University of California Press, 1991.

Index

Page references in italics refer to illustrations.

Boyer, M. Christine, 216
Braman, James, 212
Bridwell, Lowell, 211
Bureau of Governmental Research
(BGR), 209, 210, 211, 212
burial: underground, 155; during
yellow-fever epidemic, 105–7. *See
also* cemeteries
Burke, Joseph, 198, 199
Burr, Aaron, 28, 33

Cable, George Washington, 121, 155; on
yellow-fever epidemic, 101
Caernarvon crevasse, 181–83, *182, 183,*
193; effect on levees-only policy of,
189; effect on trappers of, 182–83,
185, 187; environmental effects of,
185; visitors to, 183–84. *See also*
Poydras (Louisiana)
Café du Monde, 202, 215–16
Cairo (Illinois), 2
Caldwell, Councilman, 75
Camboden Castle (trade vessel), 90, 91,
92
canals: drainage through, 154; enthusi-
asm for, 81; navigational, 31, 43;
projected, 128, 130
Capdevielle, Paul, 147
Carmichael, William, 35
Carrollton river gauge, 181, 184
Carson, Rachel: *Silent Spring,* 201
Cartwright, Samuel, 107, 108–9
cemeteries, *106;* in yellow-fever epidemic,
104–6
Charity Hospital (New Orleans), 88,
100, 108
Charleston (South Carolina), 207
Charlevoix, Pierre-François Xavier, 6–7
Chicago: environmental history of, 10;
waterfront of, 140
cholera, 116
Citizens Flood Relief Committee
(CFRC), 161, 171–81; dealings with
flood victims of, 186; and destruction
of levee, 173–74, 177–81; and MRC,
176; propaganda of, 180, 184–85
City Beautiful movement, 146, 155
City Planning Commission of New
Orleans, 197, 199
civil law (Louisiana), 20, 24–25; vs.
common law, 37; digest of, 41–42;
waterfront under, 124. *See also* servitude, riparian
Civil War: commercial community following, 120; effect on New Orleans
of, 119–21

Claiborne, William: in batture controversy, 31–32, 33, 39; and Fulton
group, 53
Claiborne Avenue (New Orleans), *219;*
belt line at, 140, 141; deforestation of,
216, *218*
Clermont (steamboat), 53, 84
Cline, Isaac, 172–73, 177
cognitive mapping, 8
Cole, Thomas, 103
Columbia River, 195
commerce: with Americans, 35, 57;
effect of railroads on, 81–82, 120,
121–22; effect of technology on, 63,
72, 73, 79; in grain, 133, 135–36; on
Mississippi, 14, 34–35, 51, 57; in
Mississippi Valley, 51, 53, 80–82,
121–22; during Reconstruction,
121–24; regulation of, 70; reshaping
of routes of, 81. *See also* free trade, on
Mississippi
commercial community, New Orleans's,
15, 49; advocacy of canals by, 130–31;
American, 71, 72–76; after Civil War,
120, 127; control of waterfront by, 96;
Creole, 72, 75–76; and Democratic
Ring, 139; and flood of 1927, 172,
173, 186, 189; on Levee Board, 166;
in riverfront expressway controversy,
205; steamboats and, 53; struggle with
railroads of, 138–42; on vagrancy
laws, 219; view of quarantines of,
91–92; in yellow-fever epidemic,
94–95, 113
Committee of One Hundred, 139
Congress, U.S.: and construction of
jetties, 131; flood control hearings of,
190, 191; levee legislation of, 169, 170
Conseil de ville (New Orleans): in batture
controversy, 20, 31–32, 46–47; and
control of waterfront, 24, 70–71;
Creoles on, 71, 72; on levees, 47
Coolidge, Calvin, 176, 189, 192
cordelling, 51
Corthell, E.L., 132, 140, 141
cotton trade, decline in, 135
Cram, Mildred, 153
Cramer, Zadok: *Navigator,* 68
Creoles: acclimation of, 98, 107; Ameri-
can threats to, 71; in batture case, 30,
36; on Conseil de ville, 71, 72; and
Jefferson, 33; prodevelopment views
of, 48
Cronon, William, 122; *Nature's Metrop-
olis,* 10
Crossman, A.D., 111

Text: 10/13 Sabon
Display: Sabon
Compositor: Impressions Book and Journal Services, Inc.
Printer and Binder: Edwards Brothers, Inc.